HENRY VIII

AND THE MEN WHO MADE HIM

HENRY VIII
AND THE MEN WHO MADE HIM

TRACY BORMAN

Atlantic Monthly Press
New York

Printed in the United States of America

First published in Great Britain in 2018 by Hodder & Stoughton
An Hachette UK company

First Grove Atlantic Edition: January 2019

Library of Congress Cataloging-in-Publication data available for this title.

ISBN 978-0-8021-2843-0
eISBN 978-0-8021-4640-3

Atlantic Monthly Press
an imprint of Grove Atlantic
154 West 14th Street
New York, NY 10011

Distributed by Publishers Group West

groveatlantic.com

19 20 21 22 10 9 8 7 6 5 4 3 2 1

Also by Tracy Borman

The Private Lives of the Tudors:
Uncovering the Secrets of Britain's Greatest Dynasty

Thomas Cromwell:
The Untold Story of Henry VIII's Most Faithful Servant

Witches: James I and the English Witch Hunts

Queen of the Conqueror:
The Life of Matilda, Wife of William I

Elizabeth's Women:
Friends, Rivals, and Foes who Shaped the Virgin Queen

King's Mistress, Queen's Servant:
The Life & Times of Henrietta Howard

Fiction

The King's Witch

For John Ashworth, with love

CONTENTS

PREFACE

'The son was born to a greater destiny'

In 1537, King Henry VIII instructed his favourite court painter, Hans Holbein, to begin work on a huge mural to decorate the wall of his privy chamber at Whitehall Palace. The timing was significant. Henry had just emerged from one of the most testing years of his reign. A jousting accident had left him with a painful, debilitating wound to his leg, which provided a salient reminder of his mortality. The failure of his second wife, Anne Boleyn, to give him a male heir had resulted in her execution. As yet there was no sign that her successor Jane Seymour would fare any better, which cast doubt upon the king's virility. Meanwhile, the turbulence of Henry's religious reforms had sparked widespread rebellion, shaking his belief in the unquestioning love of his subjects. Little wonder that Holbein was now tasked to create an image of kingly and dynastic invincibility.

It would be Holbein's most ambitious commission to date. Although the finished mural was destroyed by fire in 1698, the details have been passed down to us, thanks to a copy that was made for Charles II, as well as to the cartoon that Holbein used for transferring the composition to the wall. It was intended to project the might of the Tudor dynasty, and showed Henry flanked by his wife and his late parents, Henry VII and Elizabeth of York.

Visitors to the privy chamber at Whitehall were overawed by the life-sized image of the king that faced them as soon as they walked through the door. Henry 'stood there, majestic in his splendour . . . so lifelike that the spectator felt abashed, annihilated in its presence'.[1] Adopting an aggressive, warrior-like pose, he stands with his legs spread apart and his hands on his hips. With one hand he reaches towards an ornate dagger that hangs at his waist. He is gloriously arrayed in sumptuous clothes and glittering jewels, and his large codpiece and heavily padded shoulders leave no doubt as to his strident masculinity.

This would become the iconic image of Henry VIII and would be replicated in a host of subsequent portraits. In creating it, Holbein did more to shape the king's public persona than any of the able men and ministers who surrounded him.

But Holbein's masterpiece also reveals a deeper secret about the real man behind this intimidating exterior. At the centre of the picture is a Latin inscription. It describes the achievements of Henry and his predecessor:

> Between them there was great competition and rivalry and [posterity] may well debate whether father or son should take the palm. Both were victorious. The father triumphed over his foes, quenched the fires of civil war and brought his people lasting peace. The son was born to a greater destiny. He it was who banished from the altars undeserving men and replaced them with men of worth. Presumptuous popes were forced to yield before him and when Henry VIII bore the sceptre true religion was established and, in his reign, God's teachings received their rightful reverence.[2]

In short, Henry had achieved more than his father. He had annihilated those who had opposed his rule and had established his supremacy over the Roman Catholic Church and papacy, thus ensuring his everlasting fame as England's greatest king.

This message was reinforced by the composition of the painting. Even though Henry VII is higher up in the picture than his son, his pose is much more hesitant. He leans on a pillar and is shown in slight profile, his finely featured face suffused with an air of languor. Henry VIII forms a dramatic contrast. He faces straight ahead, as if staring down an opponent, and is the very image of vibrant power. Holbein's original design had shown Henry in the same conventional profile as his father, so this change had almost certainly been at the instigation of his royal master.

That Henry felt the need to assert his superiority over his late father at this point in his reign betrays his deep-seated insecurity, as well as the fear of parental disapproval that still plagued him almost thirty years after Henry VII's death. The father had filled the treasury, subdued his over-mighty subjects and sired four healthy children to continue the Tudor dynasty; the son had depleted the royal coffers thanks to his extravagant lifestyle and futile military campaigns, provoked dissent and rebellion, and had only a daughter to show from twenty-eight years of marriage.

But thanks to Holbein, Henry VIII was able to convince posterity that *he* was the mightier king. The artist had created an image of invincibility that not only overawed Henry's subjects, but would echo down the centuries, making him the most famous – and feared – king in English history.

Holbein was one of many men who made Henry, but his influence was arguably greater than most, certainly in terms of shaping his master's public image. In the eyes of the king, though, it was his predecessor who had the greatest hold over him. Henry VII had been a cold and distant father, but he had also established a model of kingship that his son had consistently failed to emulate. Commissioning Holbein to distort history through the Whitehall mural was therefore a defiant gesture by a man who privately resented and feared his late father for the rest of his days.

INTRODUCTION
'The changeableness
of this king'

'Divorced, beheaded, died, divorced, beheaded, survived.' The familiar mnemonic for remembering the six wives of Henry VIII also reminds us that it is the women in his life who have defined him. The fact that he married more times than any other monarch in British history has superseded every other aspect of his larger-than-life character, and his turbulent reign.

Remarkable though Henry's marital history is, it is not what defines him. Far more influential than the women in his life were the men with whom he was surrounded. Although he was raised in a predominantly female household, the overbearing, often suffocating, presence of his father Henry VII dominated his early years. The sudden death of his elder brother Arthur at the age of just fifteen propelled Henry into the limelight, and, once king, he gathered around him a coterie of high-spirited young men to keep him entertained. During the course of his thirty-seven-year reign, he would attract some of the brightest minds of the sixteenth century: from omnipotent councillors such as Cardinal Wolsey and Thomas Cromwell to the renowned scholars Thomas More and Desiderius Erasmus, and the arrogant, ruthless members of the aristocracy, such as the dukes of Buckingham and Norfolk. In his private domain, meanwhile, he was attended by an array of different men: servants, barbers, physicians, fools and other lesser-known characters whose job it was to attend to Henry's every need, to entertain him and to listen to his confidences. It was these men who shaped Henry into the man – and monster – that he would become. And he, in turn, dictated their fates.

Henry formed numerous close attachments to men throughout his life. A few were stable and enduring, but most burned brightly and were quickly extinguished. The king's favour was notoriously fickle. Indulged in childhood, he had little patience for anything that displeased or bored him, and in later life his growing paranoia made him even more unpredictable. The Imperial ambassador Eustace Chapuys, who spent more time with Henry than any other foreign envoy, once observed that he despaired of forming 'a judgment, considering the changeableness of this king'. The Spanish Chronicle agreed that 'when the King took a fancy to anyone he carried it to extremes', but that he could withdraw it just as suddenly.[1]

This book will tell the story of England's most famous monarch through the lens of the men who surrounded him: relations, servants, ministers, rivals, confidants and companions. It will follow a chronological structure based upon Henry's life, drawing in the many and varied characters at appropriate points in the narrative. As such, it will provide a fresh perspective on this much-studied monarch: a biography from the outside in.

Henry's relationships with the men who surrounded him reveal much about his beliefs, behaviour and character. They show him to be capable of fierce, but seldom abiding loyalty; of raising men only to destroy them later. Many of his closest companions were drawn from the noble classes, but the fact that he vested most power in men of humble birth suggests a deep-seated insecurity about his own position. He loved to be attended and entertained by boisterous young men who shared his passion for sport, but at other times he was more diverted by men of intellect, culture and wit. Often trusting and easily led by his male attendants and advisers during the early years of his reign, he matured into a profoundly suspicious and paranoid king whose favour could be suddenly withdrawn, as many of his later servants found to their cost. His natural generosity and gregariousness was offset by the fact that he was used to getting his own way by the time he became king, which made him intolerant and impatient when he considered that he had been ill-served by his men. His cruelty and ruthlessness would become ever more apparent as his reign progressed, but the tenderness that he displayed towards those he trusted proves that he was never the one-dimensional monster that he is often portrayed as. In short, Henry's personality is revealed in all its multi-faceted, contradictory glory by his relationships with the men who made him.

The story of these men is played out with a cast of hundreds, if not thousands. To include all of the men in Henry's life would require a multi-volume study, which in turn would dilute the central themes of this book, notably the king's character and tastes, the motives for his decisions and the impact of his actions, the creation and evolution of his image from Renaissance prince to tyrant, and the legacy that he bequeathed to the men who survived him. I have therefore focused the narrative upon those men who wielded the greatest influence upon Henry's life, or who illustrate different aspects of his character and reign.

That is not to say that the men who do not feature are not worthy of further study. They include William Reskymer, page of the chamber, and Sir John Godsalve, administrator and MP, both of whom were immortalised by Holbein during his years at Henry's court. The seasoned courtier Anthony Knyvet, who was also lieutenant of the Tower of London, and Richard Gibson, deputy Master of the Revels, who from 1510 until his death in 1534 was actively involved in the production of every major tournament and revel at court, also have fascinating stories to tell, but are beyond the scope of this narrative.

In their place is a dazzling and eclectic cast of characters: some 'mad' (Sir Francis Bryan, the so-called 'Vicar of Hell'), some 'bad' (the arch-schemer, Stephen Gardiner), but none as 'dangerous to know' as Henry VIII himself, who dominates the narrative as he did his times. There are also the men whose stories have, until now, remained in the shadows: Sir William Butts, Henry's favourite physician, Will Somer, his fool, and Sir Thomas Cawarden, who superintended some of the most spectacular entertainments of the later reign, reminding Henry of his glorious younger days. It is these men who helped to shape the character, opinions and image of their king, and whose hidden history lay behind the Tudor throne.

'The king's second born son'

THE YEAR 1486 began with a momentous event. On 18 January, the citizens of London lined the streets in hopes of catching a glimpse of their new king, Henry VII, who had been crowned just eleven weeks before. As he made his way to Westminster Abbey once more, it was to take as his bride Elizabeth of York. Their union would mark the end of more than thirty years of bitter civil strife, in which two rival branches of the Plantagenet dynasty had battled for supremacy. Thereafter, the red rose of Lancaster would be intertwined with the white rose of York to represent a single, united dynasty: the House of Tudor.

But the marriage promised more to Henry than the end of civil war. Elizabeth of York's blood was unquestionably royal. She was the eldest daughter of Edward IV and, with both of her younger brothers presumed dead after their disappearance in the Tower during the brief, bloody reign of her uncle Richard III, she was the most senior representative of the House of York. Although her new husband was the chief Lancastrian claimant, he could hardly boast the same pedigree. Henry's great-grandfather had been the son of John of Gaunt (the third son of Edward III) and his long-standing mistress Katherine Swynford. The new king was thus descended from an illegitimate branch of the royal family. His father Edmund Tudor, meanwhile, had been the child of Henry V's queen, Catherine of Valois, by her Welsh page. With such a dubious bloodline, Henry desperately needed to strengthen his right to the throne by marrying well. And the sooner he could beget an heir on his new wife, the better.

According to the humanist scholar, priest and diplomat, Polydore Vergil, who penned a history of England during his many years there, Elizabeth had been appalled by the idea of marrying the man who had usurped the York throne. 'I will not thus be married,' she declared, 'but, unhappy creature that I am, will rather suffer all the torments which St Catherine is said to have endured for the love of Christ than be united with a man who is the enemy of my family.'[1] If his account is true, then she soon suppressed her 'singular aversion'. The lure of the throne must have offered a strong enticement, and Elizabeth might have reflected that it was better to marry the king than to be palmed off on one of his followers. It was not an age when women were at liberty to choose for themselves.

Besides, if his pedigree was questionable, the first Tudor king at least presented an impressive sight to his subjects. His contemporary biographer Vergil described him as 'extremely attractive in appearance', with a 'slim, but well-built and strong' figure, above the average height, and a 'cheerful' face, which became animated when he spoke. Francis Bacon agreed that he was of a 'comely personage, a little above just stature, well and straight limbed, but slender', and added that his face was 'a little like a churchman'. He was also 'wise and prudent', shrewd in business and 'not devoid of scholarship'.[2] Having spent much of his adult life in exile in Brittany, Henry had honed his military skills in readiness for the day when he would launch an invasion of England and claim the crown that his indomitable mother, Lady Margaret Beaufort, had always insisted was his by right. The new king had spent most of these formative years surrounded by men, his uncle Jasper Tudor foremost among them. But even though he enjoyed a reputation for piety, he had not entirely resisted the temptations on offer in Brittany and had sired a bastard son, Roland de Velville.

Although Henry was naturally reserved and introspective, which earned him the reputation of a serious and sober-minded monarch, in the company of close family and friends he was much more relaxed and convivial. Vergil describes him as 'gracious and kind and . . . as attentive to his visitors as he was easy of access. His hospitality was splendidly generous.'[3] The new king's privy chamber accounts include payments to jesters, minstrels, pipers and singers. He liked to gamble and, despite his reputation as a miser, he thought nothing of waging substantial amounts on card games. He was also very fond of sport and employed two professional tennis players to help improve his game. He always took care to dress in magnificent style, anxious to project an image of majesty that might disguise his questionable claim to the throne.

Henry's bride was no less magnificent. Aged nineteen at the time of her marriage, Elizabeth of York was nine years younger than Henry and in the full bloom of youth. She was tall like her father Edward IV and, with her lustrous blonde hair and rosebud mouth, had inherited the famed good looks of both of her parents. Elizabeth was also intelligent and a shrewd political operator, having lived her life at court. The Venetian envoy described her as 'a very handsome woman, and of great ability'.[4]

Expectations were high for this union of the warring houses of York and Lancaster. 'Everyone considers [the marriage] advantageous to the kingdom,' observed one foreign ambassador, adding that 'all things appear disposed towards peace'.[5] But Henry looked for more from his bride than the resolution of conflict. She had to fill the royal nursery with children and thus secure the future of his fledgling Tudor dynasty.

The new queen did not disappoint. Just eight months after the wedding, she gave birth to a son, Arthur. The name was significant: Henry had displayed King Arthur's red dragon on his banner at Bosworth, and Elizabeth's own father had claimed descent from the legendary hero. At a stroke, Arthur's birth rendered his father significantly more secure on his throne. Now he could boast a male heir, as well as a wife of unquestionable royal blood. His Yorkist rivals had been dealt a crushing blow.

The precious infant was soon moved to Farnham in Surrey, along with a sizeable and costly household.[6] Security was of paramount importance, and the king made sure that only men of proven fidelity were chosen to care for this tiny scion of the House of Tudor. The personnel included Arthur's wet nurse, dry nurse, yeomen, grooms and, at the head of the nursery, lady governess. The most senior official was the king's cousin, Sir Reginald Pole, who was appointed chamberlain of the prince's household.

The same attention to detail was applied to Arthur's education. The respected scholar John Rede, formerly head of Winchester

College, was appointed tutor and devised a classical curriculum for the infant prince. Almost from the moment that he took his first, tottering steps, Arthur also began the physical training that formed an important part of a royal heir's education. He must be a prince in the Renaissance model, as skilled in riding and combat as he was in languages and rhetoric.

Although Elizabeth had been quick to conceive her first child, it would be more than two years before she fell pregnant again.[7] In late October 1489, the queen entered her confinement at the palace of Westminster, where she herself had been born, and on 28 November she gave birth to a daughter. The arrival of a girl tended to be something of a disappointment in royal and noble families, and the London Grey Friars chronicler did not even trouble to record the infant princess's arrival. She was christened Margaret two days later in honour of her paternal grandmother. Henry's reaction to the birth of his daughter is not recorded. Although he must have hoped for a son to strengthen his dynasty, Margaret would still prove useful in forging an international alliance through marriage.

The queen soon assumed responsibility for the upbringing of her new daughter. This was entirely in keeping with royal tradition, whereby the male heir was groomed for kingship by specially appointed tutors and attendants, leaving the other royal children to the care of their mother. Elizabeth had been raised by her mother, Edward IV's scandalous queen Elizabeth Woodville, so she knew what was expected of her.

As well as playing an active role in her daughter's upbringing, Elizabeth also resumed her wifely duties shortly after the birth. Less than a year later, she was pregnant again. The child who would grow up to be England's most famous king may have been conceived at Ewelme in Oxfordshire: Henry VII and his queen had stayed there in October 1490.[8] Today, it is a picturesque village in the heart of the Chilterns, but in the late fifteenth century it was a place of some status, with strong links to the powerful de la Pole family, who were close blood relatives of the queen.

The queen's pregnancy proceeded without incident, and she chose Greenwich as the place for her third confinement. Originally built in 1453 as 'Bella Court' by Humphrey Duke of Gloucester, regent to the young King Henry VI, the palace had been taken over by the king's formidable wife, Margaret of Anjou, who renamed it 'Placentia' and carried out a series of substantial improvements. Soon after coming to the throne, Henry VII had enlarged the palace further, refacing the entire building with red brick and changing its name to Greenwich. Even so, the palace was considerably smaller than the other royal residences in London. But it was the queen's favourite house. She may also have wished to retreat to the relative quiet and privacy of this, the easternmost royal palace in the capital, for her first summer birth.

There is no surviving record of when Elizabeth arrived at Greenwich, but it is likely to have been in late May or early June, when her pregnancy had entered its ninth month. Her husband was preoccupied with the threat posed by Perkin Warbeck, a young man claiming to be Richard, Duke of York, the younger of the 'Princes in the Tower'. This second 'pretender' constituted a significant risk to Henry's throne because he had secured a powerful patron in the form of Margaret of Burgundy, sister of the Yorkist king Edward IV and therefore aunt to Henry's queen. Many in England were willing to give him credence, and the old antipathies between York and Lancaster that had torn the country apart for so many years looked set to be revived. 'The rumour of Richard, the resuscitated duke of York, had divided nearly all England into factions, filling the minds of men with hope or fear,' recounted Polydore Vergil.[9] Deeply insecure about his right to the throne and increasingly paranoid about any rival claimants, the king was plunged into the greatest crisis of his reign so far.

What Henry needed to secure his dynasty and send a powerful message to his enemies was another son. The four-year-old Prince Arthur was thriving under the care of his tutors and household, but in this age of high infant mortality one male heir was not enough. It was therefore to his great satisfaction when news arrived that his wife had been safely delivered of a boy on 28 June. Interestingly, though, his indomitable mother, Lady Margaret Beaufort, seemed to pay less attention to the birth of her new grandson than to his elder siblings. She had recorded the precise time of Arthur and

Margaret's births in her Book of Hours, but merely noted the date of this latest prince's arrival – and even then had to correct it.[10]

The second Tudor prince was named after his father and baptised in the church of the Observant Franciscans, close to the palace at Greenwich. This would have pleased the king, whom Vergil noted was 'especially attached to those Franciscan friars, known as Observants, for whom he founded many convents so that with his help this brotherhood should flourish for ever in his kingdom'.[11] Even though Prince Henry was just the 'spare heir', his father did not stint upon the arrangements. The church was lavishly decorated with cloth of gold and damask, rich tapestries and cypress linen. A temporary wooden stage was erected, on which stood a silver font brought over from Canterbury Cathedral. The tiny prince was conveyed there, wrapped in a mantle of cloth of gold trimmed with ermine.[12] Richard Fox, Bishop of Exeter and a close adviser to the king, presided over the ceremony.

If royal protocol was observed, Henry would have remained at court until he was three months old. It was at this tender age that royal babies were then established in their own household, separate from their parents. As only the second-born son, however, Prince Henry was not afforded such a privilege, and instead joined his sister Margaret at the Palace of Sheen. Their mother loved this beautiful and tranquil residence, which lay eight miles west of London. She had spent many of her own childhood years here, and it had strong associations with her own mother, to whom it had been bequeathed by Edward IV. The royal nursery was a predominantly female environment, supervised by the queen. Elizabeth's gentle and affectionate nature formed a welcome contrast to the prince's seemingly cold and distant father, and his domineering paternal grandmother. She doted on her younger son, and he returned her love in equal measure. It is likely that young Henry learned to read and write from his mother, and there are similarities in their handwriting.[13]

When Henry was three years old, his mother appointed Elizabeth Denton, one of her own gentlewomen, as head of the royal nursery. However, 'Lady Mistress' Denton continued to draw a salary from the queen's household, which suggests that the latter continued to spend a great deal of her time at Sheen. There was one significant male influence present almost from the moment of his birth, however, because another member of his mother's household to whom he was introduced was her cupbearer (and illegitimate brother), Arthur Plantagenet.

With his auburn hair, athletic build and easy manner, Arthur was every inch a Yorkist. One friend described him as 'the pleasantest man in the world'.[14] He certainly enjoyed all of the pleasures on offer at court, and was particularly fond of jousting and fine wine. The same would be said of Henry in later years. Elizabeth was as keen to shape the character as she was the intellect of her younger son, and judged her half-brother to be an ideal role model. Henry soon established a close bond with his uncle, and later reflected that Arthur had been 'the gentlest heart living'.[15] Such warmth contrasts sharply with his more restrained, respectful references to his father. Their closeness would endure, with only one notable interruption, for many years to come, and Arthur would serve his nephew faithfully until the end of his days.

The queen had fallen pregnant very soon after Henry's birth, and in June 1492 she began her fourth confinement at Sheen. This resulted in the birth of another daughter, Elizabeth, on 2 July. The event was tinged with sadness because the queen's mother had died a few weeks before, on 8 June. The royal nursery subsequently transferred to Eltham Palace, south-east of London. Eltham had been an important royal residence for almost 200 years, and the favourite home of the queen's father, Edward IV, who had built the magnificent great hall, which still survives today. Prince Henry would have been presented with a reminder of his maternal grandfather every time he visited the great hall because Edward's *rose en soleil* emblem was carved above the entrance. Already, the one-year-old prince was beginning to physically resemble this popular Yorkist king.

Although the contemporary records include only a handful of references to Prince Henry's early years at Eltham, they suggest that he enjoyed a very comfortable, even indulgent, upbringing. There were numerous servants to attend to his needs and those of his siblings, and for his entertainment, there was a troupe of minstrels and a fool named John Goose. It is likely that the young prince, along with his sisters, was present at the great court gatherings, which were dictated by the most important dates in the religious calendar, such as Christmas and Easter.

But Henry's presence at such occasions was always overshadowed by that of his brother Arthur. Five years Henry's senior and heir to their father's throne, it was natural that the eldest prince should claim all of the attention. From a young age, it was obvious that Arthur was growing into a serious-minded young man who closely resembled his father. He excelled at his studies and was also acquiring the military prowess expected of a future monarch. The king must have been gratified to see the shaping of his son into a ruler who would emulate his own style of kingship.

Henry's feelings towards his elder brother are not recorded. They were raised separately, and there is no evidence that they ever exchanged letters or gifts. If the younger prince harboured any resentment at being forever cast into the shadows, then he left no trace of it. Francis Bacon later recorded that, although Henry was not 'unadorned with learning . . . therein he came short of his brother Arthur'.[16] Such comparisons must have been irksome, but it is also possible that Henry grew to enjoy his status as the second in line, with its comparative lack of responsibility.

Bacon also paints a picture of Henry VII as a loving father: 'Towards his children he was full of paternal affection, careful of their education, aspiring to their high advancement, regular to see that they should not want of any due honour and respect: but not greatly willing to cast any popular lustre upon them.'[17] This is wide of the mark. There is little evidence that the king paid much heed to his younger son's upbringing (or indeed that of Henry's sisters), but he was certainly not blind to the advantages of adding to his 'lustre' in public. On 5 April 1493, for example, Henry granted his 'second born son' the office of Constable of Dover Castle and the wardenship of the Cinque Ports.[18] This ceremonial post had been in existence since at least the twelfth century and carried responsibility for five strategically important coastal towns in Kent and Sussex.

An even more prestigious appointment was to follow on 20 September 1494, when the king made his younger son Duke of York and a Knight of the Bath. The choice of title was doubly significant. Since 1362, it had been customary for the younger son of a ruling king to be made Duke of Clarence. Edward IV had gone against this tradition when he had made his second son Richard Duke of York. By choosing the same title, Henry VII was emphasising the unification of the houses of York and Lancaster, and demonstrating the king's goodwill towards his wife's family. More importantly, though, it signified that the previous holder of the title was dead, and that the 'pretender' Perkin Warbeck, who was now a potent threat to Henry VII's throne, was nothing but a fraud. This was further emphasised when the king made his son lieutenant of Ireland, which had traditionally harboured the enemies of the English crown.

A detailed account of the ceremony survives among the manuscripts of the British Library and makes it clear just how seriously the king took it. Henry VII, we are told, 'being at his manor of Woodstock determined at Allhallowtide then following to hold and keep royally and solemnly that feast in his palace of Westminster, and at that feast to dub his second son knight of the Bath and after to create him duke of York'.[19] The king and queen, together with Lady Margaret Beaufort, travelled from Richmond to Westminster for the ceremony, arriving on 28 October. The following day, the king sent for his son to be brought from Eltham 'with great honour, triumph and of great estates' and paraded through the streets of London, where he was received by the mayor, aldermen and by all the crafts in their liveries.[20]

On 30 October, the king dined in state, with his son Henry holding the towel for his ablutions. As night approached, the prince, together with the thirty young noblemen who were to be dubbed with him, was led into the parliament chamber, where baths and beds had been prepared for them. Henry's father signed him with the cross and his mother gave him her blessing, then the young prince and his fellow knights-in-waiting proceeded to bathe. Afterwards, they were ceremonially dried and went to their beds for some rest before attending chapel. Tradition dictated that they must keep vigil there, but this was too much to expect of the three-year-old prince, so he was given 'spices and confectionary' and allowed to sleep.

The following morning, after mass, the prince and his entourage were mounted on horses and rode through the palace to the Star Chamber, where the ceremony of knighting was to take place. Henry, an extrovert child, revelled in being the centre of attention. The dukes of Buckingham and Dorset placed a spur upon each of his heels, and the king then girded his son with his sword and dubbed him knight. Up until now, there is no indication in the detailed account of the day's proceedings that any concessions were made for Prince Henry's age. Only when he and his fellow knights returned to the chapel and offered their swords on the altar was the prince given some help to haul his sword into place. He then left the company and 'dined in his own chamber', rather than partaking of the rich fare that had been prepared for the public feast.[21]

The festivities continued the following day, 1 November, when the king, wearing 'his robes of estate royal and crowned', progressed to the parliament chamber, where he was greeted by all the nobles and prelates of his realm. His young son was led in by the Marquis of Dorset and Earl of Arundel, clad in a miniature version of the 'robes of estate' that his escorts wore. The king read out the form of words for conferring his son's dukedom, then 'created him duke of York with the gift of a thousand pounds per year'.[22] Afterwards, they progressed to chapel to give thanks in a solemn mass, and then on to yet another sumptuous banquet. This time, though, the prince was allowed to enjoy the feast with all the rest. If he gorged too much, then at least the main ceremonies were over so he would have time to recover from any ill effects.

A lavish tournament was held on 9 November, during which four 'gentlemen of the king' challenged all comers to run at the joust and compete for prizes of gold rings set with diamonds and rubies. This proved so popular that a second tournament was staged three days later. The king and queen attended both. Still the nobles' thirst for display was not quenched, however, for a third tournament was held on 13 November.

Although the young prince had relished his moment in the sun, it was over all too soon. When the last of the tournaments was concluded, he was escorted back to Eltham and his elder brother Arthur once more took his place at their father's side. But having tasted the delights that the royal court could offer, from that day forward Henry always hankered after more. Arthur's wedding had inspired a passion for tournaments and revelry that would grow into an all-consuming obsession by the time that Henry reached maturity. Frustration at having these delights so suddenly withdrawn may have been what prompted Henry to indulge in them to excess as soon as he was able.

To Henry's delight, events would soon prompt his father to bring his younger son to prominence once more. In the summer of 1495, the threat posed by Perkin Warbeck reached a crisis point. On 3 July the pretender landed at Deal in Kent with the support of Margaret of Burgundy. Although his small army was soon routed, Warbeck escaped to Ireland, where he found favour with Maurice FitzGerald, ninth Earl of Desmond. But he soon encountered resistance and fled to Scotland. Ever eager to seize an opportunity to annoy his southern neighbour, James IV promised Warbeck his protection and support. As well as posing a threat to his crown, Henry feared that Warbeck would disrupt the delicate negotiations that he was conducting with the powerful Spanish monarchs, Ferdinand and Isabella, for a marriage between their daughter Catherine and his son Arthur.

It may have been this that incited the king to propose a marriage alliance between his three-year-old daughter Elizabeth and the French prince, Francis (later Francis I). But he and the queen were devastated when, shortly afterwards, their daughter died at Eltham. This was the first experience of a family death for Elizabeth's elder brother Henry, and it must have dealt him and his other sister Margaret a cruel blow. The princess's body was conveyed from Eltham to Westminster Abbey, where it was buried in great state.

The king's growing unease was signalled by the fact that along with the usual dignitaries and ecclesiastics, he summoned both of his sons, as well as his uncle Jasper, to parliament in October 1495.[23] This was the only recorded occasion upon which the four-year-old Henry met his great-uncle, who was sixty years his senior. The hard-bitten warrior had largely retreated from public life during the previous two years, preferring the tranquillity of his estates in Gloucestershire and Oxfordshire. His health was rapidly declining, and he had drawn up a will the previous year. It gratified him, though, to see his precious nephew, on whose behalf he had battled so hard, wielding power over his parliament, with two sons in tow. For the younger of those, this was his first experience of royal government and, given his emerging character, he is likely to have grasped it with enthusiasm. For his great-uncle Jasper, though, it would be his last. He died just two months later. The king and queen attended his funeral at Keynsham Abbey, near Bristol. Having fathered no children, Jasper left all of his property and wealth to his nephew the king.

Prince Henry's name appears in a number of royal documents the following year, which suggests that his father was minded to make more of him as he grew older. Thus, on 16 March 1496, he cited 'Henry duke of York' in an indenture granting the lordship, manor and castle of Cardiff, the county of Glamorgan and the lordship of Morgannok in south Wales to Charles Somerset, Earl of Worcester and a cousin of the king. The latter was to help keep order for the king in these lands, and if he defaulted on the terms of the indenture, they would be forfeit to Prince Henry.[24]

Two days later, Henry's mother gave birth to another girl, Mary, who joined her siblings at Eltham. In November, Prince Henry was summoned to attend parliament again.[25] By then, the young prince had risen to sufficient prominence to be mentioned in the diary of Marino Sanuto, a renowned Venetian historian. He noted that the King of England 'has two sons, Arthur, Prince of Wales . . . and the other is Duke of York'.[26]

It was probably also in 1496 that Prince Henry was assigned a new tutor at Eltham. John Skelton was a brilliant scholar who had studied at both Cambridge and Oxford, and had come to the notice of the king when he visited the latter university in 1488. Henry VII had been so impressed that he had later conferred upon him a laureateship in classical Latin rhetoric, making Skelton the first English poet laureate. In 1493, Skelton was awarded another laureateship by Cambridge, which brought him to the attention of its benefactress, the king's mother, Lady Margaret Beaufort. It may have been she who recommended the scholar as a tutor for her younger grandson.

Little is known of Skelton's earlier history. His date of birth has been estimated at being around 1460, and it is possible that he was from Yorkshire.[27] He had connections with the Percy family and also spent time at Sheriff Hutton as a guest of Elizabeth Countess of Surrey, wife of the powerful courtier Thomas Howard. It is possible that he entered royal service as early as 1488, although in what capacity it is not certain. Two years later, the celebrated writer and printer William Caxton praised Skelton for his classical learning, his skill in translation, and his 'polished and ornate terms'.[28]

It is possible that Skelton had harboured an ambition for the post of royal tutor for some time. He had certainly worked hard to flatter the king's sons. He penned a now lost verse entitled 'Prince Arturis Creacyon' to celebrate Arthur's creation as Prince of Wales in 1489. Five years later, he wrote a similarly flattering panegyric when Prince Henry became Duke of York. His efforts were rewarded shortly afterwards when he was offered the post of tutor.

Despite his impressive credentials, Skelton was something of a controversial choice. Stridently self-confident, he was opinionated, outspoken and bursting with ideas, humour, languages and verse. As such, he presented a stark contrast to the more sober tutors usually favoured by the royal family. But the queen approved of her mother-in-law's choice, shrewdly judging that Skelton was an ideal match for her irrepressible younger son, who would have quickly tired of a more conventional tutor. His appointment also won praise from some of the greatest intellectuals of the age.

Two years after being employed as tutor to Prince Henry, Skelton also became his chaplain. He entered holy orders in 1498 and was ordained a priest on 9 June that year. He was attached to the abbey of St Mary of Graces, close to the Tower of London, and celebrated mass there on 11 November 1498 in the presence of Henry VII, who made him an offering of twenty shillings. Being both chaplain and tutor to the young prince meant that Skelton was responsible for shaping Henry's spiritual as well as intellectual upbringing.

The scholar was quick to realise the potential of his position, and proceeded to teach Henry not just the classical curriculum of grammar, Latin and religious studies, but manners, courtesy and government. He later boasted of his influence on the young prince:

The honour of England I learned to spell
I gave him drink of the sugared well,
Of Helicon's waters crystalline,
Acquainting him with the muses nine . . .[29]

The young Henry revelled in the company of this irreverent and outspoken man, who provided a welcome contrast to his serious and restrained father. Skelton, too, enjoyed his time at Eltham and found it an inspiring environment. While in the service of the prince, he wrote or translated a number of pedagogical and morality texts, as well as works on royalty and government, reflecting the fact that he had opinions on practically any matter. That he was now in the privileged position of royal tutor did not make him any less inclined to express them. His works were neatly described as 'pithy, pleasant and profitable' in a compilation published in 1568.[30]

Away from the closeted world of the royal schoolroom at Eltham, tensions were again mounting. In September 1497, after several failed invasion attempts, the pretender Perkin Warbeck landed off the coast of Cornwall. To the king's great 'sorrow and anxiety', he soon amassed considerable support in the county, which had long proved a rebellious one for the crown.[31] After being declared Richard IV on Bodmin Moor, Warbeck marched to Exeter with his 6,000-strong army and succeeded in taking the city. Greatly alarmed, the king sent a force to attack the rebel troops. The pretender lost his nerve and fled when he heard that Henry's scouts were at Glastonbury. He was soon apprehended by the king's men at Beaulieu Abbey in Hampshire.

To everyone's surprise, the king chose clemency over brutality. After forcing Warbeck to publicly deny his claims to the throne, he welcomed him to court and treated him as an honoured guest. But the affair had clearly shaken Henry, who was growing increasingly paranoid about the security of his regime. He therefore decided to stage a series of very public displays of kingship. Having invested enormous sums in a collection of magnificent new robes, he embarked upon numerous crown-wearings and ceremonies to touch for the 'king's evil' (scrofula), which it was believed would be miraculously cured as soon as the king laid his hands upon the sufferer.

The king also gathered his family close once more. In October 1497, the six-year-old Prince Henry received a summons to Woodstock, where his father was due to receive two Italian ambassadors: Raimondo da Soncino, the secretary of Ludovico Sforza, Duke of Milan, and a special envoy from Venice. The king had spared no expense in having the palace lavishly decorated with 'very handsome' tapestries, cloth of gold and gilt chairs. The young prince must have been dazzled by the sight of the richly adorned chamber, as well as by his father's apparel, which comprised 'a violet-coloured gown, lined with cloth of gold, and a collar of many jewels, and on his cap was a large diamond and a most beautiful pearl'. This may have inspired his own love of magnificence, both of furnishings and dress, which found full expression when he became king.

After being granted a private audience with the king, the ambassadors were introduced to his family. Prince Henry stood next to his mother, who was also dressed in cloth of gold. On the other side of her was Henry's paternal grandmother. To the untrained eye, it was an impressive demonstration of the might and majesty of the Tudor regime. But beneath this tableau of family strength and harmony, the ambassadors sensed an atmosphere of tension and fear. The strain of being forever on the lookout for threats to his crown showed in Henry's bearing and build. The splendour of his dress could not disguise his spare physique and prominent cheekbones, and his hair was flecked with grey at the temples. Soncino reported that the English king was 'suspicious of everything . . . [and] has no one he can trust, except his paid men at arms'. Francis Bacon concurred that Henry was 'full of apprehensions and suspicions'.[32]

On 29 November 1498, a little under three years after the death of Jasper Tudor, Prince Henry was granted all of his great-uncle's estates. This had been agreed by Act of Parliament on 14 December 1497 and amounted to a considerable inheritance. As well as the various castles, manors, liberties and other property and lands, Henry was to be paid £40 per year (equivalent to around £20,000 today). Further annual payments linked to Jasper's estates followed: £20 from London and Middlesex and £42 from Hereford.[33] Henry would retain Jasper's income and estates for life, and they would then pass to his heirs.

The date of the Act may have been significant. Henry was then six years old, an age that was viewed as a milestone by the Tudors, who believed that it marked the beginning of the transition from childhood to adulthood. From that day forward, the child would be 'breeched' – that is, dressed in adult-style attire. With two older siblings, and having been given a number of tantalising glimpses of royal power and ceremony, Henry was eager to prove that he was ready for manhood.

The prince's status changed again – less positively – on 21 February 1599, when his mother gave birth to a son. Henry's new brother was christened Edmund three days later at Greenwich and titled Duke of Somerset. Although Henry was thriving at Eltham, the birth of his younger brother Edmund was less welcome to him than it was to his parents. Prince Henry might have still been second in line to the throne, but he was no longer the only 'spare heir'. As Bacon observed, though a brother was 'a comfort . . . to have, yet it draweth the subjects' eyes a little aside'.[34] Neither was Henry any longer the only boy in the royal nursery at Eltham, for Edmund soon joined him and his two sisters there.

From his father's perspective, however, the timing of Edmund's birth could not have been more fortunate. Perkin Warbeck had attempted to escape Henry's clutches during the king's summer progress in 1498 and was now a prisoner in the Tower of London. Even in captivity, though, he remained a figurehead for opposition to the Tudor regime. Likewise, Edward IV's nephew Edward Plantagenet, Earl of Warwick, who also languished in the fortress, had a great deal of support from the Yorkists. The birth of a third son was exactly what Henry VII needed to secure his dynasty. But it gave him only temporary respite from the fears that constantly nagged at him, and in November he decided to have both Warbeck and Warwick executed on trumped-up charges of conspiracy.

The episode served as a salutary lesson for his son Henry about the necessary brutality of kingship, and one that the young boy would never forget. But his father was far from being the tyrant that Henry himself would later become. He only used violence when he had exhausted every other course, and he flinched from harming those closest to him, as Francis Bacon observed: 'Though he were a dark prince, and infinitely suspicious; and his times full of secret conspiracies and troubles; yet in 24 years of reign, he never put down or discomposed counsellor or near servant; save only [Sir William] Stanley the Lord Chamberlain.'

Not long after Edmund's arrival at Eltham, the Dutch scholar Desiderius Erasmus paid a visit there. Born in around 1466, Erasmus had proved an excellent scholar from his earliest years, but poverty had forced him into the religious orders. As a canon regular at Stein in southern Holland, he had fallen in love with Servatius Rogerus, a fellow canon, whom he referred to as 'half my soul'.[35] Later, after moving to Paris, he was suddenly dismissed from his post as tutor to a young man called Thomas Grey. It has been assumed that he had been conducting an illicit affair with his pupil, although there is no firm evidence for this. Erasmus was not denounced for his sexuality during his lifetime, and he took pains to condemn sodomy in his works. But he always displayed a weakness for attractive young men.

It was thanks to one such man that Erasmus had chosen to visit Prince Henry and his siblings. William Blount, Lord Mountjoy, had recently been appointed by the queen to be a mentor or 'study companion' to her second son. Her choice was very deliberate: Mountjoy was just the sort of man who could shape her son into a prince in the mould of her late father and brothers. He had been introduced to Elizabeth by her chamberlain, the Earl of Ormond, who was his stepfather. The fact that his grandfather had been a close attendant of Edward IV and the Woodville family must also have recommended him to the queen. Mountjoy had also proved his loyalty to the king by helping to suppress a rebellion. His father had once cautioned him not 'to desire to be great about princes, for it is dangerous'.[36] Mountjoy evidently decided to ignore this advice.

Alongside his loyalty and military prowess, Prince Henry's new companion was exceptionally well educated and cultured. He had recently returned from Paris, where he had immersed himself in classical studies and had become acquainted with Erasmus. The Dutch scholar had been so impressed with Mountjoy that he declared himself willing to follow him even to the 'lower world' itself. He later claimed that 'the sun never shone on a truer friend of scholars'.[37] It is likely that he was as attracted by the young man's handsome looks as by his intellectual abilities.

The esteem in which Erasmus held his young English acquaintance was mutual. When Mountjoy returned to England in 1499, he invited the scholar to accompany him. Having been dismissed from his position as tutor in Paris, Erasmus was no doubt eager to try for advancement in England. He was certainly curious to meet Prince Henry, with whom he had already begun a correspondence. He was also a great admirer of Skelton, and writing to Henry that year he referred to his tutor as 'a light and glory of English letters'.[38]

Erasmus and Mountjoy were joined by another companion. Described as 'a man of singular and rare learning', the twenty-one-year-old Thomas More was a rising star in intellectual and humanist circles.[39] He hailed from moneyed rather than noble stock, and his family had a history of service to the crown and city guilds. His father, Sir John More, had studied law and was progressing rapidly through the ranks of this profession.[40] Prince Henry's maternal grandfather, Edward IV, had given Sir John permission to bear a coat of arms, and he had subsequently developed close relationships with members of Edward's and later Henry VII's councils. Particularly strong was his connection to John Morton, who had served Henry VII as Lord Chancellor and Archbishop of Canterbury since the early years of his reign.

At a time when occupations tended to follow family lines, Sir John was clearly paving the way for his son's entry into law, and had also arranged marriages for his two daughters to men of the same profession. Sir John paid for Thomas to study Latin at St Anthony's School, Threadneedle Street, the finest grammar school in London. He left there in 1489 and entered the household of Archbishop John Morton. Thomas thrived in the intellectually stimulating atmosphere of Lambeth Palace, which was such a centre of culture and learning that it rivalled the court itself. The chaplain there was Henry Medwall, a talented playwright, who encouraged More's love of drama. The young man often took part in the Christmas revels that Medwall devised and gave impromptu performances. His wit and intelligence soon won the favour of Morton, who appointed More his personal attendant and was said to have boasted to his noble guests, 'This child here waiting at the table, whosoever shall live to see it, will prove a marvellous man.'[41]

As More reached his teenage years, the dichotomy of his character became apparent. His love of drama, wit and culture was countered by an extraordinarily strict discipline and self-control. The battle between the flesh and the spirit was already raging within him, and when, aged sixteen, he fell in love with a young woman, he was proud to record that he had held his passion in check. By the age of eighteen, it had become his custom to wear a hair shirt next to his skin. His unflinching piety would soon deepen into fanaticism; his passion into bigotry. But all the while he retained his humour, intellect and bonhomie, giving him the ability to converse easily with ecclesiastics, scholars, lawyers and courtiers alike. Erasmus famously described him as a man *omnium horarum*, or 'man for all seasons', and claimed that he was 'always friendly and cheerful, with something of the air of one who smiles easily, and (to speak frankly) disposed to be merry rather than serious or solemn'.[42] Only those closest to More knew the strength of the convictions that were masked by this pleasant exterior.

Archbishop Morton realised More's potential, and in 1492 he secured him a place at Canterbury College, Oxford. More studied there for two years and followed the ordinary curriculum of the liberal arts: grammar, rhetoric and logic. He returned to London shortly afterwards and, urged on by his father, entered an Inn of Chancery to study law. There, he 'very well prospered' and on 12 February 1496 he was formally admitted to Lincoln's Inn, where he remained until he was called to the bar five or six years later.[43] More's sojourn at Lincoln's Inn equipped him with a great deal more than legal expertise. It was a time of intense intellectual, spiritual and cultural development that shaped his outlook and beliefs. He cultivated a number of leading intellectuals, such as John Colet, the future Dean of St Paul's, the scholar and cleric William Grocyn, and Thomas Linacre, who had taught him Greek.

One of the most significant friendships that More forged during these years was with Erasmus. The two men met thanks to Mountjoy, with whom Erasmus was staying in Greenwich when he visited England in the summer of 1499. Mountjoy held More in some esteem, and invited him to pay a visit to Greenwich after Erasmus's arrival. It was a meeting of minds between More and Erasmus, who were united by their humanist principles and intellectual brilliance. Nature had never fashioned anything 'gentler, sweeter and happier than the character of Thomas More', Erasmus subsequently enthused in a letter to a friend.[44] They established a warm friendship that would last for the remainder of More's life.

It was probably Mountjoy who suggested that he and his three companions should visit the royal nursery at nearby Eltham. More and Erasmus, who were both hungry for advancement, agreed to the plan. They arrived to find all four royal children assembled in the great hall to greet them. The scions of the House of Tudor presented an appealing sight in their fine attire. Ten-year-old Margaret was the eldest; her sister Mary was just three and Edmund was still a baby. But Erasmus later recalled that it was the eight-year-old Henry who had made the greatest impression. Writing with the benefit of hindsight, he claimed that the young prince looked 'somehow like a natural king, displaying a noble spirit combined with peculiar courtesy'.[45] Although Erasmus's description may have been coloured by his knowledge that Henry was destined for the throne, there is little doubt that the young man was already a force to be reckoned with.

The prince had proved a precocious student, and by the time he met Erasmus and his friends he was widely versed in the classics, rhetoric and languages. Among his possessions at Eltham was *De Officiis* by Cicero, which Henry proudly inscribed 'Thys boke is myne'.[46] He no doubt anticipated the visit of these renowned scholars with great excitement. His love of learning was known to Thomas More, who arrived with a gift of writing to present to Henry. This put his companion Erasmus at a disadvantage, and he was mortified that he had arrived empty-handed. Henry evidently noted this, and when they all dined together afterwards, he could not resist challenging Erasmus to write him something. Seizing his chance to make amends, the Dutch scholar immediately rushed back to Greenwich and composed a flattering ode to England and its royal family. Entitled *Prosopopoeia Britanniae Maioris*, it ran to ten pages – an impressive feat, given the haste with which he had written it. If he thus redeemed himself for the lack of a gift, however, he failed to secure the hoped-for position at court. Erasmus left England a few months later, disillusioned with 'those wretched courtiers'.[47] But Henry would never forget their meeting, and they struck up a correspondence that would stimulate and shape the prince's intellect and ideals for many years to come.

If Henry lamented Erasmus's departure, he was far from lacking in intellectual stimulation, thanks to the continuing efforts of his tutor, John Skelton. He also delighted in the company of Lord Mountjoy, which sparked Skelton's jealousy. Desperate to claw back supremacy over the prince, his tutor penned the *Speculum Principis*, or 'mirror for princes', a guide to behaviour that he presented to Henry in 1501. In a deliberate side-swipe at his rival, he urged his young charge to 'love poets' because 'athletes are two a penny but patrons of the art are rare'.[48]

But by now it was clear that Skelton was losing the battle for influence over the prince. He was also growing increasingly frustrated with the strictures of a court position. These two factors combined to send Skelton on a self-destructive course. He vented his frustration in a series of controversial satirical texts mocking the social and sexual competitiveness at court. His most notorious work was *The Bowge of Court*, in which he cast himself as 'Drede', a man of learning and 'virtue', who finds himself on a ship steered by Fortune and filled with people hoping to make their way to court.[49] He is surrounded by thieves, gamblers, pimps and potential murderers, all of whom flatter and scheme against each other relentlessly and try to involve Drede in their plots.

Skelton's non-conformism might have been what initially recommended him as a tutor to the precocious young prince, but he had overstepped the mark. Henry's father had enough rebellious subjects to deal with; he could not tolerate one within his son's household. The timing and circumstances of Skelton's departure are not clear. He was still in post on 29 April 1502, when 'the Duke of York's schoolmaster' received a gift of 40 shillings from the king.[50] But it is possible that this was a pay-off, because Skelton disappears from the court records thereafter. By April 1504, he had moved to Diss in Norfolk and was rector of the parish church of St Mary's, a post that he held until his death. This new position brought him wealth but little satisfaction. The force of nature that had dominated Prince Henry's household was hardly suited to the quiet life of a country clergyman. He certainly had plenty of time to reflect upon his impetuous and ill-advised actions, and he evidently soon resolved to claw his way back to royal favour.

By the time that Skelton left Eltham Palace, Henry had resumed his position as the only male child in the royal nursery. His younger brother Edmund died at Hatfield in June 1500, aged just fifteen months. The cause of his death is not recorded. On 22 June, his tiny coffin was 'conveyed honourably' through the streets of London with 'many noble personages' in attendance.[51] The infant prince was buried next to his sister Elizabeth at Westminster Abbey with what must have been considerable ceremony because the chief mourner was Edward Stafford, third Duke of Buckingham, one of the foremost noblemen of the realm.

Born in 1478, Buckingham had royal blood in his veins. His mother, Katherine Woodville, was the sister of Edward IV's queen, and therefore the aunt of the current queen. Like the Tudors, he could also trace his descent from Edward III's son John of Gaunt, through the Beaufort family. Buckingham and his brother Henry had been made wards of Lady Margaret Beaufort upon her son's accession in 1485. A year after taking part in Prince Henry's creation as Duke of York, he had been made a Knight of the Order of the Garter. Fiercely ambitious and stridently self-confident, Buckingham was always conspicuous at the great gatherings of court. He also had a keen sense of the superiority of his birth and always took care to dress lavishly – and expensively. On one occasion, he was said to have worn a gown worth £1,500 (equivalent to more than £700,000).

There is no record of Henry's reaction to the death of his younger brother, but having now lost two infant siblings in the space of five years, he had learned a salutary lesson about how tragically short life could be. He had a diversion, however, in the form of John Holt, who arrived at Eltham shortly after Skelton's departure in order to take up the post that he had vacated. Holt was a far more conventional choice as tutor. A fellow of Magdalen College, Oxford, in 1496 he had been appointed grammar master in the household of Archbishop Morton at Lambeth Palace. It was no doubt Morton who brought him to the attention of the king, and in 1502 Henry selected him for the post of tutor to his second son.

There is little evidence of the impact that Holt had upon his new pupil, who was eleven by the time of Holt's appointment. Besides, Henry was more diverted by a new companion who had joined the household at Eltham. Henry Guildford was two years older than the prince, and his family was of proven loyalty to the crown. His father, Sir Richard, had joined Henry VII in exile in Brittany and had helped to plan his campaign to seize power from Richard III. As king, Henry had rewarded him with a rapid succession of promotions, including Master of the Horse, knight of the king's body and councillor. Guildford also assumed special responsibility for the security of his royal master, a sign of the trust that this increasingly paranoid king invested in him. He had been present when Prince Henry had been made Duke of York in 1494, and had also been tasked with negotiating the marriage between his brother Arthur and Catherine, daughter of the Spanish monarchs Ferdinand and Isabella.

Another indication of the king's favour towards Sir Richard Guildford was that he had attended his wedding to Joan Vaux, his second wife, who fell pregnant soon afterwards and gave birth to a son, Henry, in 1489. Joan was subsequently appointed to the household of the queen. Despite the favour that the couple enjoyed, they were forever in debt, thanks in no small part to Guildford's mismanagement of their finances and estates. He had been forced to surrender his exchequer post in 1487 when some irregularities were discovered in his financial affairs, and he was later arrested for debt. The Guildfords' precarious finances may have prompted them to secure a position at court for their son Henry, who was appointed cupbearer to the king's younger son at Eltham.

Prince Henry and his new companion were like two peas in a pod. Physically, they resembled each other, both being well-built, athletic boys. Like the prince, Guildford had an irrepressible energy and loved jousting and sport. He also delighted in the entertainments on offer at court. These may have inspired the role that he would fulfil later in his career in royal service.

While his son was forging what would be a lifelong friendship with the younger Tudor prince, Sir Richard and his fellow commissioners had at last reached an agreement for the marriage of the elder prince. The negotiations had dragged on for nine long years, becoming embroiled in the shifting allegiances of foreign affairs, as well as the question of the Spanish princess's dowry. This was eventually set at 200,000 crowns (equivalent to around £2.5 million today) and a proxy betrothal sealed the bargain at Woodstock in 1497. But it would be a further two years before the proxy marriage took place, followed by another ceremony in 1500.

On 2 October 1501, Catherine finally arrived in England. Just shy of her sixteenth birthday, she was exquisitely pretty with strawberry-blonde hair, a smooth, pale complexion and large dark eyes – more an English rose than a typical Spanish beauty. An exceptionally devout young woman, she had benefited from an excellent education and was praised for her skill in Latin, as well as her knowledge of classical and vernacular literature. The Spanish humanist Juan Luis Vives greatly admired her abilities, and Erasmus regarded her as a model of Christian womanhood.

Catherine's parents had insisted that she must not meet her betrothed until the day of the wedding. The English king was not pleased with this arrangement, and after a diplomatic impasse, he rode to intercept her as she made her way in a ceremonious procession to London, insisting that he would see her 'even if she were in her bed'.[52] Catherine received him courteously, but it was an awkward meeting, thanks to neither being able to speak the other's language. Even so, Henry left satisfied that the Spanish princess was a fitting bride for his son and heir.

Prince Arthur himself arrived shortly afterwards. Now aged fifteen, he had grown into a tall young man with a slight frame and the pinched features that were typical of the Lancastrian line. By contrast, the younger Tudor son was all Yorkist: tall, athletic, and bursting with energy and *joie de vivre*. Passionate and imperious, Henry was far from being a naturally subservient 'spare heir'. Although the surviving portraits show a passing resemblance between the two brothers, there was a delicacy about Arthur that formed a sharp contrast to Henry's robustness. Intellectually, Henry was the equal of his brother, although in recent years Arthur had gained an advantage from being taught by the renowned humanist scholars Bernard André and Thomas Linacre, and he knew the works of Homer, Cicero and Ovid by heart. Most useful was his fluency in Latin, which meant that he and Catherine were able to converse far more freely than she had with his father.

Catherine was so delighted with their first meeting that she threw an impromptu party that evening. She and her ladies danced to the music that her minstrels played. Prince Arthur joined in 'right pleasant and honourably', but he respected the strictures laid down by his future parents-in-law and refused to dance with his bride, choosing Joan Guildford (mother of his brother's companion) as his partner instead.[53]

The next morning, Catherine and her entourage embarked on the final stage of the journey to London. At Kingston-upon-Thames, ten miles south-west of the city, she was greeted by the Duke of Buckingham, who rode at the head of an impressive retinue of three to four hundred horsemen all clad in red-and-black livery. He escorted Catherine to her lodgings in Lambeth, where she was to await the beginning of two weeks of elaborate pageantry and entertainments to mark her marriage, including the wedding ceremony itself.

On 12 November, Catherine made her formal entry into London, her cavalcade slowly making its way through the city streets, which were lined with thousands of people craning to catch a glimpse of the Spanish princess. Among them was Prince Henry's acquaintance, Thomas More. Although he was full of praise for the 'charming young girl' who 'thrilled the hearts of everyone', he was scathing of her ladies, who all wore black so as not to outshine their mistress. 'Except for three, or at the most four, of them, they were just too much to look at,' he wrote to a friend. 'Hunchbacked, undersized, barefoot pygmies from Ethiopia. If you had been there you would have thought they were refugees from hell.'[54]

Meanwhile, at Eltham, Prince Henry was being groomed for a starring role in the proceedings. Although the king had paraded his younger son in public on a number of previous occasions, this was to be by far the highest profile event. Henry had been accorded the honour of escorting his future sister-in-law from her lodgings in the Bishop's Palace at Lambeth to St Paul's Cathedral, where her marriage to Arthur would at last be solemnised. The ten-year-old prince may already have heard favourable reports of the beautiful

Spanish princess from More, Guildford and others. He certainly seemed to be half in love with the idea of her already.

The wedding was scheduled for 14 November, and on that day thousands of Londoners turned out to see one of the most dazzling processions in royal history. The city was also crowded with dignitaries from across the kingdom, including a number of high-ranking young gentlemen from Prince Henry's entourage. Principal among them was Lord Mountjoy, who was rapidly rising in favour with the king himself and would later be appointed to the council.

Both Prince Arthur, who arrived first at St Paul's, and his bride were dressed in white, which was unusual for the time. It may have been to ensure that they were clearly visible to the crowds that thronged the streets, or as a symbol of their purity and youth. Even so, their outfits were far from plain. Catherine was described by one admiring observer as being dressed from head to toe in 'costly apparel both of goldsmith's work and embroidery, rich jewels [and] massy chains' as she rode on a horse 'bedecked with glittering gold bells and spangles'.[55]

But it was Prince Henry who stole the show at the wedding. Although there is no record of how he was dressed, his regal bearing and charisma won the admiration of the crowds. Here was a prince in the mould of his Yorkist forebears: tall, auburn-haired and full of energy and charm. Even though he was the younger of the two Tudor princes, he looked far more robust than Arthur, who appeared gaunt and ill. Catherine's physician, Dr Alcaraz, was shocked by her groom's frailty and claimed that he had 'never seen a man whose legs and other bits of his body were so thin'.[56]

According to the same source, Arthur was in such an enfeebled state that he was unable to consummate the marriage. Alcaraz later recalled that: 'The Prince had been denied the strength necessary to know a woman, as if he was a cold piece of stone, because he was in the final stages of phthisis [consumption].' This is contradicted by other accounts, such as Edward Hall's *Chronicle*, which asserts: 'This lusty prince and his beautiful bride were brought and joined together in one bed naked and there did that act, which to the performance and full consummation of matrimony was most requisite and expedient.'[57] Arthur himself, having emerged from the bedchamber the following morning with a 'good and sanguine complexion', was quick to boast of his sexual prowess. He loudly demanded a cup of ale, 'for I have this night been in the midst of Spain'.[58]

Prince Henry did not know it, but whether or not his brother's marriage to Catherine had been consummated would have profound implications for his own life. He saw Arthur shortly afterwards when, accompanied by their father and a 500-strong entourage, they processed in great state to St Paul's for a thanksgiving ceremony. If Henry noticed that there was anything amiss with his elder brother's health or demeanour, then it was not recorded. To the crowds who had re-emerged from their houses to watch the king and his two sons lead the procession, everything appeared as it should be.

This impression was reinforced by the week of festivities that was staged in Westminster to celebrate the marriage. If the seemingly endless round of tournaments, pageants and dancing tired Prince Arthur, they were a source of constant delight to his younger brother. One of the evening entertainments took place at Westminster Hall, which was splendidly bedecked with arrases and displays of the royal plate. Catherine and her ladies, 'in apparel after the Spanish guise', danced two 'bass dances' – a stately dance in which the feet do not leave the floor. But her new brother-in-law had no patience for such formal displays, and when he took to the floor with his sister Margaret, 'perceiving himself to be encumbered with his clothes, [he] suddenly cast off his gown, and danced in his jacket'. The assembled dignitaries were delighted at this display of youthful exuberance, and even Henry's father, who was always anxious to ensure that royal dignity was maintained, showed 'right great and singular pleasure'.[59]

Once the festivities had been concluded at Westminster, the royal party travelled ten miles west to the magnificent palace of Richmond, which the king had ordered to be swiftly completed in time for the final stage of the wedding celebrations. Although he is not mentioned, it is likely that Prince Henry was among the guests, given his position in the royal family and the fact that he had proved such a resounding success in the proceedings so far. All too soon, it was time to bid goodbye to his elder brother and pretty sister-in-law, aware that with the conclusion of the festivities, he would return to the relative seclusion of Eltham.

Arthur's wedding had temporarily propelled his younger brother into the spotlight. But it was to have a far more lasting impact upon Henry than that. Not long afterwards, when Arthur and Catherine had taken up residence at Ludlow Castle, the prince fell dangerously ill. The cause of his malady has been debated ever since. There were rumours of a 'great sickness' in the area, which may have been the sweating sickness, plague or influenza. But Arthur's health had been fragile for some time, and it is likely that he had been suffering from tuberculosis. Either this alone proved fatal, or it weakened his immune system so that he fell prey to the local contagion. A contemporary record claimed that 'a pitiful disease and sickness' of 'deadly corruption did utterly vanquish and overcome the blood'.[60]

On 2 April 1502, after just twenty weeks of marriage, Arthur died. At a stroke, his younger brother's status and expectations were transformed. Henry was now not merely the spare, but the heir to the throne.

2

'Having no affection or fancy unto him'

WHEN NEWS OF Prince Arthur's death was brought to the king at Greenwich, he was utterly devastated. He went at once to find the queen, who 'with full great and constant comfortable words' tried to console him. With remarkable self-control, Elizabeth set aside her own grief and reminded her husband that they still had 'a fair prince, two fair princesses' and were 'both young enough' to have more children. Only when she had returned to the privacy of her chamber did she give vent to her sorrow, weeping so uncontrollably that her attendants sent for the king to comfort her. He came at once 'and showed her how wise counsel she had given him before, and he for his part would thank God for his son, and would she should do in like wise'.[1]

The 'fair prince' who was now the sole comfort and hope of his parents – and of the kingdom – might have received the news of his brother's death with rather more mixed feelings. Shock was no doubt among them, but this stridently self-confident young prince must also have felt excitement and elation that the all-too-fleeting attention he had enjoyed at Arthur's wedding celebrations had returned tenfold – and forever.

It is interesting to speculate what might have happened between the two brothers if Arthur had not died young. Henry's personality was hardly suited to playing second fiddle for long, and he might well have played out the history of his maternal great-uncles, George, Duke of Clarence and Richard of Gloucester, whose lust for power incited them to try and overthrow the natural order of succession.

In life, his elder brother had exerted little influence over Henry, but his untimely death would have the most profound impact possible. Henry was immediately propelled to the hallowed status of 'my lord prince', heir to the throne of England. This was quick to take effect. Negotiations for a marriage between the king's younger son and Margaret of Angoulême, kinswoman to the King of France, had been well underway by the time of Arthur's death. But these were now put on hold, and talks were opened with Ferdinand of Aragon to transfer his daughter Catherine to the surviving Tudor prince. Both he and his English counterpart were anxious to uphold their connection, and by September an initial treaty had been drawn up. It was signed the following June, and specified that a betrothal should take place within two months. Perhaps out of consideration for what had happened with Arthur, whom some thought had died from having sex too young, the treaty also specified that Prince Henry must have reached his fifteenth birthday.

Nicholas Fox, a lawyer at court, was present when the king summoned his son Henry to discuss the matter of his marriage. He recorded the conversation that followed. 'Son Henry,' the king began, 'I have agreed with the King of Aragon that you should marry Catherine, your brother's widow, in order that the peace between us might be continued.' When he asked his son if he assented to the match, the prince dutifully replied that he would do as his father wished.

Henry's compliance may have been due to more than simple obedience. As a ten-year-old boy, he had been dazzled by the beautiful Spanish princess, and the idea that she was now a helpless maiden who needed rescuing would have appealed to his chivalric ideals. For her part, Catherine was enthusiastic about the prospect of marrying the handsome young Tudor prince who had escorted her to the ceremony for her first marriage.

But for the young prince to marry his late brother's wife was no straightforward matter. The Church set down strict laws about consanguinity, and Henry and Catherine were related in the first degree of affinity. Even though Catherine, supported by her chief gentlewoman Doña Elvira, insisted that her marriage to Arthur had never been consummated, a papal dispensation would still have to be sought. No sooner had the betrothal been agreed, than it was threatened by the appointment of a new pope in November 1503.

Julius II was a belligerent and forthright character, and insisted that he needed to 'consider the case more maturely'.[2]

Prince Henry himself seemed to have little or no involvement in these diplomatic wranglings. A more immediate impact of his brother's death was the change in circumstances that he experienced in the household at Eltham. The king was no longer content for his son to be attended by women: the heir to the throne must be raised in a predominantly male household. Even Henry's lady mistress, Elizabeth Denton, was transferred to the household of his grand-mother, Lady Margaret Beaufort, and replaced by several new male attendants. Most of these were young, in their late teens or early twenties, and were drawn from the households of Henry's father and late brother.

Among them was William Thomas, a devout Welshman who had served Prince Arthur at Ludlow. Ralph Pudsey, formerly a groom of the king's privy chamber, was appointed the prince's sewer and keeper of his jewellery.[3] Another of the new men was the nineteen-year-old William Compton, son of a Warwickshire landowner, who had been made a ward of Henry VII upon the death of his father in 1493, and raised among the menial servants of the royal household. Meanwhile, Sir Henry Marney, a hard-bitten and ambitious royal councillor, was put in overall charge of the household. He soon enjoyed unparalleled access to the prince, and even had a pallet bed in his young master's own chamber.

The arrival of this new contingent of accomplished young men at Eltham could not have come at a more propitious time for Henry. The boisterous young prince, now just shy of his eleventh birthday, had outgrown the attentions of his mother and lady mistress and was eager for the company of like-minded, energetic men. Along with his uncle Arthur Plantagenet and his mentor Lord Mountjoy, they could act as role models, inspiring Henry with their sporting prowess, courtly manners and political guile.

Now that her husband had taken over their surviving son's upbringing, the queen seldom visited Eltham – appreciating, perhaps, that she had no place in this male-dominated household. She was in any case preoccupied by the expectation of adding to the royal nursery, for, true to her promise to the king, she had fallen pregnant soon after Arthur's death. Payments in the household accounts to apothecaries and nurses suggest that all was not well, however, and on 2 February 1503 she was delivered 'suddenly' of a girl. Something must have gone wrong with the birth because a physician was sent for urgently. Nine days later, both mother and daughter were dead.

For all that he revelled in the company of his new male companions, Henry was devastated by the loss of his mother. The blow had hardly been softened by the fact that his father had dispatched two attendants, Sir Charles Somerset and Sir Richard Guildford, father of the prince's companion, to convey the news, rather than doing so in person. Apparently not thinking to comfort his son, the king had promptly retreated to his privy chamber and refused to see anyone except his own mother.

Grief-stricken, Prince Henry went to court with his sisters. An illuminated manuscript in the National Library of Wales shows the three siblings in their late mother's bedchamber. Margaret and Mary are sitting on the floor. They have a dignified bearing, but the fact they are in mourning for their mother is indicated by their black headdresses. By contrast, their brother Henry has given himself over to his grief. With his head in his hands, he is weeping onto the sheets of his mother's empty bed.

With his father a distant and, it seems, rather cold figure, Henry sought comfort from another of the men in his life. He had evidently remained in contact with Thomas More since his visit to Eltham four years before. Eager to help the grieving prince – and, perhaps, lay the groundwork for his own advancement – More composed a eulogy for the late queen's tomb. The 'Rueful Lamentation' was written as a farewell address from Elizabeth to her grieving family. Referring to their 'loving son', she urges the king:

Erst were you father, and now must you supply
The mother's part also, for lo now here I lie.[4]

But the king did not seem to heed this advice. For six long weeks, he remained shut away in his privy chamber at Richmond Palace, with only his mother and a small number of trusted servants for company. There, weakened by grief at his wife's death, Henry fell prey to a tubercular condition that had afflicted him during previous winters. He also developed an acute, pustular tonsillitis. As the infection spread through his lungs, his breathing became laboured and he was unable to swallow or even open his mouth. He lay like this for several days, and it seemed that he was edging ever closer towards death.

Greatly alarmed, the king's attendants resolved to keep their master's perilous condition a secret in case his enemies should seize the advantage and overthrow his regime. They would probably have concealed the king's illness from his son and heir, too, were it not for the arrival of Arthur Plantagenet. The king may have agreed to admit him out of respect for his late wife, given that he was her kin. It is not clear why he had left Eltham to attend the king, but it is possible that he had been dispatched by Prince Henry, who was anxious for news of his father. He must have wondered if yet another death in his family was about to hasten his accession to the throne.

As the weeks dragged on, the king's sickness seemed only to grow worse, and as a fever took hold, he slipped in and out of delirium. His son's body of attendants may have been preparing the prince for the prospect that he might come into his inheritance sooner than expected. Although Prince Henry was a fine young man with all the makings of a great king, the accession of a minor threatened disaster for this fledgling Tudor dynasty. Other blood claimants were still endlessly plotting the king's overthrow. How much more easily might that be achieved if they had only an eleven-year-old boy to contend with. 'A number of great personages discussed among themselves the shape of things that might come should his grace depart this life . . . [who] should have rule in England,' reported one contemporary. 'Some of them spoke of my lord of Buckingham, saying that he was a noble man and would be a royal ruler. Others spoke of Edmund de la Pole. But none of them spoke of the Prince of Wales.'[5]

At last, however, towards the end of March 1504, the king began to show signs of recovery. Soon, he was well enough to present himself to the public court and prove that all was well. There would be no minority: his son Henry would have to wait a while longer for his inheritance. But the weeks of sickness had aged the forty-seven-year-old king considerably. His hair had turned white and his face was marked with the lines of grief. Sir Hugh Conway, treasurer of Calais, whispered that the king was 'a weak man and a sickly, not likely to be a long-lived man'.[6]

The king's manner had changed as much as his appearance. He had always been naturally introverted, but had made an effort to overcome that in the interests of projecting an image of majesty. Now, even though he had re-emerged into society, he seemed to have somehow shut himself off from the world. The death of his wife and eldest son in the space of less than a year had left him feeling dangerously destabilised. The contemporary Venetian historian Sanuto spoke out Henry's fears when he observed: 'England will make a stir, and affairs there be in commotion.'[7] With just one son left to secure the future of his dynasty, he was now consumed by paranoia and suspicion.

Grief for the woman they had both adored could have united Prince Henry and his father. Instead, it was now all too clear that the prince could seek no more solace from the king than he had been able to in the immediate aftermath of his mother's death. Their relationship from this time forward suggests that his father's apparent coldness and insensitivity may have fostered a growing resentment in his young son.

If Henry VII proved unwilling to play an active role in the upbringing of his sole surviving male heir after Elizabeth's death, then the same could not be said of the boy's domineering grandmother, Lady Margaret Beaufort. She was quick to fill the void left by Henry's mother, and her influence was most immediately felt in the strict religious observances that she inflicted upon her grandson's household. Lady Margaret also introduced her grandson to John Fisher, who was appointed Bishop of Rochester in 1504.

More than twenty years Henry's senior, Fisher had gained renown as a scholar and humanist. Like his contemporaries More and Colet, he was strongly committed to educational reform, and in the same year that he was made bishop he was appointed Chancellor of Cambridge University. Erasmus frequently praised Fisher as a model of his calling, and Vergil described him as 'a man of great learning and the highest honour and piety'.[8] In religious matters, though, the young bishop was strictly conservative and determined to uphold the doctrine of the Roman Catholic Church. This chimed with Lady Margaret's own views, and he was soon high in her favour. Although he did not have a formal role in her grandson's household, he would have been a regular presence, and there is some suggestion that he acted as Henry's tutor for a time. Quite what the prince thought of this austere young cleric is not recorded, but if Fisher won his respect as a man of piety and intellect, it is unlikely that Henry sought his company as he did that of his more pleasure-loving companions.

In the same year that Prince Henry met Fisher, another of his father's churchmen had risen to the highest ecclesiastical position in the kingdom. William Warham was of relatively obscure birth, but had benefited from an excellent education and had risen steadily through the ecclesiastical ranks during Henry VII's reign. He had proved his loyalty to the Tudor regime in 1493 when he had joined an embassy to persuade Margaret of Burgundy to withdraw her support from the pretender, Perkin Warbeck. Warham had so distinguished himself on this mission that Henry VII had subsequently entrusted him to negotiate with the Spanish ambassador over the details of the marriage between Prince Arthur and Catherine of Aragon. But only now, in 1504, did the fifty-four-year-old Warham finally enjoy the fruits of his long career in diplomacy and the Church. In January, he was appointed Lord Chancellor, and three months later he was enthroned as Archbishop of Canterbury. There is no record of what, if anything, Prince Henry thought of this new appointee, but Warham would go on to play a significant part in the young man's life.

Meanwhile, Henry's attitude towards his father could hardly have been improved by news of a shocking development at court. Although the king had been utterly grief-stricken at the loss of his queen, almost as soon as he had returned from his self-imposed seclusion, he announced his intention to find a new wife. The truly shocking part, though, was that the lady he had chosen was his widowed daughter-in-law, Catherine of Aragon, who was already betrothed to his son. But the papal dispensation had proved slow in coming, and there had also been wranglings between Henry and

Ferdinand over Catherine's dowry. The latter remained a bone of contention between the two monarchs for a long time to come.

When Catherine heard that she was now being considered as a wife for her father-in-law, rather than his son, she was horrified. Although she had lived in uncertainty after Arthur's death, not knowing whether she should remain in England or return to her native Spain, she found the idea of marrying Henry VII, who was almost thirty years her senior, utterly abhorrent. In panic, she appealed to her parents to intervene. Her mother wrote at once to the English king, upbraiding him for suggesting 'a very evil thing', and demanding that he send her daughter home.

Henry demurred. His real interest in Catherine lay not so much in her youthful charms, but in the sizeable dowry that had been agreed for her marriage to Arthur, which had not yet been paid in full. He therefore intended to keep her in England as a bargaining tool. If he could marry her, better still: after all, he was maintaining her in some considerable style in a separate household. Eventually, the king agreed to drop the idea, but he continued to apply pressure on Catherine's parents to pay what was left of the dowry. Realising that they were unlikely to do so without an incentive, he revived the scheme to marry her to his son. There is no evidence that he consulted Henry on the matter.

On 23 February 1504, Henry was formally created Prince of Wales. He had not immediately inherited the title after his elder brother's death because his father had to be sure that Arthur's widow Catherine was not pregnant. If she had been carrying a son, he would have taken precedence in the succession. But it was now almost two years since Arthur's death, so the time was ripe for his brother to be invested. The previous October, Henry had inherited the dukedom of Cornwall, a title that could only be held by the monarch's eldest son. Now, at last, he was made Prince of Wales, together with the associated title of Earl of Chester. In sharp contrast to his creation as Duke of York, there were no ostentatious ceremonies or celebrations. Rather, it was a strictly political event, as the Act of Recognition that was passed by parliament shortly afterwards made clear. This confirmed the young Henry 'to be now the King's heir apparent, Prince of Wales, Duke of Cornwall and earl of Chester'.[9] It also annulled his creation as Duke of York and diverted the associated revenues to the crown.

This was proving to be a significant year for Prince Henry because on 24 June, four days before his thirteenth birthday, he left Eltham to join the royal household at Richmond. The timing was deliberate: the Tudors viewed thirteen as the age at which boys became adults. Henry had certainly grown into an impressive young man, full of learning and accomplishments. He was also strikingly handsome, with an athletic physique that had been honed by the many hours he spent hunting and at the tiltyard with his male companions at Eltham.

As such, Henry had grown into the living embodiment of his maternal grandfather, Edward IV. Some of the attributes they shared were purely genetic: the auburn hair, fair complexion, long nose and small, rosebud mouth. Henry also had the same tall, broad-shouldered physique, and was described by one contemporary as being 'most comely of his personage'. The Venetian ambassador enthused that he had 'an excellently formed head and a very well proportioned body of tall stature [which] gave him an air of royal majesty, such as has not been witnessed in any other Sovereign for many years'.[10]

Henry's character was also strikingly similar to that of his grandfather. Both men were strong-minded and ruthless, but also affable, seductive and charismatic. Like his grandfather, Henry could dominate any gathering – a skill that his father notably lacked. His restless energy and athleticism found expression in the tournament arena, where he evoked memories of his warlike grandfather with displays of military prowess. As king, he would also emulate Edward's magnificence of dress and display – like him, appreciating its political worth.

By stark contrast, this exuberant young prince seemed to share little in common, physically or otherwise, with his father. Although he was no doubt impatient to begin his training as king in earnest, the prospect of living with a man whom he hardly knew, but whom he had grown to resent, was as unappealing as it was daunting. Moreover, Henry had held sway in his own private domain at Eltham; now he would have to cede authority to his father.

This was made clear as soon as Henry arrived at Richmond, when both his staff and council were immediately absorbed into the king's own. The latter evidently intended to keep a close eye upon his son and heir, for he appointed a number of his own trusted servants to attend him. They included Sir Richard Empson, a talented but unpopular young lawyer, who was appointed a member of the prince's council. The ordinances that he had drawn up for Arthur's upbringing now equally applied to his younger son, notably that 'all the talk in his presence was of virtue, honour, cunning, wisdom and deeds of worship, of nothing that shall move him to vice'.[11]

It was with some relief that the prince learned that he was permitted to retain his beloved uncle, Arthur Plantagenet, along with a more recent appointee, Sir Henry Marney. Henry's esteem for the latter is evident from the New Year gifts of a pointed diamond and a gold tablet that he presented to him. It is not clear whether the prince's other young companions accompanied him, but the fact that Guildford, Compton and the rest are seldom mentioned during his years at Richmond suggests that they had been left behind, which can only have been a source of frustration and grief to Henry.

Royal tradition dictated that an heir should be raised apart from his parents in order to encourage independence and initiative. This had certainly been Henry's experience to date, at least with regard to his father, but the increasingly paranoid and insecure king was now determined to superintend every aspect of life at the royal court. 'Nothing escapes his attention,' remarked one observer.[12] His fears were far from groundless: every day seemed to bring news of some 'dark treason'. 'At that time men began to bend their minds to revolution, so that not only did many nobles make secret plans to overthrow the king, but also persons of the lowest birth everywhere maligned the king himself with scandalous writings and rhymes composed in the vernacular,' recalled Polydore Vergil. 'Indeed, these evil utterances returned to choke some, for those who were caught were executed.'[13]

As well as wreaking his vengeance upon the perpetrators, the king ensured that the tightest possible security was in place for himself and his son. He chose apartments for Henry at Richmond that could only be reached by way of his own, and made the same arrangements in every other residence. In stark contrast to the freedom of his life at Eltham, the prince was no longer able to go anywhere unless he was accompanied by the tightly knit body of attendants selected by his father. If ever he wished to leave the palace to hunt or joust, he was escorted out of a side door into a private park.

But the suffocating environment of his father's household could not protect Henry from all dangers. Late one evening, when he and the king were walking together through the newly built private galleries at Richmond, the floor suddenly caved in just inches from where they had come to a halt. His father, ever alert to assassins, feared that they were under attack. In the event, it soon became clear that faulty workmanship was to blame. But the incident was an uncomfortable reminder to Henry that no matter how much he tried to protect his precious son and heir, he could never completely guarantee his safety.

The king's apparently cold yet restrictive treatment of his son might well have been simple protectiveness. The loss of Prince Arthur had affected him deeply, and it is perhaps understandable that he was anxious to ensure the well-being of his sole surviving son. The Tudors were, after all, a fledgling dynasty – and, with Yorkist claimants still causing trouble abroad, a fragile one too. A secret letter from the late queen's cousin, Edmund de la Pole, reveals that he and his supporters were well aware of the fact. He wrote that if the king's 'second son Henry' were to die, then the throne would be his.[14]

It is also possible, though, that Henry's increasing paranoia about plots and conspiracies extended even to his son. One contemporary claimed that the king was 'beset by fear that his son might during his lifetime obtain too much power by his connexion with the house of Spain'.[15] Certainly, father and son clashed on a number of occasions, most notably in 1508 when the king quarrelled so violently with Henry that it seemed 'as if he sought to kill him'.[16]

But these accounts were written by men hostile to the king, and it seems more likely that his overbearing behaviour towards Prince Henry resulted more from a desire to protect him from the plots that were forever swarming about his crown. Moreover, rather than seeking to deprive him of power, the king was quick to realise that his charismatic and popular heir could bolster the stability of the

Tudor regime. The contemporary accounts record a number of instructions from the king and 'my lord the prince of Wales', which suggests that Henry was beginning to share his kingly duties with his son.[17]

If the king privately envied his heir's natural gift for public relations, this did not stop him from capitalising upon it. Shortly after the prince's arrival at Richmond, his father took him on progress. In contrast to the summer progresses of recent years, which had stayed close to London, this was much more ambitious, extending deep into the rebellious county of Kent and other parts of the South East. The royal party was to stay at the houses of all the leading men of that region so that the king might gauge their loyalty – and show off his handsome and charismatic successor.

They were still on progress when a missive arrived from Pope Julius concerning the proposed marriage of Prince Henry to his widowed sister-in-law Catherine. It was not the hoped-for dispensation, but an assurance to the English king that he was still giving the matter his careful attention. After long months of waiting, the king was deeply frustrated, and it must have soured his enjoyment of the progress. But his son was still relishing this opportunity to explore his future kingdom. After years in the shadows, he was now being fêted as the heir to the throne. It was a role to which he seemed to have been born.

All too soon, the progress came to an end and the prince returned to Richmond with his father. Once there, the king set in place the careful plans that he had made for his son's continuing education. The prince's tutor, John Holt, had died in the same month that his pupil had joined the household at Richmond, and he had been replaced by another sober grammar master, William Hone. Meanwhile, in preparation for his son's arrival, Henry had expanded the staff at the royal library, appointing William Faques, a renowned printer, scribe and importer of books. He joined another Frenchman, Quentin Poulet, who had spent the previous decade transcribing and illuminating books for the king, adding exquisitely drawn red-and-white roses to the title pages and margins, which conveniently obscured the badges of his Yorkist predecessors.

Another scholar who joined the library staff was Giles Duwes, who had served the prince and his siblings as librarian and French teacher since the 1490s. Duwes had also taught Prince Henry to sing, play the lute, recorder and virginals, and to compose songs and ballads. The heir to the throne excelled in all of these musical accomplishments, and the king was so impressed with the tutor that he added him to his own payroll with a generous salary. The young prince also proved adept at languages, and could speak French, Italian and Latin. The Venetian ambassador Sebastian Giustinian would later enthuse that Henry was 'so gifted and adorned with mental accomplishments of every sort that we believe him to have few equals in the world'.[18]

As well as ensuring that his son was well versed in the intellectual and cultural elements of his education, the king also paid careful attention to the prince's military training and 'all such convenient sports and exercises as behoveth his estate to have experience in'.[19] The traditional sporting curriculum for a royal heir included running, swimming, weightlifting, hunting and hawking. The chivalric arts of swordplay, fighting with axes and jousting were also prominent in Henry's training. The latter held most appeal for the prince, who enthusiastically embraced the cult of chivalry that pervaded his father's court.

The king was determined that the prince would look the part, too. A few months after the latter's arrival at Richmond, he ordered a set of jousting clothes for his son. They included an arming doublet of black satin with fashionable detachable sleeves, a matching arming partlet, spurs and shoes, and two dozen silk points or laces. He also commissioned a matching saddle and harness in black velvet, with gilt buckles and pendants. This striking outfit and accessories formed a stark contrast to the king's own sober attire, but it seems that he was content for his glamorous young son and heir to claim the spotlight.

The king's new interest in Henry was viewed in a positive light by some observers. 'It is quite wonderful how much the king likes the prince of Wales,' remarked the Spanish ambassador in August 1504. 'Certainly, there could be no better school in the world than the society of such a father as Henry VII.'[20] The prince did not share his enthusiasm. He had enough wisdom – and restraint – to defer to his father in public, but in private he soon grew resentful of his suffocating influence.

Prince Henry was now physically superior to his father. The king had been praised for his height, but his son, whom the Spanish ambassador described as 'gigantic', had overtaken him. In contrast to his frail, emaciated father, Henry's physical power was already formidable. Richard, Earl of Kent, was left with a broken arm after 'fighting with the prince' during a training session. Polydore Vergil enthused about his 'handsome bearing, his comely and manly features (in which one could discern as much authority as good will), his outstanding physical strength, aptness at all the arts of both war and peace . . . skill at arms and on horseback'.[21] Little wonder that the Spanish ambassador concluded there was 'no finer youth in the world'.[22]

Perhaps realising that his son needed a physical outlet, the king was content to allow him to indulge his love of tournaments and other vigorous sports. There was no shortage of opponents for the prince, who despite the restrictions of his new lifestyle succeeded in gathering about him another group of boisterous young men. They included William Hussey, Giles Capel, Thomas Knyvet and Charles Brandon. All of them were associated with the royal court, and some had served the king, so it is possible that they may have already been acquainted with Prince Henry. Certainly it would soon become obvious how much the latter esteemed them.

Charles Brandon in particular rapidly became a great favourite with the prince. He was seven years older than Henry, but resembled him so closely that some people referred to him as the prince's 'bastard brother'.[23] Brandon came from a family of proven loyalty to the crown. His father had been killed at Bosworth bearing Henry VII's standard, and Charles had subsequently grown up in the royal household. He was described by a contemporary as 'an extremely handsome man, very brave, and one of the best jousters in the kingdom'.[24] At the age of seventeen, he had shown off his sporting prowess by jousting at a tournament held to celebrate the wedding of Arthur and Catherine. Francis Bacon later noted, however, that as a result of 'having been too gay at Prince Arthur's marriage', he had 'sunk himself deep in debt'.[25] As well as becoming a close companion of Prince Henry, Brandon also served the king. By 1503, he was waiting on Henry VII at table, and four years later he was an esquire of the body. From around 1505/6, he joined the company of the king's 'spears' – a group of young men who regularly excelled in jousts and courtly display.

But the king would hardly have approved of Brandon's character, if he had known of it. He was a notorious womaniser who had got one of the late queen's ladies pregnant and promptly abandoned her in favour of her wealthy aunt, who was more than twenty years his senior. He had subsequently sold off her property to pay the debts arising from his profligate lifestyle at court, and had the marriage annulled so that he could marry her niece, who had miscarried their child out of distress.

Far from being shocked by his scandalous new companion, Henry seems to have idolised him. Brandon's recklessness appealed to a prince who was desperate for an outlet for his wilder tendencies. Before long, he was staying up late with Brandon and the other rowdy men of his household, drinking and dancing 'in his shirt and without shoes'.[26]

It was not long before the king heard of his son's wayward behaviour. Although he had been prepared to tolerate his sporting pursuits, given that they were part of a prince's training, the fact that his heir was showing such a flagrant disregard for his safety – not to mention his reputation – could not be borne. He and his ministers therefore decreed that the prince's activities with his coterie of male favourites should be 'repressed'. Henry complied with his father's wishes, but the affair served to intensify his resentment.

The curtailing of the prince's entourage meant that it now more closely reflected that of his father. The many years that Henry VII had spent in exile before becoming king, during which there had been constant threats to his security, as well as setbacks to his ambitions for the throne, had chiselled him into a distrustful and suspicious man, and those traits deepened in the later years of his reign. As a result, although he was careful to keep a magnificent court, Henry's own personal entourage diminished significantly. It included only those men who had proven their loyalty to him before he seized the crown at Bosworth. Richard Fox and Reginald Bray were prominent among them, as were the wily lawyers, Richard Empson and Edmund Dudley.

The king was therefore isolated by his own will, and few others were admitted to the tight-knit group with which he was surrounded. The fact that Henry VII chose the same companions for his more pleasurable pursuits made it more exclusive still. In contrast to his son, the king only indulged in pastimes such as hunting, shooting and cards in private. 'For his pleasures, there is no news of them,' wrote Bacon. While the jousts and revels that he staged for the public entertainments of the court were undeniably spectacular, such as when scores of rabbits and doves were released into the hall in November 1501, Henry himself was only ever 'a princely and gentle spectator'.[27] Clearly he now expected his son and heir to follow suit.

But, surrounded – and increasingly influenced – by his intimate companions, Prince Henry was impatient to throw off the shackles of his father's overweening authority. Resentful of the fact that, thanks to the king's suffocating protectiveness, he was obliged to be no more than a spectator in the public jousts that his friends took part in, he was becoming ever more restless to break free.

Irksome though it was to the prince, the king's concern for his son's well-being and reputation was understandable at a time when the negotiations for his marriage to Catherine of Aragon had reached a particularly delicate stage. It is an indication of how desperate the king was to bring it to a successful conclusion that in the closing months of 1504, he sent a 'gift' of £4,000 to Rome. Not long afterwards, Julius issued a dispatch to Queen Isabella in Spain, granting his permission for her daughter to marry Prince Henry. There was a sting in the tail, though: the wording of the dispensation clearly stated that Catherine's marriage to Arthur had been consummated. When Isabella stoutly protested that her daughter was still a virgin, Julius relented enough to have the word *forsan* ('perhaps') added to the relevant sentence.[28] Although this gave both Isabella and the English king what they needed to proceed with the marriage, the ambiguity of the wording would have far-reaching consequences in the years to come.

The matter appeared to be settled, but in June 1505, just before his fourteenth birthday, Prince Henry suddenly performed an about-turn and rejected the idea of marrying his dead brother's wife. He asserted that as the betrothal had taken place during his minority, he had not been able to object, but now that he was 'near the age of puberty', he could better judge the matter for himself. This was unlikely to have been Henry's idea, but a wily ploy on the part of his father in response to a shift in the diplomatic situation. The death of Catherine's mother Isabella in November 1504 had prompted a crisis in Spain. Even though she had named her husband Ferdinand as her successor, the natural heir to Castile was their daughter Juana (known as 'the mad' because of her mental instability) and her husband Philip, ruler of the Low Countries. Anxious to see which way the tide would turn, the English king no longer wished to ally himself too closely to Ferdinand.

At the same time as breaking off his son's marriage negotiations, the king ordered that Catherine's household be dismantled, dismissed a number of her attendants (including her beloved *duenna* Doña Elvira), and incorporated Catherine and her remaining staff into his own. The Spanish princess had long complained about her living conditions in England, which were rather less luxurious than she expected. Being part of the royal household evidently did little to improve her lifestyle, because a few months later she claimed that her attendants were 'ready to ask alms and herself all but naked'. She pleaded with her father-in-law to arrange for her to be attended by a Spanish confessor because she had 'been for six months near death'.[29] The English king appeared unmoved, however, and her letter went unanswered.

In January 1506, Henry VII was provided with the perfect opportunity to cultivate Ferdinand's rival when Philip and his wife Juana were blown off course on their way from the Low Countries to Castile, and forced to land in England. They embarked off the coast of Dorset and were met by Sir Thomas Trenchard, one of the local gentry. Trenchard had ties with another Dorset noble family, the Russells, and according to tradition he enlisted the help of the twenty-year-old John Russell to act as interpreter. The young man evidently proved adept at the task because he subsequently escorted Philip to the royal court at Windsor, where John came to the attention of Henry VII and was appointed a gentleman of the chamber the following year. He would go on to become a favourite of Henry's son.

Philip's visit was brief, but it was to have a profound effect upon the English king's son and heir. Henry VII showed his guests every courtesy and provided lavish entertainments in their honour. They included a series of jousts, which his younger son would have been desperate to take part in, being already accomplished at 'riding at the ring'.[30] The king conveyed the Order of the Garter upon Philip, who in return gave the Order of the Fleece to his son Henry.[31] The prince was entranced upon meeting this charming and cultured young potentate, who was described by a contemporary as 'handsome of face, and heavily built . . . talented, generous and gentlemanly'.[32] He already knew of him because five years before, Philip's daughter Eleanor (then aged two) had been proposed as a bride for Prince Henry. The idea was still alive in 1505, when it was reported that Henry VII was 'treating very secretly . . . to marry his son the prince of Wales to the daughter of king Philip'.[33]

Henry spent some time with Philip at Richmond. The visitor presented a model of leadership to which the king-in-waiting seemed to aspire. For the first time, he had encountered a monarch whom he was inspired to emulate. Even before Philip had left England's shores, Henry wrote to him, begging that he would send him letters in return.[34] The notion that he might be allied to this man through marriage, with either Eleanor or Catherine as his bride, held great appeal for the young prince. It may have been at least partly due to their meeting that Henry decided to take matters into his own hands and reaffirm his commitment to Juana's sister Catherine. By April 1506, their betrothal was once more being spoken of as a certainty, and in the same letter to Philip, Henry referred to her as '*ma chère et très aimée compaigne, la princess ma femme*' ('my most dear and well-beloved consort, the princess my wife').[35]

The extent to which Henry had idolised Philip was clear when, just eight months after he and Juana had set sail for Castile, the prince received news of his death from his old friend Erasmus. Henry was devastated. 'Never, since the death of my dearest mother, hath there come to me more hateful intelligence,' he confided to the scholar. He went on to upbraid Erasmus for telling him the sorrowful tidings, 'because it seemed to tear open again the wound to which time had brought insensibility'.[36]

The strength of Henry's emotions towards a man with whom he had only spent a few days contrasted sharply with his resentment towards his father. The lack of affection was apparently mutual. Reginald Pole, a cousin of Prince Henry, later asserted that Henry VII despised his son, 'having no affection or fancy unto him'.[37] Admittedly, Pole was only a child at the time and was closeted away at Sheen Priory, so it is unlikely that he was speaking from first-hand experience of the relationship. Nevertheless, it is true that Henry's father had focused most of his energies, and his hopes, on his elder son and heir, Arthur, who from his earliest years had performed a number of public duties. Prince Henry might have reflected bitterly upon the fact that at the same age as he was now, Arthur had been married and dispatched to Ludlow to command the Council in the Marches as Prince of Wales, whereas Henry had neither wife nor independence.

But Henry's relationship with his father was rather less one-dimensional than many of the contemporary sources suggest. Only later commentators, writing with the wisdom of hindsight, noticed that despite their contrasting characters, there were some notable similarities between the two Henrys. Francis Bacon's description of the father could just as easily have applied to the son: 'He was of a high mind and loved his own will, and his own way: as one that revered himself, and would reign indeed.'[38] Both he and other commentators also drew attention to the exceptional memory that the younger Henry had inherited from his father. And while they were physically very different, both men were noted as being unable to look people straight in the eye.[39]

Henry VII might have become grasping and suspicious in his later years, but for much of his reign he had been an open-handed and genial monarch who always kept a splendid court. Polydore Vergil described him as 'gracious and kind, and as attractive to visitors as he was easy of access. His hospitality was splendidly generous: he liked having foreign visitors, and freely conferred favours on them . . . He well knew how to maintain his royal dignity, and everything belonging to his kingship, at all times and places.'[40] This would be echoed by his son Henry, who as king was much better known for his splendour and generosity than his apparently dull, avaricious old father. The younger Henry was also noted for his 'self-control', which goes against many of the stereotypes of this indulged spare heir and owes much to the example of his father.[41]

Both men were praised for their bravery and athleticism, but when wronged would prove 'hard and harsh'. For all his youthful exuberance and precociousness, Prince Henry shared his father's intense piety. He carried around with him a 'bede roll', or portable aid to prayer, like a talisman, believing that it would ward off evil. This roll of parchment was only five inches wide but eleven feet long and beautifully illuminated with the Tudor rose and other royal emblems, as well as a host of religious images. The younger Henry may also have inherited his impressive intellect from his father, whom Vergil refers to as being 'not devoid of scholarship' and possessed of 'a most tenacious memory'.[42]

But if there was more common ground between Henry and his father than has often been portrayed, the latter did not provide a model of kingship that his son wished to emulate. Bacon described the king as 'sad, serious, full of thoughts, and secret observations: and full of notes and memorials of his own hand . . . keeping (as it were) a journal of his thoughts'. He claimed that this made Henry the subject of whispered mockery at court, and recalled a 'merry tale' that 'his monkey (set on as it was thought by one of his chamber) tore his principal notebook all to pieces . . . whereat the court (which liked not those pensive accounts) was almost tickled with sport'.[43]

On the rare occasions that Henry delegated business, it was only to his most trusted servants, and even then he would keep a close eye on everything they did. A shrewd description is provided by Pedro de Ayala, a Spanish envoy who visited Henry's court. 'He [the king] likes to be much spoken of, and to be highly appreciated by the whole world. He fails in this because he is not a great man. He spends the time he is not in public or in his council, in writing the accounts of his expenses with his own hand . . . He is much influenced by his mother.' De Ayala concluded that the king was 'disliked' by most of his subjects.[44] In short, for the most part Henry had provided his son with an example of how not to rule.

There is little doubt that during the closing years of the reign, the prince was becoming increasingly impatient for power. In ever greater numbers, the king's subjects were also looking to his son as the hope of the kingdom. At sixteen, Henry presented a majestic and appealing alternative to his dour old father and his grasping advisers. Among the latter, the king's councillor Richard Empson was particularly unpopular, as was his colleague Edmund Dudley. Both men were astute lawyers, and Polydore Vergil claims that they had been promoted by the king 'not so much to administer justice as to strip the population of its wealth, without respite and by every means fair or foul [they] vied with each other in extorting money'. Before long, 'they devised many fresh ways of satisfying the king's avarice while they were eagerly serving as the ministers of their own private fortunes'.[45] The people could only hope that they would not have to suffer their regime for much longer.

Even though Prince Henry had confirmed his betrothal to Catherine, his father was still hedging his bets. The death of his son-in-law Philip in September 1506 had enabled Ferdinand to wrest back power in Castile, but the English king was slow to revive their alliance and made a show of casting about for another foreign bride for his son Henry. He was also careful to keep the latter apart from Catherine, even though they were both now living at Richmond. This could have been to prevent Henry from indulging in the premature sexual experience that it was believed had hastened his brother Arthur's death. But it is also possible that it was a tactic to make the Spanish princess even more desperate to marry his son and end her rather lonely existence. If so, it worked. In 1507, Catherine complained bitterly that she had not seen the prince for four months and admitted that she would 'rather die in England' than give up the idea of marrying him.[46] Absence also made Prince Henry's heart grow fonder. He confessed to his father that he thought her 'a beautiful creature'. On New Year's Day 1508, one of the rare occasions when the couple were allowed to meet, he presented his betrothed with a 'fair rose of rubies set in a rose of white and green'.[47]

In February that year, Catherine's father dispatched his ambassador, Don Gutierre Gómez de Fuensalida, to England in order to get the protracted marriage negotiations back on track. Ferdinand rightly judged that the only way to bring them to a successful conclusion was to show the English king evidence of his daughter's considerable dowry. His ambassador was therefore accompanied by a representative of the Aragonese branch of the Grimaldi bank, who carried with him bills of exchange.

By the time of Fuensalida's arrival in March, the English king was gravely ill. Worn down by the cares of state, Henry looked much older than his fifty-one years. His body was emaciated from the tuberculosis that had plagued him for the past five years, he had lost most of his teeth and those that remained were 'black-stained'.[48] The previous month, another bout of ill health had forced him to retreat to Richmond with just a few trusted servants in attendance. He had been unable to stomach any food, and his breathing had become laboured. Indeed, such was his enfeebled state that he had been unable to make his habitual pilgrimage to Westminster on the anniversary of his wife's death.

Although the king's condition had hardly improved by March 1508, he was determined to greet the Spanish ambassador in person and prove that all was well. He therefore mustered enough strength to make his way by barge to Greenwich, swathed in blankets to keep out the chill. But it was as obvious to Fuensalida as it was to the crowds who had gathered for his arrival that he could not live for much longer.

After holding private discussions with the ambassador, the king watched the jousts that were held in his honour. By his side was Prince Henry, who was no doubt itching to take part himself. Shortly afterwards, his father was obliged to retreat to his private chambers once more and leave his son to preside over the entertainments. The prince was evidently delighted at the opportunity to hold court, free from the shackles of his father's overbearing influence. One onlooker observed that he sat 'in place of the king' at the feasts, pageants and other festivities that were held at Greenwich.[49] Henry played his part to perfection. All those present admired his congeniality, easy grace and regal presence, which contrasted sharply with the shadow of a king who lay sick in his privy chamber.

Fuensalida spied his chance. Having got little further in his negotiations with the English king, despite the visible lure of Catherine's dowry, he now focused his attentions upon the prince, rightly judging that he was keen to marry Catherine. But if he thought to secure his agreement in the king's absence, he was mistaken. The latter may have retreated from public view, but he still controlled everything that happened there through his eagle-eyed councillors. As a result, although it concerned him closely, the king's heir had little say in the matter of his marriage. The ambassador scornfully recorded that the young prince was kept under a close supervision more suited to a girl, and 'so subjected that he does not speak a word except in response to what the King asks him'.[50] He therefore abandoned this means of bringing the marriage negotiations to a successful conclusion.

Prince Henry's supremacy at court, such as it was, proved all too brief. By April, his father had begun to show signs of recovery and was able to resume some of his duties. Increasingly, though, he took refuge in the minutiae of his account books, earning himself the reputation of a miser. Polydore Vergil claimed that all the king's 'virtues' were 'obscured latterly by avarice, from which he suffered. This avarice is surely a bad enough vice in a private individual, whom it forever torments; in a monarch indeed it may be considered the worst vice since it is harmful to everyone, and distorts those qualities of trustfulness, justice and integrity by which the State must be governed.'[51]

Francis Bacon later observed that Henry's subjects speculated about the cause of his increasingly reclusive and parsimonious habits: 'Some thought the continual rebellions wherewith he had been vexed, had made him grow to hate his people; some thought it was done to pull down their stomachs and keep them low; some, for that he would leave his son a golden fleece.' He concluded, though, that it was simply the result of Henry's 'nature, age, peace, and a mind fixed upon no other ambition, or pursuit'.[52] While Henry's public image deteriorated, those closest to him realised that he was depressed and suffered 'much displeasure and sorrow' from this 'wretched world'.[53]

That summer, the sweating sickness returned to London. This was one of the most feared diseases of the age, and for good reason. It could kill within a matter of hours and would claim thousands of lives with each new epidemic. Even though the king was on progress when the disease first broke out, its tendrils soon reached beyond the capital. Three of the king's closest privy chamber servants fell prey to the infection. But as their lives hung in the balance, their master heard the news that he had been dreading. The sickness had penetrated his son's household, killing three of his chamber servants. All of his fears seemed about to be realised. He knew that his own health was fading rapidly, and now it seemed that his only surviving son was to be taken from him. The future of his dynasty suddenly seemed desperately precarious.

Against all the odds, the disease abated as quickly as it had arrived, leaving the king and his son unharmed. But by the time that they returned to the court in London, it was obvious to everyone that the king was dying. By January 1509, he was so 'sore vexed' by the symptoms of tuberculosis that he sought refuge away from the capital and moved to the manor of Hanworth in Middlesex. His mother accompanied him, as she had so many times before, but this time she summoned his three children – an indication that she knew there would be little time.

At the end of February, Henry moved to Richmond. Keen to put his son's affairs in order, he summoned Catherine of Aragon to him. By this time, few of Catherine's household believed that she would ever marry the prince and were busy making plans for her return to Spain. Catherine herself refused to give up hope, however, and she used this opportunity to urge the dying king once more to confirm the marriage. But her earnest petition prompted a furious tirade from her father-in-law, who upbraided her for speaking out in this manner. She was so shocked that she wrote at once to her father, complaining that the English king had uttered 'things which are not fit to be written to your highness'.[54] She returned to her lodgings in Windsor shortly afterwards. Henry soon regretted his outburst and sent for Catherine once more. But her confessor, Friar Diego, whom the king despised, prevented her from going. The fact that he was unable to settle his son's marital affairs left Henry 'very much vexed'. Catherine, meanwhile, seems to have finally relinquished all hope of the match and began asking to return to Spain so that she might commit herself to the religious life.

The king lingered for almost two more months, but breathed his last at around eleven o'clock on the night of 21 April, surrounded by his most trusted attendants. His death was kept secret for two full days so that his advisers could set matters in place for a smooth succession. Despite their efforts, however, rumours of the king's death were already circulating in the city on 22 April. Fearing unrest, those who were privy to the secret began to quietly stock the royal armoury. They need not have worried. Henry VIII would be the first monarch since the year 1421 to accede to the throne peacefully as a crowned king, rather than by usurpation or conquest.

On the morning of 23 April, St George's Day, Thomas Wriothesley, who was presiding over the ceremonials as Garter King of Arms and was probably in on the secret, ordered the heralds to proclaim Henry VII's largesse to the crowded presence chamber.[55] The pretence was maintained after dinner, when a door leading to the privy apartments was opened by Richard Weston, one of the king's body servants, who entered the room with a 'smiling countenance'. Aware that all eyes were upon him, he walked calmly over to Archbishop Warham and 'certain other lords' and told them that the king wished to see them. These men duly performed the charade of visiting the privy chamber for 'a good pause', and then re-emerged into the throng 'with good countenance . . . as though the king had not been dead, showing no great manner of mourning that men might perceive'.[56]

Shortly afterwards, Prince Henry progressed to the Chapel Royal for evensong. As was customary for the king and his family, he heard mass in the holyday closet, rather than the main body of the chapel. The privacy of the closet enabled its occupants to discuss confidential matters undisturbed while the service proceeded. It may have been here that the prince was finally told of his father's death.

As soon as the service was over, Henry and his entourage returned to the presence chamber for the Garter supper, throughout which 'he was served and named as prince and not as king'.[57] Only when the last dish had been taken away was his father's death finally announced. Contemporary accounts suggest that it was something of an anti-climax. There was no joyful proclamation of the new king, but rather a series of whispered conversations between his advisers. For Henry himself, though, the knowledge that he had come into his inheritance and was free at last from his controlling father filled him with joyful anticipation.

3

'Lusty bachelors'

E VEN BEFORE THE news of the English king's death had been
confirmed, the Doge and Senate of Venice instructed his ambassador 'to condole with his son and successor the new King upon his
father's demise, and congratulate him on his own accession'.[1] The
contemporary chronicler Edward Hall captured the public mood
when Henry VIII was proclaimed king on 23 April: 'Wonder it were
to write of the lamentation that was made for this prince [Henry
VII] amongst his servants, and other of the wisest sort, and the joy
that was made for his death by such as were troubled by the rigour
of his law; yet the toward hope which in all points approved the
young king did both repair and comfort the heavy hearts of those
which had lost so wise and sage a prince; and did also put out of
the minds of such as were relieved by the said king's death, all their
old grudges and rumours, and confirmed their new joy by the new
grant of his pardon.'[2]

Others were similarly quick to draw favourable comparisons
between the new king's youthful exuberance and his dour old father:

Our eclipsed sun now cleared is from the clerk
By Harry our King the flower of nature's work.[3]

Writing in the 1550s, George Cavendish reflected that the old king
had been respected for his 'inestimable wisdom', which earned him
the nickname of 'the second Solomon', but that his son was praised
as a 'natural, young, lusty and courageous prince'.[4] Polydore Vergil,
meanwhile, made little mention of Henry VII but instead emphasised
how much the new king resembled his maternal grandfather, Edward
IV: 'For just as Edward was the most warmly thought of by the

English people among all the English kings, so this successor of his, Henry, was very like him in general appearance, in greatness of mind and generosity and for that reason was the more acclaimed and approved of by all.'[5]

Henry's own reaction to the death of his father is not recorded. Hall notes that on the same day that his accession was announced, Henry left Richmond for the Tower, 'where he remained, closely and secret, with his council, until the funerals [sic] of his father were finished and ended'.[6] The new king was careful to ensure, though, that his father would be laid to rest with due pomp, observing that 'all things necessary . . . were sumptuously prepared and done'. The late king's body was brought out of the privy chamber and lay in state in three different rooms of the palace for nine days, with dirges and masses being sung throughout, and ten mourners in attendance. The corpse was then conveyed with great ceremony, draped in 'black cloth of gold' and accompanied by a magnificent train, to Westminster, where it was interred next to the body of his wife, Elizabeth.

Henry commissioned a sumptuous tomb for his parents, selecting a design by the celebrated Italian sculptor Pietro Torrigiano. Francis Bacon described it as 'one of the stateliest and daintiest monuments of Europe . . . so that he dwelleth more richly dead, in the monument of his tomb, then he did alive in Richmond, or any of his palaces'.[7] A laudatory inscription was added, praising Henry VII as 'the glory of all the kings who lived in his time by reason of his intellect, his riches, and the fame of his exploits, to which were added the gifts of bountiful nature, a distinguished brow, an august face, an heroic stature. Joined to him his sweet wife was very pretty, chaste and fruitful. They were parents happy in their offspring, to whom, land of England, you owe Henry VIII.' The monument was decorated with medallions representing the Virgin Mary and Henry's patron saints, as well as emblems of the Tudor dynasty, such as the Welsh dragon and the greyhound of Richmond. To the untrained eye, it was a lavish compliment by Henry to his late father. But its real purpose was to reinforce the strength of the dynasty that he had founded at a time when some were still minded to question its legitimacy.

Upholding royal tradition, Henry did not attend his father's funeral, but remained at the Tower. The sermon was preached by Bishop John Fisher, who hoped that he would continue to enjoy a prominent role in the new reign. But he could not resist scorning those courtiers who had so quickly turned their allegiance from the old king to the new: 'Ah king Henry, king Henry,' he lamented, 'if thou were alive again, many a one that is here present now would pretend a full great pity and tenderness upon thee.'[8]

Not long afterwards, Henry and his entourage travelled to Westminster, the seat of power, where he was to remain until his coronation, which was scheduled for June. Because he would not turn eighteen until that month, his grandmother Margaret Beaufort acted as nominal regent for the first ten weeks of the reign. During this time, the men of the council met to debate the pressing matter of how this young man, who had barely reached maturity, should be shaped into a king. Should he 'be brought up in worldly knowledge, or else in pleasure and liberty, leaving the care to his Council'? At length, they resolved 'to bring him up in all pleasure, for otherwise he should grow too hard among his subjects as the King his father did'.[9] Henry would take them at their word.

Visitors to the new king's court were soon tripping over themselves in their eagerness to praise him. The Venetian ambassador echoed the praise of many in an adulatory letter to his master in which he described Henry VIII as 'magnificent'.[10] His fellow Italian, Lodovico Falier, later claimed: 'In this eighth Henry, God combined such corporal and mental beauty, as not merely to surprise but to astound all men.'[11] Another foreign envoy agreed that his 'acquirements and qualities are so many and excellent that I consider him to excel all who ever wore a crown'.[12] Henry appeared generous, open-hearted and 'gentle' towards everyone he met, even shedding tears when he saw one foreign envoy looking ill and 'haggard'.[13] Little wonder that his subjects rejoiced that they were now in his care.

Henry's old childhood companions and acquaintances also scrambled to add their praise to the general throng. They included his former tutor, John Skelton, languishing in his remote Norfolk parish, who rushed off 'A Laud and Praise made for our Sovereign Lord the King'. This exulted in Henry's greatness as a prince who had united the Lancastrian and Yorkist lines, and confidently predicted that he would be 'sage' and 'just', and a protector of the common people. For good measure, Skelton also sent Henry a copy of the *Speculum Principis*, with the inclusion of a twelve-line eulogy on the new king's virtues. With a typical lack of subtlety, he added: 'May Jupiter Feretrius grant that I do not pass my time on the banks of the Eurotas' – an allusion to enforced idleness and under-employment.[14] Skelton's efforts seem to have been rewarded. By November 1509, he was back in London, and a contemporary record lists him as being 'late of Diss, Norfolk'.

Another man who had been influential during Henry's childhood now reaped the rewards of his former connection. Among all the voices praising the virtues of England's new king, one of the loudest was that of Thomas More, who lauded Henry's 'fiery power', 'majestic body' and striking good looks. Like others, he also flattered the new king by drawing a favourable comparison to his dull, suspicious and miserly old father: 'This day marks the limit of our slavery, the beginning of our freedom, the end of sadness, the source of joy . . . Now the people, freed, run before their king with bright faces. Their joy is almost beyond their own comprehension. They rejoice, they exult, they leap for joy and celebrate their having such a king.'[15] His flattery hit its mark. Henry, for so long subservient to his father's strictures, exulted in the image that More had created for him as the liberator of his people from oppression.

By the time of Henry VIII's accession, More had been married for four years to Jane, daughter of Sir John Colt of Netherhall in Essex. His friend Erasmus later implied that More's father had put pressure on him to relinquish his austere spiritual habits and pursue a career in law. Sir John no doubt also wished his son to marry and continue the family line. Jane Colt was the ideal choice in this respect. She gave birth to their first child, Margaret, in 1505, and two more daughters and a son followed in quick succession.[16] The Mores had made their home in Bucklersbury, in the heart of the City of London. Shortly after moving there, Thomas received a visit from his old friend Erasmus. Lord Mountjoy had persuaded the Dutch scholar to return to London soon after the accession, confidently predicting that the new king would make England a haven for men of learning: 'Heaven smiles, earth rejoices; all is milk and honey and nectar.' In case this was not incentive enough for Erasmus to visit, Mountjoy made it clear that he could expect great preferment in the new reign: 'You are about to approach a prince who can say, "Take then these riches, and be first of bards."'[17]

Thomas More was also thriving in the intellectually vibrant atmosphere of the new reign. Shortly after Henry's accession, he was appointed Justice of the Peace for Middlesex and a member of the powerful Mercers' guild. At the end of the year, he represented Westminster in Henry VIII's first parliament. His role in public affairs continued to expand rapidly the following year, when he was appointed one of two under-sheriffs for the City of London. These early promotions were an indication of the young king's favour, which would become more obvious still in the years that followed.

Francis Bacon later claimed that Henry 'had never any the least pique, difference or jealousy with the king his father, which might give any occasion of altering court or council, upon the change [succession]; but all things passed in a still'.[18] This is a beguiling image, but it is not entirely accurate. From the outset of his reign, Henry seemed intent upon emphasising how different his kingship would be from that of his late father. He immediately issued a proclamation that if any man 'had sustained injury, or loss of goods' during his father's reign, 'that he should make his humble supplication unto the King's grace, and therein express their grief, and he was ready, not only to hear them, but also to cause satisfaction to be made'. Not surprisingly, this prompted a rush of people from every corner of the kingdom, who 'speedily came unto the Court, and every man alleged and showed just occasion that they had for complaint'. The new king's council were hard pressed to deal with all of the cases, but it was soon clear that the 'rage and cry' of his subjects had the same focus: his father's despised henchmen, Richard Empson and Edmund Dudley.[19]

Henry's reaction was at once dramatic and terrifyingly brutal. He ordered that both men be thrown into the Tower, 'not to the little rejoicing of many persons, which by them were grieved'.[20] Although he stopped short of openly criticising his father's policies, this was more than implied in the notices that were issued after the arrest. Henry VII was acknowledged to be 'a most prudent and politic

prince', but his laws had been executed 'through avarice and covetousness for the filthy desire of gain . . . to the loss of many and
honest men's goods, which should now be recompensed with the
loss of their [Empson and Dudley's] heads'.[21] Most of the complaints
against the two men would not have stood up in a court of law, so
they were arrested for an altogether different crime. According to
the charges against them, during the late king's final illness, they
had ordered their friends to take arms in preparation for his death.
Compassing the king's death constituted constructive treason, and
they were duly attainted.

Even though parliament did not confirm the attainder, Henry
pushed ahead with it and had both men executed on 17 August 1510.
It was a chilling reminder that this charismatic and generous young
king had an altogether darker side. The new men who hung about
him, basking in his reflected glory, should have taken note of how
swiftly his favour could be withdrawn. They would also have done
well to observe the wording of the indictment. This made it clear
that Empson and Dudley were condemned for having governed 'the
king and his council against the wishes of the king'.[22] Through this,
Henry had issued a clear warning: he had the power to destroy
highly placed officials who failed to do his bidding.

Soon after his accession, Henry also disbanded the Council
Learned in the Law, of which Empson and Dudley had been leading
members. This controversial body had been established by his father
in 1495 to defend his position as a feudal landlord. It had dealt with
financial matters and enforced payments of debts. Although it had
been ruthlessly efficient, it had also been deeply unpopular and had
come to represent the king's grasping nature. His son therefore
wasted no time in abolishing it.

Henry also sought more positive ways to distance himself from
his father's regime. His attitude towards the aristocracy formed a
sharp contrast to that of the late king. Henry VII had been deeply
suspicious of men who boasted noble birth, and only trusted peers
of his own creation, such as his uncle, Jasper Tudor, whom he
restored to the earldom of Bedford, or Thomas Howard, Earl of
Surrey. His chosen servants were for the most part knights, such as
Sir Reginald Bray, or clergy like John Morton. 'He kept a straight

hand on his nobility,' observed Bacon, 'and chose rather to advance clergymen and lawyers, which were more obsequious to him but had less interest in the people.'[23] Henry's suspicion of the aristocracy stemmed from his deep-seated insecurity as a king whose claim to the throne did not bear close scrutiny.

Henry VIII had no such prejudice. Stridently self-confident in his position as king, he gloried in surrounding himself with the highest-ranking men of the realm. All of the new creations early in his reign were bestowed upon men from established peerage families, such as Buckingham's brother Henry Stafford, who was made Earl of Wiltshire, and William Courtenay, Earl of Devon. As well as freeing many noble families from the bonds that had placed them in his father's debt, he also invited them to take part in court revels, jousts and other entertainments, and gave them some of the most sought-after positions in the royal household.[24] In addition, he confirmed their traditional role of providing military support to the crown – a clear signal of his warlike intentions. Only later in the reign would those who benefited from the new king's largesse learn that his eagerness to create new peers was matched by his power to destroy them.

Another expression of Henry's desire to break free from the shackles of his father's reign came on 11 June 1509 when, shortly before his eighteenth birthday, he finally married Catherine of Aragon. This put an end to all the years of diplomatic wranglings and disappointments that she had endured. In marrying her, Henry claimed to be fulfilling his father's dying wish. But it smacks more of defiance: if the old king had not prevented it, he would have married Catherine years earlier.

Henry and his new bride were crowned a little under two weeks later in the midst of such ostentatious pomp and pageantry that it eclipsed anything his father had ever staged. The spectators were dazzled by the new king and queen and their entourage, decked out in cloth of gold and silver, dripping with jewels, and flanked by scores of horses, carriages and pageants. Even Edward Hall, whose chronicle is filled with detailed descriptions of court ceremonies and pageants, was almost at a loss for words to describe the spectacle. 'If I should declare what pain, labour and diligence the tailors, embroiderers, and goldsmiths took, both to make and devise garments for Lords, Ladies, Knights and Esquires, and also for the decking, trapping and adorning of coursers, jennets and palfreys, it were too long to rehearse, but for a surety more rich nor more strange nor curious works hath not been seen than were prepared against this coronation.'[25]

There followed several days of feasting, revelry and tournaments, in which Henry's male attendants played a starring role, notably Charles Brandon, Thomas Howard, Thomas Knyvet and Thomas Grey, second Marquess of Dorset. Hall marvelled at the huge temporary castle that had been built for the pageants, decorated with 'rich cloths of Arras' and 'pomegranates gilded', and described how 'out of the mouths of certain beasts, or gargoyles, did run red, white and claret wine'.[26]

Henry's grandmother, Lady Margaret Beaufort, died five days after the coronation. On her deathbed, she exhorted her grandson to show favour towards Bishop Fisher. Henry acceded to this request, and Fisher's name appears on the list of councillors during the first few years of the new reign. But the young king was not willing to obey all of his grandmother's final wishes with regard to her favourite cleric. Although she had left Fisher part of an endowment at St John's College, Henry insisted upon retaining a greater share of her lands for himself. He did, though, compensate Fisher for his loss, so their cordial relations were preserved.

For all that he tried to distance himself from the old regime, Henry had a great deal to be grateful to his father for. Henry VII had left his son a relatively stable and peaceful kingdom, and one that was considered 'great throughout the world'.[27] Moreover, the fact that the new king was able to launch his reign in such spectacular style was at least partly thanks to his father. The Venetian ambassador had been quick to criticise the late king as 'a very great miser', compared to his 'liberal' son. But he admitted: 'The King [Henry VII] . . . had accumulated so much gold that he is supposed to have more than well nigh all the other Kings of Christendom.'[28] A later ambassador concurred that the new king was 'very rich' thanks to his father, who had 'left him ten millions of ready money in gold'.[29]

This might have been an exaggeration, but thanks to his years of meticulous financial management, the old king had accumulated around £300,000 (£145 million) in cash, bonds and jewellery. Not only did this enable his son to stage spectacular celebrations for his coronation and wedding, it also left plenty of funds to support a magnificent court, a lavish wardrobe and to quench the new king's thirst for war. Little wonder that Bacon concluded: 'There had scarce been seen or known in many ages, such a rare concurrence of signs and promises, of a happy and flourishing reign to ensue, as were now met in this young king, called after his father's name Henry the eighth.'[30] Lord Mountjoy's claim that 'Our King does not desire gold or silver, but virtue, glory, immortality' was all very well, but such things came at a price.[31]

Both Henry's coronation and his wedding had been presided over by the Archbishop of Canterbury, William Warham, who was now nearing sixty years of age. Even though Warham did not fit the mould of the energetic and youthful men with whom the new king was surrounded and may have reminded Henry a little too much of his austere old father, he was content to retain him in office for now. Much as he wished to ring the changes from the last reign, he was shrewd enough to recognise talent among his father's men. Warham was no revolutionary, but he was at least a safe pair of hands and an able administrator. He oversaw the day-to-day legal matters and administration of the court, and played a prominent role in parliament. He was equally capable – and uncontroversial – in church affairs, and enjoyed positive relations with the papacy. The year after Henry's accession, he presented the new king with a golden rose sent by Pope Julius. Neither Henry nor his archbishop could have predicted just how turbulent their relationship with Rome would become in the years that followed.

Among the other men from his late father's council whom Henry was content to retain were Sir Thomas Lovell, Sir Edward Poynings and Sir Henry Wyatt, all of whom proved active in the new king's service during the first few years of the reign. Although he was later accused of filling his council with noblemen, the new king was justified in pointing out that there were 'but scant well born gentlemen; and yet of no great lands, till they were promoted by us, and so made knights, and lords: the rest were lawyers and priests, save two bishops'.[32]

Henry also showed favour to Richard Fox, now Bishop of Winchester, who had served the Tudors even before their accession to the English throne. Richard III had denied Fox a holding in Stepney because he was abroad with 'our rebel, Henry ap Tudder'.[33] After Henry VII's triumph at Bosworth, Fox had rapidly risen to become one of his most trusted advisers. In the sketch of the king on his deathbed, Fox is shown immediately to his left. Only Henry VII's groom of the stool, Hugh Denys, who is closing his master's lifeless eyes, is closer to the royal person. By the time of Henry VIII's accession, the bishop was probably in his early sixties, but the new king had enough esteem for his father's old servant to promote him to the position of Lord Privy Seal.

The Venetian ambassador claimed that already Fox was an 'alter rex' ('other king'), but hinted that the king did not altogether trust him because Henry had remarked that the bishop was 'a Fox indeed'. This is corroborated by a letter from Thomas, Lord Darcy, in August 1509. He reported that: 'The common saying with every market man that comes from London is that the Lord Privy Seal, seeing of his own craft and policy he cannot bring himself to rule the king's grace and put out of favour the Earl of Surrey, the Earl of Shrewsbury, the Bishop of Durham, Mr Marney, Mr Brandon and the Lord Darcy, now he will prove another way; which is to bring in and bolster himself to rule all with the Duke of Buckingham and the Earl of Northumberland. And doubtless fast they curse and speak evil of my Lord Privy Seal beyond measure.'[34] But if Fox really did hope to dominate the new king and his men in this way, then he had overlooked an altogether more dangerous rival who was waiting in the wings.

Henry had come to the throne as the archetypal spare heir: pleasure loving, gregarious and carefree. Being surrounded by his coterie of like-minded young favourites served to encourage his more wayward tendencies. Although he gloried in his newfound status as king, with all of the privileges and unfettered authority that it carried, Henry had little patience for the more routine – and increasingly pressing

– affairs of state, and found writing 'somewhat tedious and painful'. Instead, he lived 'in continual festival', as his new wife put it.[35] Among the many songs that he liked to practise with his companions in the privy chamber was one of his own composing, 'Pastime with Good Company'. The lyrics neatly encapsulate the young king's philosophy:

> For my pastance,
> Hunt, sing and dance,
> My heart is set,
> All goodly sport
> To my comfort
> Who shall me let?[36]

The last line reads as a challenge to Henry's late father, who had always curtailed his son's more wayward tendencies. But for all his bluff and bluster, the young king apparently still lived in some fear of his predecessor. Although he had been intensely frustrated by his father's refusal to let him joust as often as he would have liked, it took Henry a full nine months to enter the lists. Even then, he did so with the utmost secrecy, riding incognito to Richmond Park with his close companion, William Compton. Being a stone's throw from his father's favourite palace, and the one in which he had died, must have made Henry even more conscious that he was about to do something of which the late king would have severely disapproved.

Edward Hall recalls the event, which took place in January 1510: 'There were broken many staves, and great praise given to the two strangers, but specially to one, who was the king.' But then a young man named Edward Neville challenged Compton to run at him, and proceeded to 'hurt him sore' so that Compton was 'likely to die'. In the confusion that followed, someone recognised Henry and cried 'God save the king', to the astonishment of the rest of those present. Henry then drew off his helmet 'to the great comfort of all the people'. His friend Compton soon recovered.[37]

The following month, Henry joined in a revel for the first time since his accession. Many more followed in the months and years to come, each more spectacular than the last, with the king playing the starring role as shepherd, Turk, masker and Hercules, among numerous others. His father would hardly have approved of that either, but now that Henry had tasted the delights that had been denied him for so long, there was no stopping him. 'He was extremely fond of hunting, and never took that diversion without tiring eight or ten horses,' reported the Venetian ambassador. 'He was also fond of tennis, at which game it was the prettiest thing in the world to see him play.'

Henry was clearly determined to enjoy himself. 'The king being lusty, young and courageous, greatly delighted in feats of chivalry,' observed the chronicler Edward Hall.[38] Although his late brother had been named after the legendary king, it was Henry who epitomised Arthurian folklore. He gathered around him a group of intimate friends and attendants who could join in his more chivalric pursuits, and with whom he could spend his many hours of leisure and entertainment. Many of these men were drawn from his childhood days at Eltham and were rewarded for their loyalty with positions in the new king's privy chamber. This caused some controversy among the noblemen at court, who had confidently expected appointments based upon their rank. Chief among them was the Duke of Buckingham, who grumbled that the young king 'would give his fees, offices and rewards to boys rather than noblemen'.[39]

Henry transformed his privy chamber from the tightly knit and functional body of attendants that had served his father, into a vibrant social centre, filled with as many as fifty 'lusty bachelors' who shared the king's passions and pastimes.[40] They became notorious for their boisterous and intemperate behaviour, which was both mirrored and encouraged by their royal master. But, tellingly, although they were educated enough to provide diverting company, they were all intellectually inferior to their royal master. This is how Henry willed it: his male companions should complement rather than outshine him.

Principal among them was Henry's favourite companion, Charles Brandon. The seventeenth-century antiquarian William Dugdale described him as 'a person comely of stature, high of courage and conformity of disposition to King Henry VIII, with whom he became a great favourite'. Commenting on a service that Brandon had performed for his royal master, one of his rivals admitted that he had a 'gentle heart and natural zeal towards his Majesty in this as in all other things'.[41]

The two men had long shared a passion for jousting, and there had been an element of hero worship as Henry had regularly watched Brandon show off his prowess in the tournament field during his father's reign. As soon as he became king, he made Brandon central to the tournaments and revels of his own court. At the coronation tournament in June 1509, Henry's old companion stood out among the five other challengers in an all-gilt armour.

Brandon played an ever more distinctive role in the tournaments during the years to come, and he was the king's sole partner in challenging the rest of the court. In the revels, meanwhile, he was the only participant who was dressed the same as his royal master – a sure sign of his influence. Edward Hall recalls one New Year's Eve when Henry and Brandon appeared clad in 'cloth of silver, and lined with blue velvet, the silver was pounced in letters, so that the velvet might be seen through . . . and all their hose, doublets and coats were of the same fashion cut and of the same stuff'. He concluded: 'This strange apparel pleased much every person, and especially the Queen.'[42]

A series of rapid promotions followed. When Brandon's uncle died in January 1510, he succeeded to the post of marshal of the King's Bench, and in November 1511 he became marshal of the king's household. These were influential positions and greatly enhanced Brandon's standing at court, making him more than just a companion to his royal master.

Another close friend of the king was William Compton. Nine years older than Henry, he had served him since his youth and was now one of his most trusted confidants and jousting companions. That he was high in Henry's favour was so well known that service to Compton was soon regarded as a surrogate for direct service to the king. An indication of the king's affection towards him is that Compton was given the most privileged position in the entire privy chamber: that of groom of the stool. While in theory this post required attendance upon the king when he visited his close stool, Henry expanded both the duties and prestige so that Compton became a kind of personal assistant, as well as keeper of the privy purse. As such, he was required to accompany his royal master wherever he went. The two men were soon as thick as thieves.

Compton also acted as the king's most confidential messenger. Only a man of impeccable discretion could have undertaken this task, because it involved conveying messages to Henry's wife and mistresses. Thanks to this element of his role, Compton became embroiled in the sexual dalliances of his sovereign. Within a year of his accession, Henry had started an affair with Anne Hastings, the married younger sister of the Duke of Buckingham. Compton soon began acting as intermediary between the couple, and according to one member of the court he arranged their secret trysts in his own home on Thames Street. However, rumours soon began to circulate that Compton was taking advantage of his position and had begun an affair with Anne Hastings himself. These appeared to have been confirmed when Buckingham found him in his sister's room. Compton insisted that nothing untoward had passed between them, and Henry upbraided the duke for his 'interference'. But Anne's husband was so incensed when he heard of the matter that he sent her to a convent sixty miles from court.[43] If Compton had been guilty of sexual transgression, then Henry soon forgave him. There was certainly no diminution of trust between the two men.

As groom of the stool, Compton controlled access to his royal master. In an age when access was the surest means to preferment, this imbued Compton with considerable influence. As well as attending Henry in his most intimate moments, he occupied lodgings directly beneath the king's privy chamber, linked by a private staircase, so that he could be on hand at a moment's notice.

Within a year of Henry's accession, Compton was referred to by the Spanish ambassador as the 'privado' or favourite of the king. In 1511, the French ambassador agreed that Compton enjoyed more 'crédict' with Henry than any other servant, and that he was richly rewarded for his service.[44] There were many others in the privy chamber who vied for the same level of favour.

Among them were the esquires of the body, whose role was to watch over their royal master at all times. They included two men who had served the king since his youth: Henry Guildford and William Fitzwilliam. Described as a 'lusty young man [and] well

beloved of the King', Guildford excelled at keeping Henry entertained. During the New Year festivities in January 1510, for example,
he and his half-brother Edward accompanied the king on a private
jest one morning. The three men burst into Queen Catherine's
chamber dressed as Robin Hood and his men 'in short coats of
Kentish Kendal', and proceeded to entertain her with their dancing
and boisterous behaviour.[45] The following year, Guildford designed
a lavish stage set for the Twelfth Night revels. The centrepiece was
a moving mountain that, when it drew close to the king, suddenly
opened and revealed a troupe of Morris dancers.

Guildford was clearly fascinated by design and construction,
because in the remarkable portrait of him painted by Holbein, he
is wearing a hat-badge decorated with a clock and surveying instruments. His talents won him the honour of being appointed Henry's
Master of the Revels, a prestigious post that was responsible for
court festivities. Several other notable performances that Guildford
devised or took part in are listed in the contemporary sources, and
among the collections of the British Library is a volume of songs
that he promoted, including a selection of lyrics written by the king
himself.[46]

William Fitzwilliam, meanwhile, was Henry's regular companion
at the hunt. Appointed cupbearer to the king on his accession, he
had remained one of his closest attendants. It was said that he
understood the king's 'nature and temper better than any man in
England'.[47] What distinguished Fitzwilliam from Henry's other
companions and courtiers was his refusal to become embroiled in
factional politics. A straightforward and loyal man, he was solely
committed to the king's service.

The same could not be said of his fellow esquire, Thomas Boleyn,
a man who would wield considerable influence over the king and
his court in later years. Boleyn epitomised the grasping and ambitious
courtier so reviled by Henry's old tutor Skelton. In his early thirties
by the time of Henry's accession, he was one of the oldest members
of the privy chamber and had begun his service at court in the old
king's time. Having proved his loyalty to the Tudor regime by helping
to defeat the Cornish rebels in 1497, he had attended the wedding
of Henry's brother Arthur to Catherine of Aragon, and the following

year had accompanied the prince's elder sister Margaret to Scotland for her marriage to James IV.

Eager to boost his social credentials, Boleyn had made an extremely advantageous marriage to Elizabeth Howard, eldest daughter of the second Duke of Norfolk. He was appointed an esquire of Henry's privy chamber upon his accession, and was made a Knight of the Bath at the coronation two months later. A man of learning as well as ambition, Boleyn spoke Latin and French better than anyone at court, and Henry employed him on a number of important diplomatic missions.

Boleyn's appeal for Henry lay in the fact that he shared his warlike ambitions. As such, he stood out among the more cautious advisers at court. For all that he was a consummate political operator, Thomas also had an excellent knowledge of horses, hounds and bowls, which made him an ideal companion for the king. He regularly took part in tournaments, such as those held at Greenwich in May 1510, when he was the king's opponent, and at Westminster the following year, when he donned the guise of a pilgrim from Santiago de Compostela. If he was less raucous than Henry's younger companions, Boleyn knew how to keep the king amused, and once appeared in fancy dress for a Christmas celebration at court. His son George also appeared in the Christmas revels of 1514, at the age of just twelve. Thanks to his father's influence, George was appointed a page two years later.

The other esquire in Henry's privy chamber was Edward Neville who, like Thomas Boleyn, had been appointed at the beginning of the reign and had attended the late king's funeral. A member of one of the oldest and most powerful families in the kingdom, he was a distant cousin of the king.[48] The two men looked so alike that they were often mistaken for brothers. Neville once interrupted a banquet by bursting in as part of a group of masquers. One of those present mistook him for the king, which George Cavendish did not find surprising, given that he was 'a comely knight of goodly personage that much resembled the King's person in the mask than any other'.[49] Their physical similarity has given rise to speculation that Neville was an illegitimate son of Henry VII, but there is no evidence to support this.

Neville was a natural performer and accomplished singer, with a liking for 'merry songs'. One of the verses he composed reveals a scornful view of the lower-ranking courtiers and advisers with whom Henry liked to surround himself: 'Trusted knaves should be put down, and lords should reign one day.'[50] He shared his royal master's twin passions for jousting and hunting, and was one of the principal challengers at court for the first ten years of the reign, becoming Master of the Buckhounds in 1516. He was a ferocious opponent, as William Compton had found to his cost at the impromptu joust held at Richmond in January 1510. Far from being angered by the episode, Henry had been greatly impressed by Neville's prowess and had shown him even greater favour from that day forward, showering him with gifts and standing as godfather to his second son. He also made the most of Neville's combat skills, enlisting him in a number of military campaigns and knighting him for his efforts.

Henry appointed a number of other military men to be part of his inner circle. Thomas Howard's father and grandfather had prospered under the Yorkist kings, and Richard III had granted them the dukedom of Norfolk. They had subsequently fought for him at the Battle of Bosworth, and had therefore been under a political shadow during the early years of Henry VII's reign. Neither were they of particularly impressive stock, being merely a family of small East Anglian landowners. But their rehabilitation was signalled by Thomas Howard's marriage to the king's sister-in-law Anne, one of the daughters of Edward IV, in 1495, when he was aged twenty-two. Thereafter, his career in royal service progressed rapidly. He distinguished himself in military service, and earned a knighthood for his efforts against the Scots in 1497. By the time of Henry VIII's accession, Howard was rapidly becoming one of the most influential men in the realm.

Thomas Howard did not fit the physical mould of so many of Henry's other men. He was described by the Venetian ambassador as 'small and spare in person, and his hair black', but in a portrait painted later in his life his diminutive stature is disguised by rich apparel and the many symbols of office that he wears.[51] The same ambassador thought him a 'prudent, liberal, affable and astute' man who 'associates with everybody'. But this pleasant exterior masked a brutal, ruthless nature, as even those closest to him would discover.[52] His second wife, Elizabeth, observed that he was a master at the courtly art of dissembling, and could appear as amicable to his enemy as to his friend. She knew this better than most. Although he took pains to present himself as a respectable married man, he had a mistress and became violent and abusive towards his wife in private.

If he knew of Howard's less savoury characteristics, Henry was still content to show him favour, and in 1510 he appointed him to the Order of the Garter. Like Brandon, Howard played a prominent role in the coronation tournament. The fact that the young king showed such favour towards Howard so early in the reign suggests that their association pre-dated his accession. It is possible that Howard had been among the men appointed to Henry's household at Eltham, although there is no direct evidence to support this.

Having been given an entrée into the new king's service, Thomas Howard was quick to take advantage by proving himself adept at the pursuits so favoured by Henry. He became a regular partner to the young king at cards and dice, and on one occasion won £45 from him. Although he was no great intellectual, he was fluent in French, understood the game of courtly chivalry and romance, and knew enough of literature to pass as a companion to this most cultured of Renaissance princes. Appreciating his courtly abilities, as well as his martial prowess, the new king bestowed more honours upon him. He also enlisted him in various military campaigns, and appointed him Lord Admiral in 1513 – a post that he held for twelve years. When Howard's father was created Duke of Norfolk in 1514, Thomas inherited his former title as Earl of Surrey, and within two years he was a member of the council, an institution that he soon came to dominate. It was the powerbase from which he would carve out a position of substantial influence as the reign progressed.

Howard's younger brother Edward also found favour in the new reign. In his early thirties at the time of Henry's accession, he was one of the older members of the new king's entourage, but was still physically fit. While Henry viewed the elder Howard brother as a capable statesman, he cherished the younger one as a friend and companion. Edward was far more rumbustious and fun-loving than the wily Thomas, and he always bested his brother at the court tournaments. Henry warmed to him immediately, and less than a month after his accession he made Edward his standard-bearer. Along with the likes of Charles Brandon, William Compton and Henry Guildford, Edward Howard was like the elder brother that Arthur had never been to Henry. He and his peers provided guidance and approbation, and their royal master sought to impress them with his kingly stature and martial prowess.

Edward Howard proved particularly influential over Henry in the military sphere, and encouraged his young master's thirst for war. Having grown up in the border country, Howard had a loathing for the Scots and longed for a showdown with James IV. In 1511, Bishop Fox received news that Howard 'marvellously incenseth the king against the Scots, by whose wanton means his grace spendeth much money and is more inclined to war than peace'.[53] When this reached the ears of Edward's father, who was committed to maintaining peace between the two countries, he was furious and went at once to urge the king not to listen. But such was Henry's esteem for Edward that he sent his father away with a flea in his ear, showing him 'such manner and countenance . . . that on the morrow he departed home again and is not yet returned to court'.[54]

Edward's brother-in-law, Sir Thomas Knyvet, had been one of Henry VII's esquires of the body and had risen to prominence in the tournaments of May and June 1507. He soon became a favourite with the new king too, and played a leading role in the tournaments and revels at court. Henry heaped honours upon his companion, making him Knight of the Bath at his coronation, bearer of the king's standard a month later, and Master of the Horse in February 1510.

Henry Courtenay, Earl of Devon, was also rapidly becoming a favourite with the young king. Courtenay was of royal blood, being the grandson of Edward IV and Elizabeth Woodville, whose second-youngest daughter Katherine had married William Courtenay, Earl of Devon. This made him a first cousin of the king. Courtenay had spent most of his childhood at court and had been taught by Henry's tutor, Giles Duwes. He was described by one contemporary as 'the king's near kinsman, and hath been brought up of a child with his grace in his chamber'.[55]

But Courtenay's royal blood had been tainted by treason. His father William had been high in Henry VII's favour until he had been discovered to be conspiring with his wife's cousin, the Yorkist pretender Edmund de la Pole, Earl of Suffolk. He had been sent to the Tower and attainted, living out his days under threat of execution. William had been released early in Henry VIII's reign but had died shortly afterwards and his earldom had passed to his son, who succeeded in reversing his father's attainder. Henry clearly enjoyed the company of his cousin, who shared the young king's exuberance and lust for life. His account books record the winter sports in which he and his royal master indulged at Greenwich: indoor tennis and shuffleboard, as well as a snowball fight.[56] By 1519 Courtenay was one of the select group of courtiers who were given daily livery and apartments within the royal household, and his influence continued to grow during the years that followed.

Another scion of the House of York to enter the new king's service was Henry Pole, eldest son of Lady Margaret Pole, daughter of Edward IV's younger brother George, Duke of Clarence. Born in around 1492, Henry was the eldest of the Pole brothers and became a royal ward after his father's death in 1504, Henry VII being careful to keep those of the House of York close to his throne. The new king evidently upheld his father's strategy because Henry Pole was recorded as one of the attendants at the coronation in June 1509. He appears in the royal household accounts on a number of occasions during the following three years and is referred to as a sewer, which was a prestigious position that entailed waiting upon the king when he dined. He went on to serve the king on his military campaigns, earning a knighthood and the title Lord Montagu for his efforts. During the course of his service, he became acquainted with the Neville family, and later married Jane, the daughter of Sir Edward Neville's brother George, third Baron Bergavenny. In the tightly knit world of the nobility, this marriage linked Pole with Bergavenny's father-in-law Edward Stafford, Duke of Buckingham, and they often gambled together. It would prove a hazardous connection.

The new king liked to be surrounded by men drawn from all walks of life, however, and as well as his higher-ranking companions, he was served in his privy chamber by a host of more humbly born male attendants. By dent of their regular attendance, through which they established a close bond with their royal master, these men were able to exert a level of influence that was far from negligible. Many of them were drawn from families who had served at the royal court for generations. Considerations of security were paramount in this most intimate of court departments, so it made sense to choose men of proven trustworthiness. Thus, for example, Sir John Gage held the posts of esquire of the body, comptroller, Vice Chamberlain and Lord Chamberlain under both Henry VII and Henry VIII. His son entered the royal household as a lowly groom during the latter's reign, but rose through the ranks to become Master of the Household.

If an attendant pleased Henry, then he would reward him with promotions. For example, Richard Cecil had risen from the post of page and then groom to become a yeoman in the privy chamber. As well as dressing the king, he was also in charge of accessories, weapons and hunting equipment. His family would remain in favour throughout the Tudor period.[57]

Among the most important positions held by the lower-ranking men who served Henry was that of tailor. These men were, after all, responsible for crafting the king's public image. Eager to establish his own style, and to distance himself from his late father, Henry replaced the latter's tailor, Stephen Jasper, with a man named William Hilton. Hilton served in this post until his death in 1519, and was replaced by a Frenchman, John de Paris, which perhaps reveals Henry's desire to keep up with the latest fashions from the court of his great rival.[58] Henry did retain his father's embroiderer, William More, who continued in this post until 1518, when he was succeeded by two more Williams: Mortimer and Ibrgragve.

The task of caring for the king's priceless clothes was no less responsible than that of making them. For much of the reign it fell to Nicholas Bristowe, who served as clerk to the Wardrobe of Robes and Beds. An extremely assiduous and conscientious man, Bristowe invented a painstakingly detailed system for monitoring deliveries of material to court in order to ensure that none of the items went missing.

The other men involved in ensuring that the king was presented in as magnificent a style as possible included his barber, a man named John Penn. Perhaps more than any other of Henry's body servants, he had to be exceptionally trustworthy, given that his job involved putting a blade to the king's throat on a daily basis.

Next in line were Henry's physicians, who would take it in turns to examine their royal master every morning. They were joined in the king's privy chamber by the royal apothecaries and, when the need arose, by his personal surgeons. The king's interest in his physical health bordered on the obsessive. Perhaps due to the early death of his brother, as well as his father's resulting paranoia about the well-being of his sole surviving male heir, Henry grew up to be something of a hypochondriac.

Along with the officials who attended him in his private apartments, Henry also became well acquainted with other servants at court. They included Richard Hill, the sergeant of the cellar. Despite his lowly rank, he became a frequent gambling partner of the king. It is to Henry's credit that he did not treat such 'below stairs' staff as invisible, but got to know them as individuals. If they pleased him, he would seek out their company and, occasionally, reward them with gifts and other honours.

That he was comfortable in the company of men who were so far beneath him in the social strata might also betray something of Henry's deep-seated insecurity. Like his father, he was painfully aware of the fragility of the Tudor dynasty, which was still in its infancy and which some of the ancient noble families neither wanted nor expected to survive. After all, the Tudors' claim to the throne did not bear close scrutiny, and there were others with royal blood that was untainted by bastardy. While the new king appointed high-ranking nobles to positions of influence at court, this was often a case of keeping his enemies close. When it came to his personal attendants, he preferred men of more humble origins whom he could trust entirely.

The same was true of a rising star in Henry's service who would soon come to dominate the young king and his court.

4

'His Majesty's second self'

DESCRIBING THE KING's activities a year after his accession, Edward Hall noted that he had spent time 'exercising himself daily in shooting, singing, dancing, wrestling, casting of the bar, playing at the recorders, flute, virginals, and in setting of songs, making of ballads . . . there were kept both jousts and tournaments: the rest of this progress was spent in hunting, hawking and shooting'.[1]

It is telling that there is no mention of affairs of state in this description of his new lifestyle. There was something rebellious in Henry's flagrant disregard for state business, which formed a sharp contrast to the old king's ways. Henry VII had not allowed 'any near or full approach, either to his power or to his secrets', and had spent endless hours toiling over account books, correspondence and other minutiae of government. His son could not have been more different. He had witnessed first-hand how his father had worn himself down with the endless business and cares of his kingdom, and that he had not been any more loved by his people for it: indeed, they had despised his closed, suspicious nature. 'There were many who rather feared than loved him,' observed Polydore Vergil; 'his sole interest was to ensure his safety by supervising all details of government; through which preoccupation he at last so wore out his mind and body that his energies gradually declined, he fell into a state of weakness and from that, not long after, came to his death.'[2]

Little wonder that the new king decided to leave the management of such affairs to others. 'Although always intelligent and judicious, he nevertheless allowed himself to be so allured by his pleasures, that, accustomed to ease, he for many years left the administration of the government to his ministers,' recalled an Italian envoy some years later.[3] This presented an opportunity that Thomas Wolsey was quick to grasp.

In his late thirties by the time of Henry's accession, Wolsey was an exceptionally capable and ambitious churchman and administrator who had risen rapidly through the ranks during the previous reign. His burgeoning career at court was at odds with his origins. He was the son of an Ipswich tavern keeper and butcher, but had earned his position through ability, hard work and the sheer force of his personality. Wolsey shared more in common with the new king's rumbustious and extrovert companions than with his fellow solemn-faced clerics. But he had the added refinement of sophistication and an exceptional intellect.

Wolsey was 'very apt to learning' and had graduated from Oxford at the age of just fifteen, earning himself the nickname of the 'boy batchelor'. He went on to study for a degree in theology at Magdalen College, which was a natural choice for anyone seeking a career in the Church. But from the beginning, Wolsey's ambitions also extended to the political sphere. His academic career had provided him with his first contacts with the court. He may have taught the sons of the Marquess of Dorset, who subsequently secured him the rectory of Limington in Somerset in October 1500.

But Wolsey's ambitions lay far beyond that of parish priest. He went on to secure positions in the household of Henry Deane, Archbishop of Canterbury (Warham's predecessor), and of Richard Nanfan, treasurer of Calais. Nanfan helped Wolsey to his first court appointment in 1507, as chaplain. Part of Wolsey's genius lay in his ability to spot potential – in patrons as well as protégés. According to his contemporary biographer, George Cavendish, he soon attached himself to Richard Fox, Bishop of Winchester, and Sir Thomas Lovell, Chancellor of the Exchequer, shrewdly judging that they enjoyed 'most rule in the council and . . . be most in favour with the king'.[4] Before long, he had so ingratiated himself with both men that they recommended him for a diplomatic mission to the Emperor Maximilian in Flanders. Wolsey later boasted that he had amazed Henry VII by completing the visit in just three and a half days – which, if true, would have been a staggering feat in an age when travel by road and sea was both slow and hazardous. More diplomatic missions soon followed, each one of a more complex nature than the last.

Wolsey's conscience was as flexible as his principles, and despite being by now a high-ranking member of the Church, he began a liaison with a woman known as Mistress Lark. This resulted in the birth of two children, both of whom he acknowledged and helped to careers in the Church. His enemies decried his 'lechery' and 'fornication', while others could not help but applaud his audacity and undoubted ability. Although no admirer of Wolsey, the controversial scholar and religious reformer William Tyndale described him as 'a man of lust and courage and bodily strength'.[5] At turns plain speaking and a flatterer, Wolsey employed wit and charm as much as he did threats, and spoke with what Cavendish described as a 'filed tongue'.[6]

Distinguished churchman, able administrator and man of the world, with what the Venetian ambassador described as a 'very active and assiduous mind in matters of business', Wolsey proved an irresistible combination of talents and morality to the new king.[7] According to Polydore Vergil, in the early days of the new reign, Wolsey's old patron Richard Fox pushed him forward as a counter to his adversary Thomas Howard. If this is true, then Fox would soon regret it. Vergil also notes that, in characteristic style, Wolsey was quick to spot the men who could secure him the king's favour, including Henry's closest friend, Charles Brandon. Wolsey threw himself into their boisterous circle, 'singing, laughing, dancing and playing with the young courtiers' as if he was truly one of them, rather than a man of the cloth.[8]

According to Cavendish, Wolsey, 'whose head was full of subtle wit and policy', perceived 'a plain path to walk in towards promotion'. Upon being introduced to the new king, he assured him 'that he shall not need to spare any time of his pleasure for any business that should necessary happen in the council as long as he being there'.[9] Henry immediately warmed to this quick-witted and charismatic man, who presented a welcome contrast to the more sober ministers whom he had inherited from his father. The fact that Wolsey, like a number of the other men who were intimate with the king, was a few years older than Henry suggests that the young king may have been searching for a father figure. Henry VII's influence had often been suffocating, but now that it was entirely absent his son perhaps felt a certain vulnerability alongside the heady freedom of being king.

An indication of Henry's esteem for Wolsey came in June 1509, when he appointed him Dean of Hereford. In November, Wolsey replaced Henry VII's official Richard Hobbs as Almoner, an ancient and prestigious court post that involved distributing largesse on the king's behalf, and dealing with the numerous supplicants who applied for it. Although on the surface this appeared a rather mundane office, it enabled the holder to become involved in all manner of legal, financial and ecclesiastical matters. Crucially, it also involved regular attendance upon the king. Therein lay the real prize of so many court appointments, and it was up to the office holder to make the most of the opportunity.

Wolsey was more alive to this than most. As royal Almoner, he became involved in so much of the king's business that within two years of Henry's accession, he was *de facto* chief minister. Formally admitted to the council in 1511, before long he was managing all of its affairs. As well as keeping himself busy, he also significantly increased the routine work of the council so that their presence was required more often at Westminster, leaving Wolsey free to attend the king on a regular basis.

The Almoner had been quick to realise that there was a vacuum in the heart of Henry's government – and he had been even quicker to fill it. The king's affairs were routinely handled by a group of between eight and twelve councillors, who usually met in the Star Chamber at Westminster. Henry himself was rarely present at these meetings: indeed, he was often many miles away on progress or at one of his palaces outside of London. But because he was the nominal head of the council, they could not act without his assent. This meant that someone was required to act as an intermediary between the king and council, finding out his opinion on matters of state, seeking his approval, and securing the seal of the royal signet on state documents. Wolsey filled this role perfectly. In contrast to his more noble peers, he did not consider it beneath his dignity to scurry about the capital or countryside carrying messages to and fro. The gains were worth it: Wolsey soon realised that he could put his own spin on matters when presenting them to the king, in order to influence his decision. Likewise, he became Henry's mouthpiece – a position that carried enormous power. Before long, therefore, Wolsey had transformed the role of messenger into that of royal deputy.

At the beginning of Henry's reign, a number of his father's councillors had still been in service and routinely countersigned royal documents, but soon they found themselves supplanted by the royal Almoner, who increasingly interposed between themselves and the monarch. Rather than consulting with his fellow councillors, Wolsey's strategy was to 'first make the king privy of all such matters (as should pass through their hands) before he would proceed to the finishing or determining of the same whose mind and pleasure he would fulfil and follow to the uttermost'.[10] As a result, the council often did little more than rubberstamp a policy that Wolsey had drawn up with the king's sanction. 'Thus the almoner ruled all them that before ruled him,' Cavendish shrewdly observed.[11]

Perhaps more than any other courtier, Wolsey appreciated the importance of maintaining regular access to his sovereign. He soon established a routine of meeting Henry once a week for lengthy discussions. When the king was away on progress, his minister made sure to keep him fully informed of court affairs by letter, and would sometimes visit him if he judged the matter would be best communicated in person.

Wolsey soon had the measure of his king. Henry was intelligent and well educated, but he had a short concentration span and was easily bored. His Almoner therefore made sure to read and précis all the documents that were sent to him, and then offered his royal master a brief list of options on every issue requiring a decision, making sure to weight them in favour of his own preference.

Henry was 'wonderfully pleased' with this state of affairs, which suited him perfectly.[12] Wolsey flattered him into believing that he was making all of the decisions, when really he was for the most part approving those that his official had put in place. Few others were fooled. 'It came to such a pass', observed a contemporary chronicler, 'that the King intervened in nothing, and this Cardinal [Wolsey] did everything.'[13] One aghast contemporary remarked that

Wolsey 'assumed that he could undertake nearly all the offices of state by himself'.[14] Meanwhile, a foreign envoy reported to Rome that 'the king can do nothing of the least importance without him [Wolsey] and esteems him among the dearest friends'. The Venetian ambassador agreed that Wolsey enjoyed 'extreme influence with the King'.[15] Little wonder that Henry's other men were soon courting the Almoner's favour as the surest route to influence.

One of the many reasons why Henry liked Wolsey so much was that, unlike the more senior officials, he actively encouraged, rather than disapproved of, the king's indulgent lifestyle. 'So fast as the other councillors advised the king to leave his pleasures and attend to the affairs of the realm, so busily did the Almoner persuade him to the contrary,' observed George Cavendish, 'which delighted him much, and caused him to have the greatest affection and love to the Almoner.' Cavendish was not exaggerating his master's favour when he claimed that 'no man was of that estimation with the king as he was'.[16]

According to Polydore Vergil, Wolsey also played upon his royal master's love of fine jewels and other decorative pieces as a means of securing his agreement for whatever matter he put before him. He claimed that the Almoner often 'brought out some small present or other, a beautifully fashioned dish for example or a jewel or ring or gifts of that sort, and while the King was admiring the gift intently, Wolsey would adroitly bring forward the project on which his mind was fixed . . . Henry praised Wolsey's diligence so highly that a few days later he said openly (and not by way of a joke) that Wolsey would rule not only himself but Francis [the King of France] as well.'[17] It is unlikely that the king was literally dazzled into agreeing to whatever Wolsey proposed, but Vergil's account does give an impression of the skill with which Wolsey handled his royal master. He was the first of Henry's men to realise – and exploit – the fact that the young king could be quite easily manipulated.

Wolsey also proved a generous host, and regularly entertained the king at his growing number of residences. Cavendish, who served in Wolsey's household, describes the lengths to which his master would go to delight the king: 'There wanted no preparations of goodly furniture with viands of the finest sort that might be provided for money or friendship. Such pleasures were then devised for the king's comfort and consolation as might be invented by man's wit imagined. The banquets were set forth with masques and mummeries in so gorgeous a sort and costly manner that it was an heaven to behold.'[18] In staging such spectacular entertainments for his royal master, Wolsey appreciated what many of his rivals did not: Henry loved to mix business with pleasure. Indeed, he made little distinction between the two. This 'young and lusty' king, who was 'disposed all to mirth and pleasure', was far more likely to agree to a matter of state over a hearty meal or diverting masque than he was in the more staid environment of the council chamber.[19]

For all that he revelled in the king's favour, Wolsey was shrewd enough to realise the dangers of seeming to overreach himself. He was therefore always careful to present his policies as the king's, and to involve his royal master at the most apposite moments. As the seventeenth-century church historian John Strype observed: 'Wolsey, though he knew how to indulge the King in his pleasures, yet he reminded him sometimes of business too.'[20] The Almoner also realised that for all his eagerness to return to more diverting pursuits, his young master was neither gullible nor pliant, but could be unpredictably astute and challenging in his responses. He therefore had to prepare for any eventuality.

If Wolsey's noble rivals resented his rapid rise to favour, they were also perplexed by his obvious knack for dealing with a king who, though charming and gregarious, could also be fickle and quick-tempered. How could he, the son of a butcher, understand the workings of a majestic mind so much better than the men who were born to do so? What Wolsey had appreciated was that behind the new king's mask of affability lay a nascent insecurity and paranoia, expressed in a need for unquestioning loyalty and devotion from those closest to him.

Wolsey also recognised in this typically indulged 'spare heir' the desire to be surrounded by men who would cater to his every whim. 'All his endeavour was only to satisfy the king's mind,' observed Cavendish, 'knowing right well that it was the very vain and right course to bring him to high promotion.'[21] There was no shortage of men at court to do the king's bidding, but Wolsey was always there first, fulfilling each task quickly and effectively, so that before long he could anticipate his master's needs before Henry knew them himself. Tyndale noticed that he was 'obsequious and serviceable and in all games and sports the first and next at hand'.[22] Cavendish concurred that his master was 'most earnest and readiest among all the council to advance the king's only will and pleasure without any respect to the case'. Henry himself soon realised that in Wolsey he had 'a mete instrument for the accomplishment of his devised will and pleasure [and] called him more near unto him and esteemed him so highly that his estimation and favour put all other councillors out of their accustomed favour that they were in before'.[23]

Henry was also drawn to Wolsey as a man of intellect and taste, and the latter both encouraged and broadened his knowledge of literature, recommending texts for his erudition. As a result, his esteem increased beyond what was expected for a king towards his minister. According to Cavendish, Henry 'conceived such a loving fancy' towards Wolsey that he liked to have him always close at hand.[24] In a heavily symbolic gesture, Henry also gave him a gift of property: a fine house in St Bride's, Westminster, that had formerly belonged to his father's despised official, Richard Empson. The new king's favour towards Wolsey was also expressed in a rapid succession of honours. In April 1510, he was made registrar of the Order of the Garter, an extraordinarily prestigious post. A rash of ecclesiastical promotions followed.

One matter about which Henry confided in Wolsey was his need for an heir. Forasmuch as he liked to be surrounded by men, to serve and entertain him, the young king was an attentive and loving husband to his wife Catherine. In contrast to her marriage to his brother Arthur, there was no doubt that this one had been consummated. It is likely that by the time of their joint coronation in June 1509, Catherine was already pregnant. Henry and his kingdom rejoiced at the prospect of a fertile marriage. His mother had filled the royal nursery with heirs, and it looked as if his wife was set to do the same. However, just seven months into the pregnancy, Catherine went into labour and was delivered of a stillborn daughter. The royal couple were embarrassed as well as distressed, and tried to keep the tragedy a secret. Catherine remained in seclusion for

many weeks afterwards, but by the time she emerged she was already
pregnant again. This time, she carried the child to full term, and in
the early hours of New Year's Day 1511, she was delivered of a boy.

Henry was ecstatic when he heard that he had a son. Tiny though
he was, from the moment he drew his first breath, the infant prince
was the most important man in his father's life: Henry now had an
heir to secure the Tudor dynasty. The boy was named after his father,
and the news of his arrival was proclaimed across London, prompting
days of public rejoicing. Prince Henry's christening was conducted
with great pomp and ceremony, and his parents attended the magnificent jousts and pageants that were held on 12 and 13 February at
Westminster to celebrate the birth.

It would be one of the most lavish and expensive entertainments
ever staged in Henry's reign. Edward Hall described the great mountain that was built for one of the pageants, 'glistening by night, as
though it had been all of gold and set with stones, on the top of
which mountain was a tree of gold, the branches and boughs fringed
with gold, spreading on every side over the mountain, with roses
and pomegranates'.[25] In ebullient mood, the king himself took part
in the ensuing tournaments, assuming the role of 'Couer Loyal'
(Loyal Heart) as his loving wife looked on. Charles Brandon and
Henry Guildford rode out, clad in russet silk and cloth of gold. Sir
Thomas Knyvett, Sir Edward Neville, Thomas Grey and Thomas
Boleyn were also noted among the combatants.

Other jousts and pageants followed, each more extravagant than
the last. Henry's men played a prominent role in all of them.
Guildford entered the stage in a castle of 'russet sarcenet' decorated
with gold letters, while Brandon rode out disguised as a religious
person with a pilgrim's hat and staff, and a long beard reaching down
as far as his saddle. Their royal master proceeded to run twenty-eight
courses, breaking twelve lances and winning the prize as challenger.
Edward Hall concluded that thanks to the 'excellency of the king's
person', it had been the greatest tournament ever seen in England.[26]
But it would also be one of the last of its kind.

As royal tradition dictated, the tiny prince was soon after established in a household of his own, served by no fewer than forty-four
male attendants. The king, meanwhile, expressed his thanks to God

by going on pilgrimage to Walsingham in Norfolk, the most popular of all the shrines scattered across the kingdom. But shortly after his return, disaster struck. Prince Henry, the chief hope of his father and the kingdom, died suddenly at the age of just two months. The cause of his death was not recorded.

Henry was devastated. Orders were issued that no one should seek to comfort him or the queen in case they sparked a fresh outpouring of grief. Drawing on his considerable faith, the king tried to comfort Catherine, who had fallen into 'much lamentation', by assuring her that it must be God's will and urging her not to rail against it. But as his infant son was laid to rest at Westminster, Henry must have felt as if he was being punished by the God in whom he had always placed so much trust.[27]

More misery was soon heaped upon the young king's shoulders. In May 1511, Henry sent a force to Spain in support of a crusade against the Moors of North Africa led by his father-in-law, Ferdinand of Aragon. It proved a disastrous expedition. By the time that Henry's troops arrived, they were no longer required, and proceeded to disgrace themselves by getting drunk and wreaking havoc on the streets of Cadiz. Many hundreds then fell sick from the flux and died. The king's friend Henry Guildford, who had resisted joining in their antics, also fell ill, and the command of Henry's forces was transferred to Thomas Howard. It was a poisoned chalice, and Howard soon lamented to Ferdinand: 'What shall the king our master report of our slothfulness, which hath spent innumerable treasure and nothing gained?'[28]

Despite the ignominious failure of Henry's troops, his father-in-law was so impressed with their original commander that he knighted Guildford on 15 September. Henry was a good deal less pleased with him and Howard when they returned to England soon afterwards, and he threatened to string them up from the highest gallows. But his anger soon passed, and on 30 March 1512 Guildford was sufficiently back in favour to receive a knighthood at Westminster.

Undeterred by the failure of this first military expedition, Henry started planning another. This time, he called on Ferdinand to support him in reconquering Guyenne in southern France, which had been lost by Henry VI in 1453. He assigned the command to Thomas Grey, second Marquess of Dorset who, for all his skill in the tournament arena, had never been tested in the field of combat. Although the king had every confidence in him, Grey's inexperience in battle soon became apparent, and the expedition proved another ignominious failure. To make matters worse, Ferdinand reneged on his pledge to support the English troops and instead tried to persuade the marquess to join his own attack on Navarre. But Grey refused to break his orders, and while he and Ferdinand argued, his men fell sick from too much heat and wine.

Within months, they mutinied and returned to England, bringing the marquess – who was also dangerously ill – with them. In order to cover his own duplicity, Ferdinand told his son-in-law that Grey was solely responsible for the failure. To his credit, Henry refused to cast the blame on the marquess alone, but to satisfy Ferdinand he staged a show trial. Grey knelt before his sovereign but, weakened by sickness, his knees gave out and he had to beg permission to stand for the rest of the proceedings. He suffered no further repercussions, and although he was never entrusted with another command, he was soon restored to as much favour as he had enjoyed before.

Undeterred by yet another military failure, in May 1512, Henry declared war on France. He had been lusting for military glory even before his accession, and he was not lacking in warlike companions to encourage him. Most of these were drawn from his privy chamber, whereas his more sober councillors cautioned against taking aggressive action. Foremost among them was John Fisher, who urged his royal master to adopt a more cautious approach and not deplete the treasury with an expensive and unnecessary war. But Henry hated to be contradicted by a man whom he associated with his penny-pinching father's regime, and he deprived Fisher of political power from that day forward.

By contrast, Henry's former tutor John Skelton spied an opportunity to advance himself by encouraging the king's lust for glory. Skelton had remained in London since returning upon his former pupil's accession, and by 1512, he was calling himself the *'orator regius'*, or king's spokesman.[29] Although this was more a self-appointed than an official position, Henry does seem to have employed him on a range of diplomatic, secretarial and poetical duties.

Skelton was quick to publicise his new status. He wrote two self-congratulatory poems, dedicating himself to Calliope, the muse in Greek mythology who presides over eloquence and epic poetry. He also penned a Latin epitaph for the tomb of Henry VII in Westminster Abbey, lauding the late king for his many virtues, which included instilling fear in the French and Scots.[30] Eager to exert an influence over his former pupil once more, Skelton sent the king a chronicle of the Third Crusade, which recounted the exploits of his ancestor Richard the Lionheart. Damning of the French and filled with nationalistic fervour, he evidently hoped to inspire Henry for the war with France, which was looking more likely by the day.

Skelton soon warmed to his role as royal propagandist and warmonger, shrewdly judging that it was guaranteed to win him favour with a young king desperate for military fame. Meanwhile, Henry's like-minded associates were making preparations to join the campaign. Foremost among them was Edward Howard, whom Henry appointed admiral of the fleet that he had assembled in April 1512 to protect the seas between Brest and the Thames estuary. Howard was given the command of no fewer than eighteen ships and 3,000 men. A brave and energetic captain, he distinguished himself in this service and was said to have captured sixty French vessels before the year was out. Henry was so impressed that he made him Lord Admiral and a Knight of the Garter.

The same year, Howard's brother-in-law, Sir Thomas Knyvet, described as a man of 'great courage' and military prowess, was given the command of the *Regent*, one of the largest ships in Henry VIII's navy.[31] Meanwhile, Henry Guildford and Charles Brandon captained one of Henry's largest ships, the *Sovereign*. On 10 August, the two men were forced to watch helplessly as Knyvet was killed during an engagement with the French outside Brest, and went down in the burning wreck of the *Regent*. Edward Howard, who had also been there that day, vowed to avenge his death before he saw the king again.

Henry himself was deeply affected by Knyvet's loss, although he concealed it from all except those closest to him. Wolsey confided to his old patron Bishop Fox: 'To see how the king taketh the matter and behaveth himself, ye would marvel and much allow his wise and constant manner. I have not on my faith seen the like.'[32] That Wolsey should have known Henry's true feelings about Knyvet's death is also revealing about his own relationship with the king. In a very short space of time, the Almoner had become one of Henry's closest companions and confidants, and observers such as Fox recognised that a special relationship existed between the two men. Meanwhile, the king so revered Knyvet's memory that he appointed the latter's son Henry as a gentleman of his privy chamber, and also honoured four of his brothers with offices at court and in the navy.

Though he also lamented Knyvet's demise, Henry's friend Brandon profited from it when he was appointed Master of the Horse in his place two months later. This was a role to which Brandon, with his love of the joust and hunting, was entirely suited. More honours were to follow. To the knighthood that had been conferred upon him in March 1512 was added promotion to the Order of the Garter in April 1513. Not long afterwards, Brandon was betrothed to Sir Thomas Knyvet's eight-year-old stepdaughter, Elizabeth Grey, heiress to the barony of Lisle. He had purchased her wardship from the king, and their betrothal enabled him to be created Viscount Lisle. As well as giving him greater equality with his noble peers at court, this title also enabled Brandon to assume increasingly prestigious military commands. He raised a substantial retinue of men to support his royal master's invasion of France in the summer of 1513. Henry appointed him as high marshal of the army and gave him the charge of 3,000 men.

Meanwhile, Edward Howard tried to make good his promise to try to avenge Knyvet's death. Courageous to the point of recklessness, on 25 April 1513 he insisted upon leading the attack on his opponent's flagship in person, despite lacking supplies. He was forced over the side of his galley and drowned by the weight of his armour. Before he fell to his death, he took off the silver whistle that was the Lord Admiral's badge of office, and threw it into the sea. He left behind a wife, Alice, and two illegitimate sons. He commended one of them to the care of the king, and the other to 'my special trusty friend' Charles Brandon.

Edward's brother Thomas was now free at last to emerge from the shadow of his popular, charismatic and courageous younger brother. On 4 May he arrived at Plymouth, to where his late brother's fleet had retreated, and took over the command. Thomas was a very different style of commander to his late brother, however. Whereas Edward had inspired the love of his men, Thomas bullied his troops into action with threats and bursts of temper. This may have been effective in the short term, but it spelt danger for his future campaigns.

On 30 June, Henry crossed the Channel with a sizeable retinue. Polydore Vergil describes how he had 'hand picked' the 'flower of men in their military prime' from among his entourage.[33] Principal among them was Thomas Grey, Marquis of Dorset, who was given the command of the army. Determined not to be outdone by his master's warlike companions, Wolsey was also there and had the command of 200 men.

Upon landing, the king and his army marched to Thérouanne, which was situated about thirty miles inland from the English-held town of Calais, and laid siege to it. When the French tried to relieve the town, Henry and his allies triumphed at the so-called 'Battle of the Spurs' on 16 August. In retaliation, James IV of Scotland, who had concluded an alliance with the French king, crossed the English border on 22 August. He and his troops were crushed at Flodden by an English army under the command of Thomas Howard on 9 September, and James IV was killed.

The same month, Henry and his forces captured Tournai. A number of his men benefited from the victory. Wolsey was appointed administrator of the diocese, while Sir Henry Guildford was created a knight-banneret. Some of Henry's other childhood companions were also present at Tournai. William Blount, Lord Mountjoy, had been a regular presence at court since the beginning of the reign, and in 1512 had been appointed chamberlain to Catherine of Aragon. He had married one of her ladies-in-waiting shortly after Henry's accession, which brought him into regular contact with the new queen. Before long, he enjoyed the privileged position of being favoured by both the king and his consort. In early 1513, the king had put Blount in charge of transport for the war against France, and in September he departed for Calais with a force of 500 men. After the capture of Tournai, Blount was appointed acting lieutenant, bailiff, and later governor of the city, a post that he would hold until January 1517.

The young king's illegitimate uncle, Arthur Plantagenet, had also joined the 1513 campaign. Arthur had remained close to Henry after his accession, and had regularly taken part in feats of arms at court. In 1511, he had married Elizabeth Dudley, the widow of Henry VII's despised official Edmund. The marriage had been arranged by the new king, perhaps as a penance for his brutality towards Elizabeth's first husband. Arthur's loyalty towards his nephew was as strong now as it had been during Henry's childhood. Having initially joined the naval effort during the 1513 campaign, he almost lost his life in the shipwreck of the *Nicholas of Hampton* in February. Undeterred, he joined the king's invasion of France that summer and was rewarded with a knighthood in October.

Of all the men who shared in the triumph of Tournai, though, it was Charles Brandon who enjoyed the greatest honour. He led a successful assault on one of the city gates, which proved instrumental in persuading the citizens to surrender to his royal master. As a reward, Henry gave him the outlying castle of Mortain. He and Henry had fought alongside each other in mock combat for many years: now they were brothers in arms, revelling in genuine military glory. This was the apogee of Brandon's relationship with Henry, and his favour and influence now seemed unassailable.

The young king's warlike nature formed a dramatic contrast to Henry VII, whose foreign policy had been dictated by cautious diplomacy. Perhaps the younger Henry, who had displayed his martial prowess from a tender age, viewed it as a means of proving himself against his father, even though the latter's approach was arguably more sensible. Certainly, he was evoking memories of his chivalric grandfather, Edward IV, who had won his crown on the battlefield. It also reveals the strength of Henry's natural desire to win – a desire formed during the indulgent early years of his upbringing as the spare heir, with little thought for weightier concerns. But Henry would find to his cost that there was a wide – and expensive – gulf between the victories won in the tournament field and those for which he hankered overseas.

5

'The servant is not greater than his lord'

Not long after his triumph at Tournai, Henry journeyed to Mechelen in Flanders to visit Margaret of Austria, Duchess of Savoy and sister of Philip the Handsome, whom the English king had so admired. He took with him his favourite companion, Charles Brandon.

Margaret had already heard of Brandon's influence with Henry. Her agent, who had been stationed with the English army, reported that Henry's favourite was a 'second king'.[1] When she met him in person, she was left in no doubt of his strident self-confidence. Brandon flirted with her so openly that it sparked rumours of a betrothal. When Henry made his friend Duke of Suffolk on 1 February 1514, speculation intensified – so much so that bets were placed in London on the likelihood of the marriage. A joust held in May set the rumours flying once more. Henry and Brandon appeared clad in white and black armour respectively, both holding staves on which was written: 'who can hold that will away'. Edward Hall was in no doubt that the display 'was judged to be made for the duke of Suffolk and the duchess of Savoy'.[2]

When she heard the rumours, Margaret was deeply shocked. As princess of Asturias, Duchess of Savoy and Regent of the Netherlands on behalf of her young nephew, the future Charles V, she was one of the most powerful women in Europe and her pedigree was impeccable. Brandon might be one of the highest-ranking members of Henry VIII's court, but his rise to prominence had been entirely due to the king's favour, rather than his own credentials. Moreover, his womanising ways were notorious. Margaret therefore demanded that Henry put a stop to the rumours and cancel Brandon's planned visit to the Netherlands to raise troops for the following year's campaigning. The English king complied with her wishes, but he refused to order his favourite to marry Elizabeth Grey, Lady Lisle, as Margaret wished. He was not prepared to sacrifice his friend's happiness to Anglo–Imperial amity.

Margaret was not alone in her scornful view of Henry's closest favourite. Always quick to discredit any rivals to his influence with the king, Erasmus ridiculed him in a satire of Persius. In a not very subtle reference to Brandon's position as Master of the Horse, he quipped that the king had turned his favourite from a stable boy into a nobleman. In a similar vein, Polydore Vergil noted that 'many people considered it very surprising that Charles should be so honoured as to be made a duke'.[3]

If he heard such jibes, Brandon could afford to brush them off. Whereas during the first three years of the reign, he had shared the limelight at court with the likes of Thomas Knyvet and Edward Howard, their deaths in the French war left him increasingly alone at the centre of their circle. As a result, he played an ever more prominent role in the king's entertainments. In the revels, for example, he began to be the only participant dressed identically with the king, and in the jousts he was Henry's sole partner as the pair challenged the rest of the court.

Although many at Henry's court resented Brandon's rapid rise to power, one man who did not was Thomas Wolsey. This may have been because the two men dominated different spheres of Henry's life – Brandon the private and military, and Wolsey the political and ecclesiastical. Each neatly counterbalanced the influence of the other, and it was therefore in Wolsey's interests for Brandon to remain in power. He could not risk his being replaced by a man who sought to trespass into Wolsey's domain.

However, a diplomatic move by Wolsey inadvertently led to his colleague's disgrace. In the summer of 1514, he brokered a peace between Henry and the ageing Louis XII of France. To seal the bargain, the English king's beautiful young sister Mary was offered up in marriage. In August, Brandon journeyed to France to take part in a tournament staged in celebration of the marriage, which took place in October. He was accompanied by the king's favourite jouster, Thomas Grey, Marquess of Dorset, whom Henry never missed an opportunity to show off. But while Dorset performed his part to perfection, Brandon would soon plunge himself into disgrace. It is likely that by the time he reached France, Brandon had struck up a dangerous flirtation with the bride-to-be. Even before he had left England, he had talked to Henry about the potential of a marriage. Although he was already betrothed to Elizabeth Grey, he evidently had a different lady in mind. Princess Mary had also raised the subject before she set sail for France, asking her brother if she could choose her second husband for herself if Louis died.

For now, though, everything proceeded according to Wolsey's plan. Brandon returned to England after the jousts, and his master's twenty-year-old sister was married to the fifty-four-year-old French king at Abbeville. But within three months, Louis was dead – worn out, it was rumoured, by the exertions of the marriage bed. The unsuspecting English king sent his chief favourite, Brandon, back to France to accompany Mary home. It was an ill-advised choice. Although he was well aware of the consequences, Brandon's desire for the king's sister was so strong that he married her in secret shortly after his arrival. The news soon reached the English court. 'A report circulates, and it is said publicly, that she [Mary] is married again to the English Duke of Suffolk,' reported the Venetian ambassador Giustinian, 'which, if true, is important, and very surprising.'4

This was the greatest scandal of the reign to date, and there was widespread outrage that Brandon had so overreached himself. 'Ye have failed him which hath brought you up of low degree to be of this great honour,' Wolsey upbraided him. It was a telling remark and one that revealed a little, perhaps, of how Wolsey viewed his own relationship with the king.5 For all that he loved to flaunt his newfound wealth and magnificence, Wolsey knew that without the king's favour he was just the son of a butcher. He could ill afford to be so condescending to Brandon, who was of considerably higher birth, but Wolsey was ever a man to exploit his advantage.

Henry himself was furious at his favourite's betrayal. He had trusted Brandon utterly and had courted criticism by heaping honours upon him during the previous five years. But no matter how high he had raised him, he did not see Brandon as being of sufficient status to marry his sister, a princess of the blood. Polydore

Vergil's claim that he had made Brandon Duke of Suffolk 'to enable him more properly to be related to the king in marriage, this future development being already decided upon by Henry', is highly unlikely, given his fury when he heard the news.[6] The other men who vied for Henry's favour rejoiced that Brandon had destroyed his standing at court more swiftly – and completely – than they could ever have done.

Frantic with worry, and no doubt regretting his hasty action, Brandon wrote to his royal master, giving his side of the story and pleading for forgiveness. Mary, he said, had gone out of her way to seduce him, and insisted: 'she would never have none but me'. Fearing that she would be married off to another foreign husband, she had sworn to Brandon that she would 'rather . . . be torn in pieces', and had proceeded to burst into tears. 'Sir, I never saw woman so weep,' Brandon assured his master, and begged that the only way he could comfort her was to agree to marriage. He ended with a protestation of his utter subservience to his royal master. 'Your Grace knoweth best I never sought other remedy against mine enemies but your Grace . . . for it is your Grace that has made me . . . and holden me up hitherto, and if your [pleasure] be so for to do, I care not for all the world.'[7]

Brandon also wrote to Wolsey, pleading with him to intervene on his behalf. The two men were united by their desire for an alliance with France, and in trying to persuade Wolsey to support him, Brandon claimed that Francis I had approved the match. He also reminded Wolsey that, together with the king, they stood alone against 'the council as all the other nobles of the realm' in promoting an Anglo–French alliance.[8] Wolsey assured Brandon that he was his 'firm friend' and that he would do everything possible to bring the matter to a 'successful conclusion'.[9] He added the warning, though, that he alone was fighting Brandon's corner and that his enemies were using the controversy as an excuse to destroy his relationship with the king. Brandon knew this all too well. A few days before receiving Wolsey's letter, he had heard that one of Norfolk's appointees in Mary's household had urged her 'to beware of me [Brandon] of all men, for he knew that you [Wolsey] and I had meddled with [the] devil, and by the puissance of the said [devil] we kept our master subject'.[10] Back at court, meanwhile, Thomas Howard was playing an altogether deadlier game by producing evidence that Brandon was in league with the French king and demanding that he be brought back to face treason charges.

Although Wolsey was willing to help Brandon when he thought that his only – admittedly serious – misdemeanour was a clandestine marriage, when Brandon admitted the extent of his misconduct, the chief minister was appalled. 'To be plain with you,' Brandon wrote, 'I have married her heartily and lain with her, insomuch [as] I fear me that she [may] be with child.'[11] Wolsey knew that this was too great a sin to be swept aside by his master, and angrily upbraided his ally. His fury was partly due to the fact that it was down to him to break the news to Henry and thus take the brunt of the royal wrath. This was predictably severe. 'Cursed be the blind affection and counsel that have brought ye to [this],' Henry ranted. 'Such sudden and ill-advised dealing shall have sudden repentance.'[12]

The king was momentarily distracted from his anger at his favourite's betrayal by the advent of Louis XII's successor. Aged twenty at the time of his accession, Francis I was three years younger than Henry. By rights, he should never have got anywhere near the French throne, being only the first cousin of the king. But Louis' lack of direct heirs made Francis a serious contender. He had jousted at Louis' wedding to Princess Mary, and the ageing French king had been heard to remark: '*Ce grand jeunehomme, il va tout gâcher*' ('That big lad – he'll ruin everything').[13]

Like Henry, Francis was the archetypal Renaissance prince: cultured, well educated and a great patron of the arts. Before long, it was said that he presided over the most cultured court in the world. Tall and athletic, he excelled at jousting, hunting, archery, falconry, tennis and wrestling. Striking rather than handsome, Francis had brown hair and a neatly trimmed beard. His most notable feature was his enormous nose, which earned him the nickname '*le roi grand-nez*'. Irresistibly charming and renowned for his sexual prowess, he kept a string of mistresses and fathered numerous children – including seven children by his wife Claude, which was a source of particular envy for his English rival. It was obvious to everyone that this young man, who was very much 'given to pleasure', revelled in every aspect of his life as king.[14] Like Henry, he was something of a mummy's boy and allowed his indomitable mother, Louise of Savoy, to act as regent whenever he was away.

Boasting considerable wealth, Francis created a building legacy every bit as impressive as Henry's. Early in his reign, he commissioned the magnificent Château de Chambord, which was inspired by the architectural styles of the Italian Renaissance and may even have been designed by Leonardo da Vinci. Many more sumptuous palaces followed, including the Château du Louvre, which he transformed from a medieval fortress into a masterpiece of Renaissance splendour.

That his English counterpart was already jealous of the man who would become his greatest rival is evident from a conversation that he had with the Venetian ambassador, Sebastian Giustinian. '"The King of France, is he as tall as I am?"' Henry demanded. 'I told him there was but little difference,' the ambassador recalled. 'He continued: "Is he as stout?" I said he was not; and he then inquired, "What sort of legs has he?" I replied, "Spare." Whereupon he opened the front of his doublet, and placing his hand on his thigh, said, "Look here! and I have also a good calf to my leg." He then told me that he was very fond of this King of France,' Giustinian concluded.[15]

Over the months and years that followed, Henry scrutinised his agents' reports of his rival, and it is an indication of his insecurity that as well as boasting of his own accomplishments whenever the occasion arose, he also began to emulate Francis's style and habits. For example, Giustinian noted that Henry wore his hair 'straight and short, in the French fashion'.[16] If he heard that the King of France had built a magnificent new palace, then Henry would do the same. He also tried to outshine Francis as a patron of artists, musicians, poets and architects, but there was little he could do to equal the visit by Leonardo da Vinci to the French court, or the fact that Francis kept the *Mona Lisa* in his bathroom. More significantly, neither could he match his rival's ability to sire male heirs. Within four years of coming to the throne, Francis already had two sons. It must have been galling for Henry to stand as godfather to the younger of them, who was named in his honour. His claim, not long afterwards, that if he himself were to die without a male heir, he would leave his throne to Francis, is unlikely to have been genuinely made.

Francis's feelings towards Henry are rather harder to discern. Certainly, he had less cause to feel jealous of his English rival. His kingdom dwarfed Henry's, and with two sons already, his dynasty was a good deal more secure. Politically and militarily, he had much more to fear from Charles, son of Philip the Handsome and heir to three of Europe's leading dynasties: the Houses of Valois-Burgundy, Habsburg and Trastámara. But even when he had come into his full inheritance, the physically ill-favoured Charles would be no threat to Francis on a personal level. The same could not be said of Henry VIII, who arguably excelled the French king in looks and intellect, who was his equal in chivalry and martial prowess, and whose court was challenging the pre-eminence of Francis's in cultural brilliance and prestige. Moreover, the French king's claim to his throne was much shakier than Henry's was to his own. In short, although Henry's jealousy of Francis might be better documented, the rivalry was by no means one-sided.

In the battle of one-upmanship that soon raged between the English and French kings, Henry drew upon the support of his childhood tutor, John Skelton. Still clamouring for an official role at court, the poet fired off a series of verses, all glorifying the bravery and prowess of the English king in France. Henry was delighted with them and gave Skelton enough hope of future work for him to take up residence in London on a more permanent basis.

As well as acting as the king's propagandist, Skelton also assumed responsibility for entertaining the court. He wrote a number of satires during the early years of Henry's reign, many of which served not only to amuse the king and his courtiers, but to poke fun at Skelton's rivals. They included Sir Christopher Garnesche, a prosperous knight from East Anglia who had served Henry in France and subsequently been appointed his gentleman usher. Garnesche retaliated with a series of satirical attacks on Skelton, although none of these have survived. As well as singling out individual opponents, Skelton also took up a theme that he had rehearsed many times during the king's childhood: that of the fickleness and backbiting of the court, which he attacked in 'Against Venomous Tongues'.

Thanks to the rise of the printing press, Skelton's influence soon spread well beyond the court. It made his works accessible to a much wider social spectrum, and thereby enhanced his value to the king as a propagandist. Skelton's poems and texts acted as the press releases of the day, inspiring loyalty and devotion to this warlike young king.

The disgraced Duke of Suffolk and his new wife returned to England in early May 1515. Henry travelled to meet them at Birling in Kent as they made their way home. No record survives of their meeting, but it must have been uncomfortable, to say the least. The council had urged Henry to have Brandon imprisoned or executed upon his return to England. After all, marrying a princess royal without the king's consent was, technically, treason. But Wolsey had skilfully played on his royal master's lingering affection for his sister and favourite to persuade him that they should be let off with a heavy fine. Henry agreed, and the couple were charged with raising £24,000 – equivalent to more than £11 million today. Although this was a staggering sum and would have spelt bankruptcy for Brandon, it was to come from Mary's dower lands in France and was spread over a twelve-year period.[17] Henry was further mollified by the surrender of Mary's jewels and plate, along with half of her dowry and the wardship of Brandon's ousted fiancée, Lady Lisle.

It may have been at the king's insistence that Brandon and Mary married in public shortly afterwards. Henry could not have tolerated any suggestion that their secret marriage was not valid – or, worse, that it had not taken place at all, and his sister was therefore Brandon's whore. The ceremony was held on 13 May 1515 in Greenwich and attended by Henry and members of his court, a sign that the king had forgiven his favourite in public, if not – quite – in private. The Venetian envoy reported with some astonishment that Henry had 'maintained his former friendship for the Duke, which would appear incredible, but is affirmed by the nobility at the Court'.[18]

The controversy was a clear demonstration that for the young king, personal considerations always outweighed political ones. No matter how damning the case might be against one of his men, if they had succeeded in winning his affection, then he was prepared to forgive them. Only as age and paranoia began to overtake him did the loss of faith in a one-time favourite prove both more permanent and more deadly.

Within a few short weeks, it seemed that Brandon enjoyed as great a level of favour with his royal master as he had always done. In August, Giustinian reported that the duke 'governs, commands, and acts with authority scarcely inferior to that of the King himself'.[19] But, as a relative newcomer to court, the Italian had missed the subtle shift that had occurred in Brandon's status. In the years that followed, the duke spent long periods away from court as he worked to build up his private estates. A few days before their marriage, Henry had granted Brandon what remained of the confiscated estates of his predecessors, the Pole dukes of Suffolk. This was anathema to Brandon's rival Thomas Howard, and set the two men on an even greater collision course as they sought to dominate East Anglia. Brandon proceeded to augment the Pole lands to their former level by buying out the grantees to whom Henry and his father had given many of their manors.

Henry clearly missed his old companion, and both he and Wolsey encouraged Brandon and Mary to attend court more regularly. The king needed his friend for more than just company, however. He was plagued with worry about the threat posed by Richard de la Pole, whose Yorkist blood made him a dangerous contender for the throne. In exile on the Continent, Pole had proved successful at whipping up support from Henry's rivals, particularly in France. Henry therefore supported Brandon's efforts to take ownership of the entire Pole estate, thus securing the loyalty of the local gentry. But Brandon never quite succeeded in either. Despite his standing with the king, he did not command the same respect in his estates as the Poles, whose pedigree had far exceeded his.

Brandon's standing at court was also compromised by his new wife's French connections. Even after Henry's share had been deducted, Mary's dower income from France amounted to some £4,000, which was larger than Brandon's income from all other sources. French ambassadors therefore tended to treat him as being in their pay, and Brandon's unflinching enthusiasm for Anglo–French amity resulted in his being excluded from policy-making when the tide had turned the other way. Moreover, Henry and Wolsey tended to use his chronic indebtedness to mould him to their desires. This rendered Brandon little more than a puppet of both the English and French kings, with only limited ability to express his own views.

But if Brandon was unable to dominate the political arena as the 'second king', he still reigned supreme in the tournaments and other sporting entertainments. From 1517, he became Henry's leading opponent rather than his teammate. Edward Hall describes how on one occasion, 'The king ran at the duke of Suffolk viii courses, and at every course brake his spear.'[20] Their friendship had begun at the jousts, and it was restored there too. From thenceforth, Suffolk's name often appears in the descriptions of court tournaments and other entertainments. He was particularly prominent at the Christmas festivities at Greenwich in 1524, when he and Henry disguised themselves as knights besieging the specially built 'Castle of Loyalty'. Only when they 'threw away their robes' did the audience recognise them, and were greatly astonished.[21]

Brandon's disgrace – albeit temporary – had opened the door for Henry's other companions to win greater favour. They included Sir Henry Guildford, who after spending several summers campaigning abroad had now settled back at court. In recognition of his loyal service, the king had granted him a range of new responsibilities. Foremost among them was that of Master of the Horse, one of the most sought-after positions at court, which the king bestowed upon his long-standing servant on 6 November 1515. The following year, Guildford was made a councillor. Ambitious though he was for Henry's favour, however, Guildford does not seem to have been politically motivated, and the records show that he seldom attended council meetings. Instead, he remained first and foremost a personal servant of the king. This was made clear several years later when Guildford was undertaking another military commission in France, and Henry recalled him because he was short of attendants in the privy chamber.

By contrast, Thomas Wolsey had been busily accumulating even greater powers than he had enjoyed in the first few years of Henry's reign. His political success had been mirrored by a series of rapid ecclesiastical preferments: Dean of York in February 1513, Bishop of Lincoln a year later, and Archbishop of York in July 1514. The crowning glory of his church career came in September 1515, when he was made a cardinal. According to Giustinian, this dazzling promotion had been thanks to 'the suit of this most serene King [Henry], who, with might and main, is intent on aggrandizing him'.[22] Little wonder that people began to whisper that Wolsey had ambitions to be pope. Within the space of just six years, he had come to dominate both the religious and political life of Henry's kingdom. 'English affairs thus daily prospered,' observed Vergil, 'and in this prosperity Thomas Wolsey gloried exceedingly, as though he alone were responsible for the great good fortune in that his authority was now supreme with the king.'[23]

Contemporaries were quick to recognise the fact. With more than a touch of envy, Erasmus observed that Wolsey governed 'more really than the king himself'. The Venetian ambassador Giustinian, meanwhile, described him as 'the right reverend Cardinal, in whom all the whole power of the State is really lodged', and 'who really seems to have the management of the whole of this kingdom'. He concluded that Wolsey was the only one of Henry's men 'who, for authority, may in point of fact be styled *ipse rex*', and that 'should it be requisite to neglect either the King or the Cardinal, it would be better to pass over His Majesty'. Another foreign envoy concurred that 'the right reverend Cardinal of York . . . by reason of his most excellent qualities, governs everything alone, the King not interfering in any matter, but referring the whole to him, whether it relate to foreign or domestic policy, so that foreign envoys fancy themselves negotiating not with a Cardinal, but with another King'. The Doge of Venice told Wolsey that the world considered him to be 'his Majesty's second self'.[24] Far from taking offence at such claims, Henry reinforced them. In 1515, he instructed Pope Leo X to 'pay the same regard to what Wolsey shall say as if it proceeded from the lips of the King himself'.[25] Shortly afterwards, he appointed the Cardinal Lord Chancellor, when Archbishop Warham resigned the post.

Realising that his pre-eminence was unchallenged, Wolsey soon set aside his former caution and grew dangerously arrogant. 'Acquiring so many offices at almost the same time, [he] became so proud that he considered himself the peer of kings,' observed Vergil. He went on to claim that the Cardinal was 'more hated, not only on account of his arrogance and his low reputation for integrity, but also on account of his recent origin [i.e. appointment as Bishop of Lincoln]'.[26] Eager to dazzle people into forgetting his humble origins,

Wolsey surrounded himself with magnificence. In the same year that he was made Archbishop of York, he began building Hampton Court, a palace so opulent that it rivalled those of his royal master. Similarly lavish building projects were executed at Cardinal College, Oxford, St Bride's (or Bridewell), York Place and at his country houses.

All Wolsey's residences were luxuriously decorated. Ambassadors reported that he owned enough tapestries to change his hangings every week. 'Soon he began to use a golden seat, a golden cushion, a golden cloth on his table,' reported another contemporary, 'and when he went on foot, he had his hat – the symbol of his Cardinal's rank – carried before him by a servant, and raised aloft like a holy idol, and he had it put upon the very altar in the king's chapel during divine service.'[27]

Wolsey's extravagance attracted widespread criticism. When the reformer Robert Barnes told him that the gold on his crosses would help many poor people, the Cardinal went on the defensive: 'Whether do you think it more necessary that I should have all this royalty, because I represent the king's majesty's person in all the high courts of this realm, to the terror and keeping down of all rebellious treasons, traitors, all the wicked and corrupt members of this commonwealth; or to be as simple as you would have us?'[28] Wolsey had a point. Henry's preference for leisure pursuits meant that he was content for his chief minister to represent him at a whole manner of high-profile meetings with distinguished guests, including heads of state. It was important that Wolsey reflected the status and magnificence of his sovereign on such occasions. Moreover, his ecclesiastical appointments – most notably that of Cardinal – demanded a level of pomp and ceremony. That said, however, Wolsey undoubtedly enjoyed the finer things in life, and he also delighted in emphasising his superiority over the highly born noblemen at court who vied for the king's favour.

According to Vergil, 'several leading counsellors, when they saw so much power coming into the hands of one man, gradually withdrew from court'. They included the two most influential churchmen in the kingdom, William Warham and Richard Fox, as well as the dukes of Norfolk and Suffolk. Whether they were absenting themselves because they knew they could never aspire to Wolsey's influence, or because they had lost respect for Henry for being so easily manipulated by this low-born minister, is not certain. Given the self-seeking nature of court life, however, it is more likely to have been the former, and this is supported by what happened next. Before they left, the men sought an audience with Henry and urged him 'not to suffer any servant to be greater than his master: they borrowed this saying from Christ, who, in the gospel according to St John, says to his disciples: "Verily, verily, I say unto you, the servant is not greater than his lord."' The king assured them 'that he would make it his first business diligently to ensure that any servant of his was obedient and not autocratic'.[29]

But the Cardinal paid little heed to the growing ranks of his enemies, which made his position dangerously vulnerable as time went on. 'Wolsey, with his arrogance and ambition aroused against himself the hatred of the whole country,' claimed one eyewitness, 'and by his hostility towards the nobility and the common people, caused them the greatest irritation through his vainglory . . . He was, indeed, detested by everyone.'[30] Erasmus concurred that he was 'feared by all and loved by few if any', and Thomas More, who had been called a fool by Wolsey, quipped: 'God be thanked the king our master hath but one fool on his council.'[31]

For now, though, Henry seemed to care little for his chief minister's growing arrogance and was content to let him flaunt the advantages of his position. If he was troubled by the hostility that Wolsey was attracting among the other men at court, then he did not show it. The young king might have been easy to manipulate, but he was also pragmatic in his choice of advisers. For all his unpopularity, Wolsey was performing his duties far more effectively than any of his peers, and Henry had no intention of disrupting a state of affairs that was so entirely serving his interests.

Rather, Henry provided Wolsey with ample signs of his esteem. All of the king's letters to his chief minister during these years are written with great affection and warmth. 'Mine own good Cardinal', he began one. 'I recommend me unto you with all my heart, and thank you for the great pain and labour that you do daily take in my business and matters.' In another, he assured Wolsey that he was able to confide in him 'as heartily as heart can think'. Aware of how hard the Cardinal worked on his behalf, he urged him to take some rest so that he might 'the longer endure to serve us', and signed the letter: 'with the hand of your loving master'.[32]

That he trusted his chief minister implicitly is obvious from a letter written shortly after Wolsey was made a Cardinal. In it, the king confided two pieces of news 'which be so secret that they cause me at this time to write to you myself'. The first and most important of these was that: 'I trust the queen my wife be with child.'[33] Having had so many false hopes of an heir, Henry had learned to be discreet if ever Catherine showed signs of pregnancy. There is no evidence that he confided in anyone but Wolsey about this, the matter that affected him most closely.

This latest pregnancy seemed to be progressing well, though, and on 18 February 1516, Catherine gave birth to a girl, Mary. She might not have been the son and heir that Henry had hoped for, but the infant princess was at least healthy and there was still the prospect that sons would now follow, as Henry himself rather tactlessly pointed out. Nevertheless, the news was greeted with a lukewarm response, mirroring the king's own disappointment. The Venetian ambassador reported that he intended to offer congratulations on behalf of his master, but added: 'Had it been a son, I should already have done so.'[34] Wolsey, too, shared his royal master's regret, but he could at least console himself with the fact that Henry had seen fit to name him as one of the godparents to the infant princess.

Henry's mood darkened in the days following his daughter's birth. After seven years on the throne, he still had no male heir, which meant that no matter how many treaties or wars he might successfully (and expensively) conclude, his dynasty was dangerously insecure. This seems to have provoked the king's deep-seated sense of inferiority with regard to his late father, whose first son had been born within a year of his accession. When Giustinian sought an audience with him on 11 March, he was shocked to find him 'more irritated than I could ever have imagined'. The ambassador tried to placate him by thanking him for being such a committed supporter of the Venetian Republic. 'You speak the truth,' Henry spat back, 'for I have done more for you than my father ever did . . . Be assured, Domine Orator, that I have now more money and greater force and authority than I myself or my ancestors ever had.' Perceiving that the king 'seemed to wax wrath', Giustinian tried his best to calm him, but to no avail.[35] The ghost of Henry's father always calm him at moments of crisis, reminding him of his inadequacies. As he did on this occasion, Henry always railed against it, venting the frustration that he had been unable to express when his father lived.

The year after Princess Mary's birth, Henry's chief minister fell prey to the sweating sickness. The king was aghast when he heard the news, and for a few anxious days, Wolsey's life was despaired of. But the Cardinal was one of the fortunate few to survive the disease, and he swiftly resumed his duties, attending the celebrations to mark the conclusion of a defensive league with the Archduke Charles (the future Charles V). Henry had evidently been shaken by the episode, though, and remained solicitous for his health, writing in his own hand to thank Wolsey for his great pains and urging him to take some rest 'to the intent you may the longer endure to serve us'.[36]

By 1518, Wolsey was back to full health and applied himself to Henry's service with characteristic energy, negotiating a new alliance with France. By October, the treaty of Universal Peace had been agreed, whereby his master's infant daughter was betrothed to Francis's son and heir. This was a triumph for Wolsey and one that he was quick to capitalise upon, delivering an oration in praise of peace that was widely acclaimed.

Delighted though he was by this prestigious match for his daughter, by the time of her birth, Henry had already begun an affair with one of his wife's ladies-in-waiting, Elizabeth Blount. Courtiers had noted that he danced with the attractive young 'Bessie' at the New Year celebrations held at Greenwich the previous year. Quite when she became the king's mistress is not clear. Although it was perfectly acceptable for him to seek sexual gratification during his wife's many pregnancies, Henry liked to be discreet in his affairs. Before long, it was rumoured that he was 'in the chains of love' with Bessie, although he was careful not to show any outward preference for her.[37]

In autumn 1518, as the queen was preparing for her sixth lying-in, Bessie fell pregnant. It was a bitter pill for Catherine to swallow when, a few months after giving birth to another stillborn daughter, she learned that her lady-in-waiting had had a healthy boy. In case there was any doubt that he was the king's, Bessie named this 'goodly man child of beauty like to the father and mother' Henry FitzRoy.[38]

Henry had employed customary discretion in dealing with his mistress's pregnancy, and had instructed Wolsey to arrange her confinement at a suitable distance from court. The cardinal's choice might seem surprising: the Augustinian Priory of St Laurence in Blackmore, Essex. But Wolsey knew that the brethren could be trusted to turn a blind eye to this latest inmate, just as they had to the other ladies with whom the king had consorted there in the past.

When Henry learned that he at last had a son, he abandoned his discretion and openly acknowledged the boy as his own. A christening was held and Wolsey was appointed godfather to the infant boy. FitzRoy might be illegitimate, but he had proved that the king was capable of fathering a healthy boy. With only a daughter and numerous obstetric disasters to show for a decade of marriage, Henry knew that his subjects and international rivals had started to whisper that the problem might lie with him. Now it was clear, to Henry at least, that his wife was to blame. Aged thirty-three, Catherine was considered to be nearing the end of her fertile years, whereas her twenty-eight-year-old husband was evidently still very much in his prime.

Henry's infant son had not only restored his belief, and pride, in his virility; he had planted a dangerous seed in his father's mind about the validity of his marriage.

6

'Youths of evil counsel'

EVER SINCE HIS accession in January 1515, Francis I had been a thorn in Henry's side. The English king veered between bouts of intense jealousy towards his French rival, and overblown expressions of love and amity for him, during which he would seek to emulate his court and habits. He was going through one such phase in 1518. Francis sent an embassy to the English court that year which included a number of his most highly favoured men, or *'mignons'*, for whom he had recently created the new rank of *'gentilhomme de la chambre'*. Not to be outdone, Henry created a replica post in his own inner sanctum. The gentlemen of the privy chamber were thus established and soon became the most sought-after appointments in Henry's service. That one of the most important positions at the English court came about because of the king's insecurity and jealousy towards Francis reveals the profound impact that the latter had upon his reign.

Prominent among the new appointees was Francis Bryan, one of the wildest of Henry's male companions. Bryan's father had been a knight of the body to Henry VII and was vice chamberlain to Catherine of Aragon, and his mother Margaret was governess to Princess Mary. Francis himself had come to court at a very young age and, like his royal master, had soon developed a passion for jousting, gambling and tennis. Edward Hall noted that Bryan was one of two young men (the other being Nicholas Carew) whom the king 'delighted to set forth' at the tilts in April 1515.[1] So vigorously did Bryan pursue his sporting interests that he lost an eye during a later tournament, in which Henry also took part, and was obliged to wear an eye-patch thereafter. Bryan was also an accomplished soldier, diplomat and man of letters, and many at court fell prey to his acerbic wit and irresistible charm. Although he had not attended university and was not formally trained in rhetoric, he was naturally skilled in the arts of eloquence, as his letters testify. But he preferred talking to writing, and often complained that it would take him a week to write what he could say in an hour.

Surrounded as he was by sycophants, Henry was beguiled by Bryan's natural irreverence, not to mention his frankness. He would tell the king the truth when nobody else dared. Florentius Volusensus, a Scottish humanist who knew Bryan well, recalled that he was 'accustomed to speak familiarly to the King'. Rather less approvingly, the Abbot of Woburn observed: 'The said Sir Francis dare boldly speak to the King's Grace the plainness of his mind and that his Grace doth well accept the same.'² Jealous courtiers viewed this as over-familiarity, but Bryan cared little for that – and neither did his royal master, who appreciated his frankness. Bryan also made Henry laugh with his endless stream of jokes, and treated him as a friend rather than a king. Henry loved him for it. The two men also shared a love of clothes, and no matter how neglectful Bryan might have been of court etiquette, he was always careful to dress in rich apparel of the latest fashion.

As one of the king's new gentlemen of the privy chamber, Bryan accompanied his royal master on a visit to the French court in 1518, the same year as his appointment. There, unfettered by the conventions of his own court, Henry went on the rampage with Bryan, each donning a disguise as they took to the streets of Paris. Bryan was more sexually promiscuous and a good deal less bashful than his royal master, and he was said to have demanded 'a soft bed then a hard harlot'. One disapproving member of Henry's court noted that the king and his 'minions', Bryan included, returned 'all French, in eating, drinking and apparel, yea, and in French vices and . . . high in love with the French court'.³

The expedition ignited a passion for overseas adventure in Bryan, the most energetic and restless of all Henry's men. During the years to come, he would be almost constantly on the move, flitting between England and the Continent in a series of diplomatic missions. His friend Sir Thomas Wyatt was both staggered and concerned by his wanderlust:

To thee, therefore, that trots still up and down
And never rests, but running day and night
From realm to realm, from city, street, and town,
Why dost thou wear thy body to the bones?[4]

Another of the gentlemen of the privy chamber who was appointed that year was Sir Nicholas Carew. Born no later than 1496, he was the eldest son of Sir Richard Carew, head of a noble family of ancient lineage. Sir Richard had been knighted by Henry VII at the Battle of Blackheath in 1497 and had later served as captain of Calais. His loyalty to the crown had secured a place at court for his son from an early age, and he was later described as being of Henry VIII's 'own bringing up'.[5]

Sir Nicholas was a groom of Henry's privy chamber by May 1511, esquire of the body and a 'cipherer' (cupbearer) in 1515, and gentleman in 1518. In the meantime, like many of his companions in the king's private apartments, he had distinguished himself in the field of combat. He had been among the contingent that Henry had taken to France in 1513, and had commanded the artillery with a personal retinue of 1,000 men. His father had also been there, along with another kinsman, Sir Edmund Carew, who had been killed at Thérouanne by a bullet that struck him as he sat at the council table. Sir Nicholas survived the campaign and was one of six favoured men to be rewarded with the gift of a coat of green velvet and cloth of silver. His position as royal favourite was made clear in the jousts held in July 1517 for the entertainment of some visiting ambassadors. Nicolo Sagudino, the Venetian envoy, was overawed by the young man's show of martial might: 'The jousts being ended, a beam was brought, some twenty feet in length, and was placed on the head of one of his Majesty's favourites, by name master Caroll [Carew], who was one of the jousters, and he ran a long way with the beam on his head to the marvel of everybody.'[6]

Carew was particularly close to two of the other favourites in Henry's privy chamber. In 1514 he married Elizabeth Bryan, sister of Sir Francis. The ties of kinship fostered a close and enduring friendship between the two men. Carew also became good friends with Charles Brandon, and would later invite him to his estate at

Beddington, south of London. But it was Henry himself with whom he won greatest favour. Indeed, he soon became so intimate with the king that Wolsey accused him of being overly familiar. Born into a family distinguished for their military service, Carew both admired and understood the king's warlike nature. Their mutual lust for glory was the strongest tie that bound the two men together.

Henry's other gentlemen of the privy chamber included William Carey, who was in his early twenties at the time of his appointment. His grandfather had been a prominent Lancastrian, and his father married into the Beaufort family, which made him a distant cousin of the king. Carey shared the king's sporting interests and was often to be found in the tournament field or tennis court. He was also a skilled card player and on at least one occasion won a significant sum from his royal master.

Another 'minion' to benefit from the newly created posts in the privy chamber was Henry Norris. Born in the late 1490s into a long-serving court family, he received his first royal grant in 1515 and was appointed to the privy chamber from at least 1517. By the following year, he had been entrusted with handling the king's money, and in September he was made gentleman of the privy chamber. Norris more than fulfilled what had become the unwritten qualification for members of Henry's inner circle: the ability to excel in the tiltyard. He also played a prominent part in court revels and was clearly a man of considerable charm.

Two other gentlemen were Arthur Pole, son of Lady Margaret, and William Coffin, who had served in the Tournai campaign and had subsequently been appointed to the royal household. In total, Henry appointed twelve gentlemen (including the groom of the stool), and they were marked out by their distinctive black damask gowns and doublets. Although their role was in theory confined to domestic duties, the fact that they spent so much time with the king presented an irresistible opportunity to advise and influence their royal master. For all his considerable intelligence, Henry could be easy to manipulate, as Wolsey had proven on a number of occasions. Perhaps this was the result of his vanity, which made him more susceptible to flattery than most men.

As well as serving Henry in his private apartments, his gentlemen were often dispatched on errands throughout the court and kingdom. On such occasions, they were seen not merely as messengers, but as the personification of their royal master – as if they had been able to imbibe his God-given powers through their close and constant access to his person.

Lower down the pecking order at court was Thomas Wyatt, who entered Henry's service as 'Sewer Extraordinary' in 1515. This was evidently a part-time position, for he began his studies at Cambridge the same year. Wyatt thrived in the intellectually stimulating atmosphere at St John's College, and by the time that he rose to prominence in royal service he had also gained renown as a poet. He is credited with many innovations in English poetry and, alongside his protégé Henry Howard, later Earl of Surrey, introduced the sonnet into England from Italy. Wyatt's literary prowess also won him favour with Henry, who had always prided himself on his own writing skills. He soon enlisted Wyatt on a number of important diplomatic missions.

Henry had spent the first decade of his reign filling the privy chamber with his favourites. The majority of the men who kept him company there appealed to him for their martial prowess and seemingly endless capacity for entertainments, but their close and regular access to the king imbued them with political power too. Increasingly, there was a blurring of roles between the privy chamber and the council, to the detriment of the latter – and in particular its chief, Wolsey.

The men who served Henry in his privy chamber exerted a distinct advantage over Wolsey and his fellow officials because they were his constant companions, entertaining him during his leisure hours, attending him during his most intimate moments, and even sleeping in the same room as him. As a result, they enjoyed a level of intimacy with the king that his councillors – even Wolsey – could only dream of. It was galling for the cardinal to realise that he himself was partly to blame: if he had not encouraged his master to spend so many hours at leisure, his companions would not have been able to grow so familiar – or influential. That they made the most of the opportunity had been demonstrated on numerous occasions since Henry's accession, most of which concerned the granting of royal favours.

A prime example of this occurred in 1517, when Richard Vernon of Haddon Hall in Derbyshire died, leaving a widow, Margaret. The daughter of the king's hereditary Champion, Sir Robert Dymoke, she would make a prestigious wife for any ambitious gentleman. Wolsey was fully aware of the fact, and with lightning speed petitioned her to marry Sir William Tyrwhit, one of his own servants. But one of Henry's privy chamber gentlemen, William Coffin, wanted her for himself. Together with his friend Carew, he persuaded his royal master to further his suit, and Henry duly wrote to Margaret, asking her to look kindly upon Coffin as a man 'whom we singularly favour at this time'. Wolsey was furious, and refused to be bought off by Henry with the grant of the wardship of Vernon's heir. 'My lord Cardinal is not content withal,' reported Thomas Allen to his patron the Earl of Shrewsbury, with barely concealed relish. Coffin himself wrote to the earl soon afterwards, confidently asserting that 'whatsoever noise or report is . . . made in those parts to my discomfort . . . the King continueth my good and gracious lord and so will do to the end of the matter'.[7] He was right: the marriage went ahead soon afterwards.

Wolsey was all too well aware of the danger that the men of the privy chamber presented to his own standing with Henry. The Venetian envoy Sebastian Giustiniani, who had had the opportunity to observe the king and his men at close quarters, judged that the cardinal feared Henry's minions were 'so intimate with the King that in the course of time they might have ousted him from the government'. Giustiniani shared the cardinal's view that they were 'youths of evil counsel, and intent upon their own benefit, to the detriment, hurt and discredit of his Majesty'. According to his account, Wolsey resolved to protect himself from being 'ousted . . . from the government' by striking against them first. 'By this [Wolsey] will secure the King entirely to himself.'[8]

Whether or not this intention lay behind his actions, at the beginning of 1519, Wolsey proposed a series of sweeping reforms to government administration, justice, the economy, local and national affairs. All were intended to draw his royal master into playing a more active role in governing his realm, which was the exact opposite of the strategy that Wolsey had originally adopted to win favour and influence with Henry. In order to convince the king of the need for these reforms, the cardinal presented them as a seismic break with the past and a means by which Henry could really make his mark. At the same time, he painted a picture of the privy chamber men as feckless and overindulged, and hinted that they were holding Henry back from being the king that he could be – a king, indeed, who would far outshine his father.

Wolsey could have employed no more effective means to persuade Henry to take action. Content though he had been to let his chief minister take the reins of government, Henry was aware that he had yet to make his mark as king. Military glory had proved all too fleeting, so the prospect of asserting his kingly authority at home held considerable appeal. Without hesitation, he therefore gave his full backing to Wolsey's reforms and threw himself into directing them with all the enthusiasm and energy of a man who delights in novelty.

The documents recording what happened next make it seem as if the king, rather than his chief minister, was the architect of all the reforms. 'A remembrance of such things as his grace will have to be done, and hath given in commandment to his Cardinal to put the same in effectual execution' is one such example.[9] The cardinal knew, though, that his royal master would soon lose interest: indeed, he himself had little intention of seeing through most of the reforms. 'Every one of these enterprises was great, and the least of them to our commonwealth much expedient,' observed John Palsgrave, a priest at court, not long afterwards, 'but they have been begun, and brought to no good end.'[10]

This mattered little to Wolsey. The proposed reforms had given him the excuse he needed to get rid of his rivals. With the support of the council, in May 1519, Wolsey set about purging the privy chamber of the 'minions' whom he and his fellow ministers claimed were having a deleterious influence on their royal master. The men were charged before the council with over-familiarity with the king, for having 'played such light touches with him that they forgot themselves', and for 'diverse considerations', including being 'the cause of [Henry's] incessant gambling, which has made him lose of late a treasure of gold'.

Henry, meanwhile, was presented as the victim: a master of such 'gentleness and liberality to all persons' that he had neither 'rebuked nor reproved' them.[11] It is difficult to see him in this light. Gregarious and sociable he might have been, but he was hardly the blameless and submissive victim that his councillors claimed. He had encouraged, not merely suffered, the more wayward tendencies of his privy chamber companions. But by implying that Henry's honour was at stake, the council had played a masterstroke. This was something that the chivalric-obsessed king could not ignore. 'Resolving to lead a new life, he, of his own accord removed these companions of his excesses,' recorded Guistiniani.[12] He also gave his council full authority to do everything necessary 'both for the maintenance of his honour, and for the defence of all things that might blemish the same'.[13]

Among those whose wrists had been firmly slapped was William Carey, who along with his fellow minions was 'grieved sore' when he heard the news.[14] But the greatest troublemaker was Sir Francis Bryan, whose reckless behaviour was said to have brought disgrace upon the king and his court. Bryan's partner in crime was his brother-in-law, Sir Nicholas Carew. The council at Greenwich heard how the pair had run riot during a recent embassy to France, when they 'rode disguised through Paris, throwing eggs, stones and other foolish trifles at the people'.[15]

This was the second time in the space of a year that Carew had been reprimanded. Early in 1518, objections had been raised (almost certainly by Wolsey) about the intimacy that he enjoyed with his royal master. The latter had responded by distancing himself from Carew, but he could not keep up the pretence for long. In March, Wolsey's agent reported that Carew and his wife had returned to the king's grace, 'too soon, after mine opinion'.[16]

There was to be no such reprieve now. Along with Sir Francis Bryan, Sir Henry Guildford and a number of other 'minions', Carew was exiled from court. Each of these men felt aggrieved that, for all the influence they enjoyed with Henry, Wolsey had been able to remove them so quickly. If they were angry with their master for being manipulated by his base-born minister, they did not show it. Instead, it was Wolsey himself who was the focus of their ire. His purge might have achieved its short-term objective of enhancing his own influence over Henry, but it had also increased the ranks of his enemies.

Wolsey clearly wanted to ensure that Carew would not creep his way back into favour this time because he secured him a post in Calais, where he was made lieutenant of the tower of Rysbank, guarding the entrance to the harbour. Sir Nicholas arrived there on 20 May, the day of his formal appointment. Although he was aggrieved at being sent so far away from court, he was at least afforded a comfortable living, having been granted an annuity of £109 6s 8d from the issues of the town. Those minions who escaped exile in Calais were found 'employment extra curiam (outside the court) in other parts of the kingdom'.[17]

The purge was about more than just power. Through it, Wolsey was encouraging his youthful and exuberant royal master to mature into a responsible and authoritative leader who would command the respect of his subjects and peers. In short, he was helping his royal master to grow up. It was high time Henry did so. He was now on the cusp of his twenty-eighth birthday and had ruled England for ten years. Although he was a popular and well-liked king, he had little to show for his reign beyond a depleted treasury and a few minor military victories. The alacrity with which he responded to Wolsey's proposed reforms suggests that he was already aware of the need to take greater responsibility. But for Wolsey, it was a high-risk strategy. Encouraging his royal master to mature into an authoritative, responsible king might get rid of the troublesome young men who surrounded him, but it also threatened his own hold over Henry. Having realised the full potential of his powers, the king might not want to cede so many of them to his chief minister in future. It is an indication of how much Wolsey wished to oust the 'minions' that he was prepared to take the risk.

Wolsey was not the only man who urged Henry that the time had come to change. The king's former tutor, John Skelton, expressed his support for the privy chamber purge in his ambitious morality play, *Magnificence*. This sought to persuade Henry to take care in choosing his most intimate advisers, to curb his financial excesses and to run his household efficiently. The parallels with the politics of court are even more obvious than in his other works. Set in London, it centres upon the struggle for power in the household of a 'prince', who is persuaded by irresponsible and scheming favourites to dismiss his steward, Measure. They go on to squander the prince's money, leaving him impoverished and humiliated until Good Hope, Redress, Sad Circumspection and Perseverance bring him back to good order.

These virtues were probably a thinly veiled reference to the 'four sad and ancient knights, put into the king's privy chamber' by the council that year. All of them were thought to be Wolsey's 'creatures', and were serious, hard-working men in middle age at least.[18] They included Sir John Welsbourne. The son of a Buckinghamshire landowner, little is known of him before his appointment. He was initially made a page, but rapidly rose through the ranks and was soon so firmly established in Henry's favour that he was allowed to exercise his office of controller of custom in Bristol by deputy as 'he has been retained as one of the grooms of the Privy Chamber'.[19]

Another of the new men was Sir Richard Wingfield, who was approaching fifty at the time of his appointment. The Wingfields were a distinguished Suffolk gentry family, with many years of military and diplomatic service to their credit. They had been prominent as officials at the court of Edward IV, and Sir Richard had married Katherine Woodville, one of the sisters of Edward's queen, Elizabeth. He had also found favour with the first Tudor king, serving as his esquire of the body and helping to put down the Cornish rebels in 1497. In January 1513, Wingfield had been appointed special ambassador to the Low Countries, and had taken part in the French campaign that summer. He had acquitted himself well, and early the following year he is first referred to in the records as a royal councillor. He had soon won the cardinal's trust, and Wolsey had discussed the coming purge with him, as well as giving him an assurance of a place in the new order.

Wingfield was well aware of the mockery that he and his fellow 'ancient knights' were subjected to, and at a royal banquet held at Beaulieu in September 1519, these aged men entered in masks and false white beards, and proceeded to dance gravely and silently with the queen's ladies. His self-deprecating manner, as well as his 'wise counsel', secured Wingfield the favour of the king, who soon described him as a trusted friend. But Wingfield always insisted that he owed his place to the cardinal alone.

Sir Richard Jerningham and Sir William Kingston were the other 'ancient' men with whom Wolsey filled the vacant places. Both were adherents of the cardinal and could boast distinguished service to the crown. Jerningham had been appointed a gentleman of the chamber upon Henry VIII's accession, but had spent most of the following decade abroad on a series of diplomatic missions, to which he was arguably better suited than as a companion for the king. Kingston, meanwhile, had served Henry's father as a yeoman of the chamber, and had been present at his funeral as a gentleman usher. Recognising his military ability, the new king had enlisted him in a number of campaigns, and he had been awarded a knighthood for his service at Flodden in 1513.

The ousting of Henry's 'minions' sent shockwaves across Europe. The Venetian ambassador Giustinian described it as being 'of as vital importance as any [event] that had taken place for many years', and Francis I claimed that it had resulted in 'a new world in England'.[20] Henry might have been gratified by the latter description, but the truth was that although this naturally genial king did his best to reconcile himself to his new attendants, he sorely missed his old companions. His resolve to follow Wolsey's advice and adopt a more sober life soon crumbled, and within six months of the purge, all of the ousted men had been recalled. This was one of the earliest demonstrations of Henry's fickle and changeable nature. No matter how passionately he committed himself to a cause, he could prove as easily distracted from it as a child from a toy. It was a tendency that would come increasingly to the fore as his reign progressed – with often devastating consequences for those who were caught up in his whims.

Henry was as delighted to see his former favourites as they were to be back. Eager to make amends, the king was even more generous towards them than he had been before. The spendthrift Carew had a debt of £742 (equivalent to around £280,000 today) that he had run up as sheriff of Surrey and Sussex cancelled by letters patent.

Furthermore, when he resigned his lieutenancy of Rysbank in 1520, he was granted a pension of £100.

At about the same time as Henry's favourites were welcomed back into the privy chamber, a new face appeared there. Anthony Browne was the half-brother of the king's great favourite, William Fitzwilliam. Born around 1500, he was one of the youngest of Henry's privy chamber servants and had probably been raised in the royal household. His father had been Henry VII's standard-bearer and lieutenant of Calais Castle. Despite his impeccable breeding, Browne was something of a hothead. Sir John Russell, a professional soldier and adherent of Wolsey, disparagingly remarked that Browne was 'most unreasonable and . . . one whose words and deeds do not agree together'.²¹ In 1518, Henry had recalled Sir Anthony from an embassy to Tournai for striking one of his fellow emissaries. Henry soon forgave him, though, and Browne became one of his favourite attendants during the years that followed.

Another regular attendant was Thomas More. He had been striving to enhance his position at court for almost ten years now, but he was still far from being an intimate of the young king. More's son-in-law William Roper claimed that Henry often summoned More to his private apartments in order to debate with him about 'astronomy, geometry, divinity, and sometimes of his worldly affairs'. Often, they would head up to the palace roof to consider 'the diversities, courses, motions and operations of the stars and planets', and at other times More would be invited to take supper with the king and queen and 'be merry with them'.²²

Either Roper was overstating the case, or he was confusing the chronology of his father-in-law's life, because More himself admitted that during the early years of his service to Henry, he was hardly distinguished from the many other men whom the young king showed favour towards. 'So far I keep my place there [at court] as precariously as an unaccustomed rider in the saddle,' he wrote to Fisher in 1518. 'But the king (whose intimate favour I am far from enjoying) is so courteous and kindly to all that everyone who is in any way hopeful finds a ground for imagining that he is in the king's good graces, like the London wives who, as they pray before the image of the Virgin Mother of God which stands near the Tower, gaze on it so fixedly that they imagine it smiles upon them. But I am not so fortunate as to perceive such signs of favour, nor so despondent as to imagine them.'[23] More would soon find himself propelled to the centre of court life, however, because it was at around this time that he was appointed to the council. Thereafter, his rise in Henry's favour would be rapid.

The return of the minions threatened to undermine Wolsey's position once more, but on the surface at least his power and influence seemed undiminished. Even the highest-ranking noblemen in the kingdom could not rival the magnificence of the cardinal's household, his growing portfolio of lavish properties, or his priceless collection of art and furnishings. At its height, Wolsey's household comprised no fewer than 429 members, making it second only to the king's. Seventy-three men and boys served in the kitchens alone, and in his stables he employed half as many servants as his royal master. Wolsey's influence with Henry was so widely known that competition for places in his service was almost as fierce as in the royal household itself.

The rapid succession of ecclesiastical and other preferments that the cardinal had acquired helped to fund his lavish lifestyle. The archbishopric of York brought him over £5,000 per annum, and the chancellorship added another £2,000. He also received a substantial pension from France or the empire, depending on which way his diplomacy turned, and in 1518 he obtained the revenues of the bishopric of Bath and Wells, one of the most prestigious benefices in the kingdom. By 1519, Wolsey's annual income was in the region of £9,500 (equivalent to £3.6 million today), which made him Henry's wealthiest subject.

Before long, there were whispers that the cardinal had come to rival the king himself. Aware of this, Wolsey always took care to ensure that he expressed his subservience to his royal master. Thus, for example, he gifted Henry his best singer, knowing that he admired him. But if gestures like these placated the king, they did little to convince his noble rivals that he was anything other than a dangerous upstart, intent upon their destruction. Their suspicions were at least partially justified.

Ever since entering Henry's service, Wolsey had been intent upon restricting the nobility's powers. In so doing, he was echoing the policy of his royal master's father, who had kept a tight rein on the men whose birth and estates made them a threat to his authority. But Henry VIII had relaxed these strictures, eager to win favour with the magnates of his realm. Wolsey had soon set about unpicking this. In 1511, a proclamation had been issued declaring the king's 'great displeasure' upon hearing that many of his 'lords and nobles' had been unlawfully accumulating retainers under cover of supporting the king's war effort.[24] They were ordered immediately to cease this practice or face the consequences.

In May 1516, the cardinal went further still when he made a speech in the Star Chamber, declaring that those responsible for administering justice should not regard themselves as being above the law. To prove the point, on the very same day, Henry Percy, fifth Earl of Northumberland, was summoned into court for contempt of the council's jurisdiction in private suits, and was subsequently committed to Fleet prison. This was a studied insult to one of the highest-ranking noblemen in the land, and sent out a clear message about Wolsey's intentions. His other measures included an attempt to control marriage between aristocratic families, which had been the traditional means of forging powerful alliances, sometimes against the crown. By the end of May, the cleric Thomas Allen reported 'great snarling' at court.[25]

It was not long before resentment among the nobility broke out into open aggression. Polydore Vergil claims that Thomas Howard threatened Wolsey with his dagger. Even though this is not substantiated by any other source, there can be little doubt as to the virulent hatred that Wolsey's noble rivals now harboured against him. From thenceforth, he knew that his security would increasingly rest in the king's hands alone.

Wolsey might have been protecting his own authority, and that of his royal master, with his strictures against the nobility, but he was also courting a growing body of dangerous enemies. The Duke of Buckingham, who had also fallen foul of the cardinal's policies, was heard to complain that Wolsey would undo all noblemen if he could. The chronicler Raphael Holinshed recorded: 'The duke . . . could not abide the cardinal', and had uttered 'grievous words' against him.[26] On another occasion, the duke waited on the king while he dined with Wolsey, and held a bowl of water for him to wash his hands in. After Henry had completed his ablution, Wolsey also dipped his hands in the water. This was too much for the duke to bear, and he threw the water over Wolsey's shoes. Although Wolsey brazened it out and sent Buckingham a warning to mind his manners in the king's presence, the incident had served as yet another reminder of his growing body of enemies at court.

By 1518, the chief minister had sparked such opposition that there were rumours of a plot to oust him from power. But Wolsey had taken care to convince Henry of the need to bring the aristocracy to heel. In April that year the king praised the cardinal's 'special regard for the surety of his person', and alluded to the threat posed by certain 'great personages'.[27]

In January 1519, Henry wrote to his chief minister, secretly instructing him to 'make good watch on the duke of Suffolk, on the duke of Buckingham, on my lord of Northumberland, on my lord of Derby, on my lord of Wiltshire and on others which you think suspect'.[28] That Henry should have included his best friend, Charles Brandon, Duke of Suffolk, among those whom he wished his chief minister to keep a close eye on demonstrates the extent of Wolsey's influence at this time. Henry also made it clear that Wolsey was under his protection. When his father's former solicitor-general, Thomas Lucas, slandered the cardinal, he was sent straight to the Tower.

Although Suffolk quickly allayed his master's suspicions against him with a demonstration of humble submission, Wolsey continued to stoke the king's growing paranoia about his nobles. He had a vested interest in doing so: it made more of a virtue of his own humble birth, for he could never pose a similar threat to Henry's crown. The following year, he sent a 'Privy remembrance' to Henry 'to put himself in strength with his most trusty servants in every shire for the surety of his royal person and succession'.[29] Little wonder that Thomas Howard later claimed that Wolsey had spent years plotting his destruction. According to Holinshed, when addressing the Earl of Kildare during his interrogation by the council, the cardinal told him: 'I wot [know] well (my lord) that I am not the meetest at this board to charge you with these treasons because it pleased some of your purfellows to report that I am a professed enemy to all nobility.'[30] But this account was written almost fifty years after Wolsey's death and oversimplifies the situation.

Certainly, Wolsey was determined to bring the nobility under royal control, but he did so by the carrot as well as the stick. He encouraged them to demonstrate their fidelity to the crown by hinting at desirable appointments that he could help them to, and in so doing established a network of supporters in the localities. Although he was despised by some eminent members of the aristocracy, he counted others, such as Charles Somerset, Earl of Worcester, as his friends.

The year 1519 was a significant one for Henry's foreign relations, as well as his domestic affairs. That June, the nineteen-year-old Charles V, King of Spain, Naples, Sicily and Sardinia, was elected Holy Roman Emperor. Charles's inheritance was greater than that of any European ruler in history – and certainly far greater than that of his closest rivals, Henry and Francis I. For all his power, though, the young emperor lacked the presence of these rivals. He was unattractive and ungainly, with a huge chin and protruding lower lip. Introverted and serious, he suffered from a severe stammer and eschewed the public court ceremony that Henry and Francis so revelled in. Neither was he their equal in intellect or culture. But in piety and industriousness, he far outstripped both men. He also had a fierce ambition for territory and power that spelt danger for any who opposed him.

This ambition was matched by that of Henry and Francis, both of whom had sought ways of extending their domains through an aggressive foreign policy since the beginning of their reigns. They gloried in the military aspect of kingship and personally took part in many campaigns. Francis had inherited an ongoing war in Italy from his predecessors. This came to dominate his reign, and many of his military encounters were against the newly elected Holy Roman Emperor.

In 1520, Francis made overtures to Henry as a means of countering Charles's growing power. The two kings agreed to meet in June that year on neutral territory that lay between Ardres in France and

Guines in the English Pale of Calais. The event, which would last for eighteen days, became known as the Field of Cloth of Gold because of the dazzling splendour and opulence with which it was staged. Although in theory a summit at which Henry and Francis could affirm their friendship and conclude an alliance, it turned into an expression of their intense rivalry, as each tried to outdo the other with the magnificence of their retinue and entertainments, and the various 'friendly' competitions that they entered into.

The man behind it was Cardinal Wolsey, who had long promoted amity with the French. He set his impressive organisational skills to work in creating a showpiece such as the world had never seen. Thomas Boleyn, Henry's resident ambassador to France, also played a prominent role: indeed, he could be credited with suggesting the summit in the first place. By this time, the two men were sworn enemies. Henry had promised Thomas Boleyn the comptrollership of the household in 1519, but the cardinal had obstructed the appointment. Affronted, Boleyn demanded to know if Wolsey perceived some fault in him, but was offered empty reassurances. In 1520, though, he had his revenge when the king not only appointed him comptroller but also found a position in the queen's household for Boleyn's eldest daughter, Mary.

Mary Boleyn had recently returned from France, where she had served in the household of Henry's sister Mary during her short-lived marriage to Louis XII. She had remained in France after Louis' death and had transferred to the household of Claude, wife of Francis I. A comely young woman, then in her late teens, Mary had attracted the attention of the lascivious French king, who had made her his mistress. Alarmed, her father had recalled Mary to England and, thanks to his favour with Henry, restored her reputation by having her appointed one of Queen Catherine's ladies and marrying her to William Carey, who was by then one of Henry's closest companions. The king was the principal guest at the wedding and provided the newlyweds with rooms at court, close to his own. Both Mary and her husband were among the huge entourage that accompanied the king to France in 1520 for the meeting that her father had instigated.

When Henry and his queen embarked from Dover at the beginning of June, they were accompanied by 3,000 foot soldiers and 500 horsemen, as well as all of the king's favourites and attendants. To accommodate this vast entourage, a series of lavish tents had been erected, many crafted out of the cloth of gold that gave the summit its name. The most impressive accommodation was reserved for the king: a huge temporary palace covering an area of nearly 10,000 square metres, which was built to receive him. The cost of all this splendour was staggering. The food alone for Henry and his retinue cost £7,409 (£2.8 million). For Henry, though, no expenditure was too great when it came to outshining his French rival. His deep-seated insecurity about Francis could only be suppressed – albeit temporarily – by lavish displays of magnificence.

Although Henry's father had bequeathed him a full treasury, this had soon been depleted by Henry's increasingly magnificent court and his incessant foreign campaigns. It was largely thanks to Wolsey's financial ingenuity that his royal master did not consistently live beyond his means. The chief minister reformed the taxation system so that it was both fairer and more lucrative. A new tax, or 'subsidy', was introduced that was based upon an individual's wealth. This meant that the poorer members of society paid much less than the rich. The cardinal also made frequent use of 'benevolences' – enforced loans from the nobility – which could raise vast sums. In 1522, for example, he secured £200,000 (equivalent to more than £100 million) through this means.

Wolsey's trusted friend, Sir Nicholas Wingfield, had been sent to France as ambassador in February 1520, and was charged with arranging most of the details of this spectacular event. Henry paid close attention to the martial and chivalric aspects of the meeting, and corresponded extensively with Wingfield to ensure that he had all the related matters in hand. It is a sign of the esteem in which Wingfield was held that he was able to gently tease his royal master about matching the French king's plans to bring numerous beautiful women in his train: 'I never saw your highness encumbered or find default with over great press of ladies,' he wrote.[31]

But it was the men with whom Henry was more concerned. He made sure to take with him all of his companions who had proved their prowess in the field of combat or tournament. Through them, as well as his own martial skills, he could demonstrate his superiority over Francis. But one man who did not accompany him across the Channel was Thomas Howard. Although Henry had appointed him his deputy to manage governmental affairs during his absence, it was soon obvious that Howard would enjoy only empty authority. The real power still rested in Wolsey, who took with him all of the trappings of government, including officials, secretaries and the seals with which to authenticate royal decisions. Howard, meanwhile, had been left out in the cold. As if to further emphasise the fact, his son Henry was at the same time dispatched to Ireland. The Howards' resentment against Henry's chief minister had reached boiling point by the time the royal party set sail.

As well as entrusting Wolsey with the task of creating this spectacle, the king also gave him responsibility for the more serious diplomatic business that lay behind it. The chronicler Edward Hall recalled that Henry 'by his letters patents, had given full power and authority to the same lord Cardinal, concerning all matters to be debated, touching the king and the realm, and also gave unto the same Cardinal, full strength, power and authority, to affirm and confirm, bind, and unbind, whatsoever should be in question, between him and the French king, as though the king in proper person had been there presently'.[32]

When the French councillors heard how much power the English king had vested in the cardinal, they reported it to their royal master. Wolsey had taken care to cultivate Francis since his accession, and the latter soon sent word to the cardinal that he wished to imbue him with 'the same power and authority' to treat on his behalf as Henry had given him. When Wolsey received the patent, he sent word to Francis 'that he would no such power receive, without the consent of the king of England his sovereign lord'. This was a clever move on Wolsey's part: he knew that his rivals would seize upon any evidence that he was overstepping his authority, so he was careful to defer to his royal master. Henry did not hesitate to give his approval. 'It was highly esteemed and taken for great love that the French king had given so great power to the king of England's subject,' Hall concluded.[33]

This cordial exchange set the scene for the meeting of the two kings, which took place soon afterwards. Hall describes the spectacular scene that unfolded as Henry and Francis made their way towards the meeting place. Both men were flanked by hundreds of noblemen, squires, knights, bishops and other officials, all clad in cloth of gold and silver, crimson satin, velvets of rich colours, and in the case of the officers of court, 'chains of gold, great and marvellous weighty'. But eclipsing all of his men was Henry himself, who was dressed in a garment 'of such shape and making, that it was marvellous to behold'. Fashioned from cloth of silver and damask, and 'ribbed with cloth of gold, so thick as might be', the outfit was the most sumptuous among the hundreds of others that filled the royal wardrobe. Clearly Henry was determined not to be outshone by his French rival.

The meeting had been carefully stage-managed by Wolsey so that each king would ride to the top of opposing hillsides, before descending into the valley below. The thousands of people who waited there were commanded to stand absolutely still and silent as Henry and Francis prepared to advance. When at last the two men drew level, they alighted from their horses and embraced, then 'with benign and courteous manner each to the other, with sweet and goodly words of greeting: and after few words, these two noble kings went together into the rich tent of cloth of gold . . . arm in arm'.[34]

The encounter had got off to the best possible start, but it was not long before the intense rivalry between these two men showed through the dazzling splendour that had momentarily eclipsed it. Henry might have superseded Francis in material splendour, but he was bested in the series of tournaments that followed. The carefully established rules of the tournament dictated that the two kings could not compete against each other, so Henry contented himself with showing off his prowess – and that of his companions – against a series of French opponents. He threw himself into the jousting with such vigour that one of his best horses died from exhaustion.

Although Henry and his men had shown off their athleticism and skill, he was still so desperate to prove his physical superiority over Francis that he challenged him to a wrestling match. Unfortunately, he was quickly defeated by his rival, which was a bitter blow for a king who so prided himself on his sporting prowess. But Francis also proved himself the greater gallant when, at a dinner with the English queen, he 'went from one end of the room to the other, carrying his hat in his hand and kissing all the ladies on both sides – except for four or five who were too old and ugly'. He then turned his attention to Catherine and conversed with her for a good while before 'spending the rest of the day dancing'. At the same time, Henry attended a dinner with Francis's wife Claude, but Hall deemed his efforts less worthy of note.[35]

Wolsey brought the proceedings to a formal close on 24 June, when he said mass before the two kings departed. The pretence at amity was already wearing thin, and Henry was eager to depart. The ostentatious summit had merely served to intensify his rivalry with Francis. Soon after leaving Guines, Henry made his way to Gravelines, about eighteen miles to the east, to meet Charles V. Ever mindful of the need to keep both of his powerful rivals in play, Henry entertained Charles in England just a few days before his summit with Francis. He now escorted the emperor to Calais and concluded an alliance with him there. Charles V promptly declared war on France.

The Field of Cloth of Gold might have worsened relations between Henry and Francis, but it accelerated Charles Brandon's return to favour. Brandon had played a prominent role in the jousting, and Henry was glad of his old companion at arms, whose skill outshone that of many other combatants. The summit also led to Brandon finally abandoning his pro-French stance, to the extent that three years later Henry appointed him to command an army of more than 11,000 men to invade northern France. He was accompanied by another military stalwart from the king's favourites, William Blount, Lord Mountjoy.

As Master of the Horse, Sir Henry Guildford had been a prominent member of Henry's entourage in June 1520. The contemporary descriptions of the event record that he led his master's spare mount onto the field, and that both he and the horse were richly adorned. He remained with the king for his meeting with the Emperor Charles V at Gravelines shortly afterwards. Thomas Grey, Marquess of Dorset, was also prominent at both occasions and was accorded even greater honour. At the Field of Cloth of Gold he preceded the king, on whose orders he carried the sword of state unsheathed so as not to be upstaged by the French king. Guildford and Dorset were chosen as much for their skill at arms as for their rank: their master had pulled out all the stops in order to gain the upper hand over his French rival.

Another of the king's favourites who had been present at the meeting between the two kings was Henry Courtenay, Earl of Devon. He had excelled in feats of arms against his French opponents, which had helped to offset his master's embarrassment about his own ignominious defeats. In the same year, Courtenay was rewarded with the highest honours that he had yet received at his cousin's hands: he was appointed a gentleman of the privy chamber and was sworn of the council.

Courtenay's old friend William Carey had also distinguished himself in the jousts, and now that he was allied to the powerful Boleyn family, his future in the king's service seemed assured. But his new marriage was to win him favour with his royal master in a rather unexpected way. Mary Boleyn had caught the king's eye soon after her arrival in his wife's household. The same attributes that had attracted the attention of Francis I appealed to his English rival, and within a short time of Mary's marriage she had become Henry's mistress. Their relationship was soon an open secret at court, and William Carey certainly knew of it. But service to the king came before personal concerns, and he was obliged to play the part of cuckolded husband without complaint. Henry rewarded him with grants of land, and his influence in the privy chamber continued to grow. Mary's father and brother also profited from her affair with the king. Henry granted the two men various offices in Tonbridge in Kent, close to their estate at Hever.[36] George was later granted the manor of Grimston in Norfolk.

Despite causing embarrassment on a previous excursion to France, a number of the king's hell-raising intimates had been among his entourage. They included Francis Bryan and Sir Nicholas Carew, who, along with Courtenay, staged an elaborate masque as part of the entertainments. Dressed as 'Eastlanders', their garish apparel comprised hose of gold satin, shoes with small spikes of white nails, doublets of crimson velvet lined with cloth of gold, hats from Danzig, and purses and girdles of sealskin. Thus attired, they led processions through the streets of Ardres and Guisnes, accompanied by minstrels.

The king had taken other men along for a different reason. They included Henry Percy, fifth Earl of Northumberland. The Percys were one of the most distinguished and wealthy noble families in the country, and they had traditionally enjoyed hegemony in the northern counties. But while Henry Percy's father had led the Council of the North, an administrative body established by Edward IV to strengthen his control of northern England, upon his death Henry VII had given this honour to Thomas Savage, Archbishop of York. The fifth earl's hopes that the new king would restore the leadership to him were dashed early in the reign, and his servants reported loose talk 'that if their lord had not room in the North as his father had, it should not be long well'.[37]

Henry VIII evidently did not have a high opinion of Percy, and he went on to deny him the border offices that he justifiably expected by right, and that he was best equipped to fulfil. The earl became increasingly disaffected and troublesome, and in 1516 he was imprisoned in the Fleet for contempt of the council's jurisdiction in private suits. His servants, meanwhile, were also accused of violence against a local landowner. None of this made Henry inclined to give Percy what he wanted, and instead he limited him to ceremonial roles. Thus, for example, in 1517 Percy was charged with escorting the king's sister Margaret from York to the Scottish border. He did so with bad grace and subsequently grumbled about the cost. Increasingly paranoid about any threats to his authority, Henry instructed Wolsey to keep a close eye on him. Wolsey was in a good position to do so: he had already taken the earl's young son Henry into his charge and was overseeing his education. The younger Percy was no more endearing than his father, however, and the cardinal developed a low opinion of him, not least for his lack of financial sense.

Another peer whom Henry had made sure accompanied him to France was Edward Stafford, Duke of Buckingham. As one of the highest-ranking members of the nobility, it was natural that Henry should wish Buckingham to attend, but the latter grumbled about the expense involved. According to his son's account, written many years later, the duke clashed with Wolsey during the festivities by springing to Queen Catherine's defence when she was rebuked by the cardinal.

The blue-blooded duke and the butcher's boy were natural adversaries, and Buckingham had made no secret of his dislike of Wolsey. According to Holinshed, this incited the cardinal to begin plotting his destruction: 'He [Wolsey] cast before hand all ways possible to have him in a trip, that he might cause him to leap headless.' Upon hearing the duke's slanders, Wolsey was 'boiling in hatred . . . and thirsting for his blood'.[38] But Buckingham's worst enemy was himself. He was highly strung, intemperate and had a loose tongue. As well as loudly criticising Wolsey's policies and declaring that he would govern affairs more effectively himself, he also expressed his contempt for the king's father. Perhaps he judged that this would win him favour with Henry, who despite his confident displays of kingship had always lived in his father's shadow. But if this was the case, then he had miscalculated. To make matters worse, he also boasted of his own royal blood.

Although Henry had never entrusted Buckingham with any real political power, in 1514 he had appointed him to the commission of the peace in nine English counties in which he owned extensive property. The Duke was also responsible for public order in his lordships in south Wales, but despite his efforts he was rebuked by the king in 1518 for failing to achieve results. Henry had also denied him the constableship of England, which Buckingham had successfully argued was rightfully his by virtue of his tenure of certain manors. But while the judges upheld his claim, they made the proviso that the king could dispense with his services, which Henry promptly did.

The king had not always been hostile towards Buckingham, but the latter's royal blood and overweening ambition ensured that relations were never harmonious for long. In August 1519, Henry paid a visit to the duke at his magnificent home at Penshurst in Kent, but was outraged when he saw Sir William Bulmer, a member of his own household, wearing Buckingham's livery. This earned Bulmer a public rebuke from the king, who declared: 'He would none of his servants should hang on another man's sleeve.'[39] Thereafter,

Buckingham became increasingly alienated from the king and was prone to bouts of severe ill temper, possibly also depression. He began to talk vaguely of rebellion, but was also plagued with self-doubt. Early in 1520 he told his chancellor that 'he had been such a sinner that he was sure that he lacked grace'.[40] In October, apparently on a whim, he suddenly announced an intention to go on a pilgrimage to Jerusalem.

Courting the king's disapproval was bad enough, but now that Buckingham had alienated his chief minister, his downfall was inevitable. In April 1521, he was arrested on suspicion of treason. The evidence against him was provided by members of his household, who testified that since 1512 a Carthusian monk named Nicholas Hopkins had been telling the duke of his prophecies, notably that he would one day be king. They also attested that Buckingham believed the Tudors had been cursed by God because of the unjustified execution of the Earl of Warwick in 1499 (the duke had been among the jury), and that was why Henry VIII had failed to produce a male heir. His loose-tongued remarks also included grumblings against Wolsey and the reluctance of his fellow nobles to get rid of this low-born upstart. Even more damning was his reference to his father's plans to stab Richard III to death. Kings were clearly dispensable to a man who saw the throne as his by right.

Hopkins had apparently also advised Buckingham to make himself popular with the people in order to prepare for his accession. In the indictment, the duke was charged with trying to bribe the king's guard with expensive clothes, and with building up his following with supernumerary officials. Much was made of the fact that he had also sought permission to take an armed guard of 300 to 400 men with him to establish his authority in his Welsh lordships. Buckingham's chancellor, Robert Gilbert, allegedly confessed that his master had accused Wolsey of practising witchcraft in order to retain the king's favour, and of being Henry's 'bawd'.

None of these charges bore close scrutiny, and the case depended heavily upon speculation about the duke's intentions. Certainly he expected to be at least regent if Henry should die, and planned to take revenge on Wolsey. But only one of the prophecies about Buckingham becoming king was made after Princess Mary's birth in 1516. Nevertheless, his claim to regency was easily twisted into a design on the throne, and the fact that he had countenanced the king's death was a treasonable offence.

The duke was indicted for treason on 8 May, and five days later he was put on trial at Westminster Hall before his peers. Many of the king's most favoured men were among them, including William Blount, Lord Mountjoy, who had been active in Henry's service since his return from Tournai three years earlier, and Charles Brandon, Duke of Suffolk. Thomas Howard's father, the Duke of Norfolk, presided over the proceedings as chief judge. When Buckingham was brought to the bar, the axe of the Tower was set before him. It was an ominous sign. His rivals enjoyed the spectacle as this 'proud prince' was obliged to humbly bow before them, bareheaded.[41]

When the indictment against him was read out, Buckingham declared it to be 'false and untrue and conspired and forged to bring me to my death'.[42] But it was to no avail. On 16 May, after the evidence had been heard and the jury had returned from considering the case, the Duke of Suffolk pronounced their verdict that the duke was guilty of high treason. Edward Hall describes how Buckingham was brought to the bar 'sore chafing and sweating marvellously'. In an impressive show of grief, the Duke of Norfolk wept as he described the sentence of hanging, drawing and quartering. Buckingham was not fooled. He reiterated his innocence and told his peers that he bore them no malice. Then, turning to Norfolk, he declared: 'The eternal God forgive you my death.'[43] The axe was then twisted towards the condemned man and he was ushered out of the hall and into a barge that was waiting to take him to the Tower.

To guard against any repercussions, the wording of the attainder left no doubt about the heinousness of Buckingham's crimes. He had 'divers times . . . imagined and compassed traitorously and unnaturally the destruction of the most royal person of our said sovereign lord the king'.[44] The duke was executed the next day, the king having commuted the sentence to beheading. The speed with which it all happened suggests that Wolsey had been laying the groundwork for some time – and that he wanted to rush it through before there were any objections. A number of men who were closely involved in the case were in no doubt that Wolsey had been responsible for the duke's downfall. In reporting his death, foreign ambassadors claimed that it was due to his having spoken out against the cardinal. But Wolsey confided to the French ambassador that Buckingham's opposition to an alliance with France had been his undoing.

The duke's brother Henry might have feared the same fate – after all, he had been under scrutiny by Wolsey at the king's command. But he escaped any reprisals and continued in royal service until his death three years later. Less fortunate was the king's long-standing companion, Sir Edward Neville. His elder brother George, third Baron Bergavenny, had married Buckingham's daughter, Lady Mary Stafford, in June 1519, and had subsequently supported – or at least concealed – his father-in-law's schemes. He was committed to the Tower, surrendered all of his offices and submitted to a heavy fine, until eventually receiving a royal pardon. Sir Edward, meanwhile, was banned from the king's presence on the grounds of having favoured the duke himself. His prohibition was only lifted ten months later, but he swiftly regained some of his favour with the king, albeit on less intimate terms.

The Duke of Buckingham's execution marked a turning point in Henry's relations with his nobles. At the beginning of the reign, when his confidence was riding high, he had been content to show them every favour. But now, twelve years on and still lacking a male heir, the same nagging fears that had plagued his father had begun to sound in his ears. Wolsey, who had always been suspicious of the aristocracy, urged his master to heed the policy of his father in keeping them at arm's length, and of only making new creations in reward for proven loyalty. Henry was now ready to listen, and from that moment onwards, the only ennoblements he made were to his own 'creatures'.

In what would become a practised routine, the king divided the spoils of the fallen duke among his favourites. One of those to profit most was Sir Nicholas Carew, who had been a member of the grand jury that had indicted Buckingham. He was granted the duke's forfeited manor of Bletchingley in Surrey, and also succeeded Buckingham as steward of the park of Brasted, Kent, which brought with it an income of £40 per annum. Further grants of land and honours were to follow during the years ahead, making Carew one of the wealthiest of all the men who served in the king's privy chamber.

One of the king's men who had little need of Buckingham's lands was Thomas Grey, Marquess of Dorset. He owned land in no fewer than sixteen counties, and thanks to his favour with Henry he had enjoyed a succession of honours over the past decade, including a place on the council and the coveted role of gentleman of the privy chamber. But his magnificence landed him in trouble during the early 1520s. A fierce dispute with the Hastings family in Leicestershire spilled over into the court when George, Baron Hastings, and his father-in-law, Sir Richard Sacheverell, arrived with large retinues. Not to be outdone, Dorset promptly expanded his own already considerable body of men. This violated the law against retaining, and Wolsey brought both Dorset and Hastings before the Star Chamber, before turning the matter over to the Court of King's Bench.

Although Henry had forgiven his old jousting companion in the past, he could not allow this transgression to pass. Dorset and Hastings were bound over for good behaviour, and the marquess temporarily lost his seat on the council. But the dispute simmered on, stoked by the king's obvious preference for Dorset's side, and in 1524 a fight broke out in Leicester between Dorset's cook and a client of Hastings, which escalated into a brawl involving hundreds of men. Wolsey was forced to intervene once more, and after levying a heavy fine on both parties, he had Dorset appointed lord master of Princess Mary's council and sent off to Wales. This was an honourable position, but it deprived the marquess of his accustomed proximity to the king, and when the privy chamber was reorganised two years later, he found himself without a place.

Three months after the Duke of Buckingham's execution, a peace conference was held in Paris to try to resolve the differences between Francis I and Charles V. Spying his chance to pursue his own diplomatic objectives, Wolsey, who had succeeded in ingratiating himself with both parties, offered to arbitrate. Henry empowered him to conclude an alliance with either France or the emperor, as he saw fit, or indeed to form a confederation with both powers and the papacy too. It is an indication of the enormous trust that the king now placed in his chief minister that he gave him free rein to act on his behalf in such an important international summit.

But Wolsey was not satisfied with even this level of authority because he feared that in his absence, decisions would be made in England that ran contrary to his wishes. It was already his custom whenever he was away from court to bombard the king with letters and messengers in order to update him on progress – and, no doubt, to make sure that he was not forgotten by his fickle master. As an additional safeguard, Wolsey also selected a small group of trusted men to report back on what was happening in council. They included Richard Pace, who acted as the king's secretary for a while, and even his rival Thomas More, but he would change them if ever they showed signs of putting their interests ahead of his own.[45] Now, though, he went one step further by taking the Great Seal with him, which prevented the king from sealing letters patent without his knowledge. This was both staggeringly audacious and illegal, and it whipped up even greater resentment among the cardinal's adversaries.

Having thus protected his interests at home, Wolsey embarked for France in early August 1521. He clearly relished the position of power into which Henry had placed him and was determined to flaunt it because he travelled with no fewer than 1,000 horsemen. He presided over a conference between French and Imperial ambassadors, but was unable to bring them to agreement, and subsequently travelled to Bruges. Charles V met him at the gates of the city and embraced him as if he were an equal. Even though he had traditionally favoured France, Wolsey proceeded to negotiate an offensive alliance with the emperor against Francis I, and concluded a new treaty that committed England to declaring war in March 1523. The cardinal was rewarded with a pension of £1,200 a year, which was ostensibly to compensate for relinquishing his claims to the bishopric of Tournai.

All the while, Henry was kept up to date with his chief minister's dealings. His reaction was mixed. In one dispatch, he alarmed Wolsey by making a show of wanting to recover his rightful inheritance in France and referred to Charles as 'double-tongued', but in others he expressed his satisfaction with the cardinal's wisdom.[46] When Wolsey begged him to reimburse the £10,000 of expenses that he claimed to have laid out in Calais, Henry's pockets yet again proved deep. He granted his minister St Albans Abbey in trust, which added a further £1,000 to his yearly income. This was supplemented by the grant of further benefices during the next few years so that, by the end of the 1520s, it was estimated that Wolsey's annual income had risen to a staggering £30,000 (£9.6 million).

Meanwhile, in order to fund his master's cripplingly expensive French campaign, in 1525 Wolsey organised another benevolence, or forced loan. Known as the 'Amicable Grant', it was anything but. Previous benevolences had primarily targeted the nobility, but this one included ordinary people and the clergy. It sparked widespread discontent. Although Henry had not only approved, but probably instigated the grant, most of the blame fell upon Wolsey's shoulders, as Hall recorded: 'All people cursed the Cardinal and his coadherents as subvertor of the law and liberty of England.'[47] Wolsey's reaction was typically sanguine: 'It is the custom of the people, when anything miscontenteth them, to blame those that be near the King,' he told Thomas Howard (now Duke of Norfolk) and Charles Brandon.[48] He proceeded to let his master enjoy the glory of withdrawing the tax and pardoning his people, while Wolsey himself shouldered the responsibility for the ill-fated project. 'Because every man layeth the burden from him, I am content to take it on me,' he declared, 'and to endure the fame and noise of the people for my goodwill towards the king, and comfort of you my lords, and other the king's councillors.' He could not resist adding, though, that 'the eternal God knoweth all'.[49]

But if the king was prepared to tolerate or even encourage his chief minister's autonomy, his subjects were not. The king's old tutor John Skelton penned 'Speak Parrot', a vicious attack on Wolsey for so far overreaching himself. Using the parrot of the title as a mouthpiece, the poet pretended to be merely repeating what he had heard around the court.[50] He went on to compose a series of similarly critical verses, the most notorious of which was composed in November 1522 and entitled: 'Why come ye not to court?' Whereas before, Skelton had at least attempted to disguise – albeit thinly – the subject of his criticism, this poem was a direct and highly personal attack on the cardinal. It mentions the trouble that Wolsey was having with his eyes, and draws on the rumours that he was syphilitic. Above all, though, it criticises the chief minister for dominating his aristocratic peers and setting himself up as an equal of the king himself:

Set up a wretch on high,
In a throne triumphantly,
Make him of great estate
And he will play check mate
With royal majesty.[51]

For all Skelton's criticism of Wolsey, his own ambition for influence and preferment at the king's hands did not bear close scrutiny, particularly for a man of the Church. Moreover, there were rumours that he kept a concubine and, like Wolsey, he had at least one illegitimate child.

Although most of Skelton's poems about Wolsey were not printed until some years later, it is likely that they were circulated in manuscript form and that the subject of his attacks was well aware of them. Rather than seeking to punish Skelton, however, Wolsey seems to have decided to use the poet's pen to his own advantage. Less than a year after Skelton's most vicious attack appeared, his 'Garland of Laurel' was published, dedicated to Henry VIII and, surprisingly, Wolsey. The swift change of tack was probably due to Skelton having remembered (or having been reminded) that Wolsey had promised him a prebend – that is, revenues from a cathedral or college. With a typical lack of subtlety, Skelton chose to remind Wolsey of this in his latest poem.

7

'The most rascally beggar in the world'

THE UNPRECEDENTED POWER that Wolsey had managed to accrue at the king's hands had long invoked the jealousy of Henry's other men, and increasingly there were mutterings against him among the common people too. At Christmas 1525, Henry was forced to abandon the usual festivities because of the onset of plague in London, and he retreated to Eltham with just a small number of attendants. By contrast, Wolsey kept open house at Richmond and staged 'plays and disguisings in most royal manner', with a great many lords and ladies in attendance. Edward Hall noted that it 'sore grieved the people, and especially the king's servants, to see him keep an open court, and the king a secret court'.[1] This was soon interpreted by the cardinal's enemies as an attempt to seize the reins of power. The Venetian ambassador was scandalised to hear that the king 'leaves everything in charge of Cardinal Wolsey, who keeps a great court and has comedies and tragedies performed'.[2]

But the following year, Wolsey's influence declined sharply. This had nothing to do with his presumptuousness, and everything to do with a member of the court who had rapidly supplanted him in the king's affections. George Cavendish recalls: 'Fortune, of whose favour no man is longer assured than she is disposed, began to wax something wroth with his [Wolsey's] prosperous estate, [and] thought she would devise a mean to abate his high port; wherefore she procured Venus, the insatiate goddess, to be her instrument.'[3]

The woman in question was Anne, the younger of Thomas Boleyn's daughters. She had spent most of her youth in the household of Queen Claude, wife of Francis I. More intelligent than her sister Mary, she had thrived in the cultural vibrancy of the French court and had quickly absorbed both its manners and fashions. This set her apart from the other ladies of Catherine of Aragon's household when she arrived there in 1522. Although her date of birth is not recorded, it is likely that she was then in her early twenties.

Anne may have lacked the physical attributes that were admired at the time – her skin was far too 'swarthy' and her bosom was 'not much raised' – but she had an irresistible self-confidence and sense of style that soon attracted a coterie of admirers.[4] The king was not among them – at least, not for the first four years of Anne's service at court. He was too diverted by her sister Mary to pay her much attention. Instead, Anne began a flirtation with Henry Percy, later sixth Earl of Northumberland. This was no doubt a source of great satisfaction to her father, who had brought her to court in the hope of finding her a husband of birth and property. The courtship developed rapidly, and in spring 1523 Anne and Percy were betrothed.

Like many sons of noblemen, Percy had been sent to an influential household as part of his education. The trouble was, the household in which he served was Wolsey's, so any hope of keeping his betrothal secret was soon dashed. When the cardinal heard of it, he was furious because it flew in the face of his attempts to control noble marriages. Besides, Wolsey had already lined up a candidate of his own for Anne: James Butler, the future ninth Earl of Ormond, who also served in his household. Anne was the great-granddaughter of the seventh earl, and Wolsey judged that the marriage would help to resolve a dispute over the Ormond inheritance. The cardinal therefore arranged for the Percy betrothal to be swiftly dissolved. Tradition has it that this was at the king's insistence because he had fallen in love with Anne, but this did not happen until three years later.

Wolsey was no doubt satisfied at having so swiftly put a stop to Anne's hopes of marrying Henry Percy. But in so doing, he had made an enemy who would prove far more deadly than any of his male rivals at court. Percy was married off (unhappily) to Lady Mary Talbot, the daughter of the Earl of Shrewsbury, for whom he had been intended since his youth. Meanwhile, Wolsey's scheme to marry Anne to James Butler came to nothing, which left her free to look elsewhere.

By 1526, Anne had attracted the king's attention. It may have taken

Henry four years to notice her, but once he had, his interest rapidly turned into an all-consuming obsession. The difference between this and his previous flirtations was pronounced, and owed much to Anne's tactics. Thanks to her sister Mary, she had seen first-hand what happened to the king's mistresses: once he had bedded them, he rapidly lost interest. Anne shared her father and brother's ambition and was not therefore content to join the ranks of the king's discarded mistresses, and then be married off to whichever gentleman of the court was prepared to turn a blind eye to her indiscretions.

Having rightly judged that it was the thrill of the chase that motivated Henry, Anne steadfastly refused to give way to his increasingly persistent advances. But she cleverly gave him just enough encouragement to stoke his interest even further, telling him that although she loved him in spirit, she could not love him in body unless they were married. Although Anne has traditionally been awarded all of the credit for this tactic, it is likely that she was encouraged by her ambitious father and her uncle, the Duke of Norfolk, who were better acquainted with Henry's character and had witnessed first-hand how quickly he lost interest in his mistresses. They had also built up enough of a powerbase at court to promote Anne's cause. The two men were therefore as influential in the demise of Henry's first marriage as Anne was herself.

The idea that the king might set aside his wife and marry Anne was a shocking one, but in her favour was the fact that Henry was tiring of Catherine who, at forty, was now unlikely to bear him the son that he so desperately needed. Anne, meanwhile, was in her mid-twenties and came from very fertile stock. This made her an even more attractive prospect to the king. During the months and years that followed, Henry would grow increasingly impatient to rid himself of Catherine and marry Anne. He needed a male heir, and he needed one fast if he was to avoid leaving his throne to a minor. History had consistently proven how turbulent such minorities could be. Even though the king was only in his mid-thirties, given that life expectancy did not reach far beyond forty-five for most men, he was painfully aware that time was not on his side.

Henry's lack of a legitimate male heir had also prompted him, in recent years, to lavish great care and attention upon the upbringing of his bastard son. Edward Hall notes that Henry FitzRoy was raised 'like a Prince's child'. Although he was lodged in Durham House, a grand episcopal palace on the Strand in London, he may have spent time in the royal nursery – a letter from a woman who served there suggests so. Certainly he benefited from an excellent education, which included Latin, Greek, French and music, taught to him by some of the most renowned tutors of the age, including John Palsgrave, Richard Croke and William Saunders. But while FitzRoy had inherited his father's love of sporting pursuits and had the same restless energy, he did not share his intellect and had to be bribed to settle to his books. Always eager to please the king, though, he wrote to assure him: 'I give my whole endeavour, mind and study to the diligent appliance of all sciences and feats of learning.'[5]

It may have been an accident that befell Henry in 1525 that prompted him to consider the succession as a matter of even greater urgency. While on a hawking expedition near Hitchin in Hertfordshire, Henry attempted to pole-vault over a clay marsh. To the horror of his companions, the pole broke under his weight and he was plunged face-down into the marsh, the clay rapidly closing over his head. A quick-thinking footman in his retinue named Edmund Moody leapt into the marsh and pulled his master's face out of the clay. Seconds later and Henry would have drowned. The grateful king bestowed a pension upon his rescuer, along with a grant described as 'The Reward of Valour'.[6] It had been a salutary reminder of Henry's mortality. If he had died that day, his nine-year-old daughter Mary would have succeeded him. The prospect of a minority rule by a female sovereign was little short of disastrous in the eyes of Henry and his subjects, and made him look again at the idea of legitimising his bastard son, Henry FitzRoy.

On 23 April 1525, Henry had the young boy appointed a Knight of the Garter, and he was solemnly installed on 7 June in St George's Chapel at Windsor, where he was given the second stall on the king's side. Two months later, just after his sixth birthday, FitzRoy was created Earl of Nottingham. On the same day, the dukes of Norfolk and Suffolk brought him before the king at Bridewell Palace and he received the unprecedented honour of a double dukedom at his father's hands. He knelt before the king as Sir Thomas More read out the patents of nobility. It was the first time since the twelfth century that an illegitimate son of the king had been raised to the peerage, and Henry ensured that the conferment was made with all due ceremony. The Earl of Northumberland carried the robes, Thomas Grey, Marquess of Dorset, bore the sword, the Earl of Arundel carried the cap of estate with a circlet, and the Earl of Oxford presented the boy with a rod of gold. When the patent of creation had been read out, FitzRoy took his place beside the king on the raised dais, 'so that he takes precedence of everybody', as the Venetian envoy observed.[7] After the ceremony, there was 'great feasting and disguising' to celebrate.

Henceforth, FitzRoy was referred to as the 'right high and noble prince Henry, Duke of Richmond and Somerset'. The king's choice was significant. Both his father and grandfather had been Earl of Richmond, which made it one of the most prestigious titles in the land. The Duchy of Somerset, meanwhile, was well known for its first incumbent, John Somerset, a royal bastard who had been legit- imised after the marriage of his parents, John of Gaunt and Kathryn Swynford. Henry was so proud of his son's new titles that he himself designed his coat of arms.

As well as enhancing his prestige, the two dukedoms brought FitzRoy substantial revenues amounting to £4,845 (£1.8 million) in the first year alone. But this was not the end of the honours, for on 16 July 1525 he became Lord Admiral of England. All of this prompted speculation that the king was about to name the boy his heir. 'He is now next in rank to His Majesty,' reported a Venetian envoy, 'and might yet be easily by the King's means exalted to higher things.'[8] The queen was so afraid that the boy might supplant her daughter Mary that she made it clear to Henry that she fiercely opposed his promotion.

But for as long as the king cherished hopes of marrying Anne Boleyn, FitzRoy's position remained uncertain. Before long, everyone at court knew that Lady Anne was the king's new love interest, and this enhanced her standing and that of her father and brother, both of whom served in the privy chamber. This was a 'great grief' to Wolsey, who 'began with all diligence to disappoint that match . . . which he judged ought to be avoided more than present death'.[9]

Desperate to counter the rising power of a family who were hostile to him, and to safeguard his influence over the king, Wolsey drew up a set of detailed ordinances for the government of the royal household. He worked swiftly: the Eltham Ordinances, as they became known, were introduced towards the end of 1526.

Using the excuse of making the household more financially efficient, Wolsey's ordinances included a revision and reduction of the privy chamber staff. The cardinal personally drew up a list of the current incumbents who should be excluded, and the new men who should take their place. Principal among the casualties was Sir William Compton, groom of the stool. He had long vied for power with the cardinal, albeit in a different arena. From as early as 1516, both men had been described as 'marvellous great'.[10] But not long afterwards, the number of grants made to Compton had fallen off sharply, no doubt thanks to Wolsey's influence. Yet Wolsey had still been wary of his influence with the king because in 1523 he had arranged for him to serve on the Scottish borders. According to Polydore Vergil, Wolsey hoped that he 'might gradually cause him [Compton] to be hateful to Henry' during his long absence.[11] If this was really Wolsey's plan, it backfired. Compton's service in Scotland was the longest that he had been away from his royal master, but absence only made Henry's heart grow fonder. As soon as Compton returned, he was as high in the king's favour as ever.

Wolsey had already lined up another candidate to take Compton's place in the privy chamber: Sir Henry Norris. It was a clever choice. As well as being allied to Wolsey, Norris had ingratiated himself with the king since beginning his service in the privy chamber in 1518. By now, Norris had grown so close to Henry that he was referred to as 'du Roy le mieux aimé' ('the king's most beloved').[12] He also had considerable control over court patronage because he could choose the most apposite moment to secure his master's signature for a grant. Although widely acknowledged as a gentle, likeable man, Norris did not flinch from using his position to enhance his own power at court, and he soon became the focus of a wide network of supplicants for royal favour.

Compton, meanwhile, appeared to accept his fate without protest, perhaps because by this time he had become so great a magnate thanks to the offices he had been given by his royal master that he may have been content to relinquish the post of groom. Moreover, he was soon after appointed usher of receipts in the exchequer and granted a licence allowing him to wear his hat in the royal presence – a privilege that few men enjoyed. There is no evidence that he ever wished for more. In contrast to most other members of the king's entourage, Compton was more concerned with personal than political gain. The description of him provided by Lord Herbert of Cherbury, Henry VIII's biographer in the 1640s, as 'being more attentive to his profit, than public affairs', was probably accurate.[13] The king evidently respected him for it, and remained faithful to Compton despite Wolsey's best efforts. When the cardinal later accused Compton of living in adultery with Lord Hastings' wife, Henry showed no interest in taking the matter further. Sir William was still high in his master's favour at the time of his death, from the sweating sickness, in June 1528. In his will, he admitted that he owed his entire fortune 'to the king's highness, of whom I have had all my preferment'.[14]

Having secured the most senior position in the privy chamber for a man whom he was confident would protect his interests, Wolsey went on to orchestrate a dramatic purge of the other privy chamber posts, reducing them from around fifty to just fifteen officers. His justification was the security of his royal master, and to prevent his being constantly besieged by ambitious place-seekers. Among those who lost out was Sir John Welsbourne, who had been appointed to the privy chamber in the wake of Wolsey's previous purge of 1519. Evidently he had not proved loyal enough to the cardinal during the intervening years. However, he was given some compensation in the form of the new post of esquire of the stable, and during the years that followed he slowly worked his way back into the centre of court life.

One man who benefited from Wolsey's reforms was the king's illegitimate uncle, Arthur Plantagenet. He was appointed to the sought-after position of gentleman of the privy chamber. Arthur had served his nephew loyally since his childhood at Eltham, and Henry valued him as a trusted soldier, diplomat and administrator. As a sign of his esteem, he had created Arthur Viscount Lisle in 1523 and vice-admiral of England two years later, serving as deputy to the king's illegitimate son, Henry FitzRoy. The fact that Arthur was one of a select group of men appointed to the reorganised privy chamber in 1526 suggests that he had also won favour with Wolsey. The same was probably true of Francis Weston, a charming new arrival at court, who was described by Wyatt as 'Weston, that pleasant was and young'.[15] Weston was just fifteen when he began his service to Henry, but soon came to his notice.

It is no coincidence that all of the new men were associates of the cardinal, whereas those who found themselves without a position had threatened his influence with the king. But Wolsey never took any chances, so as part of his reforms he stipulated that the new post-holders should refrain from 'pressing his grace, nor advancing themselves, either in further service than his grace will or shall assign them unto; or also in suits, or intermeddle of any causes or matters whatsoever they be'.[16]

The fact that Henry was content for Wolsey to make such sweeping changes to the department of court that affected him most closely, and in the process to get rid of many of the men whom he counted as friends, is an indication of the unique favour that the cardinal enjoyed. But there was one exception. Henry's cousin, Henry Courtenay, Earl of Devon, was the only man to keep his place at the king's specific command. His had been an inexorable rise in Henry's favour and he had enjoyed many signs of preferment, notably his creation as Marquess of Exeter the previous year. This was only the eighth marquessate to have existed in the English peerage, and it was granted on the same occasion that Henry FitzRoy was made Duke of Richmond and Somerset. Thereafter, Courtenay's name appears regularly in the records of important court occasions, such as a tournament held on Shrove Tuesday 1527, when he accompanied the king to a joust, clad in a magnificent garment of blue velvet and white satin 'like the waves of the sea'.[17]

Wolsey resented the easy intimacy that the two cousins enjoyed, but he knew better than to protest. Neither could he halt the rise of another rival, Sir Nicholas Carew. The esteem in which Henry held his long-standing attendant had been confirmed in July 1522, when Carew had been named Master of the Horse, succeeding Sir

Henry Guildford. He acquitted himself well in the role and was subsequently entrusted by the king on a number of diplomatic missions, such as in 1527, when Henry instructed him to present the Order of the Garter to Francis I, with whom he had concluded a new treaty two years earlier.

Although he had ceded his most prestigious post, Guildford also remained in favour and was one of the few men who were assigned lodgings in the royal house under the new ordinances. He had retained his positions as comptroller of the household and chamberlain of the receipt of the exchequer, to which he had been appointed in 1522 and 1525 respectively. Both posts carried a great deal of responsibility, such as auditing accounts of court banquets and revels, and being custodian of original treaties and similarly valuable documents. Such positions could only be held by a man whom the king trusted completely. Henry's esteem for his long-standing attendant was further demonstrated in June 1525, when Guildford witnessed the granting of the earldom of Nottingham to Henry FitzRoy. The following May, 1526, Guildford was made a Knight of the Garter. This honour had twice been proposed by the other knights, but the king had passed over Guildford in favour of noble candidates. But he evidently set aside such prejudice at a time when his trust in some of his other men – notably his chief minister – was being cast into doubt.

Guildford's position at the heart of the court had enabled him to build up a distinguished circle of associates, besides the king. He was a correspondent of Erasmus and became acquainted with another renowned humanist scholar, John Colet. His penchant for lavish entertainments, meanwhile, brought him into close contact with Sir Thomas Wyatt, and they were jointly responsible for the construction of a banqueting house at Greenwich in 1526. With connections like these, it is little wonder that Guildford had survived Wolsey's purge of the privy chamber.

William Carey had also weathered the reforms. The king's affair with his wife Mary had ended the previous year, but when she gave birth to a son, Henry, in March 1526, the gossips at court claimed that the king was his father. When the new ordinances were issued, Carey was named as one of the six gentlemen waiters of the privy chamber, and was appointed lodgings on the king's side of the court. The same year, he was also made keeper of Greenwich Palace. Now that his royal master was passionately in love with Carey's sister-in-law Anne, his continued rise at court seemed assured. But Carey would not long enjoy his pre-eminence. On 22 June 1528, he died suddenly of the sweating sickness, along with Compton and several other members of the royal household.

Wolsey had not contented himself with purging his royal master's household of unwanted members: he also deprived Queen Catherine of several of her ladies whom he judged to have pro-Imperialist sympathies. The cardinal had long promoted alliance with France and was determined to remove any obstacles to that, even though his master's policy had vacillated in recent years. He knew that Catherine's hold over Henry was weakening thanks to her inability to give him a male heir, and this gave him the confidence to make such an aggressive move. When the queen complained to her husband about it, Wolsey was ready with an answer. He told his royal master that the ladies in question had been turning their mistress against Henry FitzRoy. This was a sly move, drawing attention to Catherine's own failure to produce a son. Henry made no further objection to Wolsey's purge of his wife's household, and the ladies were obliged to leave her service.

Wolsey was once more riding high. At the beginning of 1527, he threw a magnificent banquet at Hampton Court for a group of ambassadors and envoys from France. Henry himself attended, and seemed to care little for the fact that, to all appearances, he was a guest at the cardinal's court. Instead, he delighted in the masque, dancing and other entertainments that his chief minister had devised. But Wolsey had evidently heard the whispers against him, and he took the precautionary step of gifting his most magnificent residence to Henry. The king had always greatly admired Wolsey's Thames-side palace, and now that Hampton Court was his, he immediately set about making it even more extensive. He rewarded Wolsey's generosity by appointing him permanent – and extraordinarily lavish – apartments at his former home, as well as at Richmond. This meant that whenever the king was in residence, his chief minister could be close at hand.

In March 1527, Wolsey met with Francis I's envoys at Westminster to renew talks for a marriage between his master's daughter Mary and the French king's son, Charles duc d'Orléans, or even Francis himself. Determined to use this as an opportunity to demonstrate his unswerving loyalty towards Henry, Wolsey made exorbitant demands and refused to give any ground. But he also changed his proposals so often that the exasperated French ambassador described him as 'the most rascally beggar in the world and one who is wholly devoted to his master's interest'.[18] Even as Wolsey was striving on his master's behalf, however, Henry was secretly telling the French ambassadors that he wished to communicate certain matters to Francis that the cardinal did not know.

A year that had begun with such promise for Wolsey would see his relationship with Henry unravel with alarming speed. Before long, he received reports that his royal master was dining most often with the dukes of Norfolk and Suffolk, and with Thomas Boleyn. Of the three men, it was soon clear that Boleyn dominated. Thanks to the king's obsession with his daughter, he had risen from a 'bachelor knight' to a host of 'higher dignities'.[19] Foreign ambassadors reported that he was in constant attendance on the king. Jean du Bellay, the French ambassador, accused him of seeking a monopoly of influence and of leading 'the dance against the dukes and Wolsey'.[20]

All of this spelt danger for the cardinal, who had long since made an enemy of Boleyn. To make matters worse, he soon heard whispers that his royal master was dissatisfied with his conduct of the country's affairs. In panic, he urged Henry to 'conceive none opinion of me, but that in this matter, and in all other things that may touch your honour and surety, I shall be as constant as any living creature'.[21] Worse was to come. The next intelligence to reach Wolsey's ears was that the king planned to have his marriage to Catherine annulled. According to his servant Cavendish, he went at once to find Henry in his privy chamber and knelt before him for over an hour, trying to persuade him not to take such a drastic step. But Henry, for once, was not to be persuaded by the cardinal's silken words. Wolsey therefore expressed his hope that a suitable princess could be found, unaware that Henry had already fixed upon Anne Boleyn. This demonstrates the extent to which she and her male relatives had undermined Wolsey's influence. Now the Boleyns, not the cardinal, were the king's closest confidants.

While the cardinal struggled to regain control over his royal master, there arrived at Henry's court a man who would play a pivotal role in the reign, shaping public perceptions of the king for centuries to come. Hans Holbein the younger hailed from a family of artists. Born in around 1497 in Augsburg, southern Germany, he was the son of Hans Holbein the elder, a painter of some renown. His elder brother Ambrosius had also followed his father's profession, but it would be the younger Hans who would be celebrated throughout the world for his skills as a portraitist.

When he was still in his teens, Hans Holbein migrated to Basel in Switzerland with his brother, and they worked on a number of projects, largely separately. Hans soon won renown as a painter of portraits, religious pictures and wall paintings, but also as a designer of woodcuts, engravings and stained glass. In around 1518–19, Holbein was appointed town painter of Basel in recognition of his talents. His paintings were widely admired for their use of rich colours, and for the striking realism of their subjects.

Among only a few portraits that Holbein painted during his years in Basel were two studies of Desiderius Erasmus. In one of these, the Dutch scholar is shown in his study, his hands resting on one of his books. Erasmus was so impressed with the portrait that he sent it to England, where he knew it would attract considerable admiration. In August 1526, he wrote to a friend, telling him that Holbein was on his way to England to 'pick up some angels [a pun on the English coins]'.²² Erasmus would prove a powerful patron for the young artist, who won his first royal commission soon after arriving at court. A 'Master Hans' is listed in the household accounts as a decorative painter for the festivities at Greenwich in the early part of 1527.

The king was evidently impressed with his new artist because Holbein was paid the considerable sum of £4 10s. (c. £1,500) for a 'plat' showing the defeat of the French in battle. He also received the highest daily wage of any artist for creating a ceiling painting of the heavens in collaboration with the king's astronomer, Nikolaus Kratzer. Numerous other commissions followed, including decorative paintings in many of the king's palaces, window frames, table fountains, fireplaces and goldsmith's work, as well as the portraits and miniatures for which he is best known.

Enjoying the patronage of Erasmus had clearly enabled Holbein to make other influential acquaintances. Sir Thomas More's brother-in-law John Rastell was one of the creators of the Greenwich revels, and Sir Henry Guildford was in charge of the whole project. These men were well known to the humanist scholar, as was Archbishop Warham, whose portrait Holbein painted in the style of his study of Erasmus. Holbein's portrait of Sir Thomas More, which he completed in 1527, became one of his most celebrated works. Perhaps to flatter the king, he depicted More as a statesman rather than a scholar, with his gilded livery collar shown off to magnificent effect. He went on to paint a striking portrait of More surrounded by members of his family. Although Holbein had picked up a number of important commissions during his time in England, he returned to Basel after just two years, having as yet had little contact with the king whom he would go on to immortalise.

Meanwhile, Wolsey had come to realise that the only way to regain Henry's favour was to secure the annulment. Somewhat against his better judgement, he therefore employed his legatine authority to make confidential inquiries into the validity of the king's union with Catherine. The issue lay with whether the queen's marriage to Henry's brother had been consummated. Much was made of the passage in the Bible that warned: 'If a man shall take his brother's wife, it is an unclean thing . . . they shall be childless.'[23] Little matter that Henry and Catherine had a daughter, or that the Pope had sanctioned their marriage because Catherine had attested that her marriage to Arthur had not been consummated. The king had decided that God was offended with his marriage, and that was why He had denied him a son.

On 17 May 1527, Wolsey convened a secret tribunal led by himself and Archbishop Warham. Having first secured their royal master's permission to do so, they summoned Henry to appear before the court to answer a charge of living in sin with his dead brother's widow. Despite Wolsey going to great lengths to conceal the hearing, the Spanish ambassador had got wind of it the following day and placed the blame entirely on him. In the end, it mattered little that the cardinal's scheme had been discovered: proceedings came to an end on 31 May, with nothing having been achieved. Two days later, he received news of an event in Rome that changed everything. The emperor's troops had sacked the city and the Pope was now effectively a prisoner of Catherine's nephew, Charles V. Desperate though he was to give Henry what he wanted, Wolsey had to be realistic. He therefore warned his master that progress with the 'Great Matter' would be severely impeded. But the king chose not to listen and, no doubt encouraged by Anne Boleyn, he forged ahead with his plans. On 22 June, he told Catherine that he intended to have their marriage annulled. Deeply shocked, she at once dispatched a messenger to alert her nephew.

Wolsey was now swept along by events over which he had little control. In July, Henry sent him to France as 'vicegerent' to a summit at Avignon so that he could convoke as many cardinals as were at liberty, and there they would debate the Great Matter. The location was significant: it was where popes and antipopes under French control had ruled during the fourteenth and fifteenth centuries. Henry hoped that the convention would confer full powers upon Wolsey until such time as Clement was able to throw off the shackles of his Imperial captor. He would then have the authority to decide upon his royal master's annulment, and the whole thing could be signed and sealed before Clement returned to his duties.

Much as Wolsey hankered for papal power, he was loath to leave his royal master at a time when the Boleyns and Howards were conspiring endlessly against him and grasping any opportunity to blacken his name with the king. Desperate to safeguard his position, he assured Henry that he would act 'only for the advancement of Your Grace's secrete affair'.[24] He also instructed his protégé Sir William Fitzwilliam to report on whom the king was keeping company with. To his dismay, he soon received news that Henry mostly 'suppeth in his privy chamber . . . with . . . the Dukes of Norfolk and Suffolk, the Marquess of Exeter and the Lord of Rochford [George Boleyn]'.[25] Together, they played on their royal master's vulnerability as a man deeply in love in order to further the annulment and carve out influential positions for themselves in the process. Even those men who were opposed to the annulment conspired against Wolsey, notably his erstwhile ally Charles Brandon.

More ill tidings soon followed. Wolsey heard that, without consulting him, Henry had sent Thomas Wyatt and Sir John Russell, first Earl of Bedford, to petition the Pope in Rome. Russell had served Henry since the beginning of the reign and had been promoted to gentleman of the privy chamber earlier that year, probably at Wolsey's behest. This was of little comfort to the cardinal, who was aghast that Henry had taken such a step without his prior knowledge.

Wolsey could, though, console himself with the fact that one adversary was unable to capitalise upon his absence. Henry had ordered Thomas More to accompany the Cardinal on his mission. Relations between the two men were worse than ever because Wolsey had deprived More of his position as under-treasurer, which in turn had precluded him from continuing as the king's secretary. Even though Wolsey had arranged for More to be given the chancellorship of the Duchy of Lancaster in recompense, it was a poor exchange and carried none of the influence or regular access to the king that his former position had afforded. But More had remained a trusted official, and it is possible that Henry had chosen him to accompany Wolsey because he wanted him to act as his eyes and ears in France. It is also possible that Wolsey himself had requested More's presence in order to prevent him from ingratiating himself with the king during the chief minister's absence.

Another man hostile to Wolsey was present in his entourage. Sir Francis Bryan had been preoccupied by local government during the first half of the 1520s, but he had continued to be a court favourite, taking part in revels and other festivities. By 1526 he was chief cupbearer and master of the 'henchmen' (Henry's pages), with whom he lodged when at court, and by the following June he was restored to the post of gentleman of the privy chamber. Bryan had a vested interest in bringing the king's Great Matter to a successful conclusion because Anne Boleyn was his cousin. Although family ties did not always guarantee loyalty, Bryan's support for Anne is clear from the separate correspondence that he struck up with her.

Wolsey was thankful to be accompanied by a member of his own household whom he trusted implicitly – and who would soon rise to prominence at court. Stephen Gardiner was a Cambridge scholar and theologian, and as a young man he had spent time in Paris as an attendant of Erasmus. Gardiner had entered Wolsey's service in 1524, and ever since that time he had been busy exploiting his connection to the king's chief minister by building up an impressive portfolio of ecclesiastical posts. His expertise in canon law had proved extremely valuable, and he was also a skilled diplomat. The cardinal was so impressed with him that he refused to relinquish him to his royal master, who had become aware of Gardiner's talents. But Gardiner had ambitions for royal service and made sure to put himself at the king's disposal whenever the opportunity presented itself. Wolsey would learn to his cost that Gardiner was not a man whose loyalty could be relied upon.

As reports reached Wolsey that his enemies were blackening his reputation with Henry, convincing the king that his chief minister was overreaching his authority, he rushed off a series of letters to his master, all reassuring him of his unflinching devotion to his service, and vowing that every day separated from him felt like a year. The wording of one particular letter reveals the efforts to which his enemies had gone to discredit him: 'God I take to be my judge that whatsoever opinion . . . your grace hath or might conceive, I never intended to set forth the expedition of the said commission [i.e. the Avignon meeting] for any authority, ambition, commodity, private profit or lucre, but only for the advancement of your grace's secret affair,' he pleaded. 'Assuring your highness that I shall never be found but as your most humble, loyal and faithful, obedient servant . . . enduring the travails and pains which I daily and hourly sustain without any regard to the continuance of my life or health, which is only preserved by the assured trust of your gracious love and favour.'[26]

Far from being softened by the cardinal's assurances, Henry showed Wolsey's letters to Thomas Boleyn and his ally Thomas Howard, Duke of Norfolk. The two men had seen Wolsey manipulate their royal master often enough to know that it could be easily done. They succeeded in twisting Wolsey's words to such an extent that when the cardinal finally returned to England at the end of

September, he found that he was obliged to meet his master in Anne Boleyn's presence. It was an ignominious return in all respects. Hearing of Wolsey's schemes, Pope Clement had forbidden his cardinals to attend the Avignon summit, and only a handful had defied the ban – certainly not enough to push through Wolsey's proposals.

Wolsey also soon realised that he was the subject of increasingly public scorn. As part of the Christmas celebrations in 1527, the king and his court attended a 'goodly disguising' at Gray's Inn. It was compiled by John Roo, whose service as a sergeant at law had begun many years before the cardinal's rise to power. His play was a blatant attack on Henry's chief minister, taking the theme of a government dominated by negligence and 'evil order'. The performance was 'highly praised of all men', but Wolsey, knowing that he had been its target, flew into a 'great fury'. He sent Roo to the Fleet prison and 'rebuked and threatened' all of the actors who had taken part. 'Many wise men grudged to see him take it so to heart,' Edward Hall noted, whereby Wolsey insisted that he was acting not for himself but for the king, who had been 'highly displeased with it'.[27]

It now seemed that the cardinal's favour with Henry, which had been unassailable for almost two decades, had suddenly collapsed. The king had given Wolsey enormous power, had turned a blind eye to his arrogance and had stood by him when the rest of his men had expressed their hostility. He had been content to do so for as long as the cardinal had proved his worth as an administrator of unparalleled ability and efficiency. But now, even though Wolsey was every bit as assiduous in his duties as he always had been, Henry had at last begun to heed the complaints against him. What made him more receptive to them was the fact that though he still loved the cardinal, he loved Anne Boleyn more.

Wolsey's influence over the court and council declined at a correspondingly rapid rate. Shortly after his return to England, he made a speech in the Star Chamber in which he tried to win popular support with promises that there would be no further taxes for wars in France. He also railed against the emperor for the sack of Rome. But the forum in which just a few short months before he had reigned supreme was now the site of his humiliation. The contemporary chronicler Hall reported that Wolsey's rousing speech was answered by scornful laughter because 'they knew that what he said was for his own glory, and nothing should follow as he said'.[28]

In every sphere of political and ecclesiastical life, the erosion of Wolsey's influence was painfully evident. In 1528, the seemingly trifling matter of the election of an abbess of Wilton provided another battleground between the cardinal and the Boleyns. Wolsey opposed the election of Eleanor Carey, the sister of Anne's brother-in-law William, on the grounds of her sexual misconduct. Although his royal master subsequently withdrew his support for her, he rebuked Wolsey for interfering in a matter that did not concern him. Worse still, he went on to threaten the college that the cardinal was building in Oxford, telling him: 'It is reported that the goods for building the same are not best acquired, and come from many religious houses unlawfully, "bearing the cloak of kindness towards the edifying of your College", which many cannot believe.'[29]

Another sign of Wolsey's diminishing influence with the king came when Sir John Welsbourne was reappointed to the privy chamber, just two years after being ousted as part of the cardinal's reforms. In an attempt to counteract this, Wolsey had his own gentleman usher, Thomas Heneage, appointed to the privy chamber. Heneage acted as a spy for his master, sending him reports of the king's actions – and those of Anne Boleyn. Although he was clearly the cardinal's man, he made himself acceptable to Lady Anne, who used him to relay messages to Wolsey. This may have aroused the latter's suspicions because he soon stopped relying on Heneage to give him news of the court, and instead enlisted Sir John Russell for this task.

Although Wolsey's relationship with Henry had been seriously destabilised by the time he returned from France, events did not go entirely in his rivals' favour. While Thomas Howard, Duke of Norfolk, had been busy promoting his niece's cause, he had neglected a personal matter that now flared up. Like his sovereign, Norfolk had begun to tire of his wife, Elizabeth, daughter of the late Duke of Buckingham. In 1526, he had begun an affair with one of his own serving girls, Bess Holland. Far from covering it up, he cavorted openly with Bess and subjected his wife to increasingly abusive treatment. She alleged that on one occasion, he had ordered his servants to pin her to the floor until her fingers bled from scratching at the boards. Their public spats at court soon became irksome to the king, and when Elizabeth Howard began voicing her support for Queen Catherine as another ill-treated wife, Henry banished both her and her husband to their Norfolk estate. The duke was only permitted to return at the end of 1528.

Wolsey made the most of his rival's absence, and it can be no coincidence that Henry's attitude towards his chief minister began to soften at around the same time. Although the king's obsession with Anne Boleyn made him vulnerable to the malevolent gossip of Wolsey's enemies, it was clear that Henry had not altogether forsaken the man who had been his mainstay for almost twenty years. In June 1528, the sweating sickness broke out in London. While the rest of the court fled the city altogether, Wolsey only retreated as far as Hampton Court, where he risked his life so that he could carry on the business of the kingdom. Touched by his servant's loyalty and steadfastness, the king wrote at once, urging him to avoid infection and offering him medical advice. Sensing that he had regained at least some of his master's former affection, Wolsey wrote to assure him that: 'If it shall fortune the same to be the last word that ever I shall speak or write unto your Highness, I dare boldly say and affirm your Grace hath had of me a most loving, true and faithful servant.'[30]

If Wolsey succumbed to the sweat, then he lived to tell the tale. But in terms of his position at court, he knew all too well that if he did not secure the annulment for his royal master, then his days would be numbered. In late August, the French ambassador reported a conversation he had with the cardinal, who confided: 'If this marriage took place, and an heir male came of it, that he would then retire, and serve God to the end of his days.'[31] He might still retain a residue of Henry's affection, but he was enough of a realist to know that this was as nothing compared to his master's all-consuming passion for Anne Boleyn. In his favour, though, was the fact that his rivals had enjoyed no more success than he. Indeed, they were a good deal less equipped to negotiate the complex web of diplomatic relations, as the French envoy observed: 'The Duke of Norfolk and his party already begin to talk big but certainly they have to do with one more subtle than themselves.'[32] In a similar vein, the Imperial ambassador claimed that George Boleyn and the dukes of Norfolk and Suffolk 'have combined to overthrow the cardinal but as yet they have made no impression on the king, except that he shows him in court not quite so good countenances as he did and . . . he [has] said more disagreeable words to him'.[33] Even so, Wolsey could not afford to rest on his laurels. Everything now rested upon the Great Matter reaching a successful conclusion.

For the time being, though, Wolsey had more pressing matters to attend to. In August 1528, Henry dispatched Sir Francis Bryan to Rome in order to accompany Cardinal Lorenzo Campeggio on his long-awaited journey to England. Pope Clement, who had escaped from captivity after six months, had given his envoy full authority to decide the legality of the king's marriage. Interestingly, although Bryan was firmly committed to securing an annulment for his royal master, he was ideologically opposed to it. His own sympathies lay firmly with the old religion, and he insisted that no member of his household could be an adherent of the 'new learning'. He had many friends and clients within monastic houses, and he did his best to secure the king's favour and patronage towards them. Although he gained notoriety as a libertine and was fond of cracking anticlerical jokes, Bryan's faith was genuine. His motto was *Je tens grace* ('I look for salvation'), and the fictional character he inspired in one of Wyatt's satires was a man of great piety.[34] He and Wyatt were now close friends, and their faith was undoubtedly one of the strongest ties that bound them together.

Interestingly, although they were ideologically opposed to the king's desire for a break with Rome, neither Bryan and Wyatt nor the other religious conservatives among Henry's men displayed any diminution of respect for their royal master. Neither did they view him as a heretic. This does not make them hypocritical or lacking in religious fervour. Rather, they placed their loyalty to the king ahead of everything else. Thus, while they might not agree with Henry's stance, they had a strong enough sense of duty to champion it on his behalf.

On his way to Rome, Bryan had an audience with the French

king, and subsequently warned Henry that some of his advisers (by whom he meant Wolsey) were secretly supporting Catherine of Aragon's cause. Henry evidently believed him because throughout the protracted divorce negotiations that followed, Bryan became the king's most trusted emissary to both Francis and Pope Clement VII.

On 5 October 1528, the king's former adviser Richard Fox, Bishop of Winchester, died. He had largely retired from royal service in 1517, telling Wolsey: 'I have determined and, betwixt God and me, utterly renounced the meddling with worldly matters.'[35] Thereafter he had devoted himself to his long-neglected episcopal duties. Virtually blind for the last ten years of his life, he had been urged by Wolsey to retire from Winchester. But Fox was wily to the end, and refused to cede the rich bishopric to his former protégé.

Fox's death had saved him from getting involved in a matter that he privately opposed. Four days later, Cardinal Campeggio finally arrived in London. But Henry's hopes were soon dashed. Still in sway to Charles V, Clement had placed all sorts of restrictions on Campeggio's commission, which made its chances of success extremely remote. In vain, Wolsey pressed Campeggio for an amplification of his commission. To make matters worse, the following January the papal chamberlain Campano arrived with secret orders that Campeggio should destroy his commission altogether. Meanwhile, popular opposition to the annulment was mounting, and efforts to persuade Catherine to retire to a monastery had failed. Her dignified stance was winning ever more supporters to her cause. Anne Boleyn, by contrast, was despised as the 'Great Whore'.

In February 1529, the pendulum of favour appeared to swing back towards Wolsey. Henry granted the see of Winchester to the cardinal without troubling to secure the usual licence. In return, Wolsey surrendered Durham to his royal master, but the gesture backfired when Henry immediately granted the revenues to Thomas Boleyn. Meanwhile, rumours of Clement's death prompted speculation that Wolsey might be elected as his successor. At a stroke, this would have catapulted Wolsey to a position of unparalleled influence and would have solved all of his royal master's difficulties. But the rumours proved false, and Clement continued to obstruct Henry and Wolsey's efforts.

In late spring, Henry sent Wolsey to attend the peace negotiations between Margaret of Austria and Louise of Savoy, mother of Francis I. His hope was that while there, the cardinal might secure French help with the Great Matter. But the king no longer trusted his chief minister, and he issued secret instructions to Charles Brandon, Duke of Suffolk, to ask the French king if he believed the cardinal was forwarding the annulment as effectively as he might. Francis, though, was reluctant to betray Wolsey, who had proved a great ally in the past, so he simply told Henry that he ought to be managing such an affair himself. Meanwhile, the French ambassador reported that the dukes of Suffolk, Norfolk and others were persuading the king that Wolsey had not done all that he might to advance the proposed marriage of Princess Mary to the duc d'Orléans. This is supported by a letter from Suffolk to his royal master, in which he urged Henry not to 'put so much trust in [any] man, whereby he may be deceived as nigh as he can', but instead 'to look substantially upon his matters himself'.

Meanwhile, Sir Francis Bryan was continuing his efforts to further the king's cause in Rome. His methods were unorthodox and lacked the customary diplomatic niceties, and he showed the same irreverence towards the Pope that had won him favour with his king. Early in May 1529, he reported to Henry that he had revealed all to the Pope 'first by fair means, and afterwards by foul means', but admitted: 'neither fair nor foul will serve here'.[36] Later, it was alleged that Bryan had slept with a courtesan at the papal court in order to gain intelligence. Henry clearly approved of his methods because not long after Bryan's return to England in June 1529, he was dispatched to France as resident ambassador. He soon won favour with Francis I, who was a man of a strikingly similar temperament and tastes to the English king's, and appreciated Bryan's frankness. Realising this, Henry enlisted him on many similar missions during the ensuing years, even though Bryan lacked the diplomatic training and languages that were usually required for ambassadors.

With an annulment still frustratingly out of reach, Henry renewed his attentions towards his bastard son, FitzRoy. Since August 1525, the young man had been living principally in Yorkshire, at Sheriff Hutton or Pontefract, in his capacity as head of the newly resurrected

Council of the North. Thanks to the honours that had been bestowed upon him in 1525, he now commanded a full-scale ducal household which comprised 245 attendants, all of whom wore his livery of blue and yellow. They included his Master of the Horse, Edward Seymour, a young gentleman from an ancient Wiltshire family, whose father, Sir John, had attended the king during a number of notable court occasions. Edward himself would soon rise to prominence in Henry's service.

As a magnate, FitzRoy was treated with all the respect that was due to a royal prince and duke. He kept 'the state of a great prince', and presided over his court from a rich chair of cloth of gold set under a canopy of estate. His attendants and visitors all addressed him as they would a royal prince. They knew well that the king cherished his son 'like his own soul'.[37] FitzRoy seemed to love and revere his father in return, and the two wrote to each other often.

Speculation about Henry's intentions towards his bastard son had intensified in February 1527 when the king had proposed a marriage between FitzRoy and Catherine de' Medici. Although this was primarily intended to counter the interest of Henri, duc d'Orléans, and James V of Scotland, it fuelled rumours that the English king was planning to make the boy his heir. The following month, it was rumoured that Henry intended to make FitzRoy king of Ireland. This came to nothing, but FitzRoy was created lord lieutenant of Ireland on 22 June 1529. Two months later, the ten-year-old boy was summoned to parliament, where he was treated like an adult, with great respect.

FitzRoy had continued to enjoy his father's favour throughout this time, and the relationship between them was consistently good, as evidenced by the numerous gifts and affectionate letters that they exchanged. On one occasion, Henry had acknowledged their shared love of music by sending his son a lute. Wolsey had once referred to the young man as 'Your entirely beloved son, the Lord Henry FitzRoy.' When the king heard that a case of plague had been reported close to Pontefract, some forty miles south of Sheriff Hutton, he was greatly alarmed and sent orders for his son to move north. He also dispatched some remedies that he himself had devised.

The king remained closely involved in his son's upbringing,

evidently still considering making him his heir. Concerned that FitzRoy was not applying himself to his studies, he recalled him from Yorkshire and had him lodged chiefly at Windsor. He also selected a new tutor for him: the respected Cambridge scholar John Palsgrave. A renowned humanist, Palsgrave was greatly influenced by the works of Erasmus and was also a friend of More. Even though he had been tutor to Princess Mary, the king wanted to be sure that he was the right man to inspire his reluctant son with a love of learning, so he interviewed Palsgrave himself at Hampton Court. Impressed by the scholar, he told him: 'Palsgrave, I deliver unto you my worldly jewel: bring him up in virtue and learning.' The tutor vowed that he would perform 'his uttermost best to cause him to love learning and be merry at it'.[38]

Palsgrave soon proved true to his word. He found that his young student could not pronounce Latin correctly because he had lost his front teeth, which made him 'something inclined to lisp'. Though this physical impediment would be rectified when FitzRoy's adult teeth started to grow, his reluctance to learn was more of a challenge. The resourceful tutor therefore used humour to enliven his lessons, and included a comedy by the Roman playwright Plautus in the curriculum. As he ruefully admitted, FitzRoy's other attendants 'wot not whether I learn with him or play with him'. In a private letter to More, Palsgrave admitted that his efforts were being hampered by certain other members of his pupil's household, who 'would in no wise he should be learned; which were a pity, for no man, rich or poor, had ever better wit; and . . . every day more people call upon him to bring his mind from learning, some to hear a cry at a hare, some to kill a buck with his bow, sometime with greyhounds, and sometime with buck-hounds . . . besides many other devices found within the house when he cannot go abroad'.[39]

But Palsgrave proved the more persistent, and before long his efforts paid off. In July 1529, he reported to Henry that this 'excellent young prince . . . never knew his match in towardness'. He assured the king that 'without any manner fear or compulsion he hath already a great furtherance in the principles grammatical both of Greek and Latin'. The tutor could not resist adding, though, that: 'To bring this to pass was a matter of no small difficulty, as he who first taught him to read was no clerk, and did not know the true pronunciation of Latin.' He therefore told the king that it would be another year before he would be able to 'cure him of his errors', but hoped that 'the changing of his teeth' would speed up the process.[40]

Despite the considerable progress that Palsgrave made with Henry's son, his services were terminated after just one year. This may have been at the instigation of Wolsey, who was hostile towards him and had earlier obstructed his appointment to the archdeaconry of Derby. FitzRoy subsequently went to live with his former tutor Richard Croke at King's College, Cambridge. There he studied a wider curriculum with a number of other young noblemen whom his father considered suitable company. Henry would have been shocked to learn that as well as sharing his son's lessons and hunting with him, these young men were also teaching him bawdy songs.

By the time that FitzRoy moved to Windsor, his godfather was under siege. Wolsey's enemies had succeeded in persuading Henry that he was failing him. In June 1529, the king ordered a covert investigation into his adviser's activities. At the same time, Wolsey's protégé Stephen Gardiner was appointed Henry's secretary, and soon began to distance himself from his old patron. By this time, Gardiner was well known for his cunning and double-handedness. John Foxe, who deplored Gardiner's staunch Catholicism, described him as 'most cruel, so was he also of a most subtle and crafty wit, gaping round about to get occasion to let and hinder the Gospel'.[41] Although Gardiner himself claimed to be 'plain, humble, and obedient', and to 'say as I think', he became known as 'wily Winchester', following his appointment to that bishopric. His insistence that he had 'never thought of returning evil upon anyone' lacked sincerity, as Wolsey learned to his cost.[42]

Foxe's description of Gardiner's physical appearance, with his 'hanging look . . . nose hooked like a buzzard, wide nostrils like a horse, ever snuffing into the wind . . . great paws like the devil . . . the form of an outward monster', suggests that he was the very embodiment of evil. His fellow reformer Thomas Becon concurred, and claimed that the bishop's face 'is like unto the face of a she-bear that is robbed of her young ones, whose eyes continually burn with the unquenchable flames of the deadly cockatrice, whose teeth are like the venomous toshes [tusks] of the ramping lion'. [43] Both men had cause to despise Gardiner, however, and their views were undoubtedly coloured by his conservative religious stance, which would become more evident as the reign progressed.

On 25 June 1529, the king and queen were summoned to appear as part of the annulment proceedings, which were held at Blackfriars. Aware that the whisperings of the court had made his position dangerously unstable, the cardinal decided to ask the king openly: 'Whether I have been the chief inventor and first mover of this matter with your majesty for I am greatly suspected of all men herein?' Wolsey's bravery was not rewarded. Henry retorted that his chief minister had opposed him. Instead, he called upon the services of his faithful servant, Sir Henry Guildford, who was invited to testify that Catherine of Aragon's marriage to the king's late brother had been consummated. It is to Guildford's credit that, committed though he was to his royal master's cause, he refused to perjure himself and instead admitted that he was unable to offer an opinion because he had been a mere boy at the time. Robert Radcliffe, who had served Henry since the beginning of the reign, had no such scruples and gave evidence to support the king's case. His loyalty was rewarded in December that year, when he was created Earl of Sussex.

Meanwhile, the cardinal was now besieged on all sides. Catherine directed her ire at him, hurling accusations 'of treachery, deceit, injustice and evil-doing in creating dissension' and called Wolsey 'the bitterest enemy both of me and of law and justice'.[44] She then declared that she would be judged only by Rome, and withdrew from the court. Thereafter, the hearing became mired in technicalities. On 31 July, Campeggio prorogued the court to 1 October, which provoked an outraged Suffolk to bang his fist on the table and shout: 'It was never merry in England when we had cardinals among us!'[45] The contemporary chroniclers Hall and Cavendish were in no doubt that his outburst was encouraged by the king, who had utterly lost faith in his cardinal.

Undaunted, Wolsey told Suffolk: 'Of all men within this realm ye have least cause to dispraise or be offended with cardinals; for if I, a simple cardinal, had not been, ye should have had at this present no head upon your shoulders wherein ye should have a tongue to make any such report in despite of us who intended you no manner of displeasure, nor we have given you any occasion with such despite to be revenged with your [haughty] words.' Warming to his theme, Wolsey went on to express his utter commitment to his royal master – something that he had had precious little opportunity to do in the king's hearing for many weeks – and assured those present that he 'would as gladly accomplish his lawful desire as the poorest subject he hath'. Wolsey concluded with a salutary reminder to Suffolk of their erstwhile connection: 'Wherefore, my lord, hold your peace, and pacify yourself, and frame your tongue like a man of honour and of wisdom, and not to speak so quickly or so reproachfully [of] your friends; for ye know best what friendship ye have received at my hands, the which yet I never revealed to no person alive before now, neither to my glory nor to your dishonour.'[46]

Before the court had even been prorogued, Clement had made peace with Charles V and recalled the case to Rome so that he could personally preside over it. William Benet, the English envoy there, warned that this would lead to the ruin of the cardinal and the destruction of the English Church. Clement acknowledged the truth of this, but declared that he must follow his conscience.

From now on, Wolsey was increasingly made a scapegoat for Henry's failure to secure an annulment. The king's passion for Anne Boleyn had intensified even more, despite his protestation that he was of an age when 'the lust of man is not so quick as in lusty youth'.[47] He was therefore only too ready to listen to her criticism of his chief minister, which was echoed by her rapacious relatives. In their eyes, the cardinal was the only thing that stood between Anne and the throne.

The contemporary chronicler Edward Hall claims that a book containing thirty-four articles against Wolsey was given to the king soon after the failure of the Blackfriars court, wherein he 'evidently perceived the high pride and covetousness of the Cardinal and . . . with what dissimulation and cloking he had handled the king's causes: how he with fair lying words had blinded and defrauded the King'.[48] These articles were signed by a number of Henry's most highly favoured men. Sir Henry Guildford was among them, and provided evidence in parliament of the cardinal's abuse of his office. Assuming that they now had enough ammunition, Wolsey's enemies prepared to have him arrested. But the king confounded their expectations by refusing to act. He also continued to meet with his chief minister and listen to his advice on matters of policy.

Wolsey had won this particular encounter, but the rumours that there would soon be a great change at the heart of the court persisted. Henry himself seemed to confirm it when he prevented the cardinal from attending the Franco–Imperial negotiations at Cambrai. Instead, he dispatched Thomas More and Cuthbert Tunstall as his represent-atives, although by the time they arrived there was little they could do to influence the outcome. When peace was concluded on 3 August, this dashed Wolsey's hopes of using the threat of an Anglo–French alliance to put pressure on Charles V, and thereby the Pope, to sanc-tion the annulment. Worse still, Wolsey was subsequently deprived of Henry's presence for another prolonged period when the latter went on progress. Although the king still sought his chief minister's advice while he was away, he forbade him to attend court, leaving his rivals to take up the reins of power.

As had so often proved to be the case in Henry's court, one man's demise spelt another's triumph. Sir Nicholas Carew was given the honour of being sent to Bologna to obtain the emperor's ratification of the Cambrai treaty, to which England had been admitted as a signatory. This was an important move for Henry as it enabled him to mend fences with Charles V, thereby giving him hope that the emperor might change his stance on the annulment.

On 19 September, amid the gathering storm, Wolsey accompanied Campeggio to Grafton in Northamptonshire for the legate's formal leave-taking. Henry and Anne were also present, and according to the cardinal's gentleman usher, George Cavendish, they used the opportunity to humiliate the chief minister. No lodgings were provided for Wolsey, and he was obliged to sit out in the courtyard on his mule until Henry Norris took pity on him and offered the use of his own chamber so that he might change before attending the king. But another of Wolsey's servants, Thomas Alward, whose account was written just five days later, reported that because Grafton was a small house, Wolsey and Campeggio were given accommo-dation at nearby Easton Neston. Both authors concur, however, that when Wolsey, filled with trepidation, entered the king's presence and knelt before his royal master in humble supplication, Henry's affection for the cardinal was rekindled and he smilingly led him to a window embrasure, where they talked together for two hours or more, 'no [other] person being present'. Thomas Alward reported: 'A friend of mine being of the privy chamber told me at my lord's departure that time from thence there was as good and as familiar a countenance showed and used between them as ever he saw in his life heretofore.'[49]

Wolsey's enemies were confounded by this latest demonstration of Henry's abiding affection for Wolsey, which seemed to be so strong that even his failure to secure the annulment might be forgiven. Anne Boleyn was furious. She had sensed that victory over the cardinal was almost within her grasp, yet now it had apparently been snatched away. According to Cavendish, Anne was more determined than ever to wrest the king away from him, so she thwarted Wolsey's attempts to meet with his royal master the following day as arranged. She insisted that Henry accompany her to see a new hunting park nearby and made sure to take a picnic so that they would be away all day. Wolsey and Campeggio arrived just as they were setting off, and the king told them he had no time to talk, then bade a swift farewell. Again, though, Alward's account suggests that this was an exaggeration. He attests that Henry and Wolsey did meet in council that morning, and that the king went hunting later in the day. Either way, when the king rode off with Anne, it would be the last time that he ever saw his beloved cardinal.

A number of the king's other men had been witness to the events at Grafton. Principal among them were the Duke of Suffolk and George Boleyn, as well as Stephen Gardiner and Wolsey's former secretary Sir Brian Tuke, now Treasurer of the Chamber. In this dangerous world of intrigue and rapidly shifting allegiances, it was no longer certain whom Wolsey could trust, as a letter by the keeper of his wardrobe makes clear. Thomas Alward noted that these four men 'did as gently behave themselves, with as much observance and humility to my lord's grace as ever I saw them do at any time heretofore. What they bear in their hearts I know not.'[50] The Duke of Norfolk had also been among the gathering, and at dinner one evening he had taken advantage of being seated next to Wolsey. Desperate to get the cardinal away from Henry, the duke suggested that it might be advisable for Wolsey to personally oversee the selection of candidates in his province of York. Wolsey had no intention of concurring, but in the coming weeks Norfolk kept up the pressure to have him sent away from court.

It was at this turbulent time that a distinguished visitor arrived at court. Eustace Chapuys had been appointed as Charles V's ambassador to England in May 1529, and arrived in London at the beginning of September. Of about the same age as the English king, he hailed from the duchy of Savoy, which straddled the Alps between France and Italy. He had enjoyed a brilliant academic career, becoming a doctor in canon and civil law, probably at the University of Turin. He had subsequently served the Bishop of Geneva for a number of years, before being appointed as the Duke of Bourbon's representative to Emperor Charles V's court at Granada in 1526. When Bourbon had been killed leading Charles's army at the sack of Rome the following year, the emperor had taken Chapuys into his service.

That Chapuys had been quick to win favour was due to his having gained more than a decade of legal and diplomatic experience in the courts of Europe, during which time he had cultivated a range of high-level contacts. On a personal level, he was charming and erudite, but had a steely disposition and was an arch-schemer. In short, he was an ideal ambassador, and when Charles's envoy to England, Inigo de Mendoza, asked to be recalled in 1529, Chapuys was a natural choice to succeed him. It was not an easy commission, though, and Mendoza had struggled to negotiate the complex intrigues surrounding the English king's Great Matter. The fact that Chapuys had already been working on that same issue for his Imperial master, and had proved an able advocate for Queen Catherine's interests in the negotiations with Henry's representatives in April 1529, put him at a distinct advantage.

Charles's unwritten commission to Chapuys was to act as Catherine's close adviser. She was in desperate need of someone with legal and canonical training in order to steer a course through the increasingly tortuous negotiations and withstand her husband's pressure for an annulment. Chapuys soon proved his aptitude for the task. The beleaguered queen wrote to her nephew, praising his new representative: 'You could not have chosen a better ambassador, his wisdom encourages and comforts me, and when my councillors through fear hesitate to answer the charges against me, he is always ready to undertake the burden of my defence. He pays the most careful attention to all my affairs.'[51]

But while Chapuys had quickly won favour with the queen, his role as her unofficial advocate set him on a collision course with the king, and those of his men who were trying to bring the Great Matter to a successful conclusion. Henry was determined to gain the upper hand from his very first audience with the new ambassador. He dispatched Robert Henneage, a member of the council, to find out whether Chapuys would prefer to discuss the purpose of his mission with the king in Latin or French at their first meeting. Undeterred, the ambassador replied that French would be most desirable, since it was his native language and the king spoke it well. Although Henry showed him every courtesy when they eventually met, referring to Chapuys as 'so wise and so well inclined', he made it clear that he expected him 'to preserve the friendship and alliance between your master and myself'.[52] It was not a request but a demand.

Chapuys immediately had the measure of Henry. Shortly after this meeting, he reported to his master that though the English king claimed to be acting out of conscience in rejecting Catherine, he was motivated only by lust and 'malice'.[53] Unlike the other religious conservatives at Henry's court, Chapuys owed no allegiance to the English king, so his views were not tempered by the same constraints of loyalty. He recognised in this fickle and indulged king a flagrant disregard for principles. Henry wanted to marry Anne Boleyn, and he was prepared to sacrifice his own soul, and those of his people, in order to have her. If he truly believed that his marriage to Catherine had offended God, then it was because he had let himself be seduced by his own publicity.

The ambassador was also aware of the far-reaching consequences that could arise from a schism with Rome, not least the confiscation of church lands by the crown, and feared that if the Pope did not soon take matters in hand, the annulment might be settled in England. A man of infinite discretion, he trod a delicate path between trying to prevent Henry from acting precipitately and maintaining a close but clandestine contact with Catherine. He also acted as her channel of communication both to the emperor and Rome, and worked hard to undermine the woman whom he saw as being responsible for all these troubles, and to whom he referred as 'the Concubine': Anne Boleyn.

After leaving Grafton, Anne and her supporters stepped up the pressure on Henry to dismiss Wolsey from office. 'It is generally and almost publicly stated that the affairs of the cardinal are getting worse and worse every day,' reported Chapuys with barely concealed delight.[54] Although the king had prevaricated over the fate of his chief minister during the preceding few years, he was now provoked into taking more decisive action. Frustrated and humiliated at being outwitted by his rival monarchs, defied by his own people over taxation, and thwarted in his desire to marry Anne Boleyn and secure the succession, Henry was painfully aware of how far he was from achieving the vision of kingship that he had confidently embraced at the beginning of his reign. It had been a vision of an all-powerful Renaissance monarch that had been shared – and, as far as possible, facilitated – by his trusty servant Wolsey. But now this idealised image had been proved a sham and, in characteristic style, rather than admitting his part in that failure, Henry sought a scapegoat.

8

'The inconstantness of princes' favour'

ON 3 AND 6 October 1529, Wolsey presided over council meetings as usual, and on the 9th he took his place in the Court of Chancery. But on that same day, he was indicted for *praemunire* (a law prohibiting the assertion of papal jurisdiction against the supremacy of the monarch) in King's Bench. This made it clear that in accepting and deploying his legatine authority, Wolsey had acted as the agent of a foreign government, to the detriment of his own royal master. Henry was therefore sending a strong message to the Pope and all those who paid fealty to him: in England, real power rested not with the Church, but with the king.

On 18 October, Wolsey surrendered the Great Seal, and the following day his arch-rivals, the dukes of Norfolk and Suffolk, presented Wolsey's alleged offences in the Star Chamber. They also arranged for him to be swiftly replaced in all of his various offices. Suffolk was among those who benefited, being made president of the king's council.

Wolsey was enough of a political realist to know that he had little choice but to accept the charges of *praemunire* and surrender all of his property. He declared: 'I would all the world knew that I have nothing but it is his [Henry's] of right, for by him, and of him I have received all that I have: therefore it is of convenience and reason, that I render unto His Majesty the same again with all my heart.'[1] The king's officials wasted no time in taking an inventory of all the cardinal's possessions and estates, which were extensive. The French diplomat Guillaume du Bellay reported: 'Wolsey has just been put out of his house, and all his goods taken into the King's hands. Besides the robberies of which they charge him, and the troubles occasioned by him between Christian princes, they accuse him of so many other things that he is quite undone.'[2]

But Wolsey had not yet given up hope of regaining Henry's favour. A decade earlier, when he had been at the height of his influence, he had shrewdly observed that men never voluntarily surrender power, and this maxim still held true. In plotting to claw back authority, he relied upon the fact that his royal master clearly harboured a lingering regard for him, and he was determined to exploit this. On 22 October, Wolsey was offered the choice of answering to the king or parliament. Without hesitation, he chose the former. The fact that he had been given a choice at all is an indication of Henry's reluctance to destroy his faithful servant. After all, Wolsey had encompassed an exceptional range of talents and there was no obvious candidate to replace him. The king was reported as saying that the cardinal was more able to manage his business than any of his rivals who remained in power.

Nevertheless, the prospects for a return to his former authority looked bleak. When Wolsey left his grand London residence, York Place, and climbed into a waiting barge, crowds gathered in expectation of seeing him conveyed to the Tower, rather than to his house in Esher. As he was rowed westwards, humiliated, away from London, he was surprised by an unexpected demonstration of his royal master's favour. At Putney, his barge was overtaken by Henry Norris, who according to Cavendish presented Wolsey with Henry's ring and an assurance that: 'although the King hath dealt with you unkindly as ye suppose, he saith that it is for no displeasure that he beareth you, but only to satisfy more the minds of some (which he knoweth be not your friends) than for any indignation. And also ye know right well that he is able to recompense you with twice as much as your goods amounteth unto. And all this he bade me that I should show you.' Norris ended by urging the cardinal to 'take patience . . . I trust to see you in better estate than ever ye were'.[3] Overcome with relief and gratitude, Wolsey knelt in the mud to thank him for such joyful tidings. He then gave Norris two gifts for his royal master: his cross and his fool, Patch, whom the king had long admired. According to Cavendish, Patch fell into 'such a rage when he saw that he must needs depart from my lord' that it took six yeoman to carry him away.

This incident reveals much about Henry's apparently contradictory attitude towards Wolsey. On the one hand, he was content to see his former chief minister suffer the humiliation and disgrace of being thrown out of office. But on the other, he clearly still cherished enough affection for Wolsey to offer some comfort in his hour of need. The king's reassurance was no doubt sincerely made. He might have proven to be easily manipulated by Wolsey's enemies (just as he had been by Wolsey himself), but he had not forgotten the qualities that had endeared the cardinal to him for all those years. Neither had he overlooked Wolsey's steadfast and loyal service. But Henry knew that it was no longer possible to show favour to both the Boleyns and Wolsey. He had had to make a choice – in public, at least. In private, it was a different matter.

On 1 November, Wolsey received another sign of Henry's favour when Sir John Russell travelled to Esher. The king, anxious to avoid angering Lady Anne, had instructed Russell to make his visit at a time when few others would be abroad, and it was midnight when Sir John arrived. According to Cavendish, who was there at the time, Russell carried his master's reassurance that 'the king commendeth him unto you, and delivered him a great ring of gold with a turquoise for a token, and willed you to be of good cheer, who loves you as well as ever he did'.[4] Shortly afterwards, the cardinal was delighted by the arrival of 'plenty of household stuff, vessel and plate and of all things necessary'.[5]

Although in public, Henry spurned his fallen minister in order to please Anne, it is clear that in private he missed the cardinal desperately and was grieved at having brought him so low. This episode is also proof of Russell's loyalty and discretion, both towards his royal master and Wolsey. His commitment to the latter would prove costly. Meanwhile, Henry's plan to keep his support for Wolsey hidden soon proved hopelessly naïve. Despite his discretion, word swiftly got out that his ousted chief minister had been forgiven. Du Bellay even speculated: 'It is not improbable that he may regain his authority.'[6]

Wolsey had an even more valuable ally in his campaign to win back Henry's favour. Thomas Cromwell was an exceptionally talented young lawyer who had been in the cardinal's service for several years. A self-confessed 'ruffian' in his youth, Cromwell was, like his patron, of very humble origins. His father had been a black-smith and brewer, among various other trades, and Thomas had escaped the family home in Putney at a very young age to seek his fortune abroad. After serving as a mercenary in the French army, he had entered the household of a wealthy Florentine merchant and gained both experience and contacts during the years that he spent there. In 1513, Cromwell had eventually returned to England, via a spell in the trading cities of the Netherlands, by which time he was approaching his thirtieth year. His years abroad had given him an education that far excelled anything he could have hoped for in London. As well as gaining invaluable experience in trade, he had absorbed the culture of Renaissance Italy, explored the writings of ancient and contemporary scholars, and witnessed first-hand the stirrings of religious dissent that would soon shake Catholic Europe to its core.

Cromwell rapidly established himself back in London. Soon after arriving, he married a wealthy widow, Elizabeth Williams, and she bore him a son and two daughters during the years that followed. Meanwhile, Cromwell set about building up several successful busi-nesses. Drawing on the contacts he had made abroad, he soon became a prosperous merchant, as well as a money-lender, property owner and lawyer. Cromwell gained most renown in the latter profession, and it probably brought him to the attention of the cardinal. 'Such was the activity and forward ripeness of nature in him, so pregnant in wit, and so ready he was, in judgement discreet, in tongue eloquent, in service faithful, in stomach courageous, in his pen active, that being conversant in the sight of men, he could not long be unespied.'[7] Such was the judgement on Cromwell delivered by the Protestant martyrologist John Foxe. Although he was bound to extol the virtues of a man who would go on to become the architect of the English reformation, his account was not exaggerated.

It is not clear when Wolsey first enlisted Cromwell's services, but there is a general consensus that they had become acquainted by 1516. Cromwell evidently impressed the cardinal because, by 1519, he was a member of his council and soon rose to become one of his most trusted servants. Wolsey once wrote to express his gratitude for Cromwell's 'good, sad, discreet advice and counsel'.[8] Eustace Chapuys took a dim view of Wolsey's new protégé, but grudgingly admitted that he had proved his 'vigilance and diligence, his ability and promptitude, both in evil and good'.[9] The years that followed proved the truth of his statement. Cromwell served Wolsey with such diligence and commitment that he became as indispensable to the cardinal as the latter was to the king.

In stark contrast to the majority of Wolsey's sizeable household, Cromwell had stood by his patron when he had been thrown out of office and banished to Esher. It was there that he was observed weeping by George Cavendish. His tears may have been for his two young daughters, who had died of the sweating sickness just a few weeks before. His wife, too, had perished in the first bout of the epidemic that had killed William Compton and Henry Carey. But Cromwell was also bemoaning his 'unhappy adventure' at being dealt such a miserable reward for his years of 'true and diligent service' to Wolsey. As the cardinal's closest adviser, he knew that his reputation was inextricably bound with that of his master and, as he lamented to Cavendish, 'An evil name once gotten will not lightly be put away.'[10]

But Cromwell was a resourceful man and, having dried his tears, declared: 'I do intend (God willing) this afternoon, when my lord hath dined, to ride to London and so to the Court, where I will either make or mar.'[11] Cromwell's prospects did not look promising. Gifted lawyer he might be, but he was severely hampered by his lack of birth and connections. Even if he managed to secure an audience with the king, his chances of winning Henry's forgiveness for Wolsey when the latter had so many powerful enemies speaking the contrary must have seemed remote indeed.

Cromwell was resolved to save his patron from ruin, however, and in the process to ingratiate himself with the king. With help from an unlikely source, the Duke of Norfolk, he therefore secured himself a place in the parliament that opened on 3 November. Sir Thomas More set the scene by crowing about 'the great weather which is of late fallen', and asserted: 'Amongst a great flock of sheep some be rotten and faulty, which the good shepherd sendeth from the good sheep.' He went on to criticise all those men who had thought that the king 'had no wit to perceive his [Wolsey's] crafty doing . . . for his grace's sight was so quick and penetrable that he saw him, yea, and saw through him, both within and without'.[12]

Wolsey's loss had been More's gain, for he had succeeded him as Lord Chancellor, and had received the Great Seal at Henry's hands on 25 October. The letter that he had written to his friend Erasmus upon receiving this honour would prove prescient. 'I am loyal to my king, as loyal as anyone on earth can be,' he vowed. 'My inability to approve of his divorce and to argue for it in public in no way detracts from the essential loyalty I feel for him, a loyalty that will keep me from ever saying a public word in opposition to him.'[13] Although this appeared to be a firm avowal of More's loyalty to Henry, the strength of his opposition to the annulment that it hints at would become ever more apparent in the years to come.

But for now, More was higher in Henry's esteem than he had ever been. The Venetian envoy reported that he was 'in great favour with the King', and More's son-in-law William Roper describes the closeness that existed between the two men. 'For the pleasure he [Henry] took in his company, would his grace suddenly sometimes come home to his house in Chelsea, to be merry with him; whither on a time, unlooked for, he came to dinner to him; and after dinner, in a fair garden of his, walked with him by the space of an hour, holding his arm about his neck . . . as I never had seen him to do to any other except Cardinal Wolsey, whom I saw his grace once walk with, arm in arm.' When Roper told his father-in-law how fortunate he was to enjoy 'such entire favour', More replied with typical sanguinity: 'I find his grace my very good lord indeed, and I believe he doth as singularly favour me as any subject within this realm. Howbeit, son Roper, I may tell thee I have no cause to be proud thereof, for if my head could win him a castle in France . . . it should not fail to go.'[14]

If More was shrewd enough to realise that the king's favour was no guarantee of security, then he also chafed against his master's increasingly demanding behaviour. Roper claimed: 'He could not once in a month get leave to go home to his wife and children, whose company he most desired, and to be absent from the court two days together but that he should be thither sent for again.' According to his account, More resented this 'restraint of his liberty' and therefore began to suppress the 'pleasant disposition' that had so appealed to Henry, and instead 'to dissemble his nature, and so by little and little from his former accustomed mirth to disuse himself' so that he was 'no more so ordinarily sent for'.[15]

Given how greatly More had desired the king's favour, Roper's account seems unlikely. True, he was not blinded by ambition and appreciated the dangers, as well as the advantages, that influence could bring, but nothing in his subsequent actions suggests reluctance to be among Henry's circle of intimates. His hours of service became increasingly lengthy, and he would often attend his royal master after supper, discussing affairs of state with him until long into the night. As well as advancing More in Henry's favour, these late-night meetings had another effect. They provided the king with a much more detailed knowledge of state business than Wolsey had deemed necessary (or desirable) to afford him. Thanks to More, Henry was therefore at last beginning to fulfil his proper kingly duties.

Having known the king since he was a boy, More had learned how to handle him. He once let his rival Cromwell in on the secret: 'You shall, in your counsel-giving unto his grace, ever tell him what he ought to do, but never what he is able to do . . . For if [a] Lion knew his own strength, hard were it for any man to rule him.'[16] The shrewd courtier therefore cast himself and Henry's other advisers in the role of lion-tamers: they knew that their master was capable of destroying everything around him, so kept him in check by reminding him of the limits of his power. More's analogy also neatly encapsulates the extreme danger in which Henry's men lived. Their master was as volatile and deadly as a caged beast.

Wolsey's analysis of the king's character had been along similar lines. But while More presented Henry as a lion, the cardinal likened him more to a mule. The stubbornness that he had displayed in pursuing the annulment – against the wishes of his kingdom, his advisers and most of Catholic Europe – lay at the heart of Henry's being. It had been fostered during his indulged upbringing, and echoes of the spoilt child at Eltham can be clearly heard in his uncompromising attitude as king. Henry liked to win, and if matters went against him, those in attendance would feel the force of his petulant temper. A group of visiting Italian bankers had experienced this early in the reign when they had roundly beaten the king at a game of dice. In a fury, Henry had loudly accused them of cheating and had thrown them out of court.

Wolsey had also been on the brunt of his royal master's temper many times, and had willingly played the part of an indulgent parent to this petulant man-child. 'He is a prince of royal [disposition], and hath a princely heart,' he told the constable of the Tower, Sir William Kingston, 'and rather than he will either miss or want any part of his will or appetite, he will put the loss of one half of his realm in danger. For I assure you I have often kneeled before him in his privy chamber on my knees the space of an hour or two to persuade him from his will and appetite; but I could never bring to pass to dissuade him therefrom.' He ended by urging Kingston: 'If it chance hereafter you to be one of his privy council . . . I warn you to be well advised and assured what matter you put in his head; for ye shall never pull it out again.'[17]

A month after parliament opened, a petition was presented to the king that listed forty-four articles against the fallen cardinal. This had been drawn up by Norfolk and his associates, but Thomas More's name was at the top of the list of signatories. The petition repeated the earlier set of Wolsey's alleged faults, but with new embellishments, all of which attested to his abuse of power both in the Church and state. One of the more outlandish was that Wolsey had approached the king while suffering from 'the foul and contagious disease of the great pox . . . whispering in your ear and blowing on your most noble grace with his perilous and infected breath'.[18] This was a deliberate attempt to play on Henry's rampant hypochondria, which was well known throughout the court.

As well as spending hours closeted away with his physicians and apothecaries, the king also devised numerous remedies both for himself and his courtiers. In 1528, Wolsey's assiduous but anxious secretary Sir Brian Tuke confided to his master that he was suffering from a painful kidney complaint. Wolsey, who was always keen to flatter his royal master, sought his advice. But Henry either misheard or misunderstood the nature of Tuke's complaint, because when the latter next sought an audience, he 'began to tell me of a medicine for a tumour in the testicles'. Tuke tried to explain that the pain was not there but in his kidney, but Henry would not listen and insisted upon showing the hapless secretary his remedies.

A man so obsessed with health can only have been appalled by the allegations against Wolsey. The latter's enemies had made sure of their case, which they knew had to be personal as well as political in order to secure the king's assent. The cardinal had been obliged to endorse the list with his signature, perhaps under threat of further action against him. He may also have calculated that a humble submission was likely to work a positive effect on Henry, given that he had already shown signs of his abiding affection towards his former chief minister. Thanks to his strategy, and in particular to the 'witty persuasions' of his protégé Cromwell, by the time that parliament was adjourned on 17 December, there had been no act of attainder and Wolsey still retained his status as Archbishop of York and cardinal.[19] The latter afforded him protection against being tried for treason, so this was a victory of sorts.

During the weeks that followed, Cromwell increasingly adopted the role of intermediary between Wolsey and the king, travelling between Esher and the court as he relayed messages and petitions. He could rely upon precious few allies, even though a number of Wolsey's former protégés now served in the royal household. Sir Thomas Heneage had been as quick as Gardiner to disassociate himself from his former master. When Wolsey sought his help, he told him to 'content yourself with that you have . . . [for] the king will be good and gracious to your Grace'. Meanwhile, Wolsey's letters to Gardiner, begging for his 'friendly mediation', went unanswered.[20] By contrast, Sir Richard Page, who had begun his career in Wolsey's service before being appointed a gentleman of the privy chamber in 1516, proved more willing to collaborate with Cromwell, as did Sir John Russell.

Wolsey tried to cultivate another, more unlikely intermediary, with Cromwell's help. As the brother of the king's inamorata, George Boleyn was enjoying his moment in the sun. A charming, self-seeking and ruthless young man, he had all the attributes of a seasoned courtier, and thanks largely to his sister's influence he was now carving out a very lucrative career for himself. In 1525 he was appointed a gentleman of the privy chamber. Although Wolsey ousted him from that position six months later, he was not without a position for long. In 1528 he was appointed esquire of the body and master of the king's buckhounds, and the following year he was given the courtesy title of Viscount Rochford when his father was made Earl of Wiltshire and Earl of Ormond. Henry also knighted him in 1529 and, despite George's lack of diplomatic experience, sent him to France as ambassador. There were soon complaints that he was behaving arrogantly and ignoring diplomatic etiquette, but the king turned a blind eye. Neither did he heed the rumours that Boleyn was homosexual. This was considered sinful in the extreme and, if proved, would have carried a heavy penalty. But Henry was so besotted with George's sister that he was prepared to overlook any hints of transgression on the part of her brother.

At the height of his powers, Wolsey had disliked George as much as the other Boleyns, but now the wheel of fortune had turned and he urged Cromwell to buy his favour with a gift of lands from the bishopric of Winchester. George accepted the gift but had no intention of promoting Wolsey's interests. He did, though, form an alliance of sorts with Cromwell. Despite their former hostility, the pair were both genuinely committed to the cause of reform. Like his father and sister, George was described as a 'Lutheran' by Chapuys – with some justification. He and Cromwell were also united by the common aim of paving the way for George's sister to take the throne, so for a time they became allies. But it was a pragmatic rather than a personal arrangement, and there was clearly no love lost between the two men.

For all the contacts at court whom Wolsey tried to cultivate, he knew that his most persuasive advocate was Cromwell himself. Even Chapuys, who had no liking for either of the two men, admitted: 'At his master's fall he [Cromwell] behaved very well towards him.'[21] In consistently defending his fallen patron, Cromwell not only softened Henry's mind towards Wolsey but also impressed him with his own loyalty. Cromwell's quick-wittedness and obvious ability also attracted the king. Self-taught rather than formally educated, he was more intelligent and articulate than most of the nobly born members of court, and he soon gained renown as an orator. But his lack of refinement showed in what one observer described as a 'rough' style of management. While this upset his noble rivals, his direct and bullish approach appealed to a king who had spent so much of his life surrounded by sycophants and flatterers.[22]

Cromwell suspected, though, that an outspoken commoner like himself could not be anything other than a passing indulgence for Henry, and his ambitions at court were far longer term. He therefore worked hard to adopt the courtly refinements that Henry expected in his favourites and confidants. Although he once declared that 'he would not, for anything in this world, be held as a liar or dissembler', he soon learned the arts of diplomacy and duplicity that were the mainstay of court.[23] Realising that Henry liked men who shared his leisure pursuits, Cromwell began to hunt and hawk, and also became adept with a longbow. He used such pastimes to conduct informal business with other members of the court too. Chapuys often reported that Cromwell had invited him to go hunting, and that he liked to watch his hawks fly in the evenings after dinner.

Cromwell may have been lowly born compared to the other men at Henry's court, but his cosmopolitan upbringing had also given him an edge over them. The traditional xenophobia espoused by the warlike members of the king's council – men such as the dukes of Suffolk and Norfolk – often blinded them to the advantages that could be gained from cordial relations with England's continental rivals. Having spent the majority of his youth in France, Italy and the Netherlands, Cromwell shared none of their prejudice, and instead actively promoted the exchange of goods and ideas with overseas lands. Cromwell's stance was unusual enough for the French ambassador to remark upon in assessing the reasons for his success in Henry's service, claiming that he 'shows himself willing to do justice, especially to foreigners'.[24]

All of these qualities set Cromwell apart from the men who surrounded Henry. He had the same distinctiveness that had been part of Wolsey's appeal. As time wore on and Henry came to miss his loyal and able chief minister, he increasingly saw Cromwell as a possible replacement. But, given Wolsey's fate, Cromwell had to demonstrate that he was more than a mere clone of his former patron. The surest means of doing so was to succeed where the cardinal had failed. Cromwell therefore began to employ his considerable legal talents in the king's Great Matter. In so doing, he was not only enhancing his esteem with Henry, but improving his relations with his 'concubine', Lady Anne.

Cromwell knew that his credit with Anne was not high, thanks to his constant championing of Wolsey's cause. She had already lashed out at Sir John Russell for commending Wolsey to the king, and had persuaded her royal suitor to recall Russell from a diplomatic mission to France in May 1529. Anne was even 'irritated' with her uncle, the Duke of Norfolk, 'because he had not done as much against him [Wolsey] as he might'. Cromwell himself admitted: 'None dares speak to the King on his [Wolsey's] part for fear of Madame Anne's displeasure.'[25] Although he was unlikely to have had a high opinion of the woman who had been the chief architect of his patron's demise, Cromwell knew that his court career rested as much upon securing her favour as Henry's.

If Wolsey had been prepared to live out his days in quiet obscurity, things might have turned out very differently. But having enjoyed the experience of being all-powerful for almost twenty years, he was unable to relinquish it. The Imperial ambassador Mendoza had realised this when he had met the cardinal two years earlier, and had observed that he was 'too able and powerful to be suffered to live in retirement or even in disgrace'. Wolsey's enemies at court knew this too. As a result, according to Cavendish, the dukes of Norfolk and Suffolk, together with Anne Boleyn's brother George, conspired to make his life as miserable as possible: 'Daily they would send him some thing or do some thing against him wherein they thought that they might give him a cause of heaviness or lamentation.'[26]

The wily ambassador, Eustace Chapuys, had Thomas Howard's measure. After an evening as the duke's guest in 1529, he reported that he was sociable, even gregarious, but added the shrewd observation that this was always to a purpose, because the duke was driven by an insatiable appetite for power. Later that year, Norfolk sought to strengthen his hand through an audacious scheme to marry his son Henry, Earl of Surrey, to the king's daughter Mary. Appreciating the advantage that this would bring to her family, Anne Boleyn at first advanced the match. But she soon turned against it, perhaps because she wished to see Mary further ousted from the king's favour, and the idea came to nothing. Nevertheless, Norfolk had succeeded in bringing his son to the king's attention, and Henry would ask that he attend him on a number of important occasions during the years that followed.

Meanwhile, weighed down by his cares, Wolsey fell prey to illness in late December 1529. He wrote to his faithful protégé Cromwell that he was 'By the space of three hours as one that should have died.'[27] How sick Wolsey really was is not certain, but he was determined to make the most of this opportunity for courting the king's sympathy. In alarm, Henry sent Dr William Butts, who had entered royal service the previous year and had rapidly become the king's favourite physician, together with a ring as a token of his esteem.

William Butts would serve Henry and his family for almost twenty years. His first royal appointment was to the household of the king's daughter Mary, to whom his wife Margaret was a lady-in-waiting. Stubborn in his opinions and vociferous in arguments, Butts was not easy to get along with. But his straight-talking manner won Henry's respect, as did his skill in the physician's art. Butts was six years older than the king and had been born into royal service because his father had been an auditor of crown revenues. An exceptionally bright young man, he had gained a BA, MA and MD from Cambridge, and had been subsequently appointed Principal of St Mary's Hostel in the same city. As well as gaining a reputation as a gifted physician, he was also a committed humanist and was interested in the evangelical ideas that were sweeping across the Continent. They would soon ignite an all-consuming reformist zeal in the king's physician.

After examining the cardinal, Butts hastened in alarm to his royal master and warned him that Wolsey 'will be dead within these four days, if he receive no comfort from you shortly, and Mistress Anne'. Henry was horrified and immediately abandoned his customary pretence of caring nothing for his old servant. 'God forbid that he should die,' he replied. 'I pray you, good Master Butts, go again unto him, and do your cure upon him; for I would not lose him for twenty thousand pounds.'[28] He sent another ring as a further assurance of his goodwill, and even persuaded Lady Anne to enclose a token for his comfort. It was with immense relief that Henry learned of his recovery shortly afterwards. The news was a good deal less welcome to Anne, who quickly resumed her former hostility towards the cardinal.

Wolsey had been forbidden to come within seven miles of the court, but in early 1530 he moved a little closer, taking up residence at Richmond. He subsequently began courting both former supporters and enemies with gifts and promises as a means of paving his way back to court. He also relied on the few allies who had remained loyal to him. These included Sir John Russell, who seemed genuinely committed to Wolsey's cause. When he publicly defended him in February, Anne was so furious that she refused to speak to him for a month. Russell's bravery prompted her uncle Norfolk to ask whether he really thought the cardinal stood a chance of returning to favour. Russell replied that such was Wolsey's ambition and courage that he would not fail if he saw an opportunity. When the duke heard this, he was so incensed that he threatened to eat Wolsey alive.

Russell's prediction seemed to be coming true in February, when events turned more decisively in Wolsey's favour. On the second of the month, Henry sent the cardinal his furniture, and on the twelfth he at last gave him a full, public pardon. Two days later, he was formally restored to the archbishopric of York, with all of its possessions except York Place. Although Wolsey was subsequently obliged to surrender control of the see of Winchester and the abbey of St Albans, he received a considerable financial compensation in return, together with a sizeable pension and the loan of £1,000 for his northward progress. In addition, Henry granted him around £9,500 worth of plate, 'divers apparel of household', such as wall hangings, bedding and napery, eighty horses, six mules, and a wide selection of meat, fish and other victuals.[29] The king's generosity made Wolsey wealthier than the Duke of Norfolk, which is proof of where Henry's favour lay between these two rivals. Little wonder that not long afterwards, the cardinal schemed 'to make sedition between him [Henry] and my lord of Norfolk'.[30]

Wolsey largely owed his pardon to his protégé Cromwell, who

had been working tirelessly on his behalf. The pardon had bolstered Cromwell's own position too. On the same day that it was issued, his friend Stephen Vaughan wrote to congratulate him and was in no doubt that 'You now sail in a sure haven.'[31] The Duke of Norfolk was a good deal less pleased by the news of Wolsey's reprieve. He resolved to get the cardinal well away from court, and petitioned the king to order him to visit his diocese of York. When Henry agreed, Norfolk, fearing that he might change his mind, sent a message to Wolsey at once, instructing him to depart immediately.

But the wily cardinal knew his royal master well enough to cherish hopes of a return to power. His enemies might have succeeded in having him ousted because of his failure to secure the annulment, but they had proved no more effective than he at untangling the complex web of diplomatic negotiations. Until they did, there remained the possibility – likelihood, even – that Henry would recall his old chief adviser and hand him the reins of power once more. Little wonder that Wolsey proved reluctant to accede to Norfolk's urgings and eked out the delay in his departure for six weeks, pleading shortage of money, among other excuses. With every day that passed, he no doubt hoped to receive a message from the king, summoning him back to his presence. Instead, Henry sent the cardinal some attendants to help him pack. Only when they arrived on 28 March did Wolsey finally accept defeat and begin to make preparations. But when he had still not departed for York a week later, the Duke of Norfolk flew into a rage and sent the following message: 'Show him that if he go not away shortly, I will, rather [than that] he should tarry still, tear him with my teeth!'[32]

In Wolsey's absence, Henry threw all of the most trusted men who remained at court behind his Great Matter. In 1530, he dispatched Thomas Boleyn on a tour of Germany, France and Italy in order to canvass academic opinion on the annulment. Boleyn would stop at nothing to see his daughter crowned. During the tour, he encountered the Emperor Charles V at Bologna. Undeterred by the fact that the emperor had just been crowned by Pope Clement (a largely symbolic gesture given that Charles had inherited the empire eleven years earlier), Boleyn urged him to support Henry's divorce from his aunt. But Charles knew how much Boleyn stood to gain from the matter and abruptly told him 'that he [Boleyn] was not to be believed in this case, as he was a party'.[33] Not long afterwards, Boleyn met the Pope himself but refused to pay him the accustomed reverence of kissing his toe. To insult the head of the Roman Catholic Church in this way when the King of England still sought his assistance was highly risky. It has been taken as a testimony to Boleyn's anti-clericalist stance, but also betrays his arrogant belief that Henry's trust in him was unshakeable.

The void left by Wolsey's departure had also been filled by his rival, Sir Nicholas Carew. The Master of the Horse had acquitted himself well during his embassy to Bologna towards the end of the previous year, and had secured Charles V's ratification of the Cambrai treaty on 8 December. The emperor had been so impressed by Carew that when the latter left Bologna in February 1530, Charles sent him on his way with a gold chain worth 2,000 ducats. Word reached Henry's ears that Carew had 'managed the King's business here with so much prudence and dexterity, that he leaves with the greatest satisfaction to the Emperor and the Pope'.[34]

Thanks to Carew's efforts, his royal master enjoyed a renewed sense of optimism and decided to dispatch a further embassy. But while Carew had grasped the opportunity for diplomatic glory with alacrity, his own feelings about the annulment were rather more lukewarm. A religious conservative, he had strong ties of loyalty to both Catherine of Aragon and her daughter Mary, as did his wife. Lady Carew was in regular contact with the princess and urged her to comply with her father's wishes so as not to harm her standing at court. Chapuys was certainly convinced that Carew could be relied upon to support Catherine of Aragon, and he reported as much to the emperor. When Sir Nicholas was chosen to accompany the king on a visit to France in 1532 to secure Francis's support for the annulment, he confided to the Imperial ambassador that he hoped the mission would fail. If the king knew of Carew's true feelings, he was content to turn a blind eye – for now at least – and he continued to employ him on diplomatic missions.

Another man who rose to prominence at around this time was Thomas Wriothesley, who had been employed by Cromwell as a secretary since 1524, at the age of nineteen. This gifted young man, who was described by one contemporary as 'one of the wisest men in the kingdom', had benefited from an excellent education, which included a stint at St Paul's School, London, with his childhood friend John Leland and also William Paget, who would enter Henry's service too.[35] Leland seems to have been particularly impressed by him and later wrote a tribute to his qualities of mind, integrity, and handsome appearance. With flame-red hair and piercing blue eyes, Wriothesley won widespread praise for his looks. In around 1522, he proceeded to Trinity Hall, Cambridge, where Paget was again a fellow student, and his teacher in civil law was Stephen Gardiner. But Wriothesley had abandoned his studies in pursuit of a career at court.

It had proved a wise move. By 1530, he had secured enough of the king's trust to be employed as his messenger. In May that year, he was appointed joint clerk of the signet under Gardiner and remained in that post for a decade, during which time he also continued to serve Cromwell. Wriothesley's ability to serve opposing masters would mark the remainder of his career. He undertook a wide range of administrative business and became known as an effective middleman for a number of different patrons. 'He was an earnest follower of whatsoever he took in hand,' observed a contemporary, 'and very seldom did miss where either wit or travail were able to bring his purpose to pass.'[36] But if Wriothesley's loyalty to others was flexible, he was always careful to demonstrate his unswerving commitment to his royal master. His strategy soon paid dividends, for it was reported that 'the King was very fond of him'.[37]

In April 1530, Wolsey finally set off for his diocese in York, but made such a slow and stately progress that he did not reach Cawood Castle, a few miles south of the city, until June. On the way, he took care to court popularity by settling quarrels among the local gentry and confirming hundreds of children. Thanks to his generous allowance from the king, Wolsey was able to travel in some style, and it was reported that 'some men thought he was of as good courage as in times past and wanted no impediment but lack of authority'. But his constant theme in the letters that he wrote to Henry and Cromwell was his insufficient means, 'not knowing where to be succoured or relieved, but only at your Highness' most merciful and charitable hands'.[38]

Embattled and distant from court though he was, Wolsey's enemies could not take anything for granted. They were greatly alarmed when the king was reported as saying that in managing business the cardinal was a better man than any of them. This prompted them to step up their efforts to get rid of him for good. They therefore spread rumours that Wolsey was not content to limit himself to his diocesan affairs in York but had begun closet negotiations with both Charles V and Francis I in a last-ditch attempt to secure their support for an annulment. They also claimed that Wolsey was planning to put in place an interdict which would arouse so much resentment against royal policy that he himself would be the only one capable of dealing with it. Although there is reliable evidence that Wolsey had been in contact with foreign powers, and was certainly cunning enough to have devised such an interdict, it lacked his customary subtlety. The fact that Norfolk was going about reporting that the cardinal was plotting to recover his authority suggests that he had embellished the facts. The duke was, as Chapuys once observed, 'a bad dissembler'.[39]

Moreover, there is stronger evidence to suggest that Wolsey was quietly working *against* the annulment. It had been the cause of all the troubles in his relationship with Henry, so perhaps he believed that if the scheme was abandoned, it would be the surest means of securing his return to power. According to Chapuys, Wolsey sent daily messages 'to inquire how the queen's cause is progressing and why it is not more energetically pushed'.[40] He was playing a dangerous game, but had been bolstered by the widespread demonstrations of support for Catherine that he had witnessed during his slow progress north. He therefore firmly believed that the only way to restore all matters to their rightful order was for his royal master to stay true to his queen.

On 10 October 1530, Wolsey's former pupil and ally, Thomas Grey, Marquess of Dorset, died. Despite his long-standing affiliation to the cardinal, he had added his signature to the articles that condemned him. But then, Dorset's steadfast loyalty to the king had always overridden all other concerns. When he had been called to sit in judgment on Buckingham, he had not hesitated, even though his mother had been married to the duke's brother. In 1529, he had acted as a principal witness in the king's annulment proceedings, testifying that Catherine's marriage to Arthur had been consummated. His appointment to Princess Mary's household had necessitated prolonged periods of absence from court during the intervening years, but even when he had not been present himself, he had entertained the king by maintaining a troupe of actors at the royal palaces. A traditional magnate in every other sense, Dorset had never wielded his considerable landed and military resources to threaten or influence his sovereign. If his temper had occasionally landed him in trouble, then his unquestioned fidelity to Henry had always ensured that he had emerged unscathed.

Although he had arguably performed equally loyal service to the king, Wolsey was not so fortunate. In the end, it was the Pope who set the seal on his doom. On 23 October, Henry received news of an intercepted papal brief prohibiting his remarriage while the legal wranglings continued and ordering him to dismiss Lady Anne from court. The finger of blame was immediately pointed at Wolsey, not least because the French, fearing an Anglo–Imperial alliance, revealed to someone at court (possibly Anne Boleyn or her uncle Norfolk) that the cardinal had been dealing with foreign powers.

Armed with this information, the duke went at once to his royal master and convinced him that the intercepted letter had contained 'presumptuous sinister practices made to the court of Rome for restoring him to his former estate and dignity'.[41] This was a fatally decisive moment in Henry's relationship with the cardinal. Ever since Wolsey's dismissal from court, Henry had vacillated between anger and affection towards his former minister, and the prospect of his return to power had never gone away. But the poison dripped into his ears by the Duke of Norfolk had finally persuaded Henry to abandon Wolsey once and for all. On 1 November, he dispatched Walter Walsh, son of the king's former mistress Bessie Blount and now a gentleman of the privy chamber, to arrest the cardinal on a charge of high treason. Three days later, Walsh arrived at Cawood with the Earl of Northumberland and took Wolsey into custody. He reacted with characteristic sang-froid. According to Edward Hall, he upheld his dignity as cardinal but, ever the loyal servant, bowed to his royal master's authority.

Wolsey must have known that this time there was little hope of a reprieve. Henry seemed to have forsaken him, and even members of his own household had apparently betrayed him. Giovanni Passano, an envoy of Francis I, reported: 'The King says he has intrigued against them, both in and out of the kingdom, and has told me where and how, and that one and perhaps more of his servants have discovered it, and accused him.'[42] Even the French king himself, although he denied any knowledge of treachery on the cardinal's part, remarked that 'he thought ever that so pompous and ambitious a heart, sprung out of so vile a stock, would once show forth the baseness of his nature, and most commonly against Him that hath raised him from low degree to high dignity'.[43] This may have proved more damning than any other accusation levelled against the cardinal, and it made his royal master feel conflicted. Henry had been content to promote a man of such lowly birth as Wolsey in the face of criticism from his court and council, but to have it remarked upon in so scornful a manner by his chief rival was something he could not ignore.

On 6 November, Wolsey bade his household an emotional farewell and embarked upon the long journey south. With every mile that passed, he knew that he might be moving closer towards a traitor's death. Yet even now he had cause to hope because Henry had ordered that the cardinal be shown every courtesy while in captivity. The king had also made it clear that his former favourite would be afforded a fair trial. Wolsey knew that if he could secure an audience with Henry, then he might work his old charm. He therefore begged: 'That I may answer unto my accusers before the King's majesty [so] that he should hear it himself in proper person.' The cardinal knew, though, that Norfolk would do his utmost to prevent this. 'I fear me that they do intend rather to dispatch me than [that] I should come before him in his presence,' he confided to an attendant, 'for they be well assured and very certain that my truth should vanquish their untruth and surmised accusations, which is the special cause that moveth me so earnestly to desire to make my answer before the King's majesty.'[44]

Henry sent Wolsey an assurance of his continued favour and expressed his confidence that he would be able to clear his name. He even told the cardinal that he would preside over his trial in person, and that he had sent a trusted servant, Sir William Kingston, to escort him on the last stage of his journey. But any comfort that Wolsey might have derived from this was weakened by the knowledge that Kingston was, among other things, constable of the Tower. Worse still, the king had already started to value and seize Wolsey's goods and property.

In the event, though, it was Wolsey's heavenly master, not his earthly one, who decided his fate. By the time that Wolsey reached the Earl of Shrewsbury's house at Sheffield Park on 8 November, he had fallen gravely ill with dysentery. Tormented by fear and grief, he lay in a sorrowful state for two weeks, his physical condition deteriorating all the time. Shrewsbury did his best to offer comfort. 'Without fail the king favoureth you much more, and beareth towards you a secret special favour, far otherwise than ye do take it,' he assured Wolsey. The cardinal was not convinced, but gave a philosophical answer: 'As God will, so be it. I am subject to fortune, and to fortune I submit myself.'[45]

On 22 November, as Henry had promised, Sir William Kingston arrived with twenty-four men to convey Wolsey to the Tower. He offered the same assurances as Shrewsbury had conveyed, telling the cardinal that the king 'beareth you as much good will and favour as ever he did; and willeth you to be of good cheer'. He then confided to Wolsey that Henry believed none of the charges against his former favourite, but 'to avoid all suspect [suspicion] of partiality [he] can do no less at the least than to send for you to your trial, mistrusting nothing your truth and wisdom, but that ye shall be able to acquit yourself against all complaints and accusations exhibited against you'.[46]

But the cardinal knew his royal master better than to derive complete assurance from these 'comfortable words', which he judged 'be but for a purpose to bring me into a fool's paradise.' 'I know what is provided for me,' he added mournfully. Wolsey, more than most, knew how fickle Henry could be, having witnessed his volteface over the purge of the minions. Only by petitioning his master in person could he hope for a genuine reprieve. But by now, he was so ill that he could not travel for two days. On the night of 26 November, barely able to stay astride his faithful mule, he reached Leicester Abbey. The monks had assembled to greet him, and Wolsey weakly declared: 'Father abbot I am come hither to leave my bones among you.'[47]

Early in the morning of 29 November, Wolsey ate a little of the chicken broth that had been brought to him. Then, recalling that it was St Andrew's eve, a fast day, he refused to eat any more. Sensing that his end was near, he begged 'with all my heart, to have me most humbly commended unto his royal majesty; beseeching him in my behalf to call to his most gracious remembrance all matters proceeding between him and me from the beginning of the world unto this day'. He then made his confession before uttering his final lament: 'I see the matter against me how it is framed, but if I had served God as diligently as I have done the king he would not have given me over in my grey hairs.' His last thoughts were of Henry, as he told Kingston to advise the king to repress the new Lutheran heresy that was rapidly taking hold across the Continent. Incapable of further speech, he fell into a coma. The abbot was called to give him the last rites, and Wolsey died at eight o'clock that morning.[48]

Although he had done his utmost to court popularity during his sojourn in the north, Wolsey's enemies were swift to blacken his reputation. There was immediately talk of suicide, which was considered a great sin in those times, as Wriothesley recorded in his chronicle: 'Some reckon he killed himself with purgations.'[49] But there is no evidence to support the notion that Wolsey had evaded his royal master's justice in this way. He was clearly a very sick man by the time he reached Leicester – and, in his late fifties, an elderly one by Tudor standards.

Back in London, George Boleyn commissioned a masque entitled 'Of the Cardinal's Going into Hell', which was performed before the court at Greenwich. This set the tone for the rash of criticism that soon appeared in print. William Tyndale went so far as to claim that the cardinal had used necromancy to bewitch the king, and had tightened his grip on Henry by surrounding him with spies.[50] John Foxe, meanwhile, lambasted the 'ambitious pride and excessive worldly wealth of this one cardinal'.[51] Edward Hall was no less damning in his Chronicle, which first appeared in 1547. He scorned Wolsey as a deceiver, 'double both in speech and meaning . . . He was vicious of body and gave the clergy evil example.' Hall also claimed that the cardinal would 'promise much and perform little'.[52] This latter charge related entirely to Wolsey's failure to secure the king's divorce, which overshadowed all of his years of exceptional service, during which he had proved himself by far the most able minister that Henry had at his disposal.

Wolsey enjoyed no better press abroad. The Imperial ambassador Chapuys reported to Charles V: 'The cardinal of York died on St Andrew's Day about 40 miles from here, at a place where the last king Richard was defeated and killed. Both lie buried in the same church, which the people begin already to call "the Tyrants' grave".'[53]

Henry's own judgement of the man who had served him faithfully for so many years is harder to discern. On many occasions in the past, he had revealed a seemingly unshakeable affection for the cardinal. This had withstood all of the attempts of Wolsey's enemies, notably Anne Boleyn, to turn the king against him. The cardinal's death might be expected to have reignited Henry's sentimentality towards his old servant. But he made little public show of regret for his passing.

George Cavendish describes a meeting he had with the king shortly after his master's death. Henry had summoned him to Hampton Court, but when he arrived he found the king practising archery in the park. Not wishing to disturb him, Cavendish waited patiently until he was at liberty. 'At last the king came suddenly behind me, where I stood, and clapped his hand upon my shoulder,' he recalled. Henry then told Cavendish that he would speak to him after he had finished his game. Once he had loosed his final arrow, though, he strode away with one of his attendants and let the gate close behind him, shutting out the cardinal's servant. Cavendish turned to go, but not long afterwards Sir Henry Norris caught up with him and commanded him to attend the king in private.

When he entered the privy chamber, Cavendish saw the king, skulking behind a door and dressed 'in a night gown of russet velvet, furred with sables'. Henry dismissed his attendants so that he might converse with Cavendish alone. For more than an hour, he 'examined me of divers weighty matters, concerning my lord [Wolsey]', and vowed that he would gladly forfeit £20,000 if he could have him back again. But in the next breath, Henry asked Cavendish for the £1,500 that he had ordered Kingston to procure from the cardinal. At the end of this clandestine meeting, he urged Wolsey's servant: 'Let me alone, and keep this near secret between yourself and me, and let no man be privy thereof.' The king then promised to support Cavendish in his own household and offered his protection 'whensoever occasion should serve'.[54]

The exchange was as contradictory as Henry's attitude to Wolsey had been during his lifetime. His words betrayed a great deal of lingering affection towards the man who had been his mainstay for almost twenty years. But to the outside world, and Anne in particular, Henry was careful to show no regret. Edward Hall noted in his chronicle that Henry kept a magnificent Christmas that year, with all the usual 'rich masks and disports, and after that a great banquet'.[55]

Sometime later, a shockingly callous act by Henry suggests that Wolsey had ceased to matter to him at all. The cardinal was laid to rest 'very unostentatiously' in Leicester Abbey church. True to form, he had commissioned a lavish tomb from the Italian architect and sculptor Benedetto da Rovezzano, instructing him to make sure it surpassed Torrigiani's Westminster Abbey monument to Henry VIII's parents. But as a scandalised Italian envoy reported, the king ordered that the tomb be plundered for his own monument, and 'caused the Cardinal's arms to be erased from it'.[56] Not long afterwards, Henry ordered that all of Wolsey's goods be conveyed to his own palace. Had he known that even in death he would be subject to Henry's fickle will, Wolsey might have given a wry smile at what his gentleman usher called the 'inconstantness of princes' favour'.[57]

Wolsey's fall had been one of the earliest, and certainly the most dramatic, instances of Henry raising someone up and giving them all the advantages of his favour, only to later condemn them. The same pattern would be repeated with increasing frequency – and ferocity – during the years to come.

9

'The man who enjoys most credit with the king'

ARLY IN CROMWELL'S career in Wolsey's household, John Foxe had remarked: 'He seemed more mete for the king then for the Cardinal.'[1] Cromwell's rapid rise to power after his arrival at court in November 1529 certainly bears this out. Within the space of just one year, he was well on his way to replacing the fallen cardinal as chief minister to Henry VIII.

Contemporaries were quick to draw comparisons between these two low-born men. Eustace Chapuys reported on a conversation he had had with Cromwell, during which he had remarked: 'I had often regretted he [Cromwell] did not come under his master's knowledge and favour at the same time as the Cardinal, for being, as he was, a more able and talented man than the latter, and there being now so many opportunities to gain credit and power, he might undoubtedly have become a greater man than the Cardinal, while the King's affairs would have gone on much better . . . I told him that I considered the King, his master, very lucky in possessing such a man as himself under present circumstances and in these troubled times.'[2]

It is interesting to speculate whether the rise of two men of such humble origins as Cromwell and Wolsey in Henry's service was more than a coincidence. Did the king consciously choose them because of their backgrounds, rather than in spite of them? Henry had already shown himself to be comfortable around low-born men in his private domain, perhaps because of his deep-seated insecurity as a king with tainted royal blood. The same insecurity could have motivated him to appoint advisers whom he could trust not to conspire for his throne by virtue of the fact that there was not one drop of royal blood in their veins. Perhaps, too, there was an understanding between Henry and the men he promoted: they knew that just as he had raised them, so might he destroy them. Although this understanding was for the most part unspoken, the king did remind men such as Cromwell of it whenever he judged they had forgotten their place.

But there were also more positive reasons why Henry favoured Cromwell and Wolsey. Both men boasted significant skills that their noble colleagues lacked and benefited from a range of practical experience that proved useful in their royal service. They were also extremely industrious and had a staggering capacity for hard work – something that could not be said of most noble courtiers, whose positions had come to them by right. That the two men had even aspired to a career in the king's service proves that they had considerable vision and ambition. This same ambition was the driving force for both men once they had gained a foothold in Henry's service; it gave them the energy and motivation to continue striving for ever greater advancement, which in turn gave them an edge over their more complacent rivals.

Perhaps there was something here that Henry recognised in himself: as merely the spare heir for the first eleven years of his life, he too had been the rank outsider. And even though his rule was now uncontested, he never enjoyed the luxury of complacency. He was forever trying to prove himself through his feats of arms and displays of kingly magnificence. This formed a sharp contrast to the nobles with whom he was surrounded, whose natural sense of entitlement was irksome to Henry. It is to his credit that he overturned centuries of royal tradition and risked the scorn of his international rivals by making his court a meritocracy, which opened the way for men of genuine talent such as Cromwell and Wolsey.

Cromwell might have been a convenient replacement for Wolsey, but there was a significant difference in his relationship with the king. While Henry, in his younger days, had been content to leave even the weightiest of business to the cardinal, it was now clear that he intended to exercise a much tighter control. Partly this was because Henry no longer spent the majority of his time hunting and pursuing the other pleasurable pastimes of his youth, but it was also because Wolsey's failure to secure an annulment had forced him to play a more active role. 'I do not choose any one to have it in his power to command me, nor will I ever suffer it,' he told the Venetian ambassador.[3] It was a decisive moment for Henry in his relationship with the men who served him: never again would he be prepared to cede authority to the same extent as he had with Wolsey. He made it known that 'he had determined to take the management of his own affairs and had appointed several councillors'.[4]

Cromwell realised this and was always careful to let Henry decide upon matters – or at least to make him believe that he had. As he ruefully remarked to Chapuys: 'The king, my master, is a great king, but very fond of having things his own way.'[5] Towards the end of Cromwell's career, the French ambassador would reflect that the minister had been 'very assiduous in affairs . . . he does nothing without first consulting the King'.[6] The trouble was, Henry was far from consistent, and his actions did not always, or even often, derive from a clear political strategy. His capricious nature would become ever more prominent in the years to come, which made the task of anticipating the royal will fraught with danger. Moreover, it was not unusual for the king to change his mind without warning, and to lash out at those who had begun to enact what they believed was his final decision. This was the volatile and potentially deadly environment into which Cromwell now stepped.

It is not clear exactly when Thomas Cromwell formally entered the king's service. As early as May 1530, Henry's daughter Mary had sought his intercession with the king, assuring him: 'I am advertised that all such men shall first resort unto you to know the king my father's pleasure.'[7] In August, his former patron Wolsey had referred to his 'opportunities of access to the King's presence', which implies that Cromwell was already in a position of some influence.[8]

Although they had been close allies, Wolsey's death accelerated his protégé's rise to power. In the closing weeks of 1530, Cromwell was appointed a member of the council. This was an astonishing promotion for a man who had only been at court for little over a year, and contemporaries were quick to speculate about what lay behind it. Chapuys claimed that the diplomat and politician Sir John Wallop had levelled so many vicious insults and threats at Cromwell upon Wolsey's death that he had sought the king's protection. In the private audience that followed, so the story goes, Cromwell addressed Henry 'in such flattering terms and eloquent language' and promised to make him the richest king in the world. As a result, 'the king at once took him into his service and made him councillor, though his appointment was kept secret for four months'.[9] This theory is propounded by other sources, notably the Spanish Chronicle, which concurs that 'Cromwell was always inventing means whereby the King might be enriched and the crown aggrandized.'[10]

John Foxe tells a different version. He claims that Cromwell had been quietly gathering information against the bishops of the kingdom, proving that they owed a greater allegiance to the Pope than to their own king. When he had amassed enough evidence, Cromwell apparently sought an audience with Henry, but the latter was reluctant to grant it because the lawyer had been slandered 'by certain in authority about the king, for his rude manner and homely [unpleasant] dealing in defacing the monks' houses and in handling of their altars'. Sir John Russell, whose life (Foxe claims) had been saved by Cromwell several years earlier, eventually intervened and Cromwell was admitted to the royal presence. As soon as he had heard the lawyer's revelations, Henry sent him to the convocation house so that he might confront the prelates in the king's name. 'From that time forward Cromwell began to be better known and dearer unto the king,' Foxe concludes.[11]

These accounts are credible to an extent, but probably owe more to the wisdom of hindsight than the reality of the situation when Henry first met Cromwell. It is entirely possible that Cromwell used the prospect of financial gain to win favour with Henry, and that he stoked the king's resentment against his bishops, but his appeal was due to more than that. Although the king was, as the French ambassador Marillac described him, 'so covetous that all the riches in the world would not satisfy him', he was not so gullible that he could be dazzled by such promises held out to him by a man he hardly knew.[12] Neither does Chapuys' later claim that he promoted Cromwell on a sudden whim explain why the king relied on him ever more during the years that followed.

Cromwell was a man of great personal charisma, as well as ability, and had such a sharp wit that even his enemies could not help laughing at his humorous asides. He was also a man of voracious intellect, and since returning from the Continent he had built up a library so impressive that even the likes of Edmund Bonner, Wolsey's former chaplain and future Bishop of London, sought to borrow from it. Far from being cowed by authority, Cromwell had a natural irreverence and was not afraid to poke fun at or criticise even the highest-ranking members of the court.

Cromwell's success also derived from his skill at finding out men's desires – and making it his business to satisfy them. In 1517, he had accepted a commission from a church in Boston, Lincolnshire, to travel to Rome in order to secure a renewal of their papal grant to sell indulgences. Rather than joining the long line of supplicants for Pope Leo's favour, Cromwell had first gone to the trouble of ascertaining that the pontiff's greatest pleasures included hunting and sweet delicacies. He had promptly made his way to a forest where he knew the Pope would be hunting, and when Leo came riding by he attracted his attention by arranging the performance of an English 'three man's song' and presented him with a selection of sweetmeats and jellies 'such as Kings and Princes only, said he, in the Realm of England use to feed upon'.[13] The Pope was surprised and delighted in equal measure, and immediately granted all of Cromwell's requests.

By the end of 1530, Cromwell had been around Henry long enough to judge that he would respond well to a similar approach. The king's chief desire was well known to the entire court and kingdom: to set aside Catherine of Aragon and marry Anne Boleyn. Cromwell had already started work in trying to achieve this, but he rightly judged that it was not Henry's sole desire. A vain and indulged king, he was always spending lavishly in order to reinforce his magnificence, and thereby his authority. To maintain this lifestyle without bankrupting his kingdom, Henry desperately needed to swell the royal coffers. Cromwell's pledge to make him rich was therefore extremely well judged. From now on, he enjoyed increasingly privileged access to the king, and even attended him alone – a sure sign of the highest possible favour. John Foxe was not exaggerating when he described Cromwell as 'the most secret and dear counsellor unto the king'.[14]

Even though he was the lowest-ranking member of the council, Cromwell did not display any sense of inferiority. Bolstered by his favour with the king, as well as his natural irreverence, he was quick to voice his opinions. The Spanish Chronicle claimed that 'always . . . he was the first to speak' in council meetings. Quick-witted and clear-sighted, he had no patience for the long debates that were a feature of the gatherings. On one occasion, he interrupted: 'Enough of that, and let us go to business.'[15] It is easy to imagine how irksome this opinionated and outspoken newcomer was to the more established members, notably the dukes of Norfolk and Suffolk, and the aged Archbishop Warham. They hated the fact that no sooner had they got rid of one low-born upstart than he had immediately been replaced by another. George Cavendish wryly observed:

With royal eagles a kite may not fly;
Although a jay may chatter in a golden cage,
Yet will the eagles disdain his parentage.[16]

Foremost among these 'eagles' was Thomas Howard, Duke of Norfolk, who soon emerged as the chief challenger to Cromwell's authority. He had been quick to capitalise upon Wolsey's fall, as the Venetian ambassador reported in November 1530: '[The king] makes use of him in all negotiations more than any other person . . . and every employment devolves to him.'[17] Even Suffolk could not challenge his authority. Henry had made his old friend President of the Council in February 1530, but he attended council meetings so irregularly that this office lapsed after only a few months. This was at least partly due to Suffolk's private opposition to the annulment. Although he had been happy to ally himself to the Boleyns in order to get rid of Wolsey, he sympathised with Queen Catherine and, as a religious conservative, was opposed to the idea of separating England from Rome. Not wishing to risk his royal master's ire, though, he wisely distanced himself from political life as much as possible, no doubt hoping the storm would soon blow itself out.

But Norfolk was not lacking other allies. Embittered by Cromwell's rise, Stephen Gardiner soon threw in his lot with the duke. He had confidently expected the king to enhance his authority as secretary so that he might aspire to become chief minister, but Cromwell seemed to have snatched this prospect from under his nose and Gardiner despised him for it. The two men engaged in a number of verbal and written spats, but Cromwell always maintained an air of superiority, mixed with vague amusement. On one occasion, he upbraided Gardiner: 'Your said letters [were] not so friendly conceived, as I think my merits towards you have deserved.'[18]

The rivalry between the king's men was now the fiercest that it had ever been. For all that he loved a convivial court, Henry was apparently content to let his advisers battle against each other, perhaps judging that for as long as they were intent upon each other's destruction, they would not plot against him. But before long, he too seemed to have been infected by the atmosphere of suspicion and paranoia. Henry Courtenay, Marquess of Exeter, soon learned this to his cost. His royal blood inspired his enemies to spread rumours that he had his eyes on the throne. Word reached the king of talk among Courtenay's affinity in Devon and Cornwall that the marquess was heir apparent to the throne. Much as he loved Courtenay, Henry did not hesitate to have him thrown out of the privy chamber. His cousin was justifiably aggrieved because he was almost certainly innocent of any wrongdoing. The source of the rumours was a disgruntled Cornishman who accused Courtenay of unlawful retaining. But this was an act of revenge for having lost out in a land dispute with Courtenay's father-in-law after the marquess had intervened.

The level of Cromwell's involvement in Courtenay's disgrace is not clear, but there was no love lost between the two men, who were as different in ideology as they were in blood. Courtenay was firmly espoused to the old religion and knew that this rising star in Henry's court had reformist ideas that threatened to overturn all of that. But, for now, he found himself out in the cold and would have to fight to regain his place in Henry's trust.

In the battle for influence with the king that raged among those men who remained, Cromwell enjoyed a distinct advantage: he had learned from Wolsey's example. Like the late cardinal, he strove to make himself as indispensable as possible to the king. Having built up experience in a wide range of disciplines – from law and land ownership to trade and diplomacy – Cromwell soon proved himself a true polymath. Among a myriad of other tasks, he managed the sale and receipt of royal land, supervised building works at the Tower of London and Westminster, and decided the fate of prisoners and felons who were brought before him.

An indication of Cromwell's increasing pre-eminence came in January 1531, when a new parliament opened for business. Although it had been little more than a year since his first entry into the Commons, Cromwell now clearly held sway. By the end of the session in March, twenty-nine bills had reached the statute book, most of which had been instigated by him. By the summer, news had reached as far as Derbyshire that 'one Mr Cromwell penned certain matters in the Parliament house, which no man gainsaid'.[19]

But there was one legal matter above all others that Henry wished Cromwell to focus his efforts upon: the annulment. Cardinal Pole claimed that Cromwell had first planted in Henry's mind the idea of a break with Rome, and that he went on to orchestrate the whole affair. However, there is little evidence to corroborate this. Rather, during the early days of his service to the king, Cromwell appeared to be simply acting as Henry's agent and draftsman on matters relating to the divorce, working behind the scenes to carry out a policy that had been formulated elsewhere. It is likely that Cromwell soon began to play a more proactive role in proceedings, however, and the fact that he suddenly 'burst into prominence' in the matter suggests that he had been preparing the groundwork for some time.[20] He brought a much-needed fresh insight to a tired, protracted campaign, and offered his royal master a new glimmer of hope that it might soon reach a successful conclusion.

It is a sign of Cromwell's perceived influence with the king that he was soon besieged by a bewildering number of requests for assistance. Some of the highest-ranking men at court began to seek his help, including Henry's closest friend and brother-in-law, Charles Brandon, Duke of Suffolk, and the ageing Henry Bourchier, second Earl of Essex, who had served both Henry and his father in various official capacities. It was anathema to these blue-blooded courtiers to go cap in hand to the son of a blacksmith. They would never have done so if they had not been convinced of his power.

Always quick to spot potential among the men who served him, Henry began to heap further promotions on his new favourite. Early in 1531, Cromwell was appointed to act as receiver-general and supervisor of the college lands that had been acquired from the late cardinal. He was officially confirmed in this position a year later, on 9 January 1532. His associates – even those with a tenuous link to him – were quick to seek his favour. Later that year, Wolsey's illegitimate son Thomas Winter wrote a begging letter to Cromwell, assuring him: 'All my hope is in you. You are now placed in that position which I and all your friends have long wished for and you have attained that dignity that you can serve them as you please.'[21] By contrast, the Duke of Norfolk, for whom the blacksmith boy's promotion was galling, did his best to put Cromwell firmly in his place. Referring to the arrangements for the forthcoming ennoblement of his niece, he sent the following peremptory note: 'I wrote to you that you should provide crimson velvet for three countesses. The king's pleasure now is that no robes of estate shall be now made but only for my wife. I send you the pattern.'[22]

But there was little Norfolk could do to check his rival's seemingly inexorable rise in the king's favour. The greatest honour of Cromwell's royal service came on 29 September 1531, when he was appointed to the inner ring of the council. This put him directly alongside the likes of Suffolk, Norfolk and the other high-ranking members. Cromwell was the only commoner, but Henry gave him wider-reaching powers than many of his colleagues. They included overseeing criminal prosecution, customs duties and payments due to the king, as well as drafting parliamentary legislation on a raft of different issues. The latter role enabled Cromwell to gain influence over elections to the Commons, which enhanced his influence still further. He also took control of the king's legal affairs, working closely with his ally Thomas Audley, who had been appointed king's serjeant that year. By April 1533, Chapuys, that faithful weathervane of the Tudor court, was reporting to his master that Cromwell had supplanted Norfolk as the man whose favour needed to be cultivated: 'Cromwell informs me now of all court affairs and is the man who enjoys most credit with the king.'[23]

Like Cromwell, Audley's background was in law, and he had been steadily rising through the ranks since 1523. A skilful and persuasive orator, he had made his mark in parliament that year by speaking on behalf of Wolsey when Thomas More had launched an attack on the cardinal's tax demands. This had brought him to the attention of both Wolsey and the king, and it was probably the former who had arranged for him to be rewarded with a succession of honours and offices. In July 1525, he had been appointed to the king's council in the marches of Wales, and the following year he had been made attorney-general in the duchy of Lancaster. By March 1527, he was a member of Wolsey's household, and in July he entered Henry's privy chamber as a groom. When his patron fell from grace in 1529, it was rumoured that Audley had his eyes on the lord chancellorship, but he was thwarted by his rival More.

Undeterred, Audley continued to seek new preferments. Shortly after Wolsey had been thrown out of court, he was named speaker of the Commons. This was said to be at Henry's own instigation: clearly he was impressed by this able and eloquent administrator. Audley gained further renown during the so-called Reformation Parliament, which began in 1529. Working in close partnership with Cromwell, he helped to steer through a raft of legislation during the next five years that paved the way for the annulment and break with Rome. That he had secured the king's favour was revealed soon afterwards, when John Fisher, Bishop of Rochester, accused the Commons of promoting the Church's destruction and levied a series of insults against Audley and his associates.

Fisher was one of the most steadfast and outspoken conservatives in Henry's realm. Although he had robbed the bishop of political power in 1513, Henry still held him in high regard as the foremost theologian of his kingdom. Horrified by the rise of Lutheranism during Henry VIII's reign, Fisher had devoted his energies to preaching and writing against such heretical beliefs. For a time, this chimed with the king's own views and he rewarded Fisher with a public display of his esteem, putting a companionable arm around the bishop's shoulders. But the onset of the king's Great Matter rapidly soured relations between the two men. Fisher became one of its fiercest opponents – and, by default, one of the queen's most influential supporters.

Fisher's outburst against the Commons in 1529 prompted Audley to protest to his royal master at being compared to heathens and infidels. Henry did not hesitate in ordering Fisher to moderate his comments. Undeterred, shortly afterwards the bishop likened himself to John the Baptist for his belief in the indissolubility of marriage, which by implication cast Henry VIII as Herod and Anne Boleyn as Salome. He would live to regret it.

By contrast, Audley's religious sympathies were more obscure. His role in pushing through reform has led to the assumption that he was a committed Protestant. But his motivation was always to further the king's wishes, and there is little evidence to suggest that he shared the increasingly radical stance of Cromwell and his allies.

The year 1531 proved decisive for Henry. Frustrated by his wife's refusal to acknowledge that their marriage was invalid, he had Catherine thrown out of court. She was obliged to live in a succession of increasingly uncomfortable lodgings well away from London while her husband and his men put the legislation in place that would sever her ties with him forever. The king subsequently sent a delegation of his most trusted men to try to persuade the queen to submit to their master. It included the Duke of Norfolk, who had more of a vested interest in the annulment than any other. Robert Radcliffe, Earl of Sussex, was also present. He had continued to throw his weight behind the king's Great Matter since providing testimony about Catherine's marriage to Arthur.

The more reluctant members of the entourage included the Duke of Suffolk. When his royal master demanded an account of his meeting with Catherine, the duke told him that she had shown herself willing to obey her husband in all things except those which conflicted with her allegiance to two higher powers. Henry was immediately suspicious. 'What two powers,' he demanded, 'the pope and the emperor?' 'No Sire,' Suffolk replied, 'God and her conscience.'[24]

Sir Henry Guildford was another man who had been obliged to suppress his personal views in order to carry out the unsavoury task. Not only had he refused to testify against Catherine two years previously, he had also defended her in a council debate. Although his loyalty to the king made him fall in with his desires, he was ideologically opposed to the annulment and was heard to remark that all lawyers and theologians arguing for the Great Matter should be put in a cart, shipped to Rome, and there exposed for the charlatans they were.

Guildford also made clear his dislike of Catherine's rival. Anne was fully aware of this, and in June 1531 she threatened him with the loss of his comptrollership when she became queen. Undaunted, Guildford retorted that he would save her the trouble and went at once to find his royal master so that he could tender his resignation. Anne was no doubt triumphant, but she had underestimated her royal suitor's regard for his old servant. Henry refused to accept Guildford's resignation and told him he should ignore 'women's talk'. He did, though, allow Guildford a leave of absence at his home in Kent.

By November, Guildford's anger had dissipated enough for him to return to his royal master's service. He was soon as high in the king's favour as ever, and on 1 January 1532 he and Henry exchanged New Year gifts of great value. Guildford also held on to his post as comptroller of the household, but he was not to continue in service for much longer. By the time that he returned to court, his health was beginning to fail, and he died in May 1532 at the age of forty-three. That he knew he was dying is suggested by the fact that he had drawn up a will the same month and ordered his tomb, at Blackfriars church in London. Henry's reaction to the news is not recorded, but given his long-standing friendship with Guildford, he can only have been greatly saddened.

Meanwhile, a feud between two of the king's other men had erupted. Although the Duke of Suffolk had done his best to distance himself from political life so that his private disapproval of the annulment would not come to light, his erstwhile ally Norfolk was fully aware of it, and it was a growing source of friction between them. Not long after the two dukes had taken part in the delegation to the ousted queen, a fight broke out between their servants. William Pennington, a member of Suffolk's entourage, was chased through the streets of London by a mob of Norfolk's retainers, who pursued him into the sanctuary of Westminster Abbey and there stabbed him to death. When news reached Suffolk, he set out for the abbey at once with some of his men. But the king heard of it in the nick of time and ordered Suffolk's men to keep the peace. Norfolk's retainers were eventually pardoned, but although further bloodshed had been avoided, the incident had shed unwelcome light upon Suffolk's opposition to the annulment.

Anne Boleyn's pre-eminence was now uncontested. As soon as Catherine had vacated her royal chambers, Anne moved into them. It was heavily symbolic: she was now queen in all but name. Now that he was sure enough that Anne would not fall from favour, Cromwell began to ally himself more closely to her. Although she had no greater liking for Cromwell than he did for her, Anne recognised the benefits of their alliance and could not help but admire the minister's exceptional ability. Sick of the tortuous negotiations that had dominated her life for the past five years, she placed her faith in Cromwell as a man who could bring them to a swift and successful conclusion. Soon, she was referring to him as 'her man'. But for Cromwell, service to his royal master would always supersede that to any other patron – even the queen in waiting.

Anne might have been Norfolk's niece, but there was no love lost between them. The fact that she had just allied herself to one of the duke's deadliest enemies was therefore a positive advantage in her eyes. According to Chapuys, she saw in Cromwell a means to discredit her uncle with Henry: 'I hear from a reliable source that day and night is the Lady working to bring about the duke of Norfolk's disgrace with the King, whether it be owing to his having spoken too freely about her, or because Cromwell wishes to bring down the aristocracy of this kingdom, and is about to begin by him, I can not say.'[25] This is the first time that the notion of a class war raging between Cromwell and the other men of Henry's inner circle had been expressed so openly. But although it reveals the prejudices that were prevalent among its well-born members, there is no evidence that Cromwell was motivated by anything other than advancing his own cause with the king at the expense of his rivals, no matter their social position.

Cromwell soon realised the advantages of his new alliance with Anne. A favourable word from her to the king was worth more than any other voice at court, and Cromwell rapidly rose in Henry's esteem as a result. It was not long before this was expressed in a series of further promotions. On 14 April 1532, Henry awarded Cromwell his first formal office, that of Master of the Jewels. This gave him access to the royal coffers and enabled him to administer government finance from the funds brought under his control. The seventeenth-century antiquarian John Strype opined that this appointment was a sure sign that Cromwell had 'grown in great favour with the King'.[26] Another prestigious appointment followed on 16 July, when Cromwell was made clerk of the hanaper, an office in the department of the chancery, for which he received fees and other moneys for the sealing of charters, patents, writs and the like.

Thanks to lucrative offices such as these, and the seventeen others that followed during the remainder of Cromwell's career, he became one of the wealthiest men in England. Under his watchful eye, his private businesses were also continuing to flourish, and together with his court appointments it has been estimated that by 1537 his annual income was around £12,000 – equivalent to more than £3.5 million in today's money. But Cromwell's promotions brought him something arguably more valuable than monetary gain: close and regular access to the king. He now had a myriad of excuses to seek an audience with Henry. As had been proven so many times in the past, this was the greatest prize of all. Personal friendships and animosities defined Henry's relationships with his men, as well as his decisions on matters of policy, so being in his presence as often as possible was vital to succeed – and to survive.

As Master of the Jewels, Cromwell took care to consult his royal master on the crafting of any new items, such as in September 1532, when he wrote to inform Henry of progress in making a new jewel-encrusted collar that the king had designed. He assured his master: 'I have willed your goldsmith not to proceed to the making of anything in perfection until your gracious pleasure shall be further known, for the which purpose both he and I shall repair unto your highness on Saturday night or Sunday in the morning.'[27]

It was almost certainly to celebrate his appointment to this office that Cromwell commissioned Hans Holbein to paint his portrait. Holbein had recently returned to England, having found Basel no longer conducive to his advancement. The advent of the Reformation, which had swept away many of the adornments favoured by the Catholic Church, had put an abrupt end to Holbein's religious commissions and encouraged his swift return to England. Before he left the city, though, he converted to the new Protestant faith. When he heard of this, Erasmus was furious. In a letter written in 1533, he claimed that Holbein had 'deceived those to whom he was recommended'.[28]

By contrast, Holbein's newfound faith made him all the more acceptable to Henry VIII's chief minister, and the two men would collaborate in different aspects of the king's service during the years ahead. Cromwell's patronage brought Holbein ever closer to Henry, but it was the artist's extraordinary talents that won the king's esteem.

Cromwell could rely upon an excellent network of associates and attendants both at home and abroad in his pursuit of the king's business. They included Thomas Wriothesley, who had continued to act as his secretary, and was now also chief clerk of the signet and Cromwell's representative at the Privy Seal. He had proved extraordinarily diligent and shrewd, with almost as great a capacity for work as his patron. By now, the king himself was fully aware of the young man's abilities and had employed him as an agent and messenger on various overseas commissions, most of which probably related to his campaign for an annulment. Gratified though Wriothesley was by these signs of royal favour, he was frustrated by the lack of any material rewards, and in December 1532 he wrote to Cromwell from Brussels, complaining that his 'apparel, and play sometimes, whereat he is unhappy, have cost him above 50 crowns'.[29]

Meanwhile, thanks to the timely death of Archbishop Warham in August that year, Cromwell's influence also began to spread rapidly into the ecclesiastical sphere. The aged Warham had long stood as a bastion of religious conservatism, and as such was an obstacle to the break with Rome. Now that he was out of the way for good, Henry replaced him with a theologian who had been rapidly rising through the ranks in recent years.

The son of a Nottinghamshire esquire, Thomas Cranmer was born in 1489. At the age of fourteen, he went to study at Cambridge and would spend the next twenty-six years there. It took eight years to gain his Bachelor of Arts degree, which may have been because, though not lacking in intellect, he struggled to absorb information quickly, or perhaps because of his family's financial problems (Cranmer's father had died in 1501). Although he would later become a figurehead for seismic religious reform, Cranmer was a plodding, cautious student who was governed by conventional views. As such, he formed a marked contrast to Cromwell and his predecessor Wolsey, both of whom Henry had selected for their obvious quick-wittedness and ability. But it would soon become clear that Cranmer had other, gentler qualities that appealed to the king.

Having completed his Master of Arts in 1515, Cranmer was well qualified for a career in the Church. But surprisingly, given his accustomed caution, he soon afterwards decided to marry. Little is known about his bride beyond her Christian name, Joan, but it seems that Cranmer had fallen deeply in love with her. That he did not simply make her his mistress reveals his honest and straightforward nature, as well as his strong sense of morality. When she died in childbirth, along with the baby, he was so grief-stricken that he was unable to speak of it even years later. Though he could not have known it at the time, this tragedy would give him a valuable empathy with the king in future years.

Soon after Joan's death, Cranmer was readmitted to Jesus College Cambridge as a fellow – a position that had been denied him when he was married. It was a significant time to be studying theology because it coincided with the first publications of Martin Luther, the reforming German monk whose attacks on the Roman Catholic Church were gaining widespread support across the Continent. According to Cranmer's first biographer, he considered 'what great controversy was in matters of religion' and 'applied his whole study three years unto the . . . scriptures'.[30] But for now, he remained a religious conservative and loyal papist.

By 1520, Cranmer had proceeded to holy orders, and some time after 1526 he was made doctor of divinity. At around this time, he came to the attention of Cardinal Wolsey, who invited him, as one of a group of bright young Cambridge scholars, to transfer to his new foundation at Oxford, Cardinal College. Cranmer declined, but in spring 1527 he agreed to take part in a diplomatic mission to Emperor Charles V. He made some important links with Imperial diplomats and courtiers, and so distinguished himself that upon their return Wolsey introduced him to the king. Henry took an immediate shine to the young scholar and showered him with gifts, including rings of gold and silver.

From that moment, Cranmer became a firm advocate for the annulment and was employed by Wolsey on a number of other business matters, some of which had brought him into regular contact with Thomas Cromwell. By now closely aligned in beliefs and outlook, the two men quickly formed an alliance. Cranmer's theological expertise perfectly complemented Cromwell's command of the law and politics, so that together they were able to build a compelling case for the annulment.

The decisive moment came two years later, largely by chance. In the summer of 1529, the plague was rife in Cambridge, so Cranmer took refuge at the Essex home of one of his kinsmen, a Mr Cressey, which lay close to the great Augustinian abbey of Waltham Holy Cross. At the same time, the king arrived on progress as a guest of the abbey, and Cranmer's old university friend Gardiner was given accommodation at the Cresseys', along with Edward Foxe, Bishop of Hereford. They met for supper, and inevitably their conversation turned to the king's Great Matter. After listening to Gardiner and Foxe express their frustration about the Pope's intransigence, Cranmer opined: 'I do think that you go not the [most convenient] way to work, to bring the matter unto a perfect conclusion and end, especially for the satisfaction of the troubled conscience of the king's highness. For in observing the common process and frustrating delays of this your courts, the matter will linger long enough, and peradventure will in the end come unto small effect.'[31]

What Cranmer proposed as an alternative was to shift the focus of the campaign from the legal case at Rome towards a general canvassing of university theologians throughout Europe. This concept was not new, but applying it to the king's 'great cause of matrimony', as he termed it, opened up an appealing alternative to the long and tortuous negotiations with the papacy.[32] As Cranmer pointed out, the opinion of these 'divines' would 'be soon known and brought so to pass with little industry and charges, that the king's conscience thereby may be quieted and pacified'.[33] It was a brilliantly simple plan, and one that was soon put into action.

As a result of his efforts, Cranmer soon won favour with the Boleyn family and was lodged in the entourage of Anne's father at Durham Place on the Strand. Henry, too, was quick to spot his potential, and before long had placed considerable trust in this rising star of the Church. As well as his reformist ideas, Cranmer stood out because of his calm and sanguine manner. 'He was a man of such temperature of nature, or rather so mortified, that no manner of prosperity or adversity could alter or change his accustomed conditions,' remarked a later sixteenth-century commentator. His quiet, self-deprecating manner was such that whenever advancement came his way, he always seemed genuinely surprised, as if he had never sought it. This formed a sharp – and perhaps, for Henry, welcome – contrast to the forceful and outspoken men surrounding him, with their endless backbiting and jockeying for position. But Cranmer's calm exterior belied a deeply devout and passionate nature, as well as an unswerving commitment to the cause of reform. The same commentator noted that 'privately with his secret friends he would shed forth many bitter tears, lamenting the misery and calamities of the world'.[34]

One of Cranmer's closest associates was Cromwell. Recognising the formidable double act that he had in these two men, Henry ensured that all of their efforts were now focused on securing the annulment of his marriage to Catherine. While Cromwell concentrated on drawing up the legal case in London, Cranmer was appointed to a team of researchers who were drafting a theological justification for the annulment and break with Rome. The team produced two major works, the most famous of which was the *Collectanea satis copiosa* ('Sufficiently abundant collections'). This was an anthology of historical texts, many of which were drawn from Arthurian legend, which proved that the king, not the Pope, had the right to exercise supreme authority over all aspects of his realm. The other work set out the biblical justification for the annulment, based upon the teachings about it being unlawful for a man to marry his brother's wife.

Throughout this time, both Cranmer and Cromwell increasingly absorbed the evangelical ideas that were sweeping across Europe. By questioning many of the practices of the Roman Catholic Church, these helped to justify the annulment, but the two men's espousal of them was due to genuine piety as well as political pragmatism. Cromwell's closest friends were reformers, and his library contained numerous 'heretical' books that would have landed him in trouble if they had been discovered. Some of these had been supplied by his companions in the king's service, Hans Holbein and Nicholas Kratzer, who used their contacts to secure the latest texts from the Netherlands and German states.

Cranmer's beliefs, meanwhile, grew even more radical from 1532, when Henry appointed him ambassador to the German states, home of the Reformation. While there, he courted controversy by marrying again. This was a clear indication that Cranmer had decisively rejected the Roman Catholic religion, with its tradition of compulsory celibacy, and openly embraced the evangelical cause. But not long afterwards, he was alarmed to receive news that upon Warham's death Henry had chosen him as the new Archbishop of Canterbury. It was a staggering promotion, and in bestowing it Henry had bypassed the entire episcopal bench in favour of a low-ranking churchman. The leap from Archdeacon of Taunton to Archbishop of Canterbury was unprecedented. Cranmer decided to keep quiet about his marriage and, though he declared himself 'a poor wretch and much unworthy', accepted the summons.[35] He also wrote to Cromwell, expressing his anxiety about the reaction that his appointment was bound to have caused among his fellow churchmen. 'Ye do know what ambition and desire of promotion is in men of the Church, and what indirect means they do use and have used to obtain their purpose,' he urged, 'which their unreasonable desires and appetites I do trust that ye will be more ready to oppress and extinguish.'[36] Cranmer took some time to embark for England, though, and did not arrive back at court until January 1533.

This new, somewhat reluctant, Archbishop of Canterbury was all too well aware what was expected of him. Henry wanted nothing less than for Cranmer to push through the annulment. Although Cranmer had worked towards this for a number of years, he seemed overawed by the task, as well as by the honour that his royal master had conferred upon him. When Nicholas Hawkins arrived to take over from Cranmer, he was aghast to discover the humble means by which his predecessor had been living. As ambassador, Cranmer was entitled to surround himself with luxury, yet as Hawkins reported, he had been dining off tin or pewter. His successor wrote at once to request some of the king's plate for his table.

It is to Cranmer's credit that his natural modesty had never given way to the self-seeking ambition and lust for power that had seduced most other men in Henry's service. Yet he had received more than enough demonstrations of the king's esteem during the preceding years to inflate his sense of self-worth. As early as the summer of 1531, a foreign visitor to court had reported that Cranmer was a close companion of the king, and that it had become Henry's habit to discuss important matters with him in private before going public on them. Even Cranmer's ally Cromwell, who was hardly lacking in power at the king's hands, ruefully – and enviously – admitted: 'You were born in a happy hour . . . for, do or say what you will, the king will always well take it at your hand.'[37]

But Cranmer's success was due to hard work, as well as good fortune. His secretary, Ralph Morice, described the close and trusting relationship that his master developed with Henry. 'At all times when the king's majesty would be resolved in any doubt or question he would but send word to my lord [Cranmer] overnight, and by the next day the king should have in writing brief notes of the doctors' minds, as well divines as lawyers, both ancient, old, and new, with a conclusion of his own mind; which he [Henry] could never get in such readiness of none, no not of all his chaplains and clergy about him, in so short a time . . . and so, reducing the notes of them altogether, would advertise the king more in one day than all his learned men could do in a month.'[38]

Cranmer's modest, humble bearing appealed to a king who was surrounded by ambitious place-seekers. In a typical dispatch, the archbishop assured his royal master: 'I dare nothing do, unless your grace's pleasure be to me first known.'[39] This was no false humility. Cranmer's belief in the divine authority of kings in all spheres of life, secular as well as spiritual, was utterly unshakeable. He was also used to dealing with overbearing personalities. Morice records that

Cranmer remembered his 'tyrannical' schoolmaster as 'marvellous severe and cruel'.[40] At an early age, therefore, he learned how to avoid angering such men, which was invaluable training for his service to Henry. A contemporary noted that he 'always tried to please the King'.[41]

But the real secret of Cranmer's success was his genuine conviction that Henry's marriage to Catherine was invalid in the eyes of God and the law. The king was no fool: he knew that most of his other men paid lip service to the Great Matter in order to ingratiate themselves with their royal master, and feather their own nests in the process. For Henry, Cranmer therefore stood apart as the only man who understood him, and in whom he could confide anything without fear that it might be twisted to an advantage other than his own.

The same unswerving dedication to the king's will was shared by Cranmer's ally, Cromwell. By the time of Cranmer's appointment, Cromwell was making great strides towards the break with Rome – and in the process was fulfilling his alleged promise to make Henry a rich man. He was responsible for the bill that was drawn up for the 'Conditional Restraint of Annates'. This was an attempt to put pressure on the Pope by ending the payments (or annates) made to Rome by senior clerics of the first year's revenue from their benefices. The bill was passed by parliament in spring 1532 and proved a decisive step forward in the break with Rome by bringing the clergy more directly under the king's authority. It also swelled the coffers of the royal treasury, which won Cromwell even greater approval from Henry.

Within two years the bill had raised an estimated £30,000 (equivalent to around £9.6 million), which prompted Chapuys to observe: 'These are devices of Cromwell, who boasts that he will make his master more wealthy than all the other princes of Christendom.'[42] Reginald Pole later claimed that Cromwell, inspired by Machiavelli's *Il Principe*, persuaded Henry to establish himself as an amoral ruler. But both of these commentators were fiercely opposed to the reformist ideas that Cromwell espoused, and their claims were part of a bitter campaign to discredit him with the king. Although Henry had proved susceptible to manipulation, and certainly appreciated the financial gains that could be made from Cromwell's reforms, he was proud to be *'Fidei Defensor'* ('Defender of the Faith') – the title that Pope Leo X had bestowed upon him in 1521. He also had a genuine and intense piety, and would not sacrifice the Church solely for the riches that it could bring. At the heart of the matter was the invalidity of his marriage to Catherine, which Henry was now utterly convinced was offensive to God.

Nevertheless, in the eyes of those who abhorred the idea of breaking from Rome, Henry had been hoodwinked by his 'evil advisers'. The whispering campaign against them had grown ever more vicious as a result. The previous year, a scandal had erupted when a number of Bishop Fisher's servants had fallen violently ill and one had died. Foul play had immediately been suspected by those who supported this leading opponent of the king's annulment, and for once the rumours had proved right. It had been discovered that poison had been added to a cauldron of porridge in the bishop's kitchen, and a man named Richard Roose had soon been identified as the murderer. Among the many accusations that had flown about, the most outrageous was that Roose had been in the pay of the king, who was desperate to silence his outspoken opponent. Henry had been so appalled when he got wind of this that he delivered an hour-and-a-half-long speech in the House of Lords about the barbarity of the poisoning. He also instituted a new act that equated poisoning with high treason, punishable by being boiled alive. The unfortunate Roose was the first person to feel its effects.

Despite the mounting tensions, for now Cromwell could do no wrong in the eyes of his master. Spurred on by the Annates bill, Cromwell turned his attention to the Church in England, realising that there was growing resistance to his reforms. He focused his attack on the clerical abuses that he knew to be rife across the kingdom. These were now articulated in the 'Supplication against the Ordinaries [clerics]', which was presented to the king in March 1532. Significantly, this described Henry as 'the only head, sovereign, lord, protector, and defender' of the Church, and forced the Convocation of Canterbury, an assembly of bishops and clergy, to decide whether it accepted him as such.

This brought Cromwell into direct conflict with another of

Henry's men: Stephen Gardiner. Until now, the bishop had set his loyalty to the king ahead of his conservative religious views, but he was provoked into issuing a robust reply on behalf of Convocation, declaring: 'We, your most humble servants, may not submit the execution of our charges and duty, certainly prescribed by God, to your highness' assent.'[43] He also attacked Cromwell's methods, denouncing the 'sinister information and importunate labours and persuasions of evil disposed persons, pretending themselves to be thereunto moved by the zeal of justice and reformation, [who] may induce right wise, sad, and constant men to suppose such things to be true, as be not so indeed'.[44] This prompted Cranmer to confide to Cromwell: 'To be plain what I think of the bishop of Winchester, I cannot persuade with myself that he so much tendereth the king's cause as he doth his own.'[45] It was a shrewd observation.

This vicious attack on Cromwell and the reformist beliefs that he espoused made Gardiner a hero to the considerable numbers of religious conservatives in England, not least his ally Norfolk. The two men had been content to further the king's annulment as a means of bringing Anne Boleyn to power, but now that they realised it threatened to unleash a religious revolution, they were appalled. Too late, they had come to appreciate just how much groundwork Cromwell and Cranmer had been carefully laying in order to effect a seismic shift in the religious life of the kingdom. But in railing against it, Gardiner merely antagonised his royal master. Henry was so outraged that he proceeded to bully the clergy into submission. He accused them in parliament of being so submissive to the Pope 'that they seem to be his subjects, and not ours'.[46] This smacked of treason, and the clergy knew it. Four days later, Convocation reluctantly signed what has become known as the Submission of the Clergy. This acknowledged that the law of the Church would in future depend upon the consent of the king, in the same way as secular laws required his approval in parliament. Cromwell had won a significant victory over his rivals, bringing England another step closer to a break with Rome.

All of this was anathema to Sir Thomas More, who was deeply opposed to the idea of royal supremacy, as well as to the annulment. He had spent much of the previous decade hunting down heretics in England, denouncing the teachings of Luther and his followers, and publishing polemics in defence of the Roman Catholic faith. Upon his appointment to the lord chancellorship, he had confided to Erasmus that he intended to use his position to further 'the interests of Christendom'.[47] His conviction had not wavered during the years that followed, and he had written a series of long and tedious polemical tracts against heresy. In another letter to Erasmus, he urged his friend not to tolerate religious extremism: 'I am keenly aware of the risk involved in an open-door policy towards these newfangled, erroneous sects', he wrote. 'Some people like to give an approving eye to novel ideas, out of superficial curiosity, and to dangerous ideas, out of devilry; and in so doing they assent to what they read, not because they believe it is true, but because they want it to be true . . . All my efforts are directed toward the protection of those men who do not deliberately desert the truth, but are seduced by the enticements of clever fellows.'[48]

Forasmuch as he desired an annulment, Henry was just as damning of such heretics as was More, and the two men had remained exceptionally close. Only once during the years of More's ascendancy did a crack appear in their relationship. This had been prompted by the return to England in 1529 of Simon Fish, an outspoken reformer and propagandist who had recently published *Supplication for the Beggars*, a virulent attack on the clergy. In it, Fish warned Henry that the clergy were attempting to usurp the power of the state, and urged him to put an end to their manifold abuses. To More's dismay, the king invited Fish to court and 'embraced him with loving countenance'.[49] He then took him out hunting and discussed theological matters with him. Fish told Henry that he feared More would take action against him, but the king gave him a ring as an assurance of his protection and instructed him to tell the Lord Chancellor not to molest him. Fish duly did so, but More refused to let the matter lie. Realising that he could not touch the heretical author directly, he found another means to harass him. Good lawyer that he was, More pointed out that the king's protection only extended to Fish, not to his wife, who now became the target of his ire. She was only saved by the fact that she was tending her daughter, who had caught the plague, so More, fearing infection, decided to abandon his investigations.

Although he held one of the highest offices in the kingdom, from the very beginning of his term as Lord Chancellor, More was increasingly isolated from political life. He was the first holder of that office not to be *de facto* leader of the council, and his attendance at meetings was irregular at best. Admittedly, the legal business of Chancery and the Star Chamber provided more than enough to occupy his time, as did his vociferous campaign against heresy. But there can be little doubt that More's stance on the king's annulment had prompted his isolation. Henry had discussed the matter privately with him on numerous occasions, so was in no doubt of More's opposition. But the two men had reached an agreement: More would not openly voice his criticism of the scheme, and the king would not pressure him to show public support for it. Henry assured his Lord Chancellor that if he 'could not therein with his conscience serve him, he was content to accept his service otherwise'.[50] Nevertheless, More's refusal to help his royal master in this most pressing issue meant that he was ousted from the inner circle of councillors, all of whom were occupied with the annulment proceedings. Instead, he allied himself with churchmen and focused all of his efforts upon helping them to eradicate heresy.

But occupying such a high-profile position in government made it increasingly difficult for More to conceal his opposition to the king's Great Matter. When in 1531 the king confirmed his intention to separate from papal jurisdiction and make himself Supreme Head of the Church in England, as Lord Chancellor More found himself in the unenviable position of having to deliver to both houses of parliament the arguments in favour of the divorce which Cranmer had begun collecting the year before.

Unable either to openly oppose or work to prevent a policy that flew in the face of all his beliefs and principles, More asked his fellow religious conservative, Norfolk, to facilitate his resignation on the grounds of ill health. Perhaps the duke refused, because More continued in office for the time being. Behind the scenes, he supported the queen's cause so assiduously that Charles V himself wrote to thank him. Anxious not to offend his sovereign, More refused to receive the letter and also began to avoid the Imperial ambassador on the grounds that 'He ought to abstain from everything which might provoke suspicion; and if there were no other reason, such a visitation [by the ambassador] might deprive him of the liberty which he had always used in speaking boldly in those matters which concerned . . . the Queen.'[51]

More knew that he was on borrowed time as Lord Chancellor, and when the clergy finally made their formal submission to the king, he sought an audience with Henry and offered his resignation on 16 May 1532. The king reluctantly acknowledged that the position of his long-standing favourite had become untenable and therefore let him go. The Duke of Norfolk was dispatched to York Place to receive the Great Seal from More's hands. A few weeks later, More told Erasmus that he had resigned on health grounds, and that Norfolk and Audley had relayed this to parliament. In fact, parliament was not sitting at the time, and few would have believed his assertion in any case. In typically overblown language, Erasmus claimed that the news had quickly spread all over the world and had prompted 'the deep sorrow of all wise and good men'.[52]

Thomas Audley might have hoped to step into More's shoes, but although he was knighted and made keeper of the Great Seal four days later, the post of Lord Chancellor remained beyond his grasp for now. As for More, he had no intention of retiring into obscurity, and he would prove an even more troublesome opponent to the Great Matter as a private citizen than he had in public office. Free from the shackles of royal service, he proceeded to wage a vociferous campaign against government policy and published a series of bitter attacks on Protestant doctrine. In so doing, he established himself as a powerful figurehead for all of the religious conservatives who opposed the king's reforms and wanted England to remain faithful to Rome. This dealt a fatal blow to More's relationship with Henry, who now viewed him as one of the greatest obstacles to his ambitions.

By contrast, Thomas Cromwell was continuing his seemingly inexorable rise in Henry's service. The day after Sir Thomas More's resignation, Henry showed his favour towards Cromwell by granting him and his son Gregory the lordship of Romney in Newport, south Wales. By the end of the year, Cromwell had been given so many appointments and privileges that he controlled the entire domestic administration of England. All of Cromwell's promotions proved lucrative, which meant that his already considerable wealth was increased still further. His household and property grew significantly as a result, and soon he employed almost as many men as the late cardinal had. But service to the king's chief minister was no sinecure. Cromwell was by far the hardest-working member of Henry's council and he expected his attendants to follow suit. He regularly worked well beyond midnight and was often up at four o'clock in the morning, drafting 'remembrances' (memoranda) and sending out letters.

Another of Wolsey's former protégés, Sir John Welsbourne, was also enjoying a rise in Henry's favour. Having been appointed an esquire of the body in 1528, he worked steadily to prove his loyalty, undertaking an embassy to France in 1530. He was rewarded the following year when Henry made him a gentleman of the privy chamber. He would serve in this capacity for the remainder of the reign, and his name always appears in the list of those attending the great occasions of state. Spying an opportunity, Welsbourne also made himself useful to Thomas Cromwell, who enlisted him on various errands during the 1530s, notably at Abingdon Abbey, which was dissolved in 1538. Eager though he was to curry favour with the chief minister, Welsbourne bemoaned his distance from his royal master and wrote to express his hope that he might still trust 'in the goodness of the King to all those who are daily waiting on him'.[53] The years ahead would prove that his loyalty to Henry was a good deal stronger than his allegiance to Cromwell. The king later rewarded him for his service with a knighthood, and there was never any indication that Welsbourne came close to losing his position at court again, as he had during Wolsey's tenure.

Sir Francis Bryan also continued to enjoy the king's favour during this turbulent time. The court records show that throughout 1532 he served in the privy chamber for six weeks in every twelve, spending the other six weeks at his country estates. He was still one of Henry's favourite companions, and helped to take his mind off his troubles by gambling with him for high stakes at dice, cards, bowls, and a game known as 'Pope Julius'. The accounts show that he successfully used his proximity to the king to forward the suits of his friends and associates, as well as promoting his own interests. However, when the king went to Calais with Anne Boleyn in October 1532, Bryan was replaced in the retinue by Sir Nicholas Carew. This has been taken as a sign of a rift between Henry and Bryan, but if this was the case then the latter was soon back in favour because the following year he was in France again on the king's business.

Another man who had accompanied the king to Calais in 1532 was Henry FitzRoy. Upon Wolsey's fall in October 1529, Henry had entrusted the Duke of Norfolk with his bastard son's care. With the onset of plague the following summer, Henry had ordered his son back to Windsor for his protection, and Norfolk had seized the opportunity to dispatch his own son there to keep him company.

A gifted scholar, Henry Howard, Earl of Surrey, was just three years older than FitzRoy and the two young men soon struck up a close accord. Surrey later recalled with fondness the two years that he spent 'with a king's son' at Windsor 'in greater feast then Priam's sons of Troy'. They were the most formative years of FitzRoy's young life, during which he matured intellectually, emotionally and physically. Surrey later reflected over 'Our tender limbs, that yet shot up in length'. He also admitted that their regular games of tennis were disrupted whenever they 'got sight of our dame' and were enticed 'by gleams of love'. Theirs was a friendship born of shared experience and 'secret thoughts imparted with such trust'.[54]

In 1531, Henry gave his son Margaret Beaufort's former residence at Collyweston in Northamptonshire as his principal seat, although FitzRoy rarely stayed there. When he accompanied the king to Calais the following year, aged 13, he was widely admired as 'a goodly young prince full of favour and beauty' who greatly resembled his father, which was a source of satisfaction to Henry.[55] After the latter's departure, FitzRoy and Surrey stayed behind as pledges for Henry's treaty with Francis I, and accompanied him to France. FitzRoy was formally accepted into Francis's privy chamber and was lodged with his son, the dauphin. Surrey's time in France would prove a pivotal moment in his literary development, for he and FitzRoy spent time at Fontainebleau, encountering a rich array of poets and works of art from the French and Italian Renaissance.

On 25 January 1533, Henry finally married Anne Boleyn. The

ceremony, which took place at Whitehall, was attended by only a handful of his courtiers, and the fact that the date and location have remained uncertain until recent years testifies to the great secrecy with which it was conducted. It seems to have been arranged by Cromwell and Cranmer, working closely with the Boleyns and their royal master himself. Although the annulment had still not been secured, Henry was unable to wait any longer. He and Anne had almost certainly started to sleep together during the visit to Calais, and she was now pregnant. Henry knew that he must legitimise their union without delay. The legal niceties to sever him from his first wife would have to follow later.

Among the guests at the wedding was a newcomer: Lord Thomas Howard, half-brother of the Duke of Norfolk and uncle of the bride. This was Howard's first appearance at court, and little is known of his earlier life. Aged about twenty-one at the time of the wedding, he was almost forty years younger than his half-brother. His presence at such a pivotal event is an indication of how much Anne's relatives had benefited from her rise. Also present was Thomas Heneage, who had risen steadily through the ranks to become one of the leading gentlemen of the privy chamber. A court record of April 1532 had listed the gentlemen in two groups, each headed by a noble and a commoner. The king's groom of the stool, Henry Norris, led the latter, while Heneage and George Boleyn headed the other.

William Brereton may also have been present. One of nine sons born to the courtier and military man Sir Randolph Brereton, he had begun his court career in around 1521 and had enjoyed Wolsey's patronage for a time. By 1524, he was a groom of the privy chamber and worked closely with Henry Norris. Although his date of birth is not recorded, Brereton was at least a year older than the king, possibly more, which set him apart from many of his fellow privy chamber servants. He had enjoyed numerous grants of land and offices from the king during his years of service, and his favour had been confirmed in 1529 when he had married the king's second cousin, Elizabeth, daughter of Charles Somerset, Earl of Worcester. But this had invoked some jealousy at court, and Brereton's dominance of local affairs in his native Chester established him as a potential obstacle to Cromwell's plans. For the time being, though, the chief minister had other rivals to deal with.

The day after the wedding, Henry made Thomas Audley Lord Chancellor. The timing may have been significant. The fact that Anne Boleyn was already pregnant may have prompted her husband to appoint a man whom he could trust to be compliant in this post and speed through the annulment. Believing that his new wife carried his son and heir, Henry had a fresh impetus for a legislative break with Rome and the foundation of a separate Church of England. Now that he was in a position to secure this for his royal master, Audley had a greater platform for influence than he had ever enjoyed. He would soon exercise his newfound powers to the full.

Audley's new position did not lead to greater intimacy with Henry, however – at least, not initially. Rather, he seems to have managed royal business when his master and Cromwell were absent, and to have acted as a conduit between the king's council and the courts. He had little direct contact with Henry himself, but addressed any legal advice or requests for grants to Cromwell, who would then pass them on to their royal master. The tone of these dispatches is always very humble and submissive, which, although customary for those addressing the king, reflects the essentially formal nature of their relationship. So anxious did Audley appear to please the king that he has been portrayed as a sycophant. But while he certainly put off decisions until he could be sure of Henry's mind, this speaks rather of prudence than obsequiousness. In fact, Audley, like Cromwell, was a blunt, matter-of-fact character who had no patience for the flowery language of senior court servants and once complained of being 'accepted better as a poor, honest man before he became Chancellor'.[56]

Nevertheless, Audley clearly had a brilliant legal mind and was confident in asserting his professional opinion. Although the French ambassador Marillac later remarked that he 'has the reputation of being a good seller of justice whenever he can find a buyer', there is no evidence that the Lord Chancellor ever placed profit ahead of the due process of the law.[57] Neither was he afraid to contradict the chief minister, even though he relied upon him as an intermediary with the king. The year before his appointment, he had disagreed with Cromwell and Sir William Paulet, comptroller of the household, over their method of handling one of Henry's suits, arguing that they could take a fairer approach and still maintain 'the king's honour and profit'.[58] Meticulous and well prepared, Audley was an excellent choice as Lord Chancellor, and Henry could rely on him to provide the best solution on even the most complex legal issues. He also became adept at reconciling the often contradictory demands of the king's wishes with true justice. Greatly though Henry came to esteem Audley, however, it was a strictly business relationship and lacked the personal element that marked so many of his other relationships with the men who served him.

Another of the king's recently appointed officials was being kept similarly busy. In April 1533, Archbishop Cranmer presided over the Convocation that was convened to annul Henry's marriage to Catherine of Aragon. Desperate to claw back favour, Stephen Gardiner stood as counsel for the king himself. Chapuys had prepared Catherine's formal protest at the court, and he also delivered a protest to Henry on behalf of the emperor. Shortly afterwards, he presented Catherine's case to the council.

Chapuys was not alone in defending the beleaguered queen. Despite his failing health, Bishop Fisher, with whom the ambassador had been in regular communication, also attended the Convocation in April. He dissented from the majority, who had denied the Pope's authority to dispense for Arthur's marriage to Catherine. Shortly afterwards, he spoke out in public against the imminent annulment, and was promptly arrested. His custodian was Stephen Gardiner, who privately sympathised with his stance but kept his fellow bishop safely immured until June, by which time events had moved beyond Fisher's control.

Chapuys and Fisher were lone voices in their defence of the embattled queen. Sir Francis Bryan was among the majority when he provided a crucial testimony of Catherine's stubborn refusal to submit to royal authority. Thanks to such testimonies, on 23 May Henry's marriage to Catherine was finally declared null.

A little over a week later, Anne Boleyn was crowned. Gardiner made sure to be prominent at the event, much to the disappointment of Chapuys and others who believed he was on the side of the ousted queen. Cromwell also played an active part. Henry had ordered that all men with an income of forty pounds or more should receive the order of knighthood at the event or else pay a fine. With typical alacrity, Cromwell had stepped in to administer this and 'so politiquely handled the matter, that he raised . . . a great sum of money to the king's use'.[59] Hans Holbein, whose fame was spreading, was almost certainly responsible for designing one of the magnificent pageants that marked the new queen's entrance into the city.

Although he had no great liking for Anne Boleyn, the Duke of Suffolk was also prominent at her coronation. He was obliged to walk before his master's new wife and bear her crown into Westminster Abbey. At the banquet that followed he 'rode often times about the hall, cheering the lords, ladies, and the Mayor and his brethren'.[60] But his wife Mary, the king's sister, spurned the occasion. She loathed Anne so much that she could not bear to be in her presence. Though Suffolk privately sympathised with her views, he would not have dared to make such a public protest, and was no doubt embarrassed that his wife had chosen to do so.

A more surprising absentee was the new queen's uncle, the Duke of Norfolk. By the time Anne married Henry, the duke had come to despise her for her arrogant and 'unqueenly' behaviour. He also resented the fact that his position at court owed so much to his involvement with the Boleyn family. Chapuys reported that Norfolk once stormed out of Anne's chamber in a rage, bellowing that his niece was a whore because she had treated him worse than he treated his own dogs.[61] Although he had furthered his niece's interests by supporting the king's campaign for an annulment, he had not been privy to the secret plans that had led to her wedding. Embittered at being so excluded, and troubled by the reforms that the marriage looked set to bring in its wake, Norfolk set sail for an embassy in France shortly before the coronation.

Thomas More had also refused to attend Anne's coronation. Upon hearing that Henry's marriage to her had been declared valid, he had remarked: 'God give grace . . . that these matters within a while be not confirmed with others.'[62] When a delegation of bishops tried to persuade him to show his conformity by attending the coronation, he retorted: 'It lieth not in my power but that they may devour me;

but God being my good lord, I will provide that they shall never deflower me.'[63] Henry was deeply offended by More's failure to present himself, and from that day forward there was a growing sense that the former favourite would not long be allowed his liberty.

Henry's new marriage placed a number of his other men in a difficult position. Although outwardly they were obliged to conform to – even celebrate – the new state of affairs, privately many lamented Catherine's demise. This was particularly true of William Blount, Lord Mountjoy, who had served as the former queen's chamberlain since 1512. Like his peers, Mountjoy had been careful to further the king's interests in public and had been among the signatories of the open letter to Pope Clement VII in 1530, urging Henry's case. According to Chapuys, Mountjoy had subsequently changed from Catherine's attendant to her captor. Shortly before the annulment was passed, he reported that Mountjoy had been ordered to stay with the beleaguered queen to prevent her escaping from England.

In July 1533, Mountjoy headed a delegation that went to persuade Catherine to submit to the consequences of the king's new marriage and acknowledge herself as Dowager Princess. Although she had grown to trust Mountjoy, Catherine would not listen to his pleas, and he was obliged to admit defeat. Shortly afterwards, he begged to be replaced as her chamberlain. Although his loyalty to the king had dictated his actions during the previous few years, his true feelings about the annulment were revealed in a letter that he wrote to Cromwell on 10 October 1533. 'It is not my part, nor for me this often to vex or unquiet her whom the king's grace caused to be sworn unto and truly to serve her to my power,' he pleaded.[64]

Mountjoy's request does not seem to have been granted, but after his death the following November, no successor was appointed. During the last few months of his life, Mountjoy had resumed his former loyal service to Henry. He had apparently profited little from his long association with the king, however. In his will dated 14 October 1534, he asked patience of his creditors, considering that he had impoverished himself by providing for his son and being often called abroad in service of the king to whom he had been a 'slender suitor'.[65]

For the time being, the king was too preoccupied with his new wife's lying-in to concern himself too greatly with the opponents of his marriage. Anne Boleyn's pregnancy had progressed without incident, and in August she made her way to Greenwich for the birth. She had promised her husband a son, and he does not seem to have considered that there might have been any other outcome. It was therefore with grave disappointment that on 7 September he learned the news that Anne had given birth to a daughter, Elizabeth. Furious and humiliated, Henry immediately cancelled the celebrations that he had planned to herald the arrival of his new son. He had little choice, though, than to acknowledge the child as his heir. Cromwell duly drafted the Act of Succession, which was passed by parliament early the following year. The infant Elizabeth supplanted the king's elder daughter Mary, who had been rendered illegitimate by the annulment of his marriage to her mother.

The new princess was christened on 10 September. Archbishop Cranmer presided over the ceremony, and among the godparents was Henry Courtenay, Marquess of Exeter. The younger of Anne Boleyn's uncles, Lord Thomas Howard, was also in attendance. From that time onwards, he was a regular fixture at court and joined the expanding group of Howard associates.

'I shall die today and you tomorrow'

THE SAME MONTH that Princess Elizabeth was born, Henry's ille-gitimate son returned from France with his companion, the Earl of Surrey. The timing was significant. Bitterly disappointed by the birth of a girl after all the turmoil he had suffered to marry Anne Boleyn, Henry was determined to flaunt the fact that he was capable of siring healthy sons. FitzRoy's recall may also have been intended as both a punishment and a warning to Anne. Henry could have sent no clearer message about what was expected of her now.

FitzRoy's status as the king's only living son made his marriage a matter of intense interest. There had even been a suggestion some years earlier that the boy should marry his own half-sister, the Princess Mary. Aware that this would prevent the annulment of her parents' marriage, the Pope had expressed himself willing to grant a special dispensation. Perhaps not surprisingly, the king had disap-proved of the scheme and it had come to nothing. This left the way open for FitzRoy's protector, the Duke of Norfolk, who began scheming to marry the young man to his own daughter Mary. The king had no objections to such a match, and in November 1533 the negotiations were concluded.

FitzRoy was then just fourteen and his bride was about the same age. Their youth sparked fearful memories for the king. His elder brother Arthur had been just a year older when he had married Catherine of Aragon. Convinced that too much sexual activity had hastened Arthur's death, Henry ordered the couple not to consum-mate their marriage. It is possible that his son's health was already failing. A miniature painted by the artist Lucas Horenbout the following year shows FitzRoy in an open-necked nightshirt and nightcap, which suggests that he was bedridden. This must have frustrated Norfolk because an heir born of the union would strengthen his position still further, but he was obliged to be patient and wait for his son-in-law to gain in strength and years.

The duke soon had other matters to attend to. The rivalry between his ally Gardiner and their mutual enemy Cromwell was growing ever more intense. It may have been at the chief minister's instigation that Gardiner found himself dispatched to France in autumn 1533. His task was to give formal notice to Francis I of Henry's intention to appeal to a general council against Pope Clement VII's judgment that his marriage to Catherine of Aragon was valid. Gardiner's diplomatic skills seem to have been lacking, however, for he displeased the French king. He also fell foul of his own royal master for failing to commit himself absolutely to the split from Rome. He was named, along with several other conservative clerics and noblemen, in a papal dispensation allowing them to celebrate mass even in the event of a papal interdict.

By the time that Gardiner returned to court, he found that his influence with Henry had slipped even further. This was due in no small part to Cromwell, who had made the most of his absence by acting as *de facto* secretary to the king. In April 1534, he formally replaced Gardiner in this role, thus confirming his position as Henry's chief minister. Contemporaries were quick to grasp the significance. 'The credit and authority which he [Cromwell] enjoys with this King just now is really incredible,' Chapuys reported to Charles V, 'as great indeed as the Cardinal ever enjoyed, besides which he is daily receiving fresh bounties from him.'[1] By contrast, Gardiner seemed to have lost Henry's regard. Soon after his rival's promotion, he retreated to his diocese, where he remained until late 1535.

Another of the king's men who found himself out in the cold was Thomas More. In February 1534, Henry turned decisively against him by insisting that his name be included in a bill of attainder for conspiring with the so-called 'Maid of Kent', Elizabeth Barton, who had prophesied disaster if the king's marriage to Anne Boleyn went ahead. Although More has often been portrayed as living in seclusion at his home in Chelsea, seeking only peace and solitude away from the corruption and backbiting of the court, this is wide of the mark. In fact, ever since his resignation, he had continued to court controversy by engaging in a series of disputes with religious reformers, and had penned various treatises aimed at whipping up popular loathing for heretics. He was always careful to speak well of the king, and to make it clear that his attacks were aimed only at those who tried to steer Henry from the paths of righteousness, but this was not enough to protect him from the royal wrath. When the Elizabeth Barton scandal broke, Henry had no hesitation in accusing More of complicity.

Cromwell had drawn up two lists in the attainder: one against those who 'shall be attainted of high treason and suffer death except the king's majesty do pardon [them]', and the other against those who 'shall be attainted of misprision (concealment of treason) and have imprisonment at the king's will and lose all their goods'. At the king's specific command, More's name was included in the latter. He was by now so incensed with his former Chancellor that he was determined to make an example of him.

John Fisher's name was also included in the second part of the attainder. Despite his arrest in 1533, he had continued to speak out against the annulment since his ill-advised comparison of Henry to King Herod in 1529. During the years that followed, Henry had gradually given up on his attempts to win over or intimidate Fisher, instead resorting to defamation and imprisonment. It may have been this that incited the bishop to begin treasonable dealings. Since the beginning of 1532, Fisher had maintained a secret correspondence with Charles V via his ambassador Chapuys. By the end of September 1533, Fisher had begun inciting the emperor to lend his military might to opposing Henry's annulment, urging him that such intervention would be tantamount to a crusade. The king never discovered these letters, but it mattered little because his ministers had already found damning evidence of another of the bishop's connections.

In 1534, Fisher was accused of conducting several interviews with Elizabeth Barton, but of failing to report any of her disloyal prophecies to the king. Cromwell seized upon this as an opportunity to discredit this troublesome opponent and claimed that he had been neglectful in his duty to Henry. He wrote to upbraid the bishop in February 1534, having already spoken 'heavy words or terrible threats' to him.[2] The letter is one of the clearest indications of Cromwell's pre-eminence in Henry's favour at this time. 'I believe that I know the king's goodness and natural gentleness so well', he told the bishop, 'that his grace would not so unkindly handle you, as you unkindly write of him, unless you gave him other causes than be expressed in your letters.'[3]

Cromwell capitalised upon Henry's increasing paranoia about those men who had once been loyal, and used the Barton controversy to further condemn them. Henry was soon so convinced that Thomas More was plotting against him that he declared that the former Chancellor had not just colluded with Barton, but was the 'deviser' of her evil words. Ever the lawyer, More asked for a formal hearing before the Lords, no doubt confident that he could prove his innocence. Henry had no intention of giving him such a prominent arena, however, and insisted that he be interrogated by a commission of four of his other men: Cromwell, Cranmer, Norfolk and Audley. Perhaps, despite his animosity towards More, the king also hoped that they would persuade him to relent. Norfolk certainly tried hard to do so. 'Master More, it is perilous striving with princes,' he urged, 'and therefore, I would wish you somewhat to incline to the King's pleasure.'[4]

In the event, however, Henry was persuaded to remove More's name from the bill because Cromwell and his fellow commissioners shrewdly judged that parliament was unlikely to pass it if it remained. More reacted to the news in typically philosophical manner, telling his daughter Margaret: *quod differtur non aufertur* ('what is set aside is not put away').[5]

For all Henry's hostility towards More, the king knew that if his former Chancellor conformed, it would substantially improve the prospects of his subjects accepting Anne Boleyn as queen and all of the associated religious reforms. As it was, More – who was still officially a member of the council – stood as a figurehead for the old, accepted order, and even though the king denied him the opportunity to voice his objections in public, they were well enough known to be severely hampering his cause.

For his part, determined though he was not to sacrifice his principles, More was still desperate to win back his sovereign's esteem. He therefore begged for an audience with Henry, knowing that this was the surest means of achieving it. When his request was denied, he was forced to content himself with penning a letter beseeching his master that 'no sinister information move your noble Grace, to have any more distrust of my truth and devotion toward you, than I have, or shall during my life, give the cause'. He declared himself 'in my most humble manner, prostrate at your gracious feet', and assured Henry that he would forsake all of his worldly goods, liberty and even his life if he could 'meet with your Grace again in heaven'.[6]

In April 1534, More learned that Barton and five of her associates had been executed. He knew that he was living on borrowed time. As he confided to his son-in-law, he had crossed a line with Henry and 'could never go back again'.[7] Although he is always hailed – justifiably – for his bravery and unwavering principles, More harboured a terror of a traitor's death and admitted to feeling relieved that in spite of this he was able to resist the overwhelming pressure to relent. The more pressure that was heaped upon his shoulders, the more sanguine, even jovial he appeared. He adopted a gallows humour when Norfolk warned him that if he continued to defy the king, it would mean death. 'Is that all, my Lord?' More retorted. 'Then in good faith is there no more difference between your grace and me, but that I shall die today and you tomorrow.'[8]

For all that, though, More was still a shrewd man and, far from being the willing martyr that he is so often portrayed as, he tried to chart the hazardous course between upholding his principles and retaining just enough royal favour to avoid the block. Having made his stand by refusing to acknowledge Anne as queen and resigning the chancellorship, he resolved to do nothing further to provoke the king's ire. The only hope he had of achieving this was to keep his counsel. He implied as much to Cromwell in a letter of March 1534, insisting that where the king's new marriage was concerned, he would never 'murmur at it, nor dispute upon it, nor never did nor will'.[9] Given his vigorous actions against the annulment and subsequent reforms, this was somewhat disingenuous. But if he was not promising to go back on his word, he was at least vowing to be silent thereafter. And he knew his fellow lawyer Cromwell would understand that under English law silence implied consent.

Silence, though, was a luxury that More would not long be

afforded. In April, he was invited to swear to the Act of Succession. The oath's preamble included a rejection of papal authority, so if More was to comply, it would be taken as a public rejection of all his former principles. Having pored over the Act in its entirety, he told Cranmer that he was prepared to swear allegiance to the king and queen and their heirs, but that he would not sign the preamble. The archbishop consulted with Cromwell, who presented this suggestion to the king as persuasively as he could. But Henry was in no mood to compromise: More would have to put his signature to the Act as a whole, or face the consequences. It was obvious that the two men's shared history, which stretched back over four decades, did not entice the king to show any greater leniency than he would to a stranger. He expected absolute obedience from his men and would not flinch from meting out the ultimate penalty if they proved intransigent. 'This Act', More protested, 'is like a sword with two edges, for if a man answer one way it will destroy the soul, and if he answer another it will destroy the body.'[10]

Backed into a corner, he decided to adhere to his conscience rather than his king. But, aware of the repercussions, he did his best to allay his royal master's fury by refusing to give his reasons, insisting that if he 'should open and disclose the causes why, I should therewith but further exasperate his Highness, which I would in no wise do'.[11] If More hoped to thus placate the king, he was soon to learn that he had failed. Furious at More's 'obstinacy', Henry sent him to the Tower on 17 April 1534, shortly followed by Fisher, who had also refused to take the oath.[12] For the king, silence meant not consent, but opposition, and he was no longer prepared to tolerate it.

During the early days of his imprisonment, More sought solace in his writings. He penned a series of treatises on the Eucharist, one of which, the *Dialogue of Comfort*, has been described as his greatest work. A narrative on human suffering, it was undoubtedly an expression of More's own internal battle as he faced the increasingly certain prospect of death. Only if he recanted would he be allowed his liberty, but despite his terror, he was still not prepared to forsake his principles.

More's imprisonment reflected Henry's fury, but it also spelt danger for his reforms. Already More had courted widespread popular sympathy, even though his resistance had been relatively low key. Now he was holed up in the most notorious prison in the country, he had been transformed from figurehead to tragic hero. Realising this, Cromwell made several visits to the Tower, determined to heap pressure upon his rival to submit. He also acted as a barrier between More and what he knew to be the implacable wrath of his royal master. He told the prisoner that he would rather send his own son Gregory to the block than see a man who was once high in royal favour antagonise Henry further. 'The King's Highness would be gracious to them that he found comfortable,' Cromwell urged, 'so his Grace would follow the course of his laws toward them such as he shall find obstinate.' His choice of words was deliberate: he knew that More would have been stung by Henry's own accusation of obstinacy.[13]

To More, Cromwell seemed like the devil sent to tempt him, and he had no intention of conceding to this base-born heretic. The respect, even affection, that the chief minister felt towards More was certainly not reciprocated. It is interesting to speculate what might have happened if the king had gone to the Tower himself, rather than entrusting it to his most powerful servant. There can be little doubt that More would have found it a great deal more difficult to refuse him. As it was, he contented himself with continuing to profess his loyalty to Henry, for example in June 1535 when he wrote to his daughter Margaret. Even after enduring fourteen months of increasingly uncomfortable imprisonment, during which 'divers times . . . I thought to die within one hour', he still bore nothing but love for his sovereign. 'I am . . . the King's true and faithful subject and daily beadsman, and pray for his Highness and all his and all the realm.'[14]

Throughout his long sojourn in the Tower, More had continued to adhere to his policy of silence. 'I do nobody harm,' he told Margaret, 'I say none harm, I think none harm, but wish everybody good. And if this be not enough to keep a man alive, in good faith I long not to live.'[15] But if saying nothing had not been enough to save him when he was first arrested, now, as the whole kingdom watched and waited to see what he would do, only a full recantation would buy his freedom.

Quite what Henry felt about his former favourite's ongoing 'obstinacy' is not recorded. Doubtless he desperately hoped that he might relent: More had already caused enough trouble for his marriage and reforms, and he would be even more dangerous dead than alive. But there was no doubt personal regret too. Henry had loved and respected More since childhood, and even the king's considerable fury could not completely obliterate the feelings of tenderness that he had cherished for so long. The fact that, once won, Anne Boleyn had proved a disappointment as a wife and queen might have further softened Henry's attitude towards the man who had opposed her from the start. But it could never be enough to save More. If the king had excused such a high-profile advocate of the old regime from conforming to the new, it would have made a mockery of everything for which he and his ministers had striven for almost a decade.

For his part, More's former affection for his royal master had gradually been replaced by disapproval. Despite his protestations of loyalty and devotion to Henry, he had come to regard him as being as much of a tyrant as his late father. His seemingly light-hearted quip that if his head could win the king a castle in France, it would be struck off without a thought had been telling. Overlooking his own relentless persecution of evangelicals, he now presented himself as an innocent victim of a tyrant's regime.

In November 1534, parliament passed the Act of Supremacy, recognising the king as Supreme Head of the Church of England. It was the epitome of all Cromwell and Cranmer had striven for, and they now seemed at the peak of their influence with Henry. By contrast, it set the seal on More's doom. Now that the Act was in force, even more pressure was applied upon him to accept the king's status and associated reforms.

At the same time as he was putting the statutory framework in place for a religious revolution, Cromwell was beginning to introduce known reformers into the king's service. They included Christopher Mont from Cologne, who had been a member of Cromwell's service for some time and was now dispatched by his master to the Protestant states of Germany with orders to foster good relations with England. A letter from the French poet and radical Nicholas Bourbon reveals the extent to which reformers had penetrated Henry's inner sanctum. As well as Cranmer and Cromwell, whom he describes as being 'aflame with the love of Christ', he mentions the king's physician William Butts, his astronomer Nicholas Kratzer, the painter Hans Holbein and the reformist Bishop of Worcester, Hugh Latimer.[16] Bourbon had lodged with Butts at the queen's expense during a visit to London, and he said that the physician was like a father to him. To More and the other religious conservatives, it seemed that these dangerous radicals were forcing the king – and England – down the road to heresy and ruin.

In January 1535, Henry appointed Cromwell Vicegerent in Spirituals, or vicar-general. This gave him considerable new powers over the clergy, enabling him to stamp out opposition to the reforms from this influential sector, just as he had among the king's ordinary subjects. It was one of the clearest indications of Henry's faith in his chief minister that he was content for him to dominate spiritual affairs as he did political ones. But the king perhaps did not envisage just how far his minister would exercise his new powers during the years that followed. The consequences would be dramatic – not just for Henry's subjects, but for his relationship with Cromwell, pushing both to the edge of their endurance.

Where Henry was concerned, though, nothing was ever quite as it seemed. Although the king had vested enormous powers in Cromwell, who was reported to now enjoy 'supreme authority', More still had cause to hope that his fickle favour might turn once more towards him.[17] In May 1535, Chapuys sent a revealing dispatch to his master about an uncharacteristic mistake that Cromwell had made. Henry had instructed him to show the ambassador a letter that he had written to the English envoy in France, but Cromwell had forgotten to do so, perhaps because of the considerable pressure of work under which he was labouring. When he learned of this, Henry was utterly unforgiving and upbraided his minister as 'a fool and a man without discretion'.[18] It was a warning shot for Cromwell, and the minister stepped up his efforts to enforce the Act of Supremacy as if by way of recompense.

Having enjoyed little success with More himself, Cromwell resolved upon a new tactic and sent his deputy, Richard Rich, a gifted and ambitious young lawyer who hailed from a family of London mercers, to consult with the fallen Lord Chancellor. Rich had been appointed solicitor-general in 1533 and was rapidly rising through the ranks. He had already snared Fisher in May 1535 by persuading him, with honeyed words, that the king wished to know for his own conscience's sake Fisher's true opinion. Rich assured him that he could confide in strict secrecy. Fisher fell into the trap and stated that Henry was not the supreme head of the Church. His fate was sealed. Lord Chancellor Audley presided over his trial on 17 June, and the bishop was condemned to death.

Now aged sixty-five, Fisher was one of Henry's oldest servants, but the king did not hesitate to see the sentence carried out. The bishop's defiance had been confounded – albeit unintentionally – by Pope Paul III's declaration on 21 May that he intended to elevate Fisher to the position of cardinal. By making Fisher a prince of the Church, he no doubt hoped to deter Henry from taking any extreme measures against him. In fact, it had the opposite effect. Upon receiving the news of this promotion, Henry darkly quipped that he could give Fisher a red hat of his own, or else see he had nowhere to put it. He subsequently gave orders for Fisher's execution, which took place on 22 June. This was one of the clearest demonstrations yet of the king's brutality. He had always been capable of lashing out against those who defied him, but the seemingly callous way in which he dispatched the aged bishop hints at a growing ruthlessness. It would become increasingly evident as his reign progressed.

Fisher was immediately proclaimed a martyr by the Catholic authors and theologians of Europe. In England, too, there were stirrings of a martyr's cult. Reports began to circulate that Fisher's head, which had been displayed on London Bridge alongside those of other convicted traitors, was growing rosier and more lifelike every day. The rumour was recorded in a pamphlet by the Catholic polemicist Johannes Cochlaeus, which attacked Henry VIII and claimed that the victims of his regime should be accorded the status of martyrs. Alarmed, Henry commissioned one of his most skilful propagandists, Richard Morison, to write a tract refuting these claims. He went further still by ordering the destruction of the tomb that Fisher had built for himself in the chapel of St John's College,

Cambridge. His heraldic emblems were defaced, and the college statutes were in due course redrafted to eliminate all mention of him.

The brutality of the response bears the mark of Cromwell, not just his royal master. Even before Fisher's death, the chief minister had instructed Rich to turn his attention to More. During a visit to his cell in the Bell Tower on 12 June, the solicitor-general engaged the prisoner in friendly conversation. But More was not so easily drawn, and when Rich subsequently claimed that the former Chancellor had verbally rejected the king's supremacy over the Church, he was almost certainly lying. More strenuously denied it, dismissing Rich as 'always reputed light of his tongue, a great dicer and gamester, and not of any commendable fame'.[19]

Whether Rich spoke the truth, it was enough to have More indicted and brought to trial on 1 July 1535. Audley again presided over this, and Rich stood as witness for the government's case. The Lord Chancellor was subsequently criticised for allowing the weight of the conviction to rest on Rich's testimony and for overruling More's objections to this in his defence. The outcome seemed even more assured when Audley began to pass sentence on More without allowing him the opportunity to argue against his conviction. Rich's testimony may have been the lynchpin of the case, but Sir Christopher Hales, the attorney-general, declared that he was ready to convict More for his silence alone, which he claimed was 'a sure token and demonstration of a corrupt and perverse nature, maligning and repining against the statute'.[20]

Only when the verdict had been delivered did More at last break his silence. With his enemies looking on, he gave vent to a forceful and persuasive repudiation of the king's supremacy over the Church, declaring it to be 'directly repugnant to the laws of God and his holy Church'. He went on to claim that separating England from Rome would render the kingdom subject to the narrow views of England's bishops, depriving her of the universal teachings of the Pope and his bishops across the globe. 'I have, for every Bishop of yours, above one hundred,' he told the judges, 'and for one Council or Parliament of yours (God knoweth what manner of one), I have all the councils made these thousand years. And for this one kingdom, I have all

Bust of a laughing boy, thought to be the future Henry VIII aged about seven, by Guido Mazzoni, c.1498. At the time it was made, Henry was the 'spare heir' of his father Henry VII.

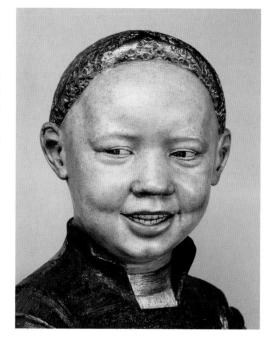

Arthur Tudor, Prince of Wales. The first-born child of Henry VII and Elizabeth of York, he was expected to inherit the throne but died in 1502, aged just fifteen.

Henry VIII. Painted around the time of his accession in 1509, this portrait shows a striking resemblance between Henry and his elder brother Arthur.

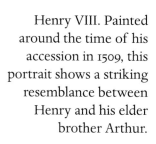

Henry VII in later life. The first Tudor king had an increasingly difficult relationship with his younger son Henry once he was his sole heir.

Henry VII (centre) with his despised lawyers, Richard Empson and Edmund Dudley. One of his son's first acts as king was to have them arrested and executed.

The royal procession to Parliament at Westminster, 1512. Henry VIII is under the canopy and is preceded by the Duke of Buckingham, carrying a sword. Henry ordered the Duke's execution for treason nine years later.

Henry VIII, 1520. This was painted the same year as his famous meeting with his French rival, Francis I.

Jousting was one of Henry VIII's favourite pastimes. Here, he jousts in front of his first wife, Catherine of Aragon, to celebrate the birth of their short-lived son in 1511.

Thomas Howard, 3rd Duke of Norfolk. Howard boasted long service to Henry VIII but was never one of his favourites.

Sir Henry Guildford, 1527. Guildford served the future Henry VIII when he was a boy and became one of his most trusted courtiers.

William Fitzwilliam, 1st Earl of Southampton, dedicated his life to serving Henry VIII and enjoyed great esteem throughout the reign.

Charles Brandon, 1st Duke of Suffolk, and Mary Tudor. Brandon had been Henry's closest friend since his youth but fell briefly from favour when he secretly married the king's sister in 1515.

Cardinal Thomas Wolsey, Henry VIII's chief adviser. Painted in c.1515-20, this shows Wolsey at the height of his powers.

Letter from Henry VIII to 'Mine own good cardinal' Wolsey, thanking him for his loyal service.

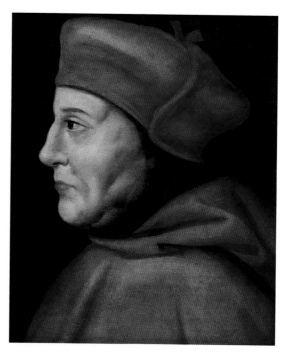

Charles V and Henry VIII. The Holy Roman Emperor was the most powerful man in Europe and one of Henry's greatest rivals.

Francis I and Henry VIII. This detail from a treaty shows the two kings in accord, but they were fierce rivals throughout their reigns.

The Field of Cloth of Gold. This magnificent and cripplingly expensive summit meeting between Henry VIII and Francis I took place in June 1520 and was masterminded by Wolsey.

Sir Thomas Wyatt, c.1535-7. Arrested on suspicion of adultery with Anne Boleyn, the poet and courtier regained his former favour with Henry and served him for the rest of his days.

Sir Nicholas Carew, Henry VIII's regular jousting companion and close friend.

Self portrait of Hans Holbein the Younger, 1542. The celebrated artist crafted Henry VIII's image as a magnificent and invincible king.

Desiderius Erasmus by Holbein, 1523. Henry met the humanist scholar when he was nine years old and revered him throughout his life.

This iconic portrait by Holbein shows Henry VIII at the height of his powers, but when it was painted in 1545 the king was grossly overweight and plagued by ill health.

Stephen Gardiner, Bishop of Winchester. A religious conservative, Gardiner fell foul of Henry VIII on a number of occasions.

Thomas Cromwell succeeded his patron Wolsey as Henry VIII's chief adviser. A religious reformer, he pushed through the king's break with Rome and established his supremacy over the English church.

This title page of *The History of the Reformation of the Church of England* shows Henry with his Archbishop of Canterbury, Thomas Cranmer, a staunch reformer.

John Fisher and Thomas More. Both men had enjoyed considerable influence with Henry VIII but were executed for refusing to take the Oath of Supremacy.

Henry FitzRoy, Duke of Richmond, c.1534. Henry considered making his illegitimate son his heir, but he died in 1536, aged seventeen.

Henry Howard, Earl of Surrey. Eldest son of the Duke of Norfolk, he was a close companion of Henry FitzRoy and the last man to be executed by Henry VIII.

Holbein's famous Whitehall Mural, completed in 1537, shows Henry VIII with his parents and third wife, Jane Seymour (bottom right).

Edward VI as a child, c.1538. Henry was overjoyed by the birth of a son and heir after almost thirty years of disappointment.

Henry VIII, 1542. This portrait by Holbein hints at the fifty-one-year-old king's expanding girth and infirmity. He is shown leaning on a staff and his beard is flecked with white.

John Russell, 1st Earl of Bedford, one of Henry VIII's most loyal and longest serving attendants.

Edward Seymour, Duke of Somerset, rose to power upon his sister Jane's marriage to Henry in 1536 and was appointed Lord Protector of their son Edward VI.

An able administrator, Thomas Wriothesley, 1st Earl of Southampton, rose to become Henry VIII's Lord Chancellor and privy councilor to his son Edward VI.

Sketch of Henry VIII by Holbein, showing the king in his later years.

Will Somer, Henry VIII's favourite jester. A 'natural fool', Somer was one of the king's most cherished companions.

Henry VIII with the Guild of Barbers and Surgeons. His favourite physician, Sir William Butts, is shown on his right (centre).

Sir William Butts, c.1543. A committed humanist and reformer, Butts was physician to Henry VIII and his family for almost twenty years.

Charles Brandon, 1st Duke of Suffolk, died two years after this portrait was painted, in 1545. He is buried at Windsor, close to his royal master.

In this illustration from the Psalter of Henry VIII, the solitary king is shown reading in his bedchamber.

Sir Anthony Denny, Henry VIII's last chief gentleman of the bedchamber. He was among the men who attended the king on his deathbed.

John Dudley, 1st Duke of Northumberland, served Henry VIII for many years but rose to prominence under his son Edward. He orchestrated a coup to place his daughter-in-law Lady Jane Grey on the throne when Edward died.

Edward VI, c.1542. Henry VIII's 'precious jewel' was just nine years old when he succeeded his father to the throne.

Henry VIII on his deathbed, pointing to his son and heir Edward VI. The vanquished pope is in the foreground, and to the new king's left are Edward Seymour, John Dudley and Thomas Cranmer.

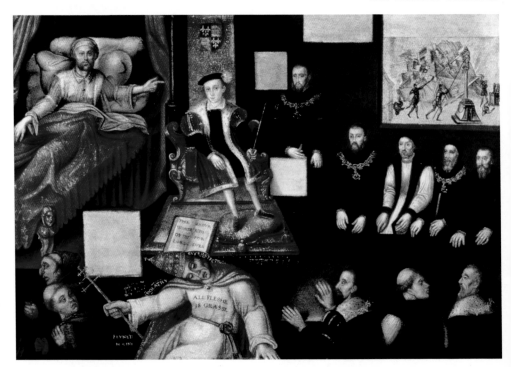

other Christian Realms.'[21] In short, England would become little more than a backwater, unable to benefit from, or play any role in, the bounty of international politics and religion.

It was More's last stand and he knew it. The relief at finally being able to express his true opinions was tempered only by the certain knowledge of the price he would pay. His sentence was the one that he had long feared: a traitor's death. This was soon commuted to beheading – ostensibly out of deference to his former office. Perhaps, in the end, Henry had relented enough to show his former favourite this final kindness – if it could be described as such. But it might equally have been prompted by a desire to appear merciful.

If the king felt any anguish at the prospect of More's death, he did not show it. No matter how much affection he cherished towards his men, if they did not do his bidding then his feelings could swiftly change to cold, implacable hostility. There may have been an element of self-preservation in this attitude. Henry would surely have been driven mad by remorse if he had allowed any more tender feelings to creep in whenever he dispatched a former friend. He was also adept at convincing himself of the justice of his actions, as the annulment had proved. And he was surrounded by men who were quick to assure him that he was right.

More, too, remained tight-lipped about his feelings towards his royal master. He had every reason to despise him – morally, ideologically and personally – but he resisted any temptation that he might have felt to speak out. His silence was typical of those who had been condemned to die: consideration for the loved ones they would leave behind often prevented any openly expressed vitriol against their king. It is equally possible, though, that even now More bore no grudge against the man whom he had admired for thirty-six years. Perhaps he believed that Henry's only crime had been in heeding the advice of his 'evil' councillors, and that they – not the king – were responsible for his impending death.

On 6 July, More was led from the Bell Tower up to the scaffold on Tower Hill. He appeared calm and in good humour, and even shared a joke with the officer who assisted him onto the scaffold: 'I pray you, master Lieutenant, see me safe up, and for my coming down let me shift for myself.'[22] In contrast to the executions of other high-profile prisoners, there were few witnesses. Henry was too fearful about the mood of the people to allow the event to become the usual crowded spectacle. Perhaps this is why More chose not to make any final speech in defence of his principles, but instead went quietly to his death.

More's head was set on a spike on London Bridge, as Fisher's had been. It was then given to his beloved daughter Margaret, and may have been buried with her in Chelsea church when she died in 1544.[23] The rest of More's remains were interred in St Peter ad Vincula, the Tower chapel that houses the bones of other eminent victims of Henry's regime. Determined to impede More's progress towards martyrdom, the king banned any accounts of the execution from being published in England. But within weeks, a French pamphlet was being circulated in London.

None of the measures that Henry and his ministers took could prevent the outrage that spread across Catholic Europe when the news of More's execution was pronounced. Henry's most powerful rival, the Emperor Charles V, upbraided the English ambassador, saying that he 'would rather have lost the best city of our dominions than have lost such a worthy counsellor'.[24] Accounts of More's life soon filled the pages of printing presses across the Continent, and even in England there was a huge underground market for biographies by the likes of William Roper and Nicholas Harpsfield. In short, More was even more troublesome to Henry in death than he had been in life.

Henry's reaction to More's execution and the subsequent backlash among his European rivals is not recorded. He expressed no regret: to do so would have been to imply that he sympathised with More's stance, which in turn would have seriously undermined his reforms, not to mention his marriage. It is possible that Henry's other men – Cromwell in particular – applied themselves to blackening More's character in the run-up to his execution so that their master did not change his mind. But it is also possible that the king was already set firmly upon his course. Henry did not flinch from punishing those who crossed him, no matter how high in his favour they might have been. And, once resolved, he rarely changed his mind.

II

'Resisting evil counsellors'

AROUND THE TIME of More's trial and execution, the king enlisted the services of a man who was to become one of his closest companions, providing him with much-needed light relief during some of the greatest crises of his reign. Will Somer is first mentioned as a member of the royal household on 28 June 1535. He was employed as a jester and seems to have struck an instant chord with Henry, who loved to laugh and had had a professional fool in his entourage since the age of ten. His father had also employed a number of fools during his reign, many of whom had been cared for together in a separate household.

Little is known of Somer's origins, so he was probably of humble birth. According to the eighteenth-century biographer James Granger, Somer 'was some time a servant in the family of Richard Farmor of Easton Neston, in Northamptonshire', but there is little evidence to substantiate this.[1] Although he is often depicted as a witty and acerbic commentator on the events and personalities of court, this owes more to the imagination of later writers than to contemporary accounts. In fact, like most other court jesters of the early Tudor period, Somer was almost certainly a 'natural fool' – that is, someone with learning difficulties. The household accounts show that a 'keeper' was appointed to care for Will. He is often mentioned in connection with a group of court musicians, so he may have danced or sung as part of his act. Contemporary likenesses show him to be lean in build with a pronounced stoop, and he was described as being 'hollow-eyed'.[2]

It might seem distasteful to modern observers that people with disabilities were a source of amusement at court, but the Tudors had a deep respect for natural fools. In one of his most celebrated and influential works, *The Praise of Folly*, Erasmus asserted that, unlike most men, fools were not tainted by sin and had a purity of thought that brought them closer to God. In a similar vein, the biblical book of 1 Corinthians asserts: 'All men are fools before God and the foolishness of God is wiser than men's wisdom.'[3]

Henry certainly treated his fools with the utmost respect – Somer in particular. Within a year of his arrival at court, Will had replaced the fool named Patch, whom Wolsey had given to Henry six years earlier. He certainly seemed to have a gift for foolery and would have his king and court in fits of laughter as he thrust his face through a gap in the arras, then proceeded to mince about the room rolling his eyes, his monkey perched precariously on his shoulder. Without respect for any authority except the king's, he was once said to have donned a ram's-horn helmet that the Emperor Maximilian had presented to Henry some years earlier.

Henry lavished gifts of expensive clothing upon his fool, and the pair spent many hours alone in the king's privy chamber. Surrounded on all sides by sycophants and intriguers, Henry evidently enjoyed being in the company of a man who was incapable of dissembling. 'They can speak truth and even open insults and be heard with positive pleasure,' observed Erasmus. 'Indeed, the words that would cost a wise man his life are surprisingly enjoyable when uttered by a clown.'[4] Nevertheless, there is evidence that Somer did occasionally use his position to influence the king. He once made a joke to draw his royal master's attention to the extravagance and waste within the royal household. This may have been at the instigation of Cromwell, who was keen to curb the household expenses.

It was probably in the same year as Will Somer's introduction to court that the celebrated artist, Hans Holbein, at last entered Henry's service. Although he is first cited as the king's painter in a 1536 publication by the poet Nicholas Bourbon, with a woodcut of the poet after a drawing by Holbein, Bourbon had left England the previous year so Holbein's appointment almost certainly dates to then. The royal accounts are inconsistent in referring to Holbein as the king's painter thereafter, but this title is always used when special payments and advances of salary are made to him with regard to his trips abroad on Henry's service. Holbein himself was proud to be in the king's employment, and in his will he refers to himself as 'the King's Majesty's servant'.

Holbein's influence on Henry's image would be profound. More than any other artist, he is responsible for creating the impression of a stridently majestic, imposing and invincible monarch, who could inspire terror and devotion among his subjects. It is also thanks to Holbein that we have such detailed representations of Henry's queens, his children and his courtiers. His strikingly realistic portrayals hold up a mirror to the king and his court. A true polymath, Holbein undertook other commissions for Henry and his queens too. One of the earliest was a table fountain that he designed for Anne Boleyn to give to the king.

Henry had other distractions during the days after Thomas More's death. The court was busily preparing for the annual summer progress, which this year was to the West Country. As usual, a number of noble houses and other grand residences were selected for the dubious honour of hosting the king and his court. But a comparatively humble dwelling was also included in the itinerary. Situated in the heart of Savernake Forest in Wiltshire, Wolf Hall was the country estate of the Seymours, a family of ancient pedigree that boasted descent from Edward III. The head of the household was Sir John Seymour, whose sons Edward and Thomas were rising to prominence at court. But it was his eldest daughter, Jane, who had inspired the king's visit.

A rather plain, unprepossessing young woman, Jane had joined the household of Henry's first wife in 1529, but upon Catherine's exile from court she had been transferred to the service of Anne Boleyn – reluctantly, perhaps, since she had greatly admired the ousted queen. The first hint that she had attracted the king's notice came in October 1534, when Chapuys reported that Henry had become 'attached' to 'a young lady' of the court.[5]

Jane was then about twenty-six years old. Apart from her pedigree, she had apparently little to recommend her. With her pasty, plump face and small beady eyes she lacked the physical attributes admired in Henry's court, and one observer dismissed her as being 'of middle stature and no great beauty'.[6] She had neither the intelligence nor the wit of the queen she served, and largely passed without notice until the king started to pay her attention. Quite what he saw in Jane was the subject of some debate, with Chapuys mischievously concluding that she must have hidden assets. But her true appeal for Henry lay in the stark contrast that she provided to his wife. Anne's seductive charms and fiery nature had kept the king in thrall for seven years, but once the two of them were married the very qualities that had attracted him soon proved irksome. An outspoken and feisty wife was not at all what Henry wanted, particularly as she had so far failed to deliver her promise of a son.

Thomas Cromwell joined his master on progress and was among the party at Wolf Hall. Nothing escaped his notice, and he was well aware of his master's growing interest in Sir John's daughter. Although outwardly loyal to Queen Anne, Cromwell had already begun to make discreet overtures towards the conservative faction at court. Shortly before embarking on the progress, he had sent his deputy Richard Rich to warn the Duke of Suffolk that the king was unhappy with him about a number of matters, and had provided details so that the duke might rectify them. In order to allay any suspicions that Suffolk might have as to why this low-born rival should suddenly be doing him favours, Cromwell had told Rich to assure him: 'I am, always have been, and ever will be his grace's poor friend.'[7]

In fact, although Suffolk was still very much a conservative, his feud with the Duke of Norfolk had continued to simmer. In the spring of 1533, Norfolk had demanded that Suffolk relinquish to him the office of Earl Marshal. The king made his old favourite comply. Another point of contention had been the fact that he had a son by the king's sister, Mary – something that the king had failed to achieve in more than twenty years of marriage. The boy, named Henry, was the only legitimate and English-born grandson of Henry VII and thus had a powerful claim to the throne. However, in June 1533, Suffolk's wife Mary died, and the following March their ten-year-old son and heir Henry followed her to the grave.

Perhaps inspired by the need to bolster his dynastic hopes, Suffolk had subsequently arranged advantageous marriages for his daughters, notably Frances, who married Henry Grey, third Marquess of Dorset. The three daughters from their marriage also had a strong claim to

the throne, which would later be exploited, with disastrous consequences. Suffolk, who was approaching fifty, similarly arranged
another marriage for himself, just three months after Mary Tudor's
death. This sent shockwaves across the court, for his chosen bride
was the fourteen-year-old Katherine Willoughby, who had been
intended for his son Henry. It proved an advantageous match for
Suffolk and gave a much-needed boost to his financial position, which
had suffered in the wake of Mary's death. The Willoughby estates
were signed over to Suffolk's heirs, and this pact was strengthened
when his teenage bride gave him a son two years into the marriage.
Despite the difference in their ages, the marriage seemed to offer
Brandon some solace during a difficult period in his relationship
with the king.

Suffolk's rival Norfolk had hardly enjoyed more success with the
king in recent times. Having absented himself before his niece's
coronation, he had attended court only rarely thereafter. By the beginning of 1535, he had grown deeply embittered about Cromwell's
dominance of the king's affairs. The growth of evangelicalism was
anathema to him, and although he had played his part in More's
condemnation, he had privately sympathised with his predicament.
Norfolk had shown a relentless energy in battling for position at
court over the past thirty or so years, but he now seemed worn
down and disillusioned. In February 1535, he had therefore retreated
to his estate at Kenninghall, and three months later he accepted
another diplomatic mission to France.

Meanwhile, Cromwell was using the king's summer progress as
an opportunity to investigate a number of religious houses in the
West Country. 'Wherever the King goes, Cromwell, who accompa-
nies him, goes about visiting the abbeys in the neighbourhood, taking
inventories of their lands and revenues, amply instructing the people
in this new sect, and dismissing from the said abbeys, convents, or
nunneries all those men or women who had professed before
reaching the age of 25, the rest being at liberty to quit or remain,
as they please,' Chapuys reported.[8] What Cromwell found, fuelled
his reforming zeal and made him determined to increase the pace
of change once he was back in London.

It was also in 1535 that the first complete modern English translation of the Bible by Myles Coverdale was published. From Cromwell's perspective, giving the people of England direct access to the word of God was a crucial part of his reforms, so he championed it enthusiastically. He had an influential ally: Hans Holbein, who was commissioned to design the frontispiece. The two men were by now closely allied and both were firmly committed to the cause of reform. Holbein's design encapsulates Cromwell's vision for the English church. Dominating the scene is Henry VIII, who sits enthroned as he distributes the Bible to the bishops in the presence of the laity. His position in the composition, directly beneath God's name, sent a clear message about his supremacy over the Church, free from the shackles of papal authority.

At the same time, Holbein produced a New Testament title page and a design for a work by the Lutheran theologian Philip Melanchthon. Together with the Bible frontispiece, these three works were probably intended as a gift for the king. The artist also produced three small woodcuts to be used in religious publications, but they did not appear until later. This may be because Henry considered them too radical: all three images show monks in the role of the biblical Pharisees, who were enemies of Christ. Holbein had learned – as his friend Cromwell would do likewise on many more occasions – that the king's enthusiasm for reform had very definite limits. Nevertheless, the religious works that he had completed would prove enormously influential in positioning Henry as the champion of reform. By now, Holbein's status as the king's favourite painter was unassailable. Having successfully completed a number of prestigious commissions, both of Henry and those close to him, he had proved that he could be trusted. Even though – as a tradesman – he was not given lodgings at court, he lived close enough for Henry to call upon him whenever he was needed, and the fact that he was given a regular salary meant that he was the king's to command.

While Cromwell was superintending profound changes in the religious life of the kingdom, his rival Gardiner was busy plotting his return to royal favour by turning his coat. He penned two treatises: one in defence of the royal supremacy and the other defending the execution of Bishop Fisher. The latter was in direct response to a pronouncement by the Pope condemning the English king for his actions. But it was the other, *De vera obedientia*, that would become Gardiner's best-known work and provide a persuasive justification for Henry's rejection of papal authority. Although on the surface it appeared that Gardiner had at last declared himself decisively for the king's reforms, his arguments were characteristically subtle and left the door open for a possible reconciliation with the Pope. Above all, he stressed the virtue of obedience – regardless, perhaps, of one's own personal opinions: 'To obey truly is nothing else but to obey unto the truth.'⁹

Gardiner made sure that both works were ready for the king's return to court in September 1535. They prompted outrage among Catherine of Aragon's supporters. Chapuys expressed surprise that the bishop had performed such a volte-face after seeming to uphold papal authority for so long. Clearly the subtlety of Gardiner's arguments was lost on him, as it no doubt was on most others who read them. Certainly they were enough to convince Henry, who was content for Gardiner to return to royal service – if not, quite, to favour.

Despite the bishop's evident lack of diplomatic skills, Henry appointed him ambassador to France. Norfolk's mission there had proved both brief and fruitless, and upon returning to England, he had withdrawn once more to his country estates. Gardiner had grave misgivings about leaving court when his chief ally was absent, but he had little choice. He would remain in France for the next three years. The fact that his embassy coincided with the most radical religious changes to take place in England since the split with Rome suggests that Cromwell had been behind his appointment, which soon seemed more like exile to Gardiner than a sign of his master's forgiveness. Shortly after arriving at the French court, he grumbled to the papal nuncio Rodolfo Pio that he had been forced to write *De vera obedientia*, hinting that it did not reflect his true beliefs.

By the time that Henry returned from his summer progress, his wife was pregnant once more. Everything now rested on whether Anne would carry the child to term (which she had failed to do with her previous two pregnancies) and, crucially, whether it would be a boy. The king's men waited and watched, ready to turn with the tide.

Towards the end of 1535, a scandal involving the queen's uncle began to unfold. Lord Thomas Howard had continued to rise to prominence since attending his niece's wedding and the christening of her daughter in 1533. In the sexually charged world of the court, to which noblemen sent their daughters so that they might make good marriages, and where clandestine affairs developed on an almost daily basis, it was perhaps inevitable that the youthful Lord Howard should form a romantic attachment. Unfortunately, though, he made a dangerous choice. Lady Margaret Douglas was the daughter of the king's sister Margaret, and half-sister to James V of Scotland. The couple apparently shared a love of poetry, and one or both of them penned a number of amorous verses contained in an anthology that still survives in the collections of the British Library.

Henry, who had long enjoyed the game of courtly love, may have encouraged their flirtation, but he certainly did not expect or wish it to go further than that. But Lord Thomas and Margaret had apparently fallen deeply in love, and early in 1536 they pledged to marry. Perhaps they knew that the king would not approve, for neither sought his permission. The consequences would be dire. When their plans were uncovered, Henry was so incensed that he had both Howard and Margaret thrown into the Tower. He suspected that it was Margaret's way of bolstering her place in the succession, considering that Henry's eldest daughter Mary had been bastardised and her half-sister Elizabeth's status was threatened by troubles in the king's marriage to Anne Boleyn. He ordered his able clerk and messenger, Thomas Wriothesley, to investigate the matter. Wriothesley evidently found enough to support his royal master's suspicions, because Henry subsequently ordered a clause to be added to the 1536 Act of Succession, making it treason to 'espouse, marry or deflower being unmarried' any of the king's female relations.[10]

Although Margaret was subsequently forgiven, Howard never would be. A bill of attainder was passed in parliament, accusing him of having been 'led and seduced by the Devil, not having God afore his eyes, not regarding his duty of allegiance that he oweth to have borne to the king our most dear and his most dread Sovereign Lord'. It went on to state: 'It is vehemently suspected and presumed maliciously and traitorously minding and imagining to put division in this realm. And to interrupt, impede and let the said succession of the crown.' It concluded by sentencing Howard to death.[11] The sentence was never carried out, but Howard remained in the Tower for the rest of his life, despite the fact that Margaret soon renounced their affair. Kept in miserable conditions, he fell sick the following year and died on 31 October 1537. Henry ordered that his body be given to his mother, the Dowager Duchess of Norfolk, to be buried 'without pomp'.[12]

If Queen Anne had been troubled by the scandal involving her uncle, she did not show it. Her pregnancy seemed to be advancing well, but Chapuys observed that although the king outwardly rejoiced in her condition, in private he 'shrank from her'.[13] Henry was also maintaining his interest in Jane Seymour, and the influence of her brothers at court was increasing as a result.

The eldest, Edward, had been introduced to court at the age of fourteen by his father, who had secured him a place as page of honour to Henry's sister Mary upon her marriage to Louis XII of France. He had subsequently taken part in a number of military campaigns and had been knighted for his bravery by Charles Brandon in 1523. Two years later, Henry had appointed him Master of the Horse to his illegitimate son, Henry FitzRoy, and in 1531 he entered the king's privy chamber as an esquire of the body. Fiercely ambitious, when it became obvious that his royal master's second marriage was faltering, Seymour did not hesitate to push his sister into the king's path, just as Thomas and George Boleyn had done with Anne. Yet again, Henry's men played a hugely significant role in directing their master's romantic decisions.

Edward's brother Thomas, who was about nine years younger, lacked the same ability, but was every bit as ambitious. He also had a dangerously reckless streak, which no doubt appealed to Sir Francis Bryan, in whose service Thomas is listed by 1530. He was in the same mould as the boisterous companions favoured by Henry in his youth, and played an active role in the social occasions of court. What he lacked in political acumen, he made up for in the tournament field, where he loved to flaunt his prowess. That there was little substance behind his showy exterior would soon become obvious, but for now his sister Jane was more than enough to make up for his shortcomings.

Sir Nicholas Carew, who despised Anne Boleyn and everything she represented, had rapidly forged an alliance with the Seymour brothers and would soon reap the rewards. Sensing which way the wind was blowing, he became more open in his support for his master's first wife, Catherine. This was demonstrated by an incident that occurred at court at around the same time as his promotion to the Garter. When Will Somer spoke well of Catherine and Mary, but called Anne a ribald and Princess Elizabeth a bastard, his royal master was so enraged that he was said to have threatened to kill the jester with his bare hands. Carew offered Somer shelter at his house at Beddington until his royal master's wrath had subsided, which was taken as a sign of his support for the ousted queen and her daughter.

Another of the king's men to distance himself from the queen and her entourage was her cousin, Sir Francis Bryan. Although he had proved a staunch supporter of Anne during her campaign to be queen, like his royal master he disapproved of her lack of decorum and her frequent outbursts of temper. At the end of 1534, he had also quarrelled with her brother George, and when he had been called up for another embassy to France the following year, he was quick to accept it – eager, no doubt, to be away from his troublesome cousins.

Meanwhile, Cromwell was keeping Anne's old rival under close scrutiny. Catherine of Aragon had suffered poor health since her exile from court. This was due at least in part to the cold and damp lodgings in which she had been housed, together with her constant fasting. Cromwell visited Catherine on occasion, and sent spies to do so on others. In late 1535, he noticed that her condition had rapidly deteriorated and reported to Gardiner that 'the dowager is in great danger'.[14] This was no exaggeration. A few days later, on 7 January 1536, Catherine died. Eustace Chapuys, who had spent the previous six and a half years championing her cause, had visited her one last time and now started a rumour that Catherine had been poisoned at the instigation of the 'Concubine'. Henry's most trusted physician, William Butts, subsequently wrote to Princess Mary's governess,

Lady Shelton, warning her to be vigilant in case Catherine's daughter was targeted next.

Meanwhile, Cromwell wrote again to Gardiner with the news, and could not resist reminding his rival of the Dowager Princess's 'sin' in marrying her late husband's brother.[15] Thomas Boleyn showed an even greater lack of sympathy, remarking that it was a pity Catherine's daughter Mary had not died too.

While Gardiner and his fellow conservatives mourned the old queen's passing, the news sparked rejoicing at court. Cromwell was quick to tell Gardiner that far from experiencing any sense of regret, their royal master was 'merry and in perfect health'.[16] Indeed, Henry was behaving 'like one transported with joy'. He ordered lavish entertainments at court and appeared 'clad all over in yellow from top to toe' with his wife and their daughter at his side.[17] Quietly, he instructed Cromwell to arrange Catherine's funeral, ensuring that it was respectful enough to the former queen without exhausting the royal coffers. It took place in Peterborough Cathedral, close to her final residence at Kimbolton. Although Cromwell had adhered to his master's instructions, Chapuys found cause to complain that Catherine had not been buried in the most sacred part of the cathedral.

Meanwhile, events at court took a dramatic turn. On 24 January, the king fell heavily from his horse while jousting at Greenwich. One report claimed that he was unconscious for two hours. Although this was written by someone who was many miles away at the time, the accident was serious enough to cause great alarm at court. It also served as a salutary reminder to Henry – and his subjects – of his mortality, and thus intensified his need to secure the succession with a son.

Yet, just five days later, on the same day that Catherine was laid to rest, Anne Boleyn miscarried again. The chronicler Charles Wriothesley claimed: 'Queen Anne was brought abed and delivered of a man child, as it was said, afore her time . . . she took a fright, for the King ran that time at the ring and had a fall from his horse, but he had no hurt; and she took such a fright withall that it caused her to fall in travail, and so was delivered afore her full time, which was a great discomfort to all this realm.' Although the two misfortunes were probably not related, Wriothesley was correct in asserting that the child Anne carried was a boy. 'The Concubine had an abortion which seemed to be a male child which she had not borne three and a half months, and on which the King has shown great distress,' Chapuys wrote in triumph to his master.[18]

Henry was bitterly disappointed. He had taken Catherine's death as a sign that God at last favoured his marriage to Anne, but now he railed at his second wife, declaring 'that he saw clearly that God did not wish to give him male children'.[19] It was soon painfully obvious that Anne's pregnancy had been her last throw of the dice. After suffering a third successive miscarriage, she must have realised that she was incapable of giving Henry what she had promised. Besides, even if she had resolved to try, her husband would not come near her. 'For more than three months this King has not spoken ten times to the Concubine . . . when formerly he could not leave her for an hour,' Chapuys reported in February 1536.[20]

Cromwell kept a close eye on all of these developments in his royal master's marriage. He also made the most of Gardener and Norfolk's absence to seize the initiative with the religious reforms. He suspended the authority of every bishop in the country so that the six canon lawyers whom he had appointed as his agents could complete their surveys of the monasteries. They soon returned with ample evidence of corruption and excess. One establishment was found to be so bad that monks turned up drunk at matins and proceeded to play cards and dice during the service. But for every allegation of abuse, there was a complaint about the methods employed by Cromwell's commissioners, who apparently bullied and threatened the monks they visited into providing the evidence that they sought, regardless of whether it was true.

However accurate the reports were, they provided Cromwell with the justification he needed to orchestrate a full-scale dissolution of the monasteries. The legislation to support this was put in place during the final session of the so-called 'Reformation Parliament', which was convened in February 1536. The following month, the Act for the Suppression of the Lesser Monasteries was passed by both the Commons and the Lords.[21] It was said that Cromwell had won favour with Henry by promising to make him the richest king in

Europe. If this was so, then he moved a step closer to achieving it when another Act was passed shortly afterwards, establishing a Court of Augmentations. This court had the power to collect the lands, property and goods of the suppressed monasteries, and to dispose of them in whatever way would be most profitable to the crown. It is telling that the most senior of the thirty or so staff were all friends and servants of Cromwell. Furthermore, as Vicegerent in Spirituals, he was able to personally control the funds that would soon come flooding into the royal treasury.

Barely had the ink dried on the new Acts than he set to work. 'Cromwell was no sluggard', observed the Spanish Chronicle, 'for he immediately sent collectors to unmake the abbeys.'[22] Once a report had been received by the Court of Augmentations, an order would be issued for the dissolution of the house in question and the diversion of its assets to the crown. These assets included not merely the revenues, gold plate and other treasures, but the vestments, pews, bells and even the lead from the roof. As soon as it had been stripped bare, the monastery would be pulled down. The devastation that this wreaked can hardly be imagined. These magnificent buildings had dominated the landscape for centuries, inspiring reverence and pride among the people who lived nearby.

The men whom Cromwell appointed to take them down, brick by brick, soon became figures of hatred. This did not deter his secretary Thomas Wriothesley who, eyeing an opportunity for aggrandisement, applied his considerable abilities to the task. With the same brutal efficiency as his patron, he undertook some of the most sensitive commissions, such as the destruction of St Swithun's shrine and the removal of all relics and treasure at his former tutor Bishop Gardiner's cathedral in Winchester.

Although the two men were linked by their past, as well as by ties of kinship, Wriothesley's passion for reform brought him into increasing conflict with the bishop. After one visitation, he wrote to assure Cromwell that 'we intend both at Hyde and St. Mary's to sweep away all the rotten bones that be called relics; which we may not omit lest it should be thought we came more for the treasure than for avoiding of the abomination of idolatry'.[23] Wriothesley did, though, profit significantly from the dissolution. As a reward for his diligence, the king granted him former monastic manors and religious houses in no fewer than eight counties.

Wriothesley also grew greatly in influence with the king, as is implied by a letter from Arthur Plantagenet's agent at court. 'Your lordship should send some loving letter unto Mr Wriothesley, giving him thanks and desiring him of continuance of his good mind toward you,' he urged. 'And if your lordship did send him some gentle remembrance . . . it should be very well bestowed. The truth is the man standeth in place where he may please and displease. It shall, therefore, be good to entertain him amongst the number of your friends.'[24] In a similar vein, Richard Morison, who knew Wriothesley well from their time together in Cromwell's service, opined: 'I was afraid of a tempest all the while Wriothesley was ever able to raise any. I knew he was an earnest follower of whatever he took in hand, and very seldom did miss where either wit or travail were able to bring his purpose to pass.'[25] An even less sympathetic observer described him as 'stout and arrogant', and another complained of his 'overmuch repugning [opposing] to the rest in matters of council'.[26]

Wriothesley's work, and many similar commissions, were viewed as acts of vandalism by large swathes of the population. Although Cromwell's associates were despised for the part that they played, by far the greatest fury and resentment was directed at Cromwell himself, who personified the radical changes that were sweeping across the kingdom.

This first phase of the dissolution brought Henry in the region of £100,000, equivalent to more than £32 million today. The annual incomes of the religious houses, meanwhile, delivered the crown a further £32,000 (£10.3 million). Little wonder that he was apparently content to allow Cromwell to continue his work, regardless of the dangerous resentment that was brewing among his subjects.

If the king experienced any unease about the scale and pace of reform, he did not show it. As Defender of the Faith, his conscience must have been pricked by the devastation that he knew had been inflicted upon the houses of God across his kingdom. But he would have taken it as a sign of weakness to display any remorse. The strong and decisive leader that Wolsey had encouraged him to become almost twenty years earlier needed to adhere to his course, no matter how tortuous it might be. In private, though, Henry was troubled by the scale of change that the break with Rome had unleashed. He was subject to increasingly dramatic mood swings, which obliged his men to tread even more carefully than before. Even those closest to him could not predict what stance he might take from one moment to the next.

For any other member of Henry's entourage, the task of administering the seismic changes in England's religious life might have proved all-consuming. But Cromwell had a staggering capacity for work. In contrast to some of the king's other men, he took each new role seriously, applying all of his energies to its successful execution, whether it was driving legislation through parliament or overseeing building works at the Tower of London. In order to manage his master's business efficiently, Cromwell employed an ever-expanding household of clerks, secretaries and messengers, but he always kept a close eye on their work. His friends expressed anxiety that he was running himself into the ground on the king's behalf, and even Chapuys was forced to acknowledge the extraordinary productivity and 'multifarious engagements' that Cromwell managed to maintain.[27]

But Cromwell's attention to detail never distracted him from the bigger picture. As well as undertaking the minutiae of the king's business, he was always careful to keep abreast of everything that was happening at court, across the kingdom and abroad. He had a sophisticated network of spies and informants who kept him abreast of affairs, and his voluminous correspondence reveals that he was as interested in the opinions of ordinary subjects as he was in those of princes and rulers.

The fact that Cromwell reigned supreme among the king's men was not entirely due to his proven ability and hard work. Securing close and regular access to the royal person had long been an essential prerequisite for favour and influence. Cromwell's various offices gave him ample reason to visit his master, and he made sure that he was almost constantly at his sovereign's side. He even managed to secure a suite of rooms at court 'to which he [Henry] can, when he likes, have access through certain galleries without being seen'.[28]

If business ever did call him away, then he would make sure to be back at court within a matter of days.

Perhaps more than any of Henry's other men, Cromwell understood the matters that lay closest to his master's heart. He was well aware of the king's growing aversion towards his second wife, and as a result he, too, began to break from Anne more decisively. Tensions between the two had been building for some time. Although Cromwell and Anne were both committed to the cause of reform, they had clashed over the dissolution of the lesser monasteries, Anne arguing that the proceeds should have been given to charitable causes, rather than swelling the royal coffers. She also accused Cromwell and his associates of lining their own pockets, and threatened to tell the king.

According to Chapuys, Cromwell had confided that the queen's animosity was so deeply rooted that she had told him 'that she would like to see his head off his shoulders'. It is an indication of how secure Cromwell felt in Henry's favour by this time that he seemed unconcerned by her threats. 'I trust so much on my master, that I fancy she cannot do me any harm,' he told Chapuys. Even though he had been regarded as Anne's 'right hand' since laying the foundations for her marriage to Henry, he had only ever been prepared to further her interests when they had corresponded with those of his royal master. He admitted as much to the ambassador, insisting that 'he had never been the cause of this marriage, although, seeing the King determined upon it, he had smoothed the way'. As if to prove the point, in April 1536 it was rumoured that Cromwell was arranging a new marriage for his master – presumably to Jane Seymour. Little wonder that he was reported to be 'on bad terms just now' with Queen Anne.[29]

The simmering hostility between Cromwell and the queen boiled over into open aggression on Passion Sunday (2 April) 1536. Anne instructed her Almoner, John Skip, to preach a sermon on a very deliberate theme at a service attended by the king and his court. The cleric duly 'explained and defended the ancient ceremonies of the Church . . . defending the clergy from their defamers and from the immoderate zeal of men in holding up to public reprobation the faults of any single clergyman as if it were the fault of all'. In case anyone was still in doubt that this was a thinly veiled attack on Cromwell's reforms, Skip 'insisted on the need of a king being wise in himself and resisting evil counsellors who tempted him to ignoble actions'. He went on to tell the story of Haman, the wicked and greedy enemy of Queen Esther in the Old Testament, who persecutes the Jews and tries to divert their riches to the royal treasury. The story ends with Haman facing death on the very scaffold that he had built for his rival, the queen's protector. The Almoner concluded that a king's councillor 'ought to take good heed what advice he gave in altering ancient things'.[30]

Both the king and his chief minister left the chapel in a rage. Skip was immediately seized and condemned for 'preaching seditious doctrines and slandering the King's Highness, his counsellors, his lords and nobles and his whole Parliament'. The fact that he escaped punishment suggests that Henry and Cromwell knew that he had merely been carrying out Anne's orders.

A little under three weeks later, Cromwell received a letter from Archbishop Cranmer, making it clear that he shared the queen's disapproval of the destruction of the monasteries. Relations between the two men had been strained for some time. In November 1535, Cranmer had written to defend himself after Cromwell had accused him of looking 'upon the king's business through my fingers, doing nothing in that matter [regarding the royal supremacy] . . . and I marvel not that you do so think, which knoweth not what I have done'.[31] Anne was quick to notice and exploit this chink in their relationship, and the knowledge that she had apparently turned his most steadfast ally against him dealt a severe blow to Cromwell.

But worse was to come, for in her next move Anne succeeded in enlisting the support of the king himself against Cromwell. Knowing that the latter favoured the Holy Roman Empire over France as England's ally, she insisted that Charles V be made to accept the royal supremacy. As the nephew of the late Queen Catherine and the most potent symbol of Roman Catholicism, aside from the Pope himself, Charles was unlikely ever to agree to this. Anne knew that if pressure was brought to bear upon him, it would gravely damage Anglo–Imperial relations and leave no other option but for Henry to ally with his great rival, Francis I. All of this could have been dismissed as bluff and bluster on Anne's part were it not for the fact that, to Cromwell's dismay, she appeared to have the full support of her husband.

Cromwell's battle for supremacy with Anne reveals a great deal about his relationship with the king. Although Henry had entrusted him with enormous power and authority, he never enjoyed the same level of influence that Wolsey had held over his royal master. Theirs had been a personal as well as a professional relationship, and Henry had cherished a great deal of affection for the cardinal. But, much as he might admire Cromwell's exceptional ability, the sharpness of his wit and his unflinching loyalty, as far as Henry was concerned theirs was a strictly business arrangement. Never again would he entrust one of his men with as much independent authority as Wolsey had exercised.

No longer the pleasure-loving prince of his younger days, Henry took a close interest in every aspect of government and made it clear to Cromwell and his fellow councillors that it was he who was in control. The fact that the king's own views were increasingly divergent from his chief minister's spelt danger for the latter. Despite breaking from Rome, Henry remained a good Catholic at heart and found some of Cromwell's more reformist ideas abhorrent. It was only a matter of time before he would begin to make his opinions more forcefully felt.

This is not to say that Cromwell did not still enjoy greater power than any other man in Henry's court. His royal master placed his advice above all others and was content to let Cromwell lead on matters that he had approved in advance, or in which he had little interest. But he wasted no opportunity to remind Cromwell and his other advisers that their power derived from him, with the implication that it could be taken away at any moment. 'It is I that made both Cromwell, Wriothesley and Paget good Secretaries,' he later boasted to William Petre, 'and so I must do to thee.'[32] Reginald Pole's claim, made in August 1536, that Cromwell 'ruled' Henry was wide of the mark.[33] Cromwell was acutely aware of this and was always careful to show the king all due deference, describing himself as 'your Majesty's most bounden' or 'humble subject and servant'. When offering his opinion, he made sure to do so with great humility, always submitting to the 'marvellous high wisdom' and 'excellent wit, prudence and long experience' of his royal master.[34]

Now it seemed that even Anne Boleyn, the woman whom Henry had shrunk from a short while before, enjoyed more favour with him than his chief minister. Cromwell knew that he had to act quickly in order to limit the damage that she had wreaked upon his relationship with his royal master. The fact that his first step was to renew his friendly overtures towards the conservative faction, now led by Sir Nicholas Carew, hints at his desperation. Despite the religious tide turning against him, Carew was still high in favour with the king and was close friends with another of his long-standing intimates, the Duke of Suffolk. Both of these men enjoyed what Cromwell never could: they were of impeccable pedigree and had been close to the king since his youth. Next to them, Cromwell seemed merely a paid adviser, esteemed by Henry for his abilities but without the ties of shared history and birth. He therefore had little choice but to use their ties to his own advantage.

Carew had also drawn the Seymour brothers into his circle. They were united by the common cause of ousting Anne Boleyn and replacing her with Jane Seymour, who was more inclined to traditional religious beliefs and was also – apparently – more pliable than her new mistress. Carew had facilitated his royal master's courtship of Jane by offering her lodgings at his house at Beddington, south of London, so that the king could make discreet visits to her in the evenings. So confident was Carew that Henry's new inamorata would soon supplant the despised 'Concubine' that he wrote to the king's daughter Mary, urging her 'to be of good cheer, for shortly the opposite party would put water in their wine'.[35]

Cromwell was not so sure. He continued to try to safeguard his position against whichever direction his master's marital affairs might take. As well as aligning himself to Carew and his faction, he also stepped up his efforts to cultivate another prominent conservative, Eustace Chapuys. Hoping to build bridges with Charles V in the wake of his aunt's death, he held a series of discreet meetings with the ambassador. He did so without Henry's knowledge or sanction, which was a risk he did not usually take. Chapuys reported that Cromwell had confided that 'as what he had said came of himself without commission from his master, I might see that he had no power to make any overture'.[36] Cromwell therefore urged Chapuys to encourage his own master to make the first conciliatory move.

When the ambassador subsequently told Henry about their conversations, the king was furious and immediately cut short their meeting. Taking Cromwell to one side, he roundly upbraided him for so far overreaching himself as to meddle in diplomatic relations. Cromwell's reaction was unexpected. Rather than meekly submitting to his master's tirade, he resolutely defended his actions, and a heated argument ensued while Chapuys and the rest of the court looked on. 'There seemed to be some dispute and considerable anger, as I thought, between the King and Cromwell,' the ambassador reported, 'and after a considerable time Cromwell grumbling left the conference in the window where the King was, excusing himself that he was so very thirsty that he was quite exhausted, as he really was with pure vexation, and sat down upon a coffer out of sight of the King, where he sent for something to drink.'[37]

Henry followed in his wake a few moments later and made a beeline for Chapuys, telling him abruptly that if he were to even consider an alliance with the emperor, then he would need to see the terms in writing. He proceeded to complain about all the wrongs that the emperor had done him during the previous years, and angrily denounced his 'great ingratitude', claiming that without Henry's support he would not have acquired such an extensive empire. Chapuys stole a glance at Cromwell, who was still sitting close by with his ally Thomas Audley, and noticed that they 'appeared to regret these answers, and in spite of the King's gestures to them that they should applaud him, neither of them would say three words'.[38]

As soon as this uncomfortable audience was over, the ambassador left court. Cromwell followed close behind and caught up with Chapuys halfway between Westminster and Greenwich. The chief minister was still smarting from having his schemes dashed in such a humiliating way, and Chapuys claimed that he was 'hardly able to speak for sorrow, and had never been more mortified in his life than with the [king's] said reply'. Cromwell went on to assure the ambassador that he had already spoken to the king about it, but his words must have sounded unconvincing even to himself. He soon gave up the pretence and admitted 'that if he had known what has taken place in this affair, he would not have meddled with it for all the gold in England, and that henceforth he would not treat with ambassadors without having a colleague'.

What Cromwell said next is the most revealing statement that he ever made about the nature of his relationship with the king. Astonished by the chief minister's candour, Chapuys reported that 'Although he had always pretended that what he said to me was of his own suggestion, yet he had neither said nor done anything without express command from the King.'[39] To concede to a man who was more of an adversary than an ally that his authority derived from, and was strictly limited by, the king is an indication of how vulnerable Cromwell was feeling at this point. Chapuys knew that the king's secretary was a master of deception and had played him false on many occasions, but he sensed that this time he spoke the truth. 'He has certainly shown himself in this an honest man,' he confided to Charles V, 'for although he knew it displeased his master, and that he incurred some danger, he would not retract anything he had said to me.'[40]

The whole sorry affair had left Cromwell feeling disillusioned as well as humiliated. 'He concluded that princes have spirits or properties which are hidden and unknown to all others,' Chapuys recorded, 'by which conversations Cromwell showed covertly his dissatisfaction at the strange contradictions of his master.' It was small consolation that, as Cromwell told Chapuys, the king had subsequently held an audience with the French ambassador, who 'came back from Court as mortified as I was the day before'. As Chapuys prepared to take his leave, a dejected Cromwell reflected: 'He who trusts in the word of princes, who say and unsay things, and promises himself anything from them, is not over wise.'[41] The beleaguered minister subsequently took a leave of absence from court, retreating to his house at Stepney and taking 'to his bed from pure sorrow'.[42]

Cromwell's relationship with Henry never quite recovered from this episode. Although he was too shrewd a man and had enough experience of courts to take the king's favour for granted, the considerable power that he had enjoyed for the past six years had given him a level of confidence that he would never again enjoy. To the naked eye, nothing had changed when he returned to court. As principal secretary, he still wielded greater influence than any of Henry's other men, but in place of his former swagger was a more tentative, deferential attitude. No longer did he presume to act in the king's name without making absolutely certain that Henry was content for him to do so, and he consulted his master on even the minutiae of court business. Whereas before he had been notoriously outspoken in council, now he hesitated to offer advice, assuring Henry on one occasion: 'This I do not write as thinking your grace needs any warning thereof being of so high and excellent wit, prudence and long experience. But that I would declare unto your Majesty how I do for my part take [perceive] the things and as I think other men should take them.'[43]

Cromwell's growing insecurity is also revealed by a 'great secret' that he confided to Chapuys. He admitted that he had been too afraid to relay an unpalatable piece of news to the king in person, so had sent him a message instead.[44] Whereas before he had sought out private audiences with Henry, now he often sent his faithful secretary Ralph Sadler to deal on his behalf. Not trusting his own considerable charm, which had worked so effectively in the past, he also employed Sadler to convey various gifts on his behalf. Soon it was noted that Sadler 'carries all the messages between the King and him'.[45]

Cromwell had been careful in his choice of intermediary, and rightly judged that Sadler's youthful charm and sharp intellect would win favour with the king. In that same year, Sadler was appointed a gentleman of the privy chamber. Cromwell might not enjoy the privilege of access himself, but having a trusted servant in Henry's inner sanctum would prove enormously useful to him in the months ahead.

It is interesting to speculate whether Cromwell kept his distance from Henry for other reasons, too. Now in his early fifties, he was one of the oldest members of the court. For all his ambition, he was perhaps growing tired of the relentless intrigue and jostling for favour, not to mention his royal master's increasingly unpredictable behaviour. He may therefore have employed the likes of Sadler out of personal preference, as well as political guile.

Increasingly distant from Henry he may have been, but Cromwell was still very much at the heart of royal affairs. He knew that in the weeks following Anne's last miscarriage, his royal master was turning ever more decisively against her. That fact, coupled with the queen's obvious antipathy towards Cromwell, was enough to convince him that the time for hedging his bets was over. To protect his position and win back favour with Henry, he had to relieve his master of his troublesome second wife and pave the way for Jane Seymour to succeed her.

The cause of Anne's downfall has been the subject of intense speculation. Much has been read into a remark that Cromwell made to Chapuys, that 'he, himself, had been authorised and commissioned by the King to prosecute and bring to an end the mistress's trial, to do which he had taken considerable trouble'.[46] There can be little doubt that Henry wanted to be rid of his second wife after her miscarriage in January 1536. He probably had in mind an annulment, but Cromwell knew that declaring the king's second marriage invalid would have made a mockery of all the tortuous legal wranglings that he had negotiated in order to end his first. Besides, the chief minister had his own reasons for wanting to remove Anne more permanently than that. She was now openly hostile towards him and had been planning her next move ever since the Passion Sunday controversy. The only way to ensure that she never regained her hold over the king was to have her convicted of treason. Chapuys, who was always at the centre of court affairs and witnessed much of what followed first-hand, was in no doubt that it was Cromwell, not his royal master, who 'planned and brought about the whole affair'.[47]

This prospect was as daunting as it was shocking. Anne was one of the shrewdest political operators at court and had fought a long and bitter campaign to be queen. She would not be easily outmanoeuvred. But she had a weakness that Cromwell resolved to exploit. Her vanity and flirtatiousness made her susceptible to flattery, and there was never a shortage of male admirers willing to indulge her.

Indeed, while most queens consort had surrounded themselves with female attendants, Anne preferred the company of men.

Some of the queen's closest male favourites were drawn from her husband's privy chamber. Principal among them was the king's groom of the stool, Henry Norris, who now enjoyed as much favour with Anne as he did with her husband. His fiercest rival was Francis Weston, who had served Henry for ten years now and was high in his favour. The privy purse accounts record him as a frequent gambling partner to the king, and the two men also regularly played tennis: in 1530 Weston won a total of sixteen angels (about £165) from four victories. This did not deter Henry from taking on his young opponent at bowls on a number of occasions. In 1532, Weston had been promoted to the sought-after position of gentleman of the privy chamber, and the following year he was made a Knight of the Bath. Although he was married, Weston proved just as popular with the ladies at court as he was with the king. George Cavendish claimed that he 'wantonly lived without fear and dread . . . following his fancy and his wanton lust'.[48] He appears as a charming, if rather shallow young man, and dangerously naïve in the world of court rivalries.

The rivalry between Weston and Norris had led to a notorious indiscretion in May 1535. The queen had playfully admonished Weston for neglecting his wife and flirting with Margaret Shelton, who was then being pursued by Henry Norris. Weston retorted that it was Anne herself, not Margaret, who prompted Norris's visits to her chamber. He slyly added that he himself loved someone in her household better than either his wife or Mistress Shelton. When Anne challenged him to name the object of his affections, he replied bluntly: 'It is your self.' Although the queen was quick to upbraid him for his impudence, the damage had been done. But she herself was responsible for an even more damning remark the following April, when she told Norris: 'If ought come to the king but good, you would look to have to me.'[49] Cromwell heard of this and other exchanges when he began making discreet enquiries among her ladies.

For now, though, it seems that Henry himself remained in ignorance. He had not been present when either of these exchanges between his wife and her male companions had taken place, and neither Cromwell nor any of the king's other men would have dared to accuse the queen of misconduct before they were sure of their case. Even though it was obvious to all that the king had tired of Anne, she had proven remarkably resilient in the past, winning back her husband's adoration when the odds had been pitted against her. Levelling an accusation of adultery against her was therefore fraught with danger and could bring the full force of Henry's wrath down upon the man who made it.

Although Cromwell was plotting Anne's downfall in the greatest secrecy, he did take another of the king's men into his confidence. William Fitzwilliam was hardly a natural ally. Even by court standards, he was notoriously fickle and would only align himself with someone for as long as they could serve his ends. Wolsey's patronage had significantly enhanced his career, yet Fitzwilliam had been one of his most outspoken defamers and had not hesitated to put his signature to the House of Lords articles that condemned him. Likewise, although privately Fitzwilliam was a religious conservative, he had attached his colours to the annulment and subsequent reforms for as long as the king himself bent that way.

Cromwell was fully aware of all this, but Fitzwilliam was too useful to him to let his failings get in the way. His half-sister, Lady Worcester, was a member of the queen's household and had a keen eye for scandal. She was therefore ideally placed to provide Cromwell with the evidence that he needed, and Fitzwilliam could in turn facilitate their meetings. He was assisted by Lady Worcester's brother, Anthony Browne, who had continued to rise in royal favour since his appointment to the privy chamber seventeen years earlier. Knighted in 1522, he had served as Henry's ambassador to France five years later and had always been in attendance at the important occasions of the reign. Like his half-brother, Browne was at heart a religious conservative, but was willing to overlook Cromwell's reformist sympathies in the interests of getting rid of Anne Boleyn. Cromwell was no more enamoured of Browne than he was of him, and once referred to him as a 'vain old beau' because of his love of finery.[50] But such personal opinions mattered little to these men in the pursuit of their political goals. Together with Fitzwilliam,

Browne soon persuaded his sister to give the chief minister what he needed.

Cromwell was assisted by another, even more unlikely ally. Henry Pole had no liking for the base-born minister, but he liked the queen even less. She stood for everything that he and his conservative associates despised and they heartily desired to rid the kingdom of her for good. In March 1536, Pole had told Chapuys that the king might want a new wife. He subsequently proved a willing accomplice to Cromwell's schemes, although the records do not detail the nature of his involvement.

Encouraged, perhaps, by Lady Worcester, a number of other ladies soon came forward. Cromwell later claimed that they had needed little persuasion. 'The queen's abomination, both in incontinent living, and other offences towards the king's highness, was so rank and common, that her ladies of her privy chamber, and her chamberers could not contain it within their breasts,' he reported to Gardiner and Sir John Wallop, the king's ambassador in France.[51] Norris wasn't the only name that was mentioned. Another was the queen's handsome young musician, Mark Smeaton, who had originally served in Wolsey's household. He had soon gained renown for his beautiful singing voice, and upon the cardinal's fall, Anne had appointed him to her entourage so that she could indulge her love of music and dancing. Even though she scorned the idea that they might converse as equals, Smeaton seems to have developed a crush on his royal mistress, and this helped to strengthen the case against her that Cromwell was quietly building.

Another member of Anne's circle was Sir Thomas Wyatt. Having distinguished himself in her husband's diplomatic service, he had been knighted in 1535, by which time he had ingratiated himself with the Boleyn faction and Anne in particular. She loved poetry and spent many hours listening to Wyatt's compositions. Thomas also shared the queen's love of France and harboured evangelical religious views. He had a reputation for loose sexual mores and seems to have developed a strong attraction for the queen. This found expression in his poetry. One of his most famous sonnets, 'Whoso list to hunt', refers to a lady with a 'fine neck', around which was written in diamonds: 'Noli me tangere [Do not touch me], Caesar's, I am.'

The most shocking allegation of impropriety against the queen, though, concerned her own brother George. Lord Rochford certainly enjoyed a close relationship with his sister. He was often in her presence, and they held many private meetings and conversations. The sources hint that his marriage to Jane Parker, who had been appointed a lady-in-waiting to Anne, was not a happy one, and he seemed to find far more solace in the company of his sister than of his wife. The fact that he and Jane had no children has cast doubt upon his sexuality – or at least his fidelity.[52] In any case, her husband's obvious preference for the company of his sister fostered in Jane a dangerous resentment that was soon to find full expression.

With one notable exception, all of these men had something in common, besides the queen's favour: they were enemies of Cromwell. Henry's chief minister had disapproved of Weston's appointment to a position of influence in the privy chamber because he was allied to a number of his enemies. Norris, meanwhile, had frustrated Cromwell's ambitions to control royal patronage. As groom of the stool, this had naturally fallen to him because he was best able to judge the right moment to present petitions to his royal master. As keeper of the privy purse, Norris had also encroached upon Cromwell's financial responsibilities as treasurer. Despite the alignment of their religious views, George Boleyn had always disliked Cromwell and, as one of Henry's principal advisers, was beginning to threaten the chief minister's pre-eminence. As a result, their fragile alliance disintegrated when Anne's influence began to waver.

The exception was Wyatt. He had long been on friendly terms with Cromwell, who was said to be 'very fond of Master Wyatt', and had even been described as the chief minister's 'minion'.[53] Their lively correspondence reveals their closeness, as does Wyatt's decision to make Cromwell executor to his father's will.[54] But the real testament to their friendship is the fact that, having gathered the shreds of evidence for the queen's adultery, Cromwell omitted Wyatt from her list of lovers, even though there was arguably more compelling evidence against him than any of the other men in Anne's coterie of male admirers.

One of Henry's other men narrowly escaped being implicated in the scandal. Sir Francis Bryan had returned from his latest embassy to France in January 1536, but had opted to spend time in the country, perhaps hoping to further distance himself from his cousin in the wake of her miscarriage. But distance from the king carried danger, too, and by April Bryan had judged that returning to court was the lesser of two evils. As Cromwell rounded up the men suspected of involvement with Anne Boleyn, Bryan was sent for in May to prove his allegiance. He had to undergo an interview with the chief minister before he was permitted an audience with the king. Either his tactic of distancing himself from the Boleyns at an early stage had paid off, or he had struck a deal with Cromwell, for he was spared any further action. To signal his favour, Henry made him chief gentleman of the privy chamber the same month and granted him £100 of the revenues of the bishopric of Winchester, much to the fury of Stephen Gardiner. It was from this time that Cromwell referred to Bryan as the 'Vicar of Hell'.

It had taken Cromwell just a week to construct his case against the queen. It was the same week that he was absent from court, when he himself had claimed to be so grief-stricken about the episode with the king that he was unable to stir himself from his bed. It had proved a perfect cover for his schemes. As soon as he returned to court on 23 April, he sought an audience with the king. Such was his sense of urgency that even though Henry was still annoyed with him for meddling in foreign policy, he agreed to see him. There were apparently no other witnesses to their conversation, and if a record of it was made, it has not survived. But Henry's subsequent actions make it clear that Cromwell's purpose in calling the meeting was to present the evidence that he had gathered against Anne.

Henry seems to have believed Cromwell's accusations – or at least, to have seen the merit in appearing to do so. It is an indication of how much the king wanted to be rid of his second wife that he was prepared to play the role of a cheated husband. This ran counter to the image that he had always aspired to of a chivalrous knight, adored by every woman he met. Now in his mid-forties, still lacking a male heir and, for all his vanity, painfully aware that he was no longer the athletic man of his youth, it was a grim prospect indeed to declare that his wife had sought sexual gratification outside the marriage bed. Henry knew that this would not just bring the condemnation of the world upon his wife's shoulders, but it would call into question his own virility.

The king was evidently prepared to suffer this personal cost in order to rid himself of Anne. Cromwell's gamble had paid off. Chapuys reported that the same month the king gave his chief minister 'a very fine house . . . well furnished'.[55] The implication was clear: Henry had rewarded Cromwell's efforts in trying to rid his master of an unwanted wife.

The king's decision to accept his chief minister's plan was quick to take effect. Shortly after their conversation, Henry presided over the annual chapter meeting of the Order of the Garter at Greenwich. The queen had confidently expected that her brother George would be elected a Knight of the Garter, but to her dismay her husband bestowed that honour instead upon her most prominent adversary, Sir Nicholas Carew.

If Anne failed to recognise this as an ominous sign, then she would soon have more certain proof that something was very seriously amiss. Cromwell was swift to capitalise upon his advantage, and the very next day his 'creature', Sir Thomas Audley, appointed two special commissions for hearing and judging pleas of the crown. Although this legal practice dated back to the thirteenth century, it was rarely used and only for the most serious cases. The purpose of the commissions was kept secret, but the fact that two courts were subsequently established in Middlesex and Kent, the location of Anne's alleged infidelities, is significant. Even more so was the list of the men chosen as jurors, which included the dukes of Suffolk and Norfolk, William Fitzwilliam and others hostile to Anne. The notable exception was her own father, Thomas, who was also called to examine the case. Whether this was a test of his loyalty to the king or an attempt to prove the impartiality of the commission is not certain, but in characteristically ruthless style, Boleyn did not flinch from the task.

The chief minister himself now began to make further enquiries into the queen's conduct. 'In most secret sort, certain persons of the Privy Chamber and others of [the Queen's side] were examined', it was reported.[56] Although she did not yet know what was afoot, Anne sensed the growing tension at court and was reported to have lashed out at Mark Smeaton and Henry Norris. These altercations prompted both men to utter words that could easily be misconstrued, and Anne's ladies were quick to report them to Cromwell. Armed with this fresh evidence, on 30 April, he had Smeaton arrested and brought to his house in Stepney, where he subjected him to intensive questioning (possibly under torture) about his relationship with the queen. The terrified young man soon capitulated. As well as admitting to a sexual liaison with the queen, Smeaton also provided Cromwell with the names of other members of her circle whom she had slept with.

Cromwell knew that this was enough. He wrote at once to his royal master, enclosing the hapless attendant's confession. The king must have experienced a range of emotions upon reading Cromwell's letter, but he somehow managed to keep his composure. He ordered that everything should proceed as normal for the traditional May Day tournament, which was to be held at Greenwich Palace the following day. He did, though, cancel the trip to Calais that had been planned for himself and Anne directly after the tournament.

Anne, too, maintained her composure, despite the gathering storm. The news of Smeaton's arrest was kept from her, but her sharp eyes and ears may have picked up on the whispered conversations and meaningful looks between her ladies. Nevertheless, it was apparently without a care in the world that she took her place next to her husband, who was revelling in the spectacle of his favourite event and 'gave himself up to enjoyment'.[57] Anne was further reassured by the sight of her beloved brother George taking part in the jousts, as well as her favourite, Henry Norris. But then suddenly, halfway through the contest, a messenger arrived in the viewing gallery and pressed a note into the king's hand. After reading its contents, Henry stood abruptly and strode out of the tournament, accompanied by a handful of attendants. 'Of this sudden departing many men mused, but most chiefly the queen,' observed Edward Hall.[58]

Anne was still reeling when she saw Henry Norris being escorted from the arena. He was ordered to accompany the king to Westminster at once, and as they rode westwards the officials revealed the full horror of his situation. Norris fiercely denied the charges of adultery with the queen, even though Henry offered him a full pardon if he confessed. This was almost certainly to coax his former favourite into admitting his crimes, and it is unlikely that he had any intention of honouring it. Norris held firm and was taken to the Tower, where he joined Mark Smeaton. William Fitzwilliam joined in Norris's interrogation, and the prisoner later alleged that he had tricked him into making a confession.

Even though his plan was falling into place exactly as he had envisaged, Cromwell was taking no chances. Such was his pre-eminence at court that he was able to assume control of access to the king so that none of the men loyal to Anne could plead on her behalf. For the next few days, Henry lived as a virtual recluse, being seen only 'in the garden and in his boat at night, at which times it may become no man to prevent him'.[59] Although he had been willing to give his chief minister free rein to direct the proceedings against the queen, he was clearly humiliated by the role in which he had been cast, as the cuckold to an adulterous wife. It hardly flattered his considerable ego, and for all his gratitude to Cromwell for acting so decisively to release him from his marriage, he may have harboured some resentment towards him for the means that he had employed.

The queen did not have long to wait before she, too, was arrested. On 2 May, Cromwell accompanied her to the Tower. Anne's uncle, the Duke of Norfolk, went with them, as did Thomas Audley. One source claims that Anne's former advocate, Cranmer, was also present. All of Henry's men were now united, it seemed, in the single aim of getting rid of this troublesome woman. Their hatred for her transcended their rivalry with each other, and they no doubt spied an opportunity to win favour with the king by being seen to bring the woman who had so wronged him to justice.

George Boleyn was taken to the Tower on the same day as his sister. This added a deliberately shocking new dimension to an already scandalous case. Adultery was one thing; incest another entirely, as the official trial papers made clear, describing it as 'most detestable against the law of God and nature'. To make matters even worse, George was accused of having claimed that Princess Elizabeth was not Henry's daughter. Cromwell was making absolutely sure of the outcome, and in the process destroying a rival whom he had long despised.

All the while, Henry remained in seclusion. It is an indication of his emotional turmoil that on the evening following Anne Boleyn's arrest, he summoned his bastard son Henry FitzRoy to attend him. Now aged seventeen, FitzRoy was widely admired as 'a goodly young lord, and a toward [one] in many qualities and feats'.[60] Like his father, he was renowned for his sporting prowess and charm. His time in France had sharpened his intellect, and he was praised for his articulate speech and refinement.

Henry had continued to show favour towards his son in recent years, and had deputised important occasions to him. In November 1534, for example, FitzRoy had hosted a feast in honour of the French admiral, and the following February he had entertained the Imperial ambassador. Keen for the young man to witness the exercise of his father's justice, in May the same year, Henry had arranged for him to attend the hanging, drawing and quartering of a contingent of men who had refused to swear the oath of succession. FitzRoy had been obliged to stand 'quite near the sufferers' as he had watched their terrible punishment being carried out.

But all the while that Henry seemed to be grooming FitzRoy for kingship, he was painfully aware that his son's health was continuing to fail. When the young man arrived in the privy chamber on the evening after Anne Boleyn had been taken to the Tower and sought his father's blessing, the king broke down, clutching his son to his breast and weeping uncontrollably. As soon as he was able to speak, he declared that FitzRoy and his half-sister Mary 'were greatly bound to God for having escaped the hands of that accursed whore, who had determined to poison them'.[61] The episode reveals a great deal about Henry's precarious mental state. As well as seeking to assuage his guilt over his wife's arrest by convincing himself and FitzRoy that she was a would-be murderess, he was also clearly distressed at the sight of his son's now obvious frailty. To Henry, it seemed that everything of which he had been so sure was about to come crashing down around him. His emotional meeting with FitzRoy suggests that as well as self-righteous anger, he was also filled with fear.

But the king could show no irresolution, for there would be still more arrests. On 4 May, William Brereton was conveyed to the same fortress where Anne's other suspected lovers were being held. This occasioned great surprise. Although, like Norris and Weston, he was a member of the king's privy chamber, Brereton had had little if any contact with the queen and was certainly not one of her favourites. Aged almost fifty, he was also considerably older than the other accused men. What was more, by the time of his arrest, he had been absent from court for long periods of time, preferring to live at his family estates in Cheshire. That he should become embroiled in the scandal of the queen's adultery is one of the clearest indications that Cromwell had cooked up the affair. Brereton had been a troublesome opponent to the progress of reform in Cheshire, obstructing Cromwell's attempts to dissolve the monasteries in that region. The chief minister had so far struggled to find a way of removing him, so he now seized his opportunity, no doubt capitalising upon the fact that Brereton was a noted seducer of women. His indictment listed four occasions upon which he had committed adultery with the queen. The fact that on at least two of these Anne had not been in the location claimed was quietly overlooked.

But if Cromwell was behind Brereton's arrest, he had nothing whatsoever to do with that of Thomas Wyatt the following day, nor of Richard Page, a gentleman of the privy chamber, three days later. Both men had been his associates for some time, so he had no wish to see them implicated. It is likely that other men close to the king, observing how Cromwell was using the plot to rid himself of his rivals, decided to follow suit. Wyatt himself later claimed that it was the 'undeserved evil will' of the Duke of Suffolk that had landed him in prison.[62] According to the Spanish Chronicle, Cromwell managed to intercept Wyatt before he was taken to the Tower and assured him that he would 'promise to stand his friend'.[63] It is telling that neither Wyatt nor Page were subsequently charged with adultery.

The last man to be taken was Francis Weston, on 5 May. Cromwell had already gathered sufficient evidence to have him arrested, but it was the queen herself who inadvertently hammered another nail into his coffin. Now that she was in the Tower, all of her conversations were carefully recorded by those who attended her, and she spoke of Weston's flirtatious manner towards her the previous year.

Sir William Kingston, governor of the Tower, was present when she made this remark, and it can be no coincidence that Weston was brought in shortly afterwards.

All of the accused men except George Boleyn were tried on 12 May. Cromwell had made sure of the verdict, and the jury did not hesitate to condemn them for 'high treason against the King for using fornication with Queen Anne, wife to the King, and also for conspiracy of the King's death'. Thomas Audley delivered the sentence. Charles Wriothesley reported with some relish that they were to be 'hanged, drawn and quartered, their members cut off and burnt before them, their heads cut off and quartered'.[64]

The following day, Sir William Fitzwilliam was dispatched to Greenwich with orders to break up the queen's household and discharge all of her servants. It was an ominous sign for Anne as she prepared for her trial, which was to be held at the Tower. Of the outcome, there seemed no doubt. On 14 May, the day before it was scheduled to take place, Cromwell confidently predicted: 'She and her brother shall be arraigned tomorrow, and will undoubtedly go the same way.'[65]

Although Anne gave 'so wise and discreet answers to all things laid against her', it was to no avail.[66] Among the twenty-six lords present, she would have seen her uncle Norfolk, holding the long white staff of his office as High Steward of England. At his feet sat his son, the Earl of Surrey, who held the golden staff of the Earl Marshal. The Duke of Suffolk was also in attendance, and it was an altogether more welcome duty than the prominent role that he had been obliged to perform at her coronation a little under three years before. Meanwhile, Cromwell's accomplice Audley attended the trial as an adviser to the panel of peers on legal matters. Assiduous though he was about the process of law, Audley could always be relied upon to further the king's cause. As well as Henry's most trusted councillors, Henry Pole was also present, and derived great satisfaction in witnessing the downfall of this upstart queen that he had helped to orchestrate.

As the most senior peer, it fell to Norfolk to deliver the verdict. That he was Anne's uncle did not make him flinch from the task in the slightest: indeed, he seemed to perform it with relish. 'Because thou hast offended our sovereign the King's grace, in committing treason against his person,' he pronounced, 'and here attainted of the same, the law of the realm is this, that thou hast deserved death, and the judgement is this: That thou shalt be brought here within the Tower of London on the Green, else to have thy head smitten off as the King's pleasure shall be further known.' Anne's brother George was condemned immediately afterwards, 'for knowing the Queen, his sister, carnally, most detestable against the laws of God and nature also'.[67] Like the queen's four other alleged lovers, he was sentenced to a traitor's death.

Of all the king's men who were involved in Anne's downfall, Cranmer was by far the most reluctant. He had remained loyal to the queen almost to the end, insisting that he could not believe her to be guilty of the charges against her because 'I had never better opinion of woman'.[68] His integrity is admirable, but it also placed him in danger. As the lone voice speaking out in favour of a woman whom his royal master wanted desperately to be rid of, Cranmer was risking his position, if not worse. The king knew that if his foremost prelate continued to defend Anne, it would prompt others to doubt her guilt. It may have been Henry himself, or perhaps Cromwell, who eventually persuaded Cranmer to change his stance and make the declaration.

As soon as Cranmer had submitted to the king's will, Henry appointed him Anne's confessor. On 16 May, Sir William Kingston, constable of the Tower, reported to Cromwell that the archbishop had visited the beleaguered queen. It must have brought her some comfort to have her faithful chaplain with her during those desperate hours when she awaited her execution. Kingston also reported that her brother, George, who was to die the following day, had begged to speak to Cromwell. If the latter sent an answer, then it has not survived. It is clear from Kingston's letter that Cromwell was arranging everything on his royal master's behalf, even down to 'the preparation of the scaffolds and other necessaries'.[69]

The sentences were carried out on 17 May. From the scaffold, Francis Weston declared his fate a warning to others not to take life for granted: 'For I had thought to have lived in abomination yet this twenty or thirty years and to have made amends.' In a similar vein,

George Boleyn told the assembled crowds: 'Desiring you all, and especially you my masters of the court, that you will trust on God specially, and not on the vanities of the world, for if I had done so, I think I had been alive as ye be now.'[70] All five men were executed on 17 May, the king having commuted their punishment to beheading. The news sent shockwaves across Europe. In Venice it was reported that 'four of his Majesty's most confidential servants' had been put to death (the fifth being Smeaton).[71] It was a salutary warning that proximity to the king carried more dangers than it did protection. Whether or not these men had been guilty apparently mattered little to Henry. They had been the means by which he had freed himself from an unwanted wife. Even those who, like Norris, had been close friends, had been sacrificed by a king who was by now as ruthless as he was cold-blooded.

Anne may have witnessed her alleged lovers being led to their place of execution on Tower Hill, and their headless bodies returned to the Tower afterwards. The same day, at a 'solemn court' held at Lambeth Palace, Archbishop Cranmer declared her marriage to the king invalid.[72] The basis for the annulment was not the queen's alleged adultery, but that she had been pre-contracted to her former suitor Henry Percy, Earl of Northumberland. Cromwell had been assiduous in trying to extract a statement from him to that effect, but Percy had consistently denied that any pre-contract had existed. He was still doing so as late as 14 May, when he told Cromwell 'that the same may be to my damnation, if ever there were any contract or promise of marriage between her and me'.[73] But his words were drowned out by the cacophony of accusations and slander that Cromwell had devised, and the king paid little heed to them.

On the same day as the five men were executed, Sir Francis Bryan, eager to justify his royal master's faith in him, took the news of Anne Boleyn's condemnation to her successor, Jane Seymour. He may also have told her that the king's second marriage had been declared null and void. The path was now clear for Jane to take Anne's place.

Anne went to her death on 19 May. All of the men who had helped to condemn her were present. When the expert executioner whom Henry had sent for from Calais struck off her head with a single stroke, Cromwell must have experienced the greatest surge of relief. He knew that it had been his neck or hers, and he had worked hard to ensure that his royal master would not grant any last-minute reprieve. Even after her execution, Cromwell tried to ensure that nobody would cast doubt upon the justice of her fate. In a letter to Gardiner and Wallop, he claimed that as well as the weight of evidence against the fallen queen, there had been even more damning details from the confessions that he had kept hidden because they were 'so abominable that a great part of them were never given in evidence but clearly kept secret'.[74]

Both Cromwell and his royal master were determined that, unlike Sir Thomas More's and other victims of Henry's increasingly brutal regime, Anne's reputation would remain as black in death as it had been in life.

'Every man here is for himself'

ANNE BOLEYN'S REMAINS, which had been hastily bundled into an old arrow chest, were barely cold by the time that her estranged husband was betrothed to Jane Seymour. They married ten days later, on 30 May 1536. Several of Henry's men were in attendance, including Sir John Russell, who had weathered the storm of Anne Boleyn's hostility towards him and was rewarded with increasing signs of favour from Henry now that she was dead. Although he had always been discreet, the strength of his disapproval of Anne and the influence that she had exerted over his beloved master was now clear. Writing to his friend Arthur Plantagenet, Viscount Lisle, shortly after the wedding, he rejoiced that the 'king hath come out of hell into heaven for the gentleness of this [Jane] and the cursedness and unhappiness in the other [Anne]'.[1]

The new queen's brothers – who were now brothers-in-law to the king – were quick to benefit from her exalted status. On 5 June, her eldest brother Edward was created Viscount Beauchamp, and before the summer was out he had also been appointed governor and captain of Jersey and Chancellor of north Wales. The greatest honour came on 22 May 1537, when he was admitted to the inner ring of the king's council. Jane's younger brother Thomas also enjoyed the bounties of his sister's dazzling rise. By the beginning of October 1536 he was a gentleman of the privy chamber, and he seems to have impressed Henry because he was granted various other honours during the years that followed.

The Seymour brothers may have been the most immediate beneficiaries of Henry's new marriage, but other men were quick to fill the posts left vacant by those who had been caught up in Anne's fall. They included Thomas Heneage, who replaced Norris as groom of the stool, as well as chief gentleman of the privy chamber, following George Boleyn's execution. A consummate courtier, he changed allegiance as deftly as he performed his duties to the king. He therefore now became a client of Thomas Cromwell, with whom he had served in Wolsey's household. Well used to being an intermediary between a powerful patron and the king, he performed this task for Cromwell and soon became responsible for securing the king's signature on important documents. Cromwell had the measure of Heneage, though, so he placed his trust in a number of other men too, notably Thomas Wriothesley and Ralph Sadler, both of whom were continuing to rise in the king's favour.

In the scramble for places and honours that followed Anne Boleyn's demise, Cromwell was undoubtedly the greatest winner. Even though cracks had begun to appear in the king's relationship with his chief minister, in dispatching the unwanted queen with such devastating effectiveness, Cromwell had once more proved just how indispensable he was to his royal master. And now he was determined to capitalise upon his regained favour with Henry by planning a new suite of legislation that would accelerate the progress of his reforms.

Cromwell's rivals expected a rather different outcome from Anne's demise. Stephen Gardiner and Sir John Wallop openly rejoiced upon hearing the news. As religious conservatives, they had never favoured their master's second marriage and the accompanying reforms, and the papal nuncio in France reported that they now hoped a reconciliation with Rome would soon follow. Meanwhile, Sir Nicholas Carew and his fellow conservatives at court hoped that their royal master's eldest daughter Mary would soon be restored to her place in the succession. After all, Elizabeth was now a bastard thanks to the annulment of her parents' marriage. Sir Francis Bryan, who was perhaps still working to distance himself from the fallen queen, was suspected of aiding their campaign.

All of this was anathema to Cromwell, and he was determined to thwart their schemes. Just because he had removed Anne Boleyn did not mean that he was willing to see the unpicking of all the reforms that had helped raise her to the throne in the first place. As far as he was concerned, having regained the king's trust and favour, his reformation could proceed on an even more ambitious scale. In order to discredit Gardiner, he enlisted Wriothesley to gather inside information about the bishop's household. It was not long before the ever-efficient secretary provided evidence of Gardiner's papist leanings that could be reported to the king. Neither was Cromwell prepared to allow Mary to be reinstated as Henry's heir. He was used to tackling that issue, having withstood pressure from Chapuys for the past three years, and responded in no uncertain terms 'that the thing is quite impossible'.[2] Mary was a potent symbol of the king's first marriage, as well as of Roman Catholicism. She had made no secret of her loathing for Cromwell and his reforms, and her constant prayer was that England would soon be returned to the papal fold.

Cromwell was swift to act when Mary was invited back to court, perhaps at the instigation of Carew and his faction, and her father subsequently 'made much of her'.[3] He persuaded Henry against restoring his eldest daughter to the succession, arguing that his European rivals would take it as a sign that he had lost confidence in his reformation and would return England to the papal fold. Cromwell shrewdly judged that his master would not wish to appear weak or irresolute in the eyes of Charles V and Francis I. He knew, too, that Henry exulted in his new status as head of the English church, and perhaps took the opportunity to remind him of all the benefits this bestowed. Nevertheless, Cromwell was enough of a realist to acknowledge that, lacking any other legitimate heirs, Henry was bound to look more favourably upon Mary. He therefore urged his royal master to set a condition upon her return to court: she must at last formally recognise her father's supremacy over the Church. Now that his short-lived alliance with Carew and his supporters was at an end, Cromwell could not resist pushing home his advantage by persuading Henry that it was these men who had been to blame for encouraging Mary's stubborn refusal to submit.

But Mary was not going to give in without a fight. When her father found her to be as unyielding as she had been before, he quickly lost patience and would have sent her to the Tower if Cranmer, ever the peacemaker, had not urged him against it. Henry subsequently ordered Cromwell to make her see reason. His chief minister had no more success, and in his frustration ranted at her for being 'the most ungrateful, unnatural, and most obstinate person living'. He warned that she should be 'much ashamed [and] likewise afraid'.[4] That Cromwell, the son of a blacksmith, should threaten the daughter of a king and queen is a sign of how secure he now felt in Henry's favour. But seeing his failure to persuade Mary, his rivals were quick to take advantage. The Duke of Norfolk led a delegation that tried to intimidate Mary into submission. When she held firm, they went even further in their threats than Cromwell had, telling her that 'if she was their daughter, they would beat her and knock her head so violently against the wall that they would make it as soft as baked apples'.[5]

In the end, help came from an unlikely source. Observing that Mary's principled stand was inflicting more harm than good upon their mutual aim to have her restored to the succession, Chapuys persuaded her to relent. The ambassador had served her faithfully since her mother's death, and while he privately sympathised with her predicament, he knew that no good could come of her ongoing resistance. On 15 June 1536, Mary at last agreed to submit to her father's will. The speed of Cromwell's reaction suggests that he may have collaborated with the ambassador. Good lawyer that he was, he knew that Mary's spoken word was not enough. She had to put it in writing. The letter that she subsequently sent to her father was drafted by Cromwell and copied by Mary 'word for word'. It left no room for doubt as to her absolute capitulation. Yet again, Cromwell had emerged triumphant from the battle for supremacy among the king's men.

If Mary cherished any hopes that her submission would lead to her restoration as heir to the throne, they were soon dashed. A new Act of Succession was passed in June 1536 that removed Elizabeth from the succession and confirmed Mary's status as illegitimate. The Act renewed speculation that Henry FitzRoy would be named the king's heir, particularly as he had been present at parliament, walking directly ahead of the king in a rich robe and cap of maintenance.[6] The previous month Henry had bestowed further honours upon the young man, appointing him chamberlain of Chester and north Wales, lord warden of the Cinque Ports, and constable of Dover Castle.

FitzRoy had also enjoyed the dubious honour of being present at the execution of Anne Boleyn, along with his friend Henry Howard. It is tempting to see this as a deliberate taunt by Henry, showing his condemned wife the fine son that she had failed to give him. But the king's boast would soon backfire. Less than two months later, FitzRoy followed Anne to the grave. His final illness seems to have been sudden. It was first reported on 8 July, and he died on the twenty-third of that month at St James's Palace. The cause of death was cited as a 'consumption', and it seems likely that he had been suffering from tuberculosis. There were also rumours of foul play. In an echo of his royal master's openly expressed fears, Wriothesley declared that the king's 'base son' had been 'privily poisoned by the means of Queen Anne and her brother Lord Rochford, for he pined inwardly in his body long before he died'.[7] But such rumours often attended sudden deaths, and there is no evidence to support this one.

Henry was deeply shocked and saddened by the loss of the son of whom he had become so proud. Strangely, though, while he had lavished honours on the young man in life, he ordered the Duke of Norfolk to arrange his funeral with as little fuss as possible. This may have been to suppress fears over the succession, since many had clung to the belief that the king would make the young man his heir. Cromwell later asserted that his master 'certainly intended to make the Duke his successor, and would have got him declared so by Parliament'.[8] Henry can hardly have hoped to keep FitzRoy's death a secret forever, but it seems that he was determined that as few people as possible would know of it for now.

The wooden coffin containing FitzRoy's body was hidden in straw and taken in secret to be quietly laid to rest at Thetford Priory in Norfolk.[9] The only mourners were two attendants who followed the coffin at a distance. But no sooner had the modest ceremony been performed than Henry sent an angry message to the duke, demanding to know why his son had not been more honourably interred. It was another indication of Henry's increasingly changeable nature. Those who served him were hard pressed to keep up. This was no doubt intentional on the part of their master. Henry was far from being indecisive by nature, so his apparent changes of mind were more likely to have been a method of control. They reminded his men that no matter how much authority he gave them, he was always one step ahead. Norfolk, though, had seen enough of the king's rages to judge that it would soon pass. When Cromwell warned him that he might face imprisonment or worse, he angrily retorted: 'When I deserve to be in the Tower, Tottenham shall turn French!'[10]

For all Henry's fears about the implications of FitzRoy's death, it was soon forgotten. The focus of attention had shifted to an extraordinary rumour that had begun to circulate about the king's daughter and his chief minister, Cromwell. It was whispered that now Mary was back in favour and likely to be restored as the king's sole heir, Cromwell planned to marry her so that he might one day inherit the throne. In a letter to Charles V, Chapuys repeated the rumour that the English king 'intends marrying her [Mary] to Master Cromwell'. The ambassador was rightly sceptical, and judged that the servants were basing their speculation 'only upon the very great favour the King has shown to his Secretary ever since his return from the visit he paid her'.[11]

But Cromwell himself fuelled the rumours shortly afterwards when he had a gold ring made for Mary. Bearing a likeness of the king and his daughter, along with an inscription about the virtues of obedience, it was clearly intended as a reward for Mary's submission. But even Chapuys was now suspicious. For his part, Henry appears to have found the whole idea of his base-born servant marrying his daughter utterly absurd. He quickly put an end to the rumours when he gave the ring to Mary himself. 'Cromwell will have to find other presents,' Chapuys wryly observed.[12]

The controversy soon died down, and court affairs were once more dominated by the rivalry between the king's men. Cromwell was not content merely to distance himself from Carew, Fitzwilliam and the other conservatives with whom he had formed a short-lived rapprochement. Aware that they were plotting to unravel his reforms, he resolved to destroy their influence with Henry for good and succeeded in having Fitzwilliam removed from the council, along with a number of other men from their party.

Cromwell also had another rival in view. The king's beloved cousin Henry Courtenay had rapidly become a thorn in the chief minister's side. The fact that Courtenay was pre-eminent in the privy chamber while Cromwell commanded the council had set them on a collision course. This, and their difference in birth and faith, made the two men natural enemies. Although they had allied for a time in order to bring down Anne Boleyn, this had been nothing more than political expediency, and as soon as she was out of the way, Cromwell had accused Courtenay, along with his ally Carew, of promoting the Lady Mary's cause too zealously. Despite being the king's closest companion and kinsman, Courtenay was no match for Cromwell's political guile, and the latter now succeeded in persuading his royal master to expel his cousin from the council. Cromwell knew that even a whiff of treason was enough to make the increasingly paranoid king take action.

There was one man whom Cromwell failed to remove from his path, however. For all his conservative beliefs, Nicholas Carew remained as close a confidant to the king as ever, and Henry had refused to give any credence to Cromwell's accusations that he had shown too much favour towards Princess Mary. The chief minister therefore devised a more subtle ploy to gradually whittle away Carew's influence by having his own protégés appointed to positions in the privy chamber, which had long been Carew's domain. Thanks to the fact that most of the men who had been implicated for adultery with Anne Boleyn had served in this court department, there was no shortage of vacant positions. Cromwell was quick to gain Henry's approval for the appointment of the trusty Ralph Sadler, along with Philip Hoby, Peter Mewtis and Anthony Denny.

Denny had served in the privy chamber since May 1533, but was now made a groom and yeoman of the wardrobe, as well as assuming informal responsibility for the privy purse and keepership of Westminster Palace.[13] A man of considerable ability, he also seems to have maintained a foothold in politics, and may have represented Ipswich in the parliament of 1535–6. A former pupil of the renowned scholar and humanist John Colet, Denny became a respected patron of humanist letters, winning praise from such leading intellectuals as Nicholas Wentworth and Roger Ascham. He was hailed as 'a favourable supporter of all good learning and a very *Maecenas* of all towards wits'.[14] Most of his friends and associates were humanists, committed to Erasmian principles and the cause of learning. All of this rendered him highly acceptable to the king.

Denny and the other new men whose appointment Cromwell arranged were also committed evangelicals, so it was a deliberate ploy on his part to surround the king with men who would promote his reforms. Interestingly, the new appointees had something else in common: they were all of comparatively humble birth. If Henrician court politics can be viewed as a class war, then Cromwell had made a strike for the common man. Carew, Norfolk and the other blue-blooded conservatives certainly saw it this way and were furious when the appointments were announced.

But Cromwell would not have been able to secure appointments for such men if Henry had not willed it. From the early years of his reign, the king had shown favour to men of lowly status, whom he could trust more than the ambitious magnates with blood ties to the throne. He also liked to be surrounded by men who could provide him with lively company, regardless of their background. It was a preference that would endure for the rest of Henry's life, which made his court a great deal more fluid than those that adhered to the more rigid social structures imposed by centuries of royal tradition.

Cromwell may have taken it as a compliment that his royal master was willing to accept his appointees, even though they lacked the noble status of his other companions. But he soon learned that there were limits to Henry's favour, when he tried to secure a place for another of his associates, Richard Morison. Although he was an exceptionally learned and accomplished young man, and had proved his worth by acting as Cromwell's agent during his travels in Italy, Morison was overawed upon meeting the king and failed to make a good impression. It took all of Cromwell's powers of persuasion to convince his royal master that Morison would prove an excellent addition to the privy chamber. In the end, Henry acceded, but his initial resistance had served as a salutary reminder to Cromwell that the goodwill he had earned from ridding the king of Anne Boleyn was far from inexhaustible.

Although Henry's chief minister recognised the limits of his power, the outside world did not. 'Cromwell rules all,' observed Reginald Pole on 8 June.[15] As if to prove the point, ten days later the king bestowed a prestigious new appointment upon him. In the wake of his daughter's execution, Thomas Boleyn was obliged to forfeit most of his privileges, and he now surrendered the position of Lord Privy Seal, which he had held since 1529. The fact that his successor was the architect of Anne's downfall made it even more galling. Further honours were to follow for Cromwell. On 6 July, Henry raised him to the peerage by creating him Baron Cromwell of Wimbledon, and he knighted him twelve days later. Of all the promotions that Cromwell enjoyed at the hands of his sovereign, this was perhaps the sweetest. Now he could deal with his noble rivals at court as an equal – by right, if not by birth.

Delighted though he was by his new status, Cromwell had been in Henry's service for long enough to know that his master's favour could be just as swiftly withdrawn. He therefore took measures to safeguard his pre-eminence by controlling access to the king even more strictly than he had done before. Although his role as secretary gave Cromwell the right to read the king's correspondence, Chapuys complained that he was deliberately withholding or misinterpreting messages that arrived for his sovereign if they did not tally with his own objectives. 'Cromwell might not have let him [Henry] know all the urgency I had made in soliciting audiences,' he wrote anxiously to the emperor.[16] Cromwell also took it upon himself to relay verbal messages from his master to those who sought an audience, which in turn enabled him to put his own spin on them if need be. In short, Cromwell was the king's spokesman, and none of those who attempted to communicate with Henry knew whether the response they received came from him or his minister. Little wonder that the Spanish Chronicle claimed: 'This Cromwell had more command even than the Cardinal had had, and the gentlemen [i.e. the Council] obeyed him as if he were the King.'[17]

All of this spelt danger, as well as power, for Cromwell. The higher the king raised him, the more he was a target for the other men at court who clamoured for influence. 'The grace and favour he had with the king/Hath caused him [to] have so many enemies,' observed the author of a play about Cromwell's life.[18] The number of Cromwell's enemies grew in direct proportion to the scale of his influence. And as had so often been the case in the past, the battle for Henry's favour polarised the religious factions at court. It was no coincidence that all those who wished to see Cromwell fall from grace were also espoused to the old religion and fiercely opposed to his increasingly radical reforms. They knew that although the king delighted in his position as head of the English church, at heart he was still a traditional Catholic and uncomfortable with some of the changes that his chief minister had introduced.

Rather than seeking a compromise, however, Cromwell went on the offensive and resolved upon even more sweeping religious reforms. The June parliament was followed by Convocation. Cromwell attended several times and, working with Cranmer, used the gathering as an opportunity to stamp out any remaining doubts about the validity of the royal supremacy. Meanwhile, another ally, Dr Edward Foxe, who had supported Cromwell's campaign for the annulment by leading the team of scholars assigned to seek out the biblical justification, had been conducting an embassy to the Lutheran princes in Saxony with the aim of forging a religious and political alliance. The negotiations had collapsed, but they inspired a set of evangelical proposals known as the Wittenberg articles that Foxe presented to Convocation upon his return. Both Cromwell and Cranmer gave them their strong backing. The latter had abandoned his former mildness and was now inflamed with an evangelical zeal, as he told his ally: 'I was ever hitherto cold, but now I am in a heat with the cause of religion.'[19] But he and Cromwell were too radical for most of those present and met with fierce opposition.

What both men needed in order to push through the reforms was their royal master's support. But while Henry could not turn his back on the Reformation without making a mockery of the annulment, his supremacy, the dissolution and all of the other benefits that it had brought him, neither was he prepared to throw his wholehearted support behind it. Instead, he sought a middle ground between the reformers and conservatives at court, which merely served to create confusion and disappointment on both sides.

Cromwell may have originally been drawn to reform for reasons of pragmatism rather than principle, but it is an indication of how genuinely committed he now was that he was prepared to risk his favour with the king by pressing him to commit. Eventually, after much persuasion by Cromwell, Henry agreed to endorse the proposal in a form that was, at best, mildly evangelical. To satisfy those inclined to reform, such as Cromwell, it cast doubt upon some of the long-cherished Catholic doctrines, such as purgatory, promoted only three out of the traditional seven sacraments as being essential for salvation, and included the words 'justification' and 'faith' in close proximity. The idea that an individual could receive God's pardon (or justification) through faith alone, rather than through actions or deeds, was the cornerstone of Protestant theology.[20] But the proposal also encouraged the use of the images and ceremonies that were synonymous with the 'old religion', and continued to assert that the body and blood of Christ were really present at the Eucharist. It may have been at the insistence of a frustrated Cromwell that a few days after it had been agreed, Convocation enacted a law that abolished a number of saints' days.

The reforms were encapsulated in ten articles, which were published in August 1536. To ensure that they were enforced, Cromwell drew up a series of injunctions. To these he added an uncharacteristically strong preamble in which he, for once, pulled rank, referring to himself as 'Lord Cromwell keeper of the privy seal of our said sovereign lord the king and viceregent to the same for and concerning all his jurisdiction ecclesiastical within this realm.'[21] He also used these injunctions to introduce additional reforms that had not been agreed by Convocation, notably an order that every parish church must provide copies of the Bible in both English and Latin. That he should do so despite the bitter experience of Henry's punishment last time he had overstepped his authority is telling. Cromwell was deeply frustrated that his royal master had used the Reformation for his own ends, and that he was far from being as genuinely committed to it as was his increasingly evangelical chief minister.

The new Lord Privy Seal's increasingly reformist stance was also courting widespread hostility among the clergy. He was all too well aware of the fact, and in a conversation with Chapuys he complained about 'the great hatred which all this English priesthood, as he called them, bore him, for his having attempted to put down the tyranny of the Church and reform the Clergy'.[22] Cromwell had always been a model of restraint, carefully withholding his opinions until he saw which way events would turn. Now, though, he seemed blinded by his evangelical zeal and lashed out at what he was convinced was the evil and corruption of the Roman Catholic Church. Chapuys was surprised by another uncharacteristically passionate outburst, and reported to his master: 'He began to rage against all these popes and cardinals, saying that he hoped the race would soon become extinct so that people might rid themselves of their abomination and tyranny.'[23]

Although Cromwell's passionate and principled stance is commendable, and certainly contradicts the commonly held view of him as a cold-hearted political pragmatist, they were qualities that rarely found lasting favour with a king who was increasingly prone to fickle and unpredictable behaviour. The French ambassador Marillac observed that the king's 'lightness and inconstancy' was such that he treated even the weightiest of matters 'as softened wax [that] can be altered to any form'.[24] Henry's favourites were obliged to change their stance just as quickly. Cromwell had been a master of this in the past, but now he seemed tired of the constant shifts in policy, wives and favour, and was determined to follow his own inclinations. It was an understandable but dangerous change of approach.

Cromwell was soon making enemies everywhere. As well as the clergy, he knew that he was deeply unpopular with his master's ordinary subjects. He strengthened his already considerable network of informers across the kingdom so that they could swiftly report any threat of rebellion. In October 1536, he wrote to one of his agents, Sir Thomas Butler, 'desiring you to be vigilant now in this queasy time'.[25] Bullish in the face of the growing opposition, Cromwell instructed his agents in the north of England: 'Set forth the king's authority as Supreme Head by all possible means. There can be no better way to beat the king's authority into the heads of the rude people in the North than to show them that the king intends reformation and correction of religion.' With all the conviction of an evangelising zealot, he concluded: 'They are more superstitious than virtuous, long accustomed to frantic fantasies and ceremonies, which they regard more than either God or their prince. They are completely alienated from true religion.'[26]

Growing as paranoid as his royal master, albeit for different reasons, Cromwell employed increasingly brutal means to root out opposition to his reforms, instructing two other agents who had apprehended a suspected papist in Worcestershire to use 'all the ways you can possibly devise to fish out of him whither he knows any man minded or disposed if he might get such opportunity to such purpose, not sparing for the knowledge hereof to pinch him with pains to the declaration of it in case good advertisement will not serve the same'.[27]

But there was little Cromwell could do to stem the tide of opposition. If anything, the brutality of his methods served to further inflame popular hostility towards the chief minister. The people also railed against two of the king's other men whom they saw as the architects of all their troubles. A popular ballad decried 'Crim Cram and Rich' (Cromwell, Cranmer and Richard Rich) and called for God to 'amend their ways'.[28] On 3 October, a group of opponents to religious reform published a list of leading evangelicals who should be murdered, and Archbishop Cranmer was at the top of it. There were so many threatening references to him thereafter that he was instructed to keep a low profile in Kent.

Nevertheless, it was undoubtedly Cromwell upon whom most of the fury was centred. As opposition boiled over into open rebellion, a proclamation was issued which urged the common men in every shire to 'rise on pain of death' and 'put down the lord Cromwell, that heretic'.[29] The first uprising took place in Lincolnshire at the beginning of October 1536 and rapidly spread across the region, fuelled by the atmosphere of suspicion and fear. It was rumoured that the cook of one of Cromwell's commissioners had been hanged, and that when his agent had reproved the perpetrators, they had 'wrapped him in the hide of a cow newly killed and caused him to be attacked and eaten by dogs, threatening to do the like to his master'.[30]

Within a week of this first outbreak, Chapuys reported that 'a great multitude of people rose against the King's commissioners' in the northern counties. Estimates of the number who had taken arms against the king varied wildly from 5,000 to 50,000. The ambassador secretly supported the rebellion and had been cultivating two of its noble leaders, lords Darcy and Hussey, for a number of years. John, Lord Hussey, boasted a long and distinguished record of royal service. He had fought for Henry VII at the Battle of Stoke in 1486, and had been appointed comptroller of his household. He had continued to enjoy favour during the reign of his son, serving on the council as knight of the wards and chamberlain to Princess Mary. But he had become increasingly disillusioned with the king and his court, which he described as 'queasy' and 'unstable', concluding: 'Every man here is for himself.'[31] Thomas Darcy, meanwhile, had also been prominent in his service to Henry VII and had received various offices and commissions from his successor. But like Hussey, he had become increasingly disillusioned with the political and religious changes of the 1530s, and had soon been excluded from any real power.

Ambassador Chapuys now dispatched his nephew to the Netherlands to ask for 2,000 hand gunners to be sent to the Humber estuary. Lord Darcy also sent a representative there to secure 2,000 hand gunners and 2,000 horse. Chapuys added a command to procure papal absolution, and offered an assurance that his representative was expected by certain nobles and others who had recently been in England as 'ambassadors'. The prospect of the violent overthrow of reform had evidently tempted Chapuys from his usual discretion, and it was only thanks to the king's respect for diplomatic privilege that, when he found out, the ambassador was spared any reprisals.

Henry was quick to react. He had lived through enough uprisings during his father's reign to know that they required a swift and sharp remedy. But in contrast to Henry VII, he did not ride out in person to command his forces. Instead, he shut himself away at Windsor and issued instructions to every 'gentleman and man of influence . . . to be ready with his power'.[32] This did not include Norfolk, whom the king – 'at Cromwell's suggestion' – had recently sent from court for expressing his opposition to the dissolution.[33] The duke was instructed to stay at Kenninghall and keep watch on his own shire.

Norfolk was outraged and immediately fired off a letter to Henry, complaining that the dispatch was 'the most discomfortable that ever came to his hands'. 'Alas, Sir, shall every nobleman save I only either come to your person or else go towards your enemies?' he demanded.

Then, with a deliberate side-swipe at Cromwell, he added: 'Shall I now sit still like a man of law? Alas, Sir, my heart is near dead, as would to God it were.' He concluded that unless he received specific orders from the king to stay put, he would 'rather set forward to the enemy, though he has only 40 horses with him, than remain at home with so much shame'.[34] The duke's anger had subsided enough by the evening for him to regret his impetuousness, and he hurried off another letter to Henry, vowing to obey his instructions and remain in Norfolk until he heard otherwise.

Before these letters reached the court, the king had already had a change of heart. Alarmed by reports of how quickly the rebel forces were swelling, Henry ordered the dukes of Norfolk and Suffolk to direct his troops. Although both men had suffered a decline in favour in recent years, their military experience was now vital to the king. By contrast, his chief minister Cromwell was obliged to remain at court. It had been many years since he had had any fighting experience, and in Henry's eyes he was merely a bureaucrat. Moreover, he was the cause of all this trouble.

Suffolk responded with alacrity, delighted to be at the heart of his sovereign's affairs once more. The Duke of Norfolk was even more gleeful upon receiving the summons. John Kite, Bishop of Carlisle, saw him shortly afterwards and claimed that 'he never saw the duke so happy as he was today, which I attribute either to his reconciliation with the King, or to the pleasure this report itself has given him, thinking that it will be the ruin of his rival Cromwell, to whom the blame of everything is attached, and whose head the rebels demand'. Chapuys concurred that the duke confidently predicted that the rebellion 'will ultimately work the ruin and destruction of his competitor and enemy, Cromwell'.[35] Suddenly, the Pilgrimage of Grace (as the uprising became known) seemed as nothing compared to the battle for supremacy that was waging among the king's men.

There was another reason for Norfolk's good mood. Although he did not hesitate to take up arms on behalf of his royal master, he secretly sympathised with the rebels and hoped that they might spark a reversal of the dissolution and other religious reforms. But, seasoned courtier that he was, Norfolk was not prepared to sacrifice his political career for the sake of his private beliefs. As Chapuys shrewdly observed, the duke was willing 'when occasion required, to defend the cause of the Church', but could not be relied upon, 'considering his inconstancy'.[36]

Among the other men whom Henry had dispatched to put down the uprising was Sir John Russell. He had served Henry on many military campaigns during his long career, and the fact that he had been partially blinded during one encounter is testament to his having been in the thick of the action. The king therefore did not hesitate to appoint him one of his chief commanders. He was sent to lead a small force at Stamford in south Lincolnshire, where he was joined by Suffolk, Sir William Fitzwilliam, Thomas Cromwell's nephew Richard and Sir Francis Bryan. But reports soon reached Henry's ears that Russell's initial response had been too hesitant. By now, the king was easily persuaded that even those closest to him had turned traitor, so Russell was promptly called to defend himself against charges of 'slackness'.[37] In truth, his caution was probably born of an awareness that the royal forces were dangerously insufficient to counter the rapidly swelling rebel ranks. Fortunately, Brandon and Fitzwilliam confirmed this, so no further action was taken against Russell for now.

When the rebellion began to spread rapidly across the northern counties, the king ordered Norfolk to go there at once and crush the rebels by force. His son Henry, Earl of Surrey, was dispatched to join the royal forces soon after. Delighted though he was by this sign of the king's trust in him, the duke soon realised that the royal forces were dangerously outnumbered here too. Members of the northern nobility, including lords Darcy and Hussey, had put their considerable military might behind the uprising and soon had six counties under their control.

Norfolk claimed that he had no choice but to negotiate a truce, promising that the king would listen to their grievances. But he had not been authorised by Henry to make such an offer, and Cromwell and others hostile to the duke at court whispered in the king's ear that he could easily have put down the rebellion if he had wished to. Chapuys also inferred as much in a letter to his master by claiming that the duke was a 'good Christian' who hoped to tacitly show the king 'that the petitions of the insurgents are lawful'.[38] In fact, this is unlikely. Norfolk and George Talbot, fourth Earl of Shrewsbury, the other leader of the royal forces, had 12,000 men between them, but the size of the rebel army had grown rapidly during the few short weeks since the first uprising in Lincolnshire and now numbered around 40,000. In alarm, the duke wrote to Henry, assuring him: 'None oath nor promise made for policy to serve you, mine only master and sovereign can distain [corrupt] me, who shall rather be torn in a million pieces than to show one point of cowardice or untruth to your majesty.'[39]

Sir Francis Bryan had carried the news of Norfolk's actions to the court. He had been appointed to act as an emissary between the king and his commanders in the north. It was typical of the man that even at the height of the crisis, he was able to make light of it. One of the rebel leaders was a man named Robert Aske who, like Bryan, had only one eye. This prompted the latter to quip: 'I know him not, nor he me . . . yet we have but two eyes.'[40] The increasingly suspicious Henry was evidently using the rebellion to test the loyalty of his men, and although Bryan's sympathies may have lain with the rebels, he was determined to carry out his orders to the letter.

In December 1536, Henry dispatched Sir John Russell to join Norfolk and Talbot at Doncaster. Sir John was now in the invidious position of being an intermediary between his increasingly paranoid royal master and the two mighty noblemen. Worse still, when he delivered the king's pardon to the rebels, he earned his master's wrath because Henry claimed that he had acted prematurely. Whether or not this was true, Henry did eventually forgive his old servant, and Russell was one of the few among the king's men who emerged from the troubles still in favour with his master. Shortly afterwards, he was appointed to the reorganised council and became comptroller of the royal household. This office had previously been held by his friend Sir William Paulet, who was now named treasurer.

Meanwhile, throughout the winter, the north remained under rebel control as Henry and Cromwell waited anxiously for news at court. Then, in February 1537, a fresh rebellion broke out in Cumberland and Westmorland. It was not authorised by the leaders of the Pilgrimage of Grace and proved their undoing. The royal forces swiftly quashed it and Henry used this flouting of the terms of their truce as an excuse to wreak vengeance upon the rebels. He ordered the immediate execution of more than 200 'pilgrims' and had the leaders brought to London for interrogation. The loss of their leaders fatally weakened the rebel forces, and the king's men were able to suppress them.

Upon arriving in London, those who had led the rebellion used the opportunity to voice their grievances against the religious reforms. They were careful, though, to place the blame on the 'evil counsellors' who surrounded the king, rather than on Henry himself. Lord Darcy was the most vociferous of all, telling Cromwell to his face: 'It is thou that art the very original and chief causer of all this rebellion and mischief, and art likewise causer of the apprehension of us that be noblemen and dost daily earnestly travail to bring us to our end and to strike off our heads.' Clearly he despised the chief minister as much for being 'base-born' as for the reforms that he had introduced. He ended with a warning: 'Though thou wouldst procure all the noblemen's heads within the realm to be stricken off, yet shall there one head remain that shall strike off thy head.'[41]

Whether all of this made Cromwell pause for thought is not recorded. He was well used to jibes about his lack of pedigree but, more than most men at court, he knew the truth of Darcy's last remark. He had seen first-hand how Henry had not hesitated to dispatch even those closest to him, including his own wife and anointed queen, Anne Boleyn. Even if he did experience a moment's terror at the prospect that his head might one day be struck off at the king's orders, there was little that he could do to safeguard against it. He had gone too far down the path of reform to retreat now, and could only hope that his master would continue to follow where he led.

Lord Darcy also attempted to incriminate another of Henry's men: Henry Howard, Earl of Surrey, whom it was claimed had privately sympathised with the rebels. The king had looked kindly on this 'foolish proud boy' since the death of Henry FitzRoy, aware of how much his son had cherished their friendship. But the king's patience soon wore thin, and Surrey's fortunes had begun to decline, thanks in no small part to his own hot-headedness. He was brought before the courts in the summer of 1537, and although the charges are not clear, it was apparently to defend himself and his family honour against accusations of disloyalty. He was subsequently sent to live confined at Windsor Castle. He later lamented his 'cruel prison' in his sonnet 'When Windsor wails':

> Thus I alone, where all my freedom grew,
> In prison pine with bondage and restraint.[42]

Surrey also bemoaned the loss of his 'noble fair', FitzRoy, and of the 'unconsidered' life they had led together. During his time at Windsor, his resentment had grown towards the 'new men' at court – notably Cromwell, whom he saw as a threat to the established order. Echoing his father Norfolk, he resolved to take upon himself the role of guardian and defender of the true nobility. But his overweening pride was laced with a dangerous blend of vanity and arrogance, as well as a reluctance to play the role expected of a courtier. Although he was subsequently restored to favour, he was increasingly critical of court life. The narrator in his poem 'Too dearly had I bought my green and youthful years' avoided the sycophancy and backbiting that were features of royal service, proudly declaring: 'And seldom though I come in court among the rest.'[43]

Another closet sympathiser with the Pilgrimage of Grace rebels was trying hard to rehabilitate himself with the king. In April 1537, Sir Francis Bryan was sent to Paris on a mission to prevent the French king from receiving the papal legation of Cardinal Reginald Pole. Pole had been tasked with drumming up support among the Catholic powers for an invasion of England. Bryan's mission had a secret – and altogether more deadly – purpose: to arrange for the kidnap or even assassination of Pole. There could have been no greater test of his loyalty, and Henry knew it. As a sympathiser with the Roman Catholic religion, Bryan was now tasked with eliminating one of its chief proponents. In the event, Pole caught word of the plan and made his escape. There were suspicions that it was Bryan himself who had sent Pole the warning. He returned to England at the end of May, anxious to prove his loyalty to the king.

The same month, lords Darcy and Hussey were arraigned at Westminster, with Henry Courtenay, Marquess of Exeter, presiding as Lord Steward. Both men were found guilty of treason and condemned to suffer the extreme penalty of hanging, drawing and quartering. In the event, though, this was commuted to beheading. Although the court record mentions Tyburn as the place assigned for Hussey's execution, Stow records that he was taken to Lincoln to undergo his sentence, in order to strike terror where the rebellion had begun. His friend Darcy was beheaded on Tower Hill on 30 June.

In contrast to some of his rivals, the Duke of Suffolk had acquitted himself well during the troubles, and his able service seemed to remind Henry of his former favourite's usefulness. Henry now commanded his old friend to move his home to Lincolnshire (where his new wife had estates) so that he could keep a close eye on this rebellious region. But Suffolk also became a regular attendee at court once more and served on the council. In 1539 he was appointed to the great mastership of the household after it had been reformed, which equated to the former position of Lord Steward, an enormous honour. Interestingly, after his return to court life, Brandon seems to have collaborated well with Thomas Cromwell, setting aside his former prejudice against this low-born royal servant.

Cromwell was grateful for allies at this juncture. Painfully aware of how precarious his position was in the wake of the Pilgrimage of Grace, he was doing everything he could to curry favour with his royal master. It seemed to be working – for now at least. The Spanish Chronicle describes how, when the last flames of rebellion had been extinguished, Henry told his chief minister: 'It seems, Cromwell, that the country does not know thee as I know thee. Whoever harms thee shall harm me.' A grateful Cromwell then knelt and kissed his sovereign's hand. Although the chronicle is not always a reliable source, it is corroborated on this occasion by a remark by Charles V, who in February 1537 had heard that 'councillor Cromwell' was 'most in favour now and has greatest influence with his master'.[44]

Although publicly defiant in resuming business as usual, privately Cromwell seems to have felt the effects of the stress under which he had been labouring since the rebellion first broke out. His accounts reveal that from February 1537, he began to receive regular visits from surgeons, 'doctors of physic' and apothecaries. Like his royal master, he was increasingly troubled by pain in one of his legs. If this gave him a new empathy with the king, he did not learn from the latter's mistake. Henry had rapidly gained weight since his jousting accident at the beginning of the previous year. This served to aggravate his leg wound (not to mention his temper) by placing additional pressure on it when he walked. Cromwell had long been a stout man, and in middle age his waist expanded even more. As a result, he, like Henry, began to walk with difficulty and his servants were obliged to purchase two stools 'to set my lord's leg on'.[45]

At no point did Cromwell allow his physical infirmities to hamper his efforts in the king's service. But those who knew him best recognised the increasing toll that these were taking. 'Much business maketh you to forget many things,' Cranmer told him, 'and yet I wonder that you remember so many things as you do.'[46] With the support of his old ally, as well as Bishop Edward Foxe, the chief minister pushed on with the religious reforms during the months following the northern uprising. Most significantly, they edited and renumbered the Ten Commandments to conform with Protestant teachings, and published their doctrines in The Institution of a Christian Man (more commonly known as the Bishops' Book), which first appeared in October 1537.

Neither did Cromwell neglect his administrative duties. Anxious to guard against future resistance, he strengthened Henry's authority in Wales, Ireland and – particularly pleasing to Henry – Calais, where he introduced a series of measures to make it like any other English borough, complete with parliamentary representation. Closer to home, Cromwell tackled the most troublesome part of the kingdom by reforming the Council of the North, an administrative body established by Edward IV. Its effectiveness had waned under the Tudors and the northern nobles had soon regained the ascendancy, as proved by the Pilgrimage of Grace. Sensing that, if properly administered, the council could be the key to royal authority, Cromwell set about filling it with men of proven loyalty to his master. Significantly, the majority of these were also of low birth, which provoked an angry response from his rival Norfolk. 'More arrant thieves and murderers be not in no realm,' he ranted. 'Borders cannot be restrained by such mean men, but that some man of great nobility should have the rule.'⁴⁷ This sparked a furious row with Cromwell, which raged for months afterwards.

In the end, the king himself was obliged to intervene. To Cromwell's delight, he told the duke in no uncertain terms: 'We will not be bound of a necessity to be served there with lords, but we will be served with such men what degree soever they be of as we shall appoint the same.'⁴⁸ This was the first time that Henry had been explicit about his attitude towards the status of the men whom he chose to favour. Ability came far ahead of nobility as a qualification for royal service. That he was prepared to make this clear, rather than simply express it through his actions as he had since the beginning of his reign, suggests that Henry was by now more uncompromising and more secure in his authority as king.

Not everything was going Cromwell's way, though. He might have strengthened his master's authority in the wake of the Pilgrimage of Grace, but the rebellion had resulted in a development at court that was to prove a significant threat to his position. During the height of the crisis, a group of leading magnates had formed a special war council to bring the rebels under control. This had proved so effective that Henry decided to establish it as a permanent 'privy council' during the spring of 1537. The new council was dominated by the Duke of Norfolk and his conservative allies. Cromwell suddenly found himself outnumbered in what had traditionally been his powerbase, and one in which he had enjoyed pre-eminence for seven years. But he was enough of a realist on this occasion to appreciate that conciliation was better than conflict, so he began to make friendly overtures towards Norfolk. As well as helping the duke to obtain some lucrative former monastic property, he even entrusted his son Gregory to his care.

It was always going to be an uneasy alliance, however, and Cromwell knew that having been deprived of any real authority on the council, he was now more reliant than ever upon the king's favour. This made him vulnerable and he knew it. For now, though, Henry seemed content to show his support for his chief minister. In May 1537, he bestowed a great honour upon Cromwell by allowing him to write on his behalf to his sister Margaret, Dowager Queen of Scotland. Cromwell was quick to carry out the commission, writing in such deferential and complimentary terms that he could not fail to win favour with the recipient. He even enclosed some cramp rings, which were believed to cure the 'falling sickness' (epilepsy), for good measure. But Cromwell was never one to let an opportunity slip, so he asked that Margaret might inform him 'from time to time' of affairs in Scotland.[49] After all, it would be a significant advantage to have the king's sister as a regular correspondent.

Highly pleased though he was at this sign that he still enjoyed the king's good graces, Cromwell did not rest upon his laurels. In fact, it is likely that he had already begun quietly working on an audacious new plan to safeguard his favour with the king once and for all.

13

'A goodly prince'

THE YEAR 1537 had so far proved a difficult one for Henry. Although he had suppressed the Pilgrimage of Grace and associated uprisings, these had made it clear just how unpopular his religious reforms were with large swathes of the population. Neither was his new marriage providing much comfort. 'Plain' Jane Seymour might have been the perfect antidote to Anne Boleyn, but now that she was Henry's wife, he found her lack of physical charms a disappointment, and his eye had already started to wander to other, more alluring women at court. Worse still, after almost a year of marriage, Jane was still showing no signs of pregnancy.

Watching in the wings, as ever, was the king's faithful minister Cromwell. He had paved Jane's way to the throne, but he knew that if she failed to – literally – deliver as a royal wife, then Henry might task him with getting rid of her, as he had her predecessor. Everything rested upon whether Jane would give Henry the son that he so craved. Now in her late twenties, she was certainly still young enough, and the number of her siblings testified to the fact that she came from fertile stock. There was thus good reason to hope.

Ever one to hedge his bets, Cromwell began discreetly to cultivate Jane's sister Elizabeth, the widowed Lady Ughtred, as a potential wife for his son Gregory. It is an indication of how high the blacksmith's son had risen that he should contemplate such a match. It would tie the Cromwells by marriage to the royal family, which would be a staggering achievement. It is not clear when Cromwell first conceived the idea. It may have been prompted by Lady Ughtred herself, who wrote to him in March 1537, asking for his help in acquiring one of the soon-to-be-dissolved Yorkshire monasteries. She had been widowed three years earlier, and pleaded reduced circumstances. This was not the first contact between them, however, for Elizabeth referred to an earlier meeting at court, when Cromwell had promised her his favour. He had proved as good as his word by arranging for her to reside for a time at Leeds Castle.

It is therefore likely that Cromwell had had the match in mind for some time. He may even have considered Lady Ughtred as a wife for himself. She was probably in her late twenties by the time that they began to correspond regularly, and even though Cromwell was more than twenty years her senior, it was common – even expected – for men of influence to marry much younger wives. Indeed, it was more unusual for women, even those of considerable means, to marry younger husbands: after all, marriages were made to produce heirs, as well as to forge alliances. Aged about seventeen, Gregory Cromwell was at least ten years younger than his prospective bride, but his father saw this as no impediment and began to prepare the ground.

Even so, the wily minister resolved not to act precipitately. He had seen a succession of royal wives and mistresses come and go during his years as Henry's chief minister, and as yet there was no reason to assume that Jane Seymour would enjoy her husband's favour more permanently than her predecessors.

But in May 1537, everything changed with the announcement of the queen's 'quickening of child'. Henry was overjoyed at the prospect of an heir. 'The king's Majesty is in as good health and disposition as I saw his grace of a long season,' reported Cromwell, 'and the more because the Queen's grace is quick with child. God by his grace send her good deliverance of such a prince long to live according to his Majesty's gracious desire.' It is no coincidence that Cromwell now began to actively pursue the idea of a marriage between Jane's sister and his son.[1] Within a month of the announcement, rumours were already circulating that Cromwell was planning a match with the queen's sister. If Jane had a son, then an alliance with her family would prove the best possible strategy.

The fact that Cromwell did not wait until the child was born before cementing the alliance with the Seymours suggests that he was once more feeling insecure at court. In July, Cromwell opened negotiations with Elizabeth's brother Edward. The newly created

Viscount Beauchamp had no great liking for Cromwell, but he was pragmatic enough to realise the advantages of an alliance with the king's most powerful minister, so the two men soon came to an agreement. The marriage was confirmed in mid-July, and the ceremony took place on 3 August in Mortlake, probably at Cromwell's property there.

This was possibly the highest point of Cromwell's career in the king's service. The fact that Henry was content to see his wife's sister marry the son of a commoner is one of the clearest demonstrations he had ever made of the esteem that he held for Cromwell. While his noble councillors and companions scorned this base-born minister, Henry apparently valued his exceptional ability and loyalty so highly that he was willing to tie their two families together. As if this was not a great enough distinction for Cromwell, two days later his royal master elected him to the Order of the Garter, the most prestigious honour in the kingdom.

Edward Seymour was quick to express his satisfaction with the marriage, and to make friendly overtures to his new ally. He wrote a fulsome letter to Cromwell on 2 September, assuring him that he wished the chief minister was with him so that he should have 'the best sport with bow, hounds, and hawks'. He asked Cromwell to pass on his commendations to the newlyweds, adding: 'I pray God to send me by them shortly a nephew.'[2]

But it was from his other sister that Seymour most urgently desired a nephew. Shortly after dispatching his letter to Cromwell, Jane had entered her confinement at Hampton Court. She went into labour a month later. Yet again, the king and his court held their breath. The entire future of the kingdom seemed to rest upon the sex of the child. If it was a boy, then Henry would have secured his dynasty, and the fortunes of at least two of his men would be assured. If it was a girl, the best that they could hope for would be for the queen to fall pregnant again quickly. The news did not arrive as swiftly as they hoped. Jane's labour dragged on for two days and three nights. Finally, at about two o'clock in the morning of 12 October, came the joyous tidings that the queen had been safely delivered of 'the most beautiful boy that ever was seen'.[3]

The king was beside himself when he heard the news. After

twenty-six years of bitter disappointment, a wife had finally given him what he most desired. This 'noble imp' at once became the most important male in Henry's life – the saviour of his dynasty and a much-needed assertion of his manhood.[4] When he first held the boy in his arms, he wept with joy. In contrast to the cancelled celebrations upon his daughter Elizabeth's birth, the *Te Deum* was sung in every parish church throughout London, their bells pealing out long into the following night. Meanwhile, 'above two thousand' cannons were fired from the Tower, and bonfires were lit across the city, around which Henry's joyous subjects gathered to drink their fill of wine.[5]

Seymour and Cromwell were similarly delighted. The latter wrote at once to Sir Thomas Wyatt at the Imperial court: 'It hath pleased almighty God of his goodness to send unto the queen's grace deliverance of a goodly prince to the great comfort, rejoicing and consolation of the King's Majesty and of all us his most humble loving and obedient subjects.'[6] Cromwell was quick to appreciate how the news strengthened his royal master's position with his continental rivals, and urged Wyatt to let the emperor know straightaway so that he, and the other princes of Europe, might share in his 'great joy and comfort'.

The tiny prince was given the name Edward at a lavish christening three days later, and was also named Duke of Cornwall.[7] As well as performing the ceremony, Thomas Cranmer stood as godfather – the clearest indication yet of the king's esteem. The Duke of Norfolk was the other godfather. His rival Cromwell was prominent in the procession to the Chapel Royal at Hampton Court, but Sir Nicholas Carew was afforded the place of honour. Carew had long been a supporter of the Seymours, and his royal master was only too glad to recognise the fact. The king also used the occasion to assert his favour towards his cousin, Henry Courtenay, who played a leading role. Meanwhile, Courtenay's wife Gertrude, daughter of the king's old companion William Blount, Lord Mountjoy, was entrusted with the privilege of carrying the precious prince to the chapel. Sir Francis Bryan, whose loyalties had been under scrutiny since the controversy with Reginald Pole in France the previous year, also appeared to be back in favour. Along with the other guests, he was there to hear the proud proclamation at court of 'Edward, son and heir to King Henry the Eight, Prince of Wales, Duke of Cornwall, and Earl of Chester.'[8]

But the celebrations at court came to an abrupt end with the news that the queen had fallen gravely ill. She continued to sicken over the next few days and died on 24 October.[9] Henry was grief-stricken. He railed against 'divine providence' for tarring the joy of his son's birth with the 'bitterness of death', and retreated to Westminster, 'where he mourned and kept himself close and secret a great while'.[10] A lavish funeral was held at Windsor shortly after-wards and, despite his barely concealed derision for the court, the Earl of Surrey was given the honour of acting as principal mourner. Cranmer presided over the ceremony 'with great solemnity'.[11]

Several of Henry's men had cause to lament Jane's passing. Her brother Edward had been created Earl of Hertford on the day of his nephew's christening, but this title was no guarantee of contin-uing influence, and the following year he was described as being of 'small power', albeit 'young and wise'.[12] Although he remained active in court and was entrusted by Henry with a number of military commissions, his sister's untimely death had proved a significant check to his political ambitions.

His more charismatic brother Thomas seemed to fare rather better. He had been knighted shortly after Edward's birth and retained his post as gentleman of the privy chamber. In March 1538, Henry favoured him with grants of former monastic land in Essex, Hampshire and Berkshire. It is an indication of Thomas Seymour's perceived influence that, a few months later, the Duke of Norfolk began scheming to marry him to his daughter Mary, widow of the king's illegitimate son Henry FitzRoy. When the king heard of it and asked Thomas's opinion, the latter replied that he preferred Cromwell to have 'the manning of the matter'.[13] Although this implies that Seymour was close to Cromwell, the only reason that he deferred to the chief minister is that he knew he would be as opposed to the match as Seymour was himself. Not surprisingly, Norfolk's schemes came to nothing.

Shortly after Jane Seymour's death, the grieving king granted Sir John Russell and his wife Anne some of the jewels belonging to the late queen. Thanks to this, and the many other grants, annuities and fees that Russell had received at his master's hands during his thirty-three years of court service, he was now a wealthy man with an annual income of around £550 (equivalent to around £170,000 today). As one of the king's longest-serving men, he understood Henry's temperament and needs better than most. This did not escape the notice of Castillon, the French ambassador, who in 1538 remarked upon the close relationship that existed between the king and his councillor in a dispatch to his own master.

In the fickle, backbiting world of the court, Russell appears as a straight-talking man of integrity. The rebel Lord Darcy had been heard to remark that Russell was among those who 'dare and will speak to the king the truth'.[14] His qualities were appreciated by others, too. Russell's loyalty towards Wolsey had stood the test of Anne Boleyn's threats, and he had also remained on good terms with Cromwell. His friends Arthur Plantagenet and his wife Honor, known more widely as Lord and Lady Lisle, relied upon him as a friend at court to advance numerous suits throughout the 1530s while they were in Calais. Arthur had been appointed governor of the town in March 1533, a strategically and diplomatically weighty position that reflected the king's trust in him.

While Jane Seymour's death had presented Henry with the chance to confirm his favour to Russell, it had dealt a severe blow to Cromwell. His brief spell as the king's in-law was at an end, and the prize that he had secured for his son Gregory had lost much of its sparkle. But his response was characteristically pragmatic. Within days, he had begun casting about for a new wife for his sovereign. Although he would remain in mourning for Jane for months to come, Henry shared Cromwell's practical outlook and spied an opportunity to boost his standing with his continental rivals by making an advantageous foreign marriage. He therefore agreed that Cromwell could begin making overtures to various potential candidates.

Meanwhile, Sir Francis Bryan, having convinced Henry of his loyalty, was sent back to France in January 1538 to try to patch up another rift that was developing between his master and Francis I. He returned there in April, by which time Henry's suspicions against him were revived thanks to some investigations that were being undertaken at Woburn Abbey in Bedfordshire, where Bryan was steward. They soon revealed that he had forged a close friendship with the abbot, Robert Hobbes. Although Hobbes had taken the Oath of Supremacy in 1535, he had made little secret of his antipathy towards the king's reforms and was steadfastly opposed to the evangelical ideas that were sweeping across the kingdom. It came to light that Bryan had lent a sympathetic ear to his treasonable utterances, and had agreed with his views on religious reforms. But Hobbes was not the only one of his conservative associates. Bryan was old friends with Arthur Plantagenet, and had once warned him of the need for discretion in finding ways to support the old faith.

Hobbes was convicted of treason in June and condemned to be hanged, drawn and quartered. If Bryan was perturbed upon hearing the news, he had more pressing matters to deal with in France, because in May 1538 Francis I and Charles V began preparing to declare a truce. Recognising the threat that this would pose to his own authority, Henry charged Bryan and Sir Thomas Wyatt, ambassador to the emperor, to join forces and prevent it. This was an extremely fragile diplomatic situation and required the utmost sensitivity, but Bryan's reckless nature got the better of him. When he was denied an audience with the French king, he vented his frustration by gambling for such high stakes that he had to be ransomed from debt by Wyatt.

When Henry heard that his ambassador had brought English diplomacy into disrepute, he flew into a fury and demanded Bryan return at once. He would never return as ambassador. The king also ordered an investigation into Bryan's embassy. Cromwell, who had long resented the influence that the 'Vicar of Hell' was able to exert over his master, was all too happy to oblige. Reports of Bryan's drunkenness, his undiplomatic exchanges with the French king, and his unrestrained dispatches, soon reached Henry's ears. Worse still, Cromwell's agents found evidence of Bryan's involvement in a scheme to reconcile England with Rome. When Henry asked to see the book of all Bryan's offices and fees, it was taken as an ominous sign. Bryan fell dangerously ill, whether from stress or a natural malady is not clear, and before long his life was feared of. This did little to evoke the king's sympathy towards his old favourite, however, and by the end of the year Bryan had been ousted from his position in the privy chamber by his own former servant Anthony Denny. Henry also formally confirmed Denny as keeper of Westminster Palace.

Bryan was not the only victim of Cromwell's investigations that year. In January 1538, the chief minister had launched a fresh attack against all forms of Roman Catholic idolatry, ordering that statues, relics and shrines be destroyed in churches and religious houses across the kingdom. He followed this up in September with a new set of vicegerential injunctions against 'pilgrimages, relics or images or any such superstition', and urged 'every Christian person' to look only to the scriptures for the true word of God.[15] To this end, he also renewed his efforts for an English translation of the Bible to be distributed to every parish in the kingdom. Such was the strength of his conviction that he even poured his own money into the project. His friend Cranmer applauded his efforts, but noted the hostility that they had engendered: 'You continue to take such pains for the setting forth of God's word . . . although in the mean season you suffer some snubs, and many slanders, lies, and reproaches for the same.'[16]

Although Cromwell was increasingly driven by a genuine passion for the reformist faith, he was still despised as a cynical and ruthless money-grabber. 'No lord or gentleman in England beareth love or favour to my Lord Privy Seal,' observed one courtier in 1538, 'because he is so great a taker of money, for he will speak, solicit, or do for no man, but all for money.'[17] Cromwell seemed to care little for the growing tide of opposition, but forged ahead with ever greater determination.

By contrast, Henry was becoming uneasy about his subjects' growing resentment. Although in private he continued to support Cromwell's reforms, in public he began to distance himself from his chief minister. The impatience that he had occasionally shown towards Cromwell in the past now became an increasing feature of their exchanges, and Henry seemed determined to keep him firmly in his place. On one notorious occasion in 1538, he even used violence towards his former favourite. George Paulet, brother of the comptroller and treasurer of the household and a friend of William Fitzwilliam, recalled: 'The King beknaveth him [Cromwell] twice a week, and sometimes knocks him well about the pate [head].' He went on to describe how the hapless minister was regularly 'well pommelled about the head, and shaken up, as it were a dog'. Little wonder that he concluded: 'I would not be in his case for all that ever he hath.'[18] While some of this may have been sour grapes on the part of a courtier who, despite his connections, never enjoyed any great advancement, the account does concur with other evidence of the king's growing irritability with his chief adviser.

Cromwell's reaction to such abusive treatment was typically restrained. He knew that if he betrayed any sign of fear or humiliation, his rivals would seize upon it. He therefore put on a show of cheerful nonchalance, as Paulet recorded: 'He will come out into the great chamber, shaking off the bush with as merry a countenance as though he might rule all the roost.' On another occasion, he described how Henry had goaded Cromwell and 'hath called my Lord Privy Seal villain, knave, bobbed him about the head, and thrust him out of the privy chamber', but that Cromwell would 'laugh' at such treatment.[19]

This latter comment is particularly revealing because it suggests that his influence was strictly limited to Henry's public life. Only the king's friends and intimates enjoyed the privilege of conversing with him in his private apartments. Cromwell's old patron Wolsey had found this problematic, which is why he had tried to restrict the number of privy chamber staff. He had succeeded for a while, but the personnel had steadily increased since his fall so that now his protégé faced the same issue. Without access to the king during his leisure hours, when he was more inclined to confide in and grant favours to his companions, Cromwell could not hope to supplant their influence.

The other leading reformer among Henry's men had also fallen foul of his master. In late January 1538, Archbishop Cranmer confronted the king about his personal revision of the Bishops' Book, published the previous year. Henry had begun work on the revisions to this key reformist text in the aftermath of Jane Seymour's death. They signalled his growing discomfort with the most radical aspects of the new doctrine, notably the evangelical message of justification by faith. Although he was renowned for his mildness and discretion, Cranmer was provoked by his master's clumsy amendments into pointing out the errors in his arguments. It was a brave man who contradicted the king at this juncture, particularly given his obvious disapproval. But while he did not succeed in changing Henry's mind, neither did he seem to incur his wrath. Cranmer wisely chose not to press the matter. To his mind, the king's will superseded all else, so he was content to suppress his difference of opinion, and would never have dreamt of challenging his royal master in public.

Cranmer was wise to tread carefully at a time when Henry was prone to swing between favouring reform and hankering after the 'old religion'. In April 1538, he had decided to recall Stephen Gardiner from his embassy in France. The bishop was quick to win favour with Henry upon his return. The seventeenth-century church historian, John Strype, observed: 'About this time Cromwell's interest was not so absolute, but Winchester sometimes got the ascendant of him with the King.'[20]

The hostility between the two men soon dominated Henry's court. 'There was continual emulation between them two, and mortal dissention, such as . . . between the wolves and the lambs,' claimed John Foxe, 'for both of them being greatly in the king's favour, the one being much more feared [Gardiner], the other was much better beloved [Cromwell].'[21] Though both men were very shrewd and able, Cromwell had a sharper wit and a lawyer's skill at presenting a persuasive argument. During a council debate at Hampton Court, when Gardiner was demurring over a matter of policy, Cromwell cried: 'Come on my Lord of Winchester. Answer the king here . . . but speak plainly and directly, and shrink not, man!' Gardiner refused to answer Cromwell, but addressed his views directly to Henry who, apparently unimpressed, 'turned his back and left the matter'.[22]

Not long after Gardiner's return, Henry dispatched Thomas Wriothesley to the Netherlands, which robbed Cromwell of a useful ally at court. Shortly afterwards, he invited Cuthbert Tunstall, Bishop of Durham, to accompany him on his progress that summer. Tunstall had made no secret of his adherence to Roman Catholic doctrine and had long stood out against Cromwell's reforms. The significance was not lost on contemporaries. George Constantine, a former servant of Henry Norris, observed that Tunstall and Gardiner together presented a substantial threat to Cromwell's power. 'I would not counsel my Lord Privy Seal to trust them too much,' he told a confidant. 'For I dare say this, that they will do the best they can to have him out, if they can see him at an advantage.'[23]

Although he was Cromwell's ally, Thomas Audley had succeeded in keeping himself one step removed from this dangerous interplay between the rival factions of the king's men. He had proved an excellent Lord Chancellor since his appointment five years before, ably facilitating the removal of any obstacles to the achievement of the king's desires, from his predecessor Thomas More to the queens who had outlived their usefulness. His standing had been further enhanced in April 1538, when he had married Lady Elizabeth, daughter of Thomas Grey, second Marquess of Dorset, which made him a cousin by marriage to the king. Henry elevated him to the peerage as Baron Audley of Walden a few months later. That he had come to trust and esteem the Lord Chancellor is also demonstrated by the fact that in September of the same year, Audley was granted permission by Henry to visit his son Edward at Havering in Essex.

This was a privilege afforded to few men at court, for the king was paranoid about his son's well-being and security. From the moment of Edward's birth, Henry had established a strict regime to safeguard his precious heir. A suite of apartments was built for the prince at Hampton Court, which lay at a safe distance from London, with its perpetual outbreaks of plague and sweating sickness. Even though the standards of preparation and cleanliness were high in the main kitchens of the palace, Henry arranged for a privy kitchen to be installed close to his son's apartments to minimise the risk of contamination. Once the prince had been weaned, which was typically at the age of two, his food was carefully prepared by a team of trusted cooks, and was tested by a servant before being given to him. His clothes were tried on before being worn in case they had been poisoned, and any new garments were first washed, dried by the fire and anointed with perfume before they were deemed fit for Edward to wear.

Neither did the king stint upon the decoration and furnishing of his young son's apartments. From his earliest moments, Edward was surrounded by every conceivable luxury. His lodgings closely mirrored those of his father in scale and magnificence. A heavily guarded watching chamber led to a presence chamber that contained a sumptuous cradle of state, which privileged visitors were permitted to approach so that they might pay homage to the infant. But this cradle was just for show, and the one in which Edward slept was protected from excessive sunlight by 'a frame of scaffold polls' over which was draped a canopy.[24]

The same strict standards were mirrored at Edward's other residences, so that wherever he and his sizeable household travelled, the king could be sure that the utmost care was being taken. Lady Margaret Bryan was appointed Edward's lady mistress. Having performed the same service for the king's daughters, as well as his illegitimate son Henry FitzRoy, she was an experienced and trustworthy choice. Most of the prince's other attendants during his infancy were female. He later reflected that he had been raised 'among the women', just as his father had been.[25] And, like Henry, they would indulge him excessively. In a dispatch to Thomas Cromwell, Lady Bryan fondly recalled that her young charge was generally 'merry' and 'marvellous pleasantly disposed'. She went on to describe an entertainment one night at Hunsdon: 'The minstrels played, and his Grace danced and played so wantonly that he could not stand still, and was as full of pretty toys as ever I saw child in my life.'[26]

But while Henry took the utmost care over his son's upbringing, he seldom visited in person. It was traditional for royal children to be brought up away from court, and Henry evidently saw no reason to flout that for his son, any more than he did for his two daughters, both of whom only appeared at court for festivities such as Christmas or Easter. When Edward's nursery moved to the king's hunting lodge at Royston in May 1538, Henry paid him a rare visit. He was observed playing with his young son, 'with much mirth and joy, dallying with him in his arms a long space and so holding him in a window to the sight and great comfort of all the people'.[27]

The fact that Henry made sure he could be seen with his son was partly due to pride at having finally sired an heir. But such public displays of fatherly affection do not seem to have been repeated in private. Of course, it could be that he was simply mirroring the relationship that he had experienced with his own father, which had mostly been conducted at a distance. But a remark made by Prince Edward in later years raises the possibility that Henry harboured some resentment against his son for the death of his beloved wife, Jane, and that either he or the boy's attendants had hinted at this. 'How unfortunate have I been to those of my blood,' Edward would lament; 'my mother I slew at my birth.'[28]

When Thomas Audley visited Havering in September 1538, he was quick to tell his royal master all about it. Setting aside his usual formality, he wrote a chatty letter that included the necessary compliments about the young prince. But the Lord Chancellor also observed that Edward's attendants were too overprotective, which was a brave statement given the king's well-known anxiety about his son's welfare. Perhaps to offset this, though, Audley also expressed his relief that the prince's household would be moving from Havering before the winter cold set in.

In the same month that Audley visited Havering, his ally Cromwell suffered a severe setback. The talks between a delegation from the Lutheran Schmalkaldic League of north German princes collapsed. Cromwell had arranged the visit and briefed Cranmer to conduct the negotiations. Although things had looked promising for a while, the king soon voiced his objections to their religious views and it became clear that their visit had been a waste of time. This prompted a rare expression of despondency by Cromwell. He told the delegates that although he inclined to their faith, 'as the world stood, [he] would believe even as his master the king believed'.[29]

Many times in the past, Cromwell had proven to be the most resilient of all Henry's men, but the incident had been such a blow to his confidence that it took him a while to recover. The Spanish diplomat Mendoza met him soon afterwards and described him as 'fearful', adding 'that there was no reason to suppose that sentiment to be feigned'. Chapuys was also surprised by Cromwell's melancholy and reported that the minister had lately 'passed many sleepless nights, and met with a thousand reproaches and objurgations' from his royal master.[30]

The truth of this was proven during the trial of the evangelical, John Lambert, in November 1538. Henry, who personally presided over it, dressed in white to emphasise his purity and delivered a powerful speech defending transubstantiation – one of the key doctrines of the Catholic Church, whereby the bread and wine are believed to become the body and blood of Christ during the Eucharist. In order to make a point, he ordered Cromwell to read out the sentence condemning Lambert. This was deliberate: if Cromwell refused, then he would be admitting that he shared the same views as the accused. John Foxe was in no doubt that this had been the work of Bishop Gardiner, whose 'malicious and crafty subtlety' had wrong-footed his rival.[31] Realising that he had been outmanoeuvred, Cromwell duly read out the condemnation, though it must have pained him to do so. But worse was to come. On the same day that Lambert was burned as a heretic, Henry issued a proclamation defending transubstantiation and clerical celibacy, another important element of the Catholic faith. For good measure, he also banned heretical books. Gardiner's triumph seemed complete.

His rival's ascendancy soon shook Cromwell from his self-pity. Always at his most deadly when under siege, he began to lash out at his enemies with increasing ferocity. One of the first to suffer by his schemes was Robert Radcliffe, Earl of Sussex, who was closely allied to Norfolk. In June 1537, he had been granted the reversion of stewardship of the royal household, once held by his father and now by the fourth Earl of Shrewsbury. But when Shrewsbury died the following year, he was succeeded not by Sussex but by the Duke of Suffolk. This was a bitter blow for the earl and a clear demonstration of the influence that Cromwell was still able to exert over their royal master. But Sussex also had himself to blame. Although he had been an early favourite of Henry and had received some of the most prestigious court appointments at his hands, he lacked the skill of his rivals, rarely attended council meetings and never quite fulfilled his potential as a member of the king's political elite. In the same year that he was passed over as Lord Steward, he was described as being 'of small power and little discretion and many words'.[32]

Having neutralised one political opponent – albeit not a man with any real influence – Cromwell began plotting to have several eminent conservatives indicted for treason. Principal among them was the king's cousin, Henry Courtenay, Marquess of Exeter. Despite his return to royal favour, Courtenay was still embittered at having been outmanoeuvred by Cromwell in 1536, and the following year relations between them reached such a nadir that it was rumoured Courtenay had been sent to the Tower for stabbing Cromwell with a dagger.

Although the marquess was close to Henry, Cromwell rightly judged that his increasingly paranoid royal master could be persuaded that he had turned traitor. He chose his moment well. The king was feeling threatened by the alliance between his great continental rivals Charles V and Francis I. With the Catholic powers thus aligned, if they chose to invade England there were many of the old faith who would turn out in support, and Henry knew it. This gave Cromwell the perfect excuse to round up several members of the Catholic faction at court.

By late 1538, Cromwell had gathered enough evidence to have Henry Courtenay arrested on a charge of treason. His alleged accomplices were Sir Edward Neville and Henry Pole, Lord Montague, who 'disliked Cromwell very much' and whose brother Sir Geoffrey Pole had informed on them during his interrogation in the Tower.[33] Cromwell also took the precaution of having Courtenay's wife Gertrude arrested. The relish with which the Lord Privy Seal undertook her interrogation is evident from a letter he wrote to his master, assuring him: 'I shall assay to the uttermost of my power, and never cease til the bottom of her stomach may be clearly opened and disclosed.' The Spanish chronicler claims that in seeking to destroy these men, Cromwell was motivated by the same loathing for 'lords who were of the blood royal' that he had harboured throughout his service to Henry.[34] But the chief minister was too pragmatic to destroy rivals because of their pedigree alone: there had to be other advantages at play.

As for Courtenay's accomplices, this was not Henry Pole's first brush with treason. He had been arrested at the beginning of the reign, and had also been implicated in the Duke of Buckingham's disgrace. He had been released after the latter's execution in 1521 and had made strenuous efforts to prove his loyalty to the crown. He had given every appearance of supporting the king's annulment and accompanying reforms, and when his brother Reginald had published his damning attack on the 'Great Matter', Henry Pole had appeared genuinely shocked and disappointed, telling him: 'If there is any grace in you, now you will turn to the right way, and then we may reckon it was the will of God that your ingratitude should show the King's meekness.'[35] He had subsequently played a prominent role in the lavish coronation feast staged for Anne Boleyn, and two years later he had been among the men who had condemned Thomas More at his trial.

But Pole's loyalty to the crown remained questionable, and Cromwell eventually secured enough evidence to have him implicated. The chief minister found out that, thanks to his court connections, Pole had secured copies of his brother Reginald's correspondence with Bishop Cuthbert Tunstall of Durham. He had also had sight of some letters that had passed between the king and Cromwell. His brother Geoffrey, meanwhile, had allegedly told his interrogators that in late 1536 Henry Pole had remarked: 'I like well the doings of my brother the Cardinal, and I would we were both over the sea, for this world will one day come to stripes.'[36]

If this seemed flimsy evidence upon which to base an arrest, Cromwell soon added more damning details, most of which were based upon gossip and hearsay. Henry Pole had been heard to express his fear many times that there would soon be no honest men left in the kingdom, and ranted that 'knaves rule about the king'.[37] He had also commented that the king's ulcerated leg would eventually kill him. The latter was an understandable remark, given that Pole would have seen the torment that his royal master suffered in private, but countenancing the king's death was still treason. Another comment he made had been even more shrewd. He was said to have remarked that Henry never made anyone whom he did not later destroy. This speaks volumes about the way in which the king kept his men in thrall through fear. Each of them had seen enough to know that no matter how high an intimate might rise in his favour one day, they could find themselves out in the cold – or worse – the next.

Whether or not Pole was guilty of the charges that were hastily gathered against him is not certain. Although some of his actions had been ill-advised, he had always outwardly conformed to Henry's regime. Moreover, at precisely the same moment that he was said to have made the damning remark about his brother Reginald, there is firm evidence that he had instead been sharply reprimanding him. The fact that his brother Geoffrey was notoriously unstable and his evidence was at best unreliable was also overlooked. But Henry Pole's real crime was one that he lacked the power to change: he had Yorkist blood coursing through his veins.

The evidence against Pole's alleged accomplice, Sir Edward Neville, was hardly more convincing. Neville had been the king's companion in the privy chamber since the beginning of the reign, but the close relationship that he had long enjoyed with Henry had wavered in recent years. Having been forgiven for his association with the fallen Duke of Buckingham, he had wisely kept a lower profile during the years that followed. An indication that he had regained the king's trust came in 1532, when Henry took him to Calais for his meeting with Francis I. Later that year, Neville had been appointed the king's standard-bearer upon the death of Sir Henry Guildford. Like Henry Pole, he had also been prominent at Anne Boleyn's coronation feast, and had further distinguished himself by becoming an eminent member of local government in Kent.

But it was Neville's elder brother George, son-in-law of the late Duke of Buckingham, who had again embroiled him in trouble by arranging various marriages that brought Neville into close kinship with the Poles and Courtenays. A religious conservative, Neville soon found affinity with these men, and as a result began to feel increasingly isolated in the privy chamber, which was largely staffed by men whom Cromwell could be sure would support his reforms. Disillusioned though he was, Neville still remained close to the king, and when Henry learned of Cromwell's plan to have Courtenay arrested, he warned Neville to stay away from the marquess.

It was too late. Sir Geoffrey Pole's confession had already provided Cromwell with ample evidence to have Neville and Henry Pole arrested. Along with Courtenay, they were charged with desiring the king's death and seeking to deprive him of his title as Supreme Head of the Church. The three men were also charged with abetting Cardinal Reginald Pole, who had been conspiring with the Pope against his sovereign since the latter's marriage to Anne Boleyn. Pope

Paul III had rewarded his efforts by making him a cardinal in 1537, and together they had tried to whip up support among the English king's continental rivals.

The similarity in the charges against Neville and Henry Pole is striking. Neville was also alleged to have criticised the calibre of men who now enjoyed the favour of his royal master. 'The king keepeth a sort of knaves here that we dare not speak,' he apparently complained, 'and if I were able to live, I would rather live any life in the world than tarry in the privy chamber.'[38] Courtenay was also recorded as having told Henry Pole: 'I trust once to have a fair day upon these knaves which rule about the king; and I trust to see a merry world one day.'[39] As for Neville, he was also alleged to have called the king 'a beast and worse than a beast'.[40] Neville's reputation was further blackened by Courtenay's wife, who under questioning alleged that his co-conspirator had dabbled in prophecy. As with Pole, any evidence that contradicted the charges against Neville was quietly ignored. In vain, the Imperial ambassador Chapuys spoke up for 'good Edward Neville'.[41] But Cromwell's voice was louder. He condemned the accused's 'miserable wretchedness and traitorous malice'.[42]

The king himself made no comment on the matter. In characteristic fashion, he proved all too ready to be convinced by rumour and hearsay, overlooking years of loyal service in the process. The indictment was duly issued and all three men went to their trial. As he had on other well-publicised occasions, Audley presided over it as lord high steward. Neville protested his innocence to the last, but it was no good. Together with Pole and Courtenay, he was condemned to death for high treason. All three men were beheaded at the Tower on 9 December 1538.

Although the king showed no regret at their passing, he did look favourably upon Neville's eighteen-year-old son Henry, to whom he was godfather. He granted the young man an annuity of £20 in October 1539 and subsequently employed him on an embassy to France. Henry Neville continued in the king's good graces and was later appointed a groom of the privy chamber – a considerable honour for the son of an executed traitor.

But for Courtenay, the destruction of his family was more

absolute. Having been attainted by parliament, his noble house was systematically dismantled after his death. The marquess was formally degraded from the Order of the Garter and his arms 'thrown down'. All of his lands, houses, and possessions were now forfeit to the crown, and a painstaking inventory was carried out to ensure that nothing was missed. Even his young son's little gilt sword, which was found inside the wardrobe of the marquess's London residence, was seized by Henry. Meanwhile, ever with an eye to the future rather than the past, the king granted many of his lands to his long-standing servant and Dorset magnate, Sir John Russell.

There would be one more victim of Cromwell's purge. Sir Nicholas Carew had continued to enjoy the king's favour during the turbulent times that had followed Anne Boleyn's demise. But he had long been a thorn in Cromwell's side, and the latter now found the means to implicate him in the same conspiracy that had sent the so-called 'White Rose faction' to the block. On 31 December 1538, Carew was arrested on suspicion of treason. It was alleged that a letter had been found at the home of Courtenay's widow that proved Carew's involvement in the three men's schemes. All of Sir Nicholas's goods were immediately seized by the king's commissioners, and he was sent to the Tower to await his fate.

Carew's sudden fall from grace prompted a rash of speculation at court. Chapuys opined that it was part of a deliberate plot to deprive Princess Mary of her allies. A later account put forward the unlikely claim that the king had turned against his long-standing attendant because of a personal quarrel. It was said that as the two men played bowls, Henry 'gave this knight opprobrious language, betwixt jest and earnest; to which the other returned an answer rather true than discreet'. Henry, 'being no good fellow in repartees, was so highly offended thereat that Sir Nicholas fell from the top of his favour to the bottom of his displeasure, and was bruised to death thereby'.[43]

Although he had almost certainly been a victim of Cromwell's schemes, Carew had set the seal upon his own fate with an ill-advised comment that he had made to the jury at Courtenay's trial. 'I marvel greatly that the indictment against the Lord Marquis was so secretly handled and for what purpose,' he told the assembled dignitaries, 'for the like was never seen.'[44] This more than hinted that Carew was sympathetic to the disgraced marquess which, taken with the other evidence that Cromwell had gathered, was enough to secure his downfall. Among the men who sat on the jury at his trial was Sir Francis Bryan, who had been out in the cold since his disgrace the previous summer, so was desperate to prove his fidelity to the king. He and his fellow jurymen convicted Carew on 14 February 1539 and Sir Nicholas was beheaded on Tower Green on 8 March.

If Hall's Chronicle is to be believed, this stalwart of the traditional Catholic faith had a last-minute change of heart. Having mounted the scaffold, he 'made a goodly confession, both of his folly and superstitious faith, giving God most hearty thanks that ever he came in the prison of the Tower, where he first savoured the life and sweetness of God's most holy word meaning the Bible in English'.[45] If this is true, there is a delicious irony in the fact that it was thanks to Cromwell's efforts that Carew, along with Henry's other subjects, had access to an English Bible.

The story is corroborated by Wriothesley, who recorded that Carew's head was not exposed on London Bridge as was the tradition for traitors, but was buried with his body in the chapel of St Peter ad Vincula.[46] Cromwell's own actions in the wake of his rival's death add further weight to the tale. Carew's property had been forfeit to the crown, which left his widow Elizabeth destitute, so Cromwell provided her with some assistance. Elizabeth's mother, Lady Margaret Bryan, wrote to thank him 'for the great goodness you show upon my poor daughter Carew, which bindeth me to owe you my true heart and faithful service while I live'.[47]

Meanwhile, Henry feared that Courtenay's execution would spark fresh trouble in his home county, so he agreed to Cromwell's proposal to establish a Council of the West in March 1539. Similar in form to the Council of the North, its aim was to bring order to another distant part of the realm that had long proven troublesome. The king's faithful servant Sir John Russell was appointed its Lord President. The fact that he was Dorset-born and had strong links in the area made him an ideal candidate. He had also just been elevated to the peerage by his royal master, and in April he was elected to the Order of the Garter. These signs of favour bound Russell even more tightly to his master, who needed a man whom he could trust completely to lead this new council.

Once Russell was established in his new role, Henry heaped more honours upon him. On 4 July, he granted him about 30,000 acres, drawn primarily from the former monastery of Tavistock in Devon and valued at £648 (c. £200,000) per annum. This doubled Russell's annual income and made him one of the richest and most powerful landed magnates in the West Country. This was fully justified: Russell needed considerable resources in order to enforce royal power effectively. To make sure of his servant's superiority, Henry also made him steward of the duchy of Cornwall and lord warden of the stannaries (tin mines). The latter post had been held by the late Henry Courtenay, and contemporaries were quick to notice how swiftly Russell had superseded him. In summer 1539, Richard Grenville observed the Courtenays were 'never more esteemed nor better beloved in these parts than his lordship is'.[48]

This was exactly what the king had intended. It was vital that the power void left by Courtenay should quickly be filled, and that all trace of him be eradicated. The message was clear: Henry's men were like chess pieces to be manoeuvred or removed from the board completely, as their master saw fit. No matter how high they might rise, if they opposed or angered the king, he would swiftly prove how dispensable – and replaceable – they were.

14

'*The greatest wretch ever born in England*'

'HOW MANY SERVANTS did he advance in haste (but for what virtue no man could suspect) and with the change of his fancy ruined again, no man knowing for what offence? To how many others of more desert gave he abundant flowers, from whence to gather honey and in the end of harvest burned them in the hive?'[1]

This damning portrayal of the king was penned by Sir Walter Raleigh, who would be the favourite of Henry's daughter Elizabeth. Admittedly, Raleigh was writing from the Tower, where he had been incarcerated by James I – another tyrannical king, as he saw it. But his embittered view did not altogether obscure the truth of his claim. Henry's relationships with the men who served him had long been subject to sudden, often violent change. And now, as the 1530s drew to a close, that was about to become even more apparent.

In January 1539, Henry's chief rivals, Charles V and Francis I, forged a new alliance. Shortly afterwards, Pope Paul III reissued the bull of excommunication against the English king that had first been served after the annulment in 1533. This left Henry desperately short of allies. He was therefore prepared to look more favourably upon Cromwell's suggestion for an alliance with Johann, Duke of Cleves, who – like Henry – had expelled papal authority from his domain. Cleves was a state of the Holy Roman Empire, but had fully embraced the religious reforms that were sweeping across other parts of Europe. The duke's eldest daughter was married to the head of the Schmalkaldic League of Lutheran princes, so if Henry were to marry his younger daughter Anne, it would bring him a suite of powerful new allies. It would also provide a significant boost to the Reformation in England. From Cromwell's perspective, it was therefore the very definition of a win–win situation.

The idea of a marriage between Henry and Anne of Cleves was not a new one. It had first been proposed just a few weeks after the death of Jane Seymour. The king had shown little interest, perhaps because he had heard that the lady was no great beauty, and nothing had been done to advance the scheme. But now the political climate had changed.

Cromwell reported to the English ambassador in France that his royal master was 'indifferent' to the question of his marriage and that he was therefore content to accept 'any person from any part that with deliberation shall be thought meet for him'.[2] But in this Cromwell was mistaken. Had he paid greater heed, he would have found ample signs that even though kings married for politics more than love, his royal master was not prepared to tie himself to just any lady, regardless of her attributes.

Having heard a number of unfavourable reports about Anne's appearance, Henry instructed his chief minister to determine whether they were true. Cromwell duly instructed his agent Christopher Mont to 'diligently but secretly enquire of the beauty and qualities of the lady'.[3] The report that Mont provided has not survived, but Cromwell subsequently assured his master of Anne's attractions, 'as well for the face as for the whole body', and also praised her virtue.[4] It is telling that Henry was not prepared to take Cromwell at his word, but instead dispatched Hans Holbein to take her likeness.

Holbein was now high in Henry's favour. He had undertaken a number of successful commissions for the king during the preceding years, notably the Whitehall mural of 1537, and a portrait of Jane Seymour shortly after she became queen. In March 1538, he had travelled to Brussels to paint another potential bride: Christina of Denmark, Duchess of Milan. After a three-hour sitting, he made his way back to London and showed his royal master the resulting sketch. Henry was utterly beguiled by the beautiful widow, who seemed to adopt a seductive pose. But Holbein's efforts were in vain: when she heard of the proposal, Christina quipped that if she had two heads, she would gladly place one at the King of England's disposal. Undeterred, not long afterwards Henry sent Holbein first to France and then to Burgundy to paint no fewer than five more ladies with whom he was considering marriage. None of these portraits survives, and the matches themselves came to nothing.

As well as painting the king's potential wives, Holbein was also commissioned to paint his son and heir, Prince Edward. Henry planned to send the portrait to Cleves in order to show off his kingly vitality. The charming portrait was completed early in 1539 and shows the prince dressed as a king in miniature, with a rattle in place of a sceptre. The image of his father, Edward has the same small dark eyes and red hair. The painting bears a Latin inscription composed by Sir Richard Morison, who had been appointed special envoy to Cleves. It reads: 'Little one, imitate your father and be the heir of his virtue, the world contains nothing greater . . . Surpass him . . . and none will ever surpass you.'[5] This neatly encapsulates what Henry expected of his son, and also echoes the self-confident inscription that he had commissioned for Holbein's Whitehall mural. Edward was tasked with exceeding the achievements of his father, just as Henry had done.

The king had come to trust Holbein more than any other portraitist, and he did not hesitate to dispatch him to Cleves in 1539, with instructions to paint both Anne and her younger sister Amelia. By now, Cromwell was also well acquainted with Holbein, and it is possible that he briefed him in advance of his journey. He also made sure that he would have first sight of the resulting sketches before they were presented to his master.

Holbein executed his commission with customary skill and efficiency, and Cromwell was evidently pleased with the results. However, he had been in Henry's service long enough to appreciate the importance of choosing the right moment to approach his master about any matters of importance. He therefore waited until Henry was in a 'very merry' mood before showing the sketches to him.[6] His patience was rewarded: upon seeing Anne's likeness, the king was instantly captivated and instructed Cromwell to begin the negotiations at once. There was some talk of sending Henry Howard, Earl of Surrey, to Cleves to assist in the task, but this does not seem to have come to fruition. Instead, the king's able Lord Chancellor Thomas Audley, whose legal skills were second only to Cromwell's, was entrusted with the mission.

But Henry was not so beguiled as to overlook the implications of such a step. He knew that the marriage would be taken as a signal of his dedication to religious reform, so he made it clear that this would be a purely political alliance. He tried to distance himself from it further by stating that responsibility for the proposed alliance would rest entirely upon Cromwell's shoulders. This sent an ominous message to his chief minister, but the latter knew that if he succeeded, then the prize would be more than worth the risks involved.

As well as Henry's marriage to Anne, his envoys were to propose that of his eldest daughter Mary to Anne's brother. This was anathema to Mary, who firmly espoused her mother's Roman Catholic beliefs. But Henry cared little for that: the primary purpose of a royal daughter was to act as a pawn in the game of international diplomacy. In the event, this part of the scheme was soon abandoned. It was rumoured that Cromwell had deliberately obstructed it so that he could marry Mary himself, but this is highly unlikely.

When negotiations were well advanced, the king became somewhat lukewarm to the idea of marrying Anne of Cleves because he saw the alliance as beneath his dignity. He therefore began making friendly overtures towards France once more. On 28 March, the new French ambassador, Charles de Marillac, arrived at court. This gave Henry cause to hope that Francis I would soon abandon his alliance with the emperor and strike up an accord with England.

If this gave Cromwell misgivings, he did not show it. As well as furthering the negotiations with Cleves, he also started planning 'a device in the Parliament for the unity in religion'.[7] It is telling that despite the demise of Henry Courtenay and the rest, Cromwell was minded to swell the ranks of his allies. At this time, there were only three men who could be described in this way: Thomas Cranmer, Thomas Wyatt and Thomas Wriothesley. Although William Fitzwilliam remained a nominal supporter, he could not be relied upon to stand by Cromwell if he fell from grace.

Thomas Audley, meanwhile, had been one of Cromwell's closest associates throughout the first half of the 1530s, but a subsequent controversy had made it clear that he could no longer be relied upon. In April 1535, he had been appointed by Cromwell to collect a new tax, which had sparked fierce opposition across the kingdom. Audley had urged Cromwell to abandon the scheme for fear of rebellion, but, according to Chapuys, the chief minister had retorted that 'the idea was not his but the King's, whose avarice and cupidity were well known to him [Audley]'.[8] This is almost certainly untrue: Cromwell was far too shrewd – and loyal – a servant to levy such an insult against the king. Whether or not Audley had reported the remark or it had been entirely Chapuys' invention, the matter was enough to convince Cromwell that the former could no longer be trusted. In the battle for influence over Henry, the two men were now ranged on opposite sides.

How tenuous Cromwell's hold upon his royal master's favour was would soon be proved. In the run-up to presenting his device to parliament, the minister had secured a seat for his ally Wriothesley, who had just returned from the Netherlands. Wriothesley was fully aware of how embattled his patron was feeling and had written to express his fears for Cromwell's safety. They proved justified.

Although Cromwell had prepared the ground for his device with the king, and the latter had seemed favourable towards it, when parliament met shortly afterwards, Henry withdrew his support and it was thrown out. The king followed this up by performing the traditional ceremonies during Easter, and celebrating Ascension Day – one of the most important observances of the Roman Catholic faith – in ostentatious style. The message to Cromwell and his fellow reformists was clear: if they continued to promote their reformist ideas, then they would be acting in direct opposition to the king.

This may be another instance of Henry exerting control by switching his stance without warning. But it is at least equally possible that he was expressing his natural inclination towards the traditional faith. He had suppressed this during the years immediately following the break with Rome, anxious not to appear weak-willed or hypocritical as his reforms took hold. He was evidently tired of the pretence, and also troubled by the obvious dissent that the Reformation was generating among his people. The time was ripe to assert his true opinions.

But in typically contradictory fashion, if Henry was no longer prepared to lend his full support to Cromwell's reforms, he still appreciated the financial benefits that could be gained from some of them. Cromwell had overseen the dissolution of the lesser religious houses which, together with the diversion of the annates, had netted Henry an estimated £2.5 million (equivalent to more than £1 billion today). This greatly strengthened his case in seeking the king's consent to dissolve the larger monasteries.[9] This was where the greatest riches were to be had, and Cromwell made sure that Henry knew just how much he stood to gain. The same parliament that had rejected Cromwell's device therefore gave its assent to this new phase of the dissolution. It was perhaps no coincidence that at precisely this moment, Eustace Chapuys, who had stood as a bastion against reform for the previous ten years, was recalled by Charles V to the Netherlands.

Cromwell was swift to act, and by the end of 1539 his commissioners had taken possession of all but a handful of monasteries. They included some of the largest and wealthiest religious houses in the kingdom, such as the abbeys of Kirkstall and Hailes. The assets that flooded into the royal treasury were staggering and made Henry one of the richest kings in Christendom. If the lesser monasteries had provided in excess of £1 billion, then the greater houses must have been worth significantly more. Perhaps to justify his title as 'Defender of the Faith', Henry promised to use his newly won gains to build many new churches and cathedrals, but there is only evidence of six being erected at his orders. Instead, he used his vast new landed estate to secure the loyalty of his nobles by granting them a portion of it, and generated more funds by selling off other parts. He also used his new riches to fund overseas campaigns, which were as exorbitant as they were self-indulgent.

Many of the monks and nuns whose houses had been dissolved now found themselves destitute. In a letter to a Burgundian acquaintance, Eustace Chapuys bemoaned their fate: 'It is a lamentable thing to see a legion of monks and nuns, who have been chased from their monasteries, wandering miserably hither and thither, seeking means to live, and several honest men have told me, that what with monks, nuns, and persons dependent on the monasteries suppressed, there were over 20,000 who knew not how to live.'[10]

At the same time as Henry sanctioned the dissolution of the larger monasteries, he turned his attention to a more personal matter. The safety and well-being of his 'precious jewel', Prince Edward, had always been uppermost in his mind, and in March 1539 he issued a series of extraordinarily detailed instructions to a group of newly named officers of the boy's household. They included Sir William Sidney, who was appointed chamberlain, and Sir John Cornwallis as steward. Lady Margaret Bryan was confirmed in her post as lady mistress, and Sir William Sidney's sister-in-law, Sybil Penne, as his nurse. Other personnel included a physician, Dr George Owen, who would serve in that capacity for the rest of Edward's life.

Henry's instructions to his son's new household stipulated that the walls, floors and ceilings of Edward's lodgings should be scrubbed clean several times a day. Everything that might be handled by the prince had also to be washed, and this applied to his attendants and visitors too. If any of Edward's household displayed symptoms of sickness, or had come into contact with others who did, they were immediately banished from his presence. Because high-ranking subjects tended to be cleaner and therefore less susceptible to disease than the lower orders, Henry ordained that only those of the rank of knight or above could attend his son. For all the seriousness of Henry's new injunctions, though, he did not overlook his son's amusement and also provided for the appointment of a company of players.

In the same month that Henry issued these new instructions for the care of his son, he received news that a former favourite had died. Thomas Boleyn had been in the political wilderness since the executions of his son and daughter three years earlier. Although he had been a guest at Prince Edward's christening in October 1537, he no longer enjoyed any of the offices or titles that he had laid claim to during Anne's ascendancy. A papal report of 1538 described him as 'wise' but 'of little power'.[11] Of all the king's men who had been his ally during his years of influence, only Cranmer – to his credit – had stood by him, intervening on his behalf in disputes over his estates. These were still unresolved at the time of Boleyn's death at Hever Castle on 12 March 1539. Perhaps not surprisingly, the king showed no sign of regret at the demise of his former father-in-law. There had, after all, been plenty of men to take his place.

A month after Boleyn's death, his old rival Cromwell was struck down by a fever and forced to take a leave of absence from court. Tormented by the thought of how his enemies would capitalise upon his absence, he wrote a desperate letter to Henry, assuring him: 'The pain of the disease grieves me nothing so much as . . . that I cannot be as I should there present and employ my power to your grace's affairs and service as my heart desires to do.'[12] Cromwell would undoubtedly have dragged himself to court despite his raging fever, but he was fully aware of his master's paranoia of sickness, so had no choice but to remain at home. Henry wrote to pardon his absence, but it provided small comfort as Cromwell imagined the advantage that his enemies must be enjoying over him.

Cromwell's sickness dragged on for several weeks, obliging him to miss parliament, which opened on 28 April. On 5 May, Audley delivered a speech in the Lords that reiterated the king's desire to control 'diversity of opinions'. In truth, Henry had allowed himself to be influenced by the conservatives during Cromwell's absence and was now backtracking on many of his reforms. Whereas Cromwell had intended that the parliament would be a vehicle for pushing through further measures, in his absence a committee was established to examine doctrine. This gave his rivals the chance to voice their opposition to the religious policies that Cromwell espoused.

Predictably, chaos ensued, with a cacophony of different voices all arguing against each other. The Duke of Norfolk made sure that he was the one who took charge. He declared that the committee was unable to reach a decision and then presented six 'questions' for the house to consider. These constituted an unravelling of Cromwell's reforms and a return to conservative religious practices. So that he and his allies would have time to drum up support for the policies among the court – and above all with the king – the duke proposed that parliament be prorogued for a week so that its members could consider the arguments.

That Norfolk and his companions had influenced Henry seemed clear from the events that now rapidly unfolded. On 7 June, he declared two days of official mourning for Isabella, wife of Charles V and niece of Catherine of Aragon. The significance of the gesture was not lost on the reformists. The leader of another Lutheran delegation to England left the same day. At around the same time, a controversy was unfolding in the English-held town of Calais. Cromwell had sent some evangelical ministers there from England in the interests of their safety. But having heard that the tide was turning at court, the deputy of Calais, Arthur Plantagenet, a religious conservative, had the ministers rounded up and sent to London for interrogation. Cromwell was incensed when he heard of this and immediately ordered him to recall the men. But Lisle ignored his commands. He would never have dared to do so a few weeks before, but the chief minister had returned to court to find his authority severely depleted.

To set the seal on Cromwell's misery, the six questions were enacted into law as the Act of Six Articles on 16 June, and a little under two weeks later they received the king's assent. The Six Articles reinforced existing heresy laws and, more significantly, reasserted traditional Catholic doctrine. Ever conscious of his public image, Henry ensured that the Act was carefully worded so that he could not be accused of irresolution, given that he had promoted religious reform so forcefully during the previous ten years. He was simply acting in response to the 'great discord and variance' that had arisen since the introduction of the reforms, and believed that 'the said articles should make a perfect concord and unity generally amongst all his loving and obedient subjects'.[13]

Archbishop Cranmer did his best to oppose the Act, and dared to speak out against it while the king was present in the House of Lords. But in characteristic style, once he had made his views known, he was not prepared to contradict his royal master any further. To demonstrate his compliance to the clause relating to clerical celibacy, as well as to protect himself, he sent his wife Margaret and their daughter back to her German relatives. Henry rewarded him for it. When Sir John Gostwick, knight of the shire for Bedfordshire, made accusations in the Commons about some of Cranmer's sermons and lectures, the king furiously upbraided him as a 'varlet' and added the ominous threat that if he did not personally apologise to Cranmer, 'I will sure both make him a poor Gostwick, and otherwise punish him, to the example of others.'[14]

Despite the assurance of his master's favour, this was one of the lowest points of Cranmer's career. His reverence for the royal will had always prevented him from contesting his master once it was clear that Henry's mind was made up, but this time Cranmer's compliance had come at a terrible personal cost. The Scottish theologian Alexander Ales, a close associate of Cranmer, recalled that, while strolling through the gardens of Lambeth Palace early one morning at the end of June, the archbishop begged him to flee England. Handing Ales a ring that the king had given him, Cranmer lamented: 'I repent of what I have done, and if I had known that my only punishment would have been deposition from the Archbishopric (as I hear that my Lord [Hugh] Latimer is deposed), of a truth I would not have subscribed.'[15]

It is interesting to speculate whether Henry would have reverted to a conservative stance so decisively if Cromwell had not been absent from court. Although he had been content to allow the introduction of ever more seismic reforms by his chief minister during the previous decade, this had only been when they had aligned with his personal desires: namely, to marry Anne Boleyn, secure his dynasty with a son, swell the treasury and enhance his own authority. Forasmuch as Henry gloried in the title of Supreme Head of the Church, he remained a Catholic at heart and was uncomfortable with the doctrine that Cromwell had promoted so enthusiastically since his arrival at court. The chief minister knew this, but had argued each case with a lawyer's tongue, employing the persuasions that he knew would sway his master. Norfolk knew it too, and as soon as his rival was out of the way, he had taken full advantage.

Interestingly, even though Henry had taken a significant step back towards the traditional religion, he evidently did not wish to choose sides. According to John Foxe, the day after confirming the Act of the Six Articles, the king held a dinner at Lambeth Palace in an attempt to reconcile Cranmer to his conservative opponents. He invited both Cromwell and Norfolk in the optimistic (and somewhat naïve) hope that the two men would agree to settle their differences in this informal setting. It was not long before a furious row erupted. Norfolk goaded Cromwell by making a disparaging remark about Wolsey. The chief minister, still smarting from his rival's victory in parliament, was easily provoked and launched a bitter tirade in defence of his former patron. The spat ended with Cromwell accusing Norfolk of disloyalty, and the duke calling him a liar.

A revealing conversation between Cromwell and Cranmer was also overheard during the course of the evening. The archbishop's secretary, Ralph Morice, recalled that Cromwell had said to his friend: 'I must needs confess that in some things I have complained of you unto his majesty, but all in vain, for he will never give credit against you, whatsoever is laid to your charge.'[16] This neatly summarises the favour that Cranmer enjoyed with Henry. Even when this increasingly paranoid king heard disparaging remarks about his archbishop, he refused to heed them. The reason for his seemingly unshakeable esteem was the fact that he knew Cranmer would always put the royal will ahead of his own opinions. The same could not be said of Cromwell and others in the king's service, and they would suffer for it.

The Lambeth Palace dinner poses an intriguing question about Henry's tactics with regard to his men. It has often been suggested that the king encouraged factions in his court so that no single individual would ever be able to dominate – a classic 'divide and rule' approach. There is certainly plenty of evidence to support this, with the rapid succession of different favourites, the predominant atmosphere of suspicion, intrigue and backbiting that Henry seemed to encourage, and his frequent, unpredictable changes of mind. Yet how much this was a deliberate ploy rather than Henry's true nature is difficult to ascertain. Royal courts had long been beset by faction and rivalries, even during the reigns of the most peaceable sovereigns. As the forum in which favour and influence were grappled over by the nation's most powerful and ambitious men, this was understandable. A naturally fickle man with a notoriously short attention span, Henry certainly did not help to foster greater accord among his courtiers and advisers, but it is perhaps overstating the case to claim that he actively encouraged rivalry between his men.

If further proof was needed of the king's fickle nature, it soon manifested itself. The Act of Six Articles prompted a rash of allegations of heresy against those evangelicals who had formerly enjoyed Cromwell's protection. Cranmer was obliged to investigate all of them, albeit reluctantly, and most of the accused were imprisoned.

Little wonder that in mid-July the French ambassador Marillac was able to confidently report that the English king had 'taken up again all the old opinions and constitutions, excepting only papal obedience and destruction of abbeys and churches of which he has taken the revenue'.[17]

But just as Norfolk and his allies were savouring victory, the king made an apparent volte-face by taking Cromwell back into his confidence and listening favourably to his reformist ideas once more. The chief minister soon felt secure enough to go on the offensive against his rivals. Joining what he thought was a purge of evangelicals, in August Stephen Gardiner accused Robert Barnes of heresy. Barnes had previously assisted the king's campaign for an annulment, but Gardiner was confident that the tide had turned decisively enough in the conservatives' favour for him to bring down this prominent reformer. He misjudged the situation, and Cromwell wasted no time in having him expelled from the Privy Council. This deprived Norfolk of one of his most powerful allies at court, and also disrupted the implementation of the Six Articles, which Gardiner had been busily preparing for. Any hope that the two men might have cherished of appealing to the king was dashed when Henry sanctioned the expulsion.

Cromwell was quick to take advantage of his master's renewed favour and secured Henry's assent to bring the long-standing negotiations for his marriage to Anne of Cleves to a swift conclusion, knowing that the match would signal a return to reform. In so doing, he brushed aside the warnings voiced by his friend Cranmer. Even though he had been one of the principal negotiators for the marriage and fully appreciated its advantages on ideological grounds, Henry's archbishop appreciated what his chief minister did not: the king needed to marry for love as much as for politics. Cranmer urged Cromwell that he 'thought it most expedient the King to marry where that he had his fantasy and love, for that would be most comfort for his Grace'. Perhaps speaking from his own experience of a German wife, he added 'that it would be very strange to be married with her that he could not talk withal'.[18] This was extraordinarily prescient of the archbishop, as events would soon prove, but his ally was too firmly set upon his course to heed the warning.

The marriage treaty was duly signed on 5 October. Even though Henry still had not met his bride, their union was now indissoluble. Cromwell was triumphant. The Spanish Chronicle recorded that his 'pleasure cannot be described at having arranged this match', but added with the wisdom of hindsight: 'It turned out wrong for him.'[19]

For now, though, Henry was as delighted with his chief minister as he was at the prospect of his new wife, and the alliance prompted him to show even more favour towards the reformers. He therefore commissioned Archbishop Cranmer to compose an official preface to the second edition of the English Bible, and on 14 November he issued a proclamation granting Cromwell responsibility for licensing all Bible translations for the next five years. This was the strongest indication yet that Henry was now once again committed to the cause of reform. Moreover, by giving his people direct access to the word of God, and thereby freeing them from centuries of relying on the intercession of priests, Henry had secured a legacy that was both far-reaching and long-lived. The king himself might still blow hot and cold on the subject of reform, but from henceforth his subjects could make up their own minds.

Cromwell and Cranmer were quick to undertake their commission. They also capitalised upon their master's favour by securing the release of the Calais evangelicals, who had been languishing in captivity for several months. The majority of them were freed in mid-November, and the two men successfully delayed proceedings against the rest.

Another man who was enjoying Henry's favour that year was Sir Richard Long, who had served as gentleman usher since 1535. He had been conspicuous at Prince Edward's christening two years later, and had been knighted in the celebrations following. By 1539, he had been promoted to the role of gentleman of the privy chamber, and Henry's trust in him was so well known that Long was able to act as his deputy on diplomatic missions. Marillac later referred to him as 'a person of authority and conduct'.[20] He would continue to enjoy the king's trust and favour during the years to come.

Sir Anthony Browne had also enjoyed his best year yet in the king's service. During the course of 1539, he had been made a privy councillor, Master of the Horse, knight of the shire and captain of the gentleman pensioners. The king had also paid him the honour of visiting his house at Battle in Sussex. All of this had spelt danger for Cromwell, for Browne was one of the men whom Gardiner could rely upon to help cause trouble for the chief minister.

Nevertheless, as 1539 drew to a close, Cromwell looked forward to the new year with greater confidence than he had enjoyed since Anne Boleyn's fall. He had triumphed over his conservative rivals and inspired the king to even more sweeping reforms than he had hitherto sanctioned. And the woman who was even now making her ponderous journey to England would set the seal on his victory as Henry's new queen. Had Cromwell learned the harsh lesson experienced by so many of the king's other men in the past, he might have been more circumspect.

Cromwell's son Gregory was among the delegation appointed to welcome Anne of Cleves when she reached Calais on 11 December, as was his ally the Duke of Suffolk. The ensuing celebrations were so magnificent that they filled many letters back to the court in London – Gregory's included. But of the lady herself Cromwell's son said little. If this gave his father cause for concern, he did not express it. Rather, he accompanied his royal master as he rode in high spirits to surprise his new wife when she finally arrived at Rochester Castle on 31 December. Henry had sent Browne ahead to greet his bride. Although it has been claimed that Sir Anthony married her as the king's proxy, this is not substantiated by the evidence.

In true chivalric tradition, Henry, along with five of his privy chamber men, donned a disguise for his meeting with Anne of Cleves, the theory being that only his true love would recognise him. Unfortunately, Anne herself was not conversant with the tradition, and when her betrothed strode into the room and planted a kiss on her lips, she was greatly 'abashed' and turned back to look out of the window. Highly affronted that his betrothed had 'regarded his coming so little', Henry flounced out and returned shortly afterwards dressed in his regal finery so that this time there could be no doubt as to his identity. Anne duly 'humbled' herself before him, and they appeared to talk 'lovingly together'.[21] But the damage had been done. Much has been made of Henry's revulsion at Anne's looks, but the real cause of his distaste was her lack of refinement. If she had been a true queen, she would have understood the game of courtly love of which the king was such a devotee. Neither was Anne the epitome of royal fashion that he expected, but she was dressed in the unflattering gowns and headdresses favoured by the Flemish court. The fact that she was said to have 'evil airs' about her did not help matters.[22]

As soon as he was able, Henry excused himself and sought a private audience with Cromwell. 'I like her not! I like her not!' he shouted at the beleaguered minister, complaining that Anne was 'nothing so well as she was spoken of'. He demanded to know 'what remedy' Cromwell proposed. But the minister, for once, was at a loss. Able lawyer that he was, he had ensured that, once signed, the marriage contract would be indissoluble. He was therefore forced to admit that he 'knew none but was very sorry therefore'.[23] The king refused to listen to reason and continued to harangue his chief minister. 'Is there no other remedy but that I must needs against my will put my neck in the yoke?' he urged.[24] Cromwell could only reiterate that there was nothing else for it but to go ahead with the wedding.

One of the first to learn of Henry's distaste for his prospective bride was Sir John Russell. Although he was an ally of Cromwell, he was too pragmatic to defend him when it was clear that the king did not wish to be appeased. A number of Henry's other men were quick to capitalise upon Cromwell's fall from grace. The Spanish Chronicle claims that Henry immediately sent for the Duke of Norfolk and Edward Seymour, telling them: 'I am determined to get rid of Anne of Cleves, and Cromwell shall not deceive me again.' There was certainly little love lost between these two men and Cromwell. The latter had once castigated Seymour for acting 'very craftily'.[25] Though they had been content to work together when it suited them, their alliance had always been fragile. As soon as the audience was over, Norfolk told his companion: 'This is the time for us to get rid of common people from our midst; you see that the King has quarrelled with Cromwell, and asks our counsel. We will advise him to take affairs into his own hands, and not be ruled so much by Cromwell.'[26] The Chronicle may not always be a reliable source, but it was accurate in claiming that Norfolk resolved to use the Cleves fiasco as a means of destroying the low-born minister once and for all.

The duke and his ally Gardiner wasted no time in causing trouble for Cromwell in both foreign and domestic affairs. As well as disrupting the Franco–Imperial alliance so that Henry was less reliant upon Cleves, they ordered a new investigation of heretics in Calais and engineered the arrest of three prominent reformers in England: Robert Barnes, Thomas Gerrard and William Jerome. All of this was useful to their cause, but they knew that it was insufficient to bring Cromwell down. What they needed was something closer to Henry's heart in order to sever his ties with his chief minister for good. Norfolk had already spied the perfect means: his niece Katherine.

Henry may have first met Katherine Howard on the same day as Anne of Cleves because she had been among the ladies appointed to serve the new queen. The date of her birth is not known, but she could have been as young as fifteen at the time. But she had gained sexual experience beyond her years, with rumours of an affair with her music teacher at the age of twelve, and then a well-testified relationship with her kinsman, Francis Dereham. Katherine's immoral past, however, had been successfully hushed up by her guardian, the Dowager Duchess of Norfolk, so she arrived at court with a reputation as unblemished as her beauty.

For Henry, it was love – or lust – at first sight. Attractive and vivacious, Katherine possessed all of the qualities that the new queen so painfully lacked. Norfolk was quick to spot his master's attraction to his alluring young niece, and he and Gardiner soon began to arrange clandestine meetings between the pair. By pushing Katherine in the king's path, Norfolk had raised the stakes for Cromwell, who was trying desperately to think of a way out of the Cleves disaster. One of the few men who remained loyal to him was Thomas Wriothesley, but the latter knew that if his patron failed to think of a solution, then he would suffer by association. 'For God's sake,' he urged Cromwell, 'devise for the relief of the King; for if he remain in this grief and trouble, we shall all one day smart for it.'[27]

But if Cromwell's friends still hoped that he might prevail, his royal master had lost faith in the man who had served him diligently for the past decade. Henry secretly instructed his agent and diplomat Thomas Vaughan, a close friend of Cromwell, to go to Cleves and find out more about a previous betrothal between Anne and François, heir to the duchy of Lorraine. According to the Spanish Chronicle, Vaughan found evidence to suggest that Anne had actually been married to François, but as soon as negotiations began for a betrothal with Henry, her father had had him taken away. François had apparently 'died of grief' a short time later.[28] If true, this provided ample grounds for an annulment.

The Spanish Chronicle tells how, armed with this information, Henry summoned Cromwell. 'If thou didst know that Anne of Cleves was married, why didst thou make me marry her?' he demanded. Cromwell was greatly 'grieved' upon hearing this, but retorted: 'If your Majesty leaves her, everybody will be saying what a many wives you have.'[29] The king flew into a rage at such insolence and ordered Cromwell out of his presence. Although the king's fury at Cromwell is well substantiated, it is unlikely that the minister would have stoked it further by making such a remark. Cromwell had suffered enough of his master's temper to know that it would be more quickly diffused if he proved compliant.

In fact, far from contradicting Henry, Cromwell agreed to investigate the rumours that Vaughan had reported. He questioned Anne's ambassadors closely about the nature of her betrothal to François, but they emphatically denied that a marriage had taken place and promised to have a copy of the original contract sent to England as proof. Meanwhile, Anne agreed to sign a notarial instrument swearing that she was free to marry. In despair, Cromwell returned to his master and admitted that nothing further could be done. He later reflected that the king had been 'very much displeased' and complained that he was 'not well handled'.[30] Although Henry insisted that he would not go through with the marriage, he knew that he had no choice.

On 3 January 1540, Henry formally greeted his bride on Blackheath Common amid great ceremony. To the untrained eye, everything was as it should be, but those who could get close enough noticed the look of profound disappointment on the king's face. Three days later, the wedding took place. The aged Earl of Essex, Henry

Bourchier, had been assigned the dubious honour of leading the bride down the aisle, but on the morning of the wedding he was nowhere to be found, so the task was transferred to Cromwell. The chief minister was hardly more enthusiastic about his role than his royal master was about his. Unlike the latter, though, he was relieved of his responsibility at the eleventh hour when Bourchier finally materialised. Archbishop Cranmer was obliged to preside over the ceremony, which proceeded without incident – or any semblance of joy on the part of the groom.

Henry had been prepared to honour the alliance by playing his part in the ceremony, but his dedication to royal duty did not extend to the marriage bed. A detailed account of the wedding night still survives among the records of the reign, and for good reason: the king wanted there to be no doubt that the marriage had not been consummated. According to the account, Henry ran his hands all over his new wife's body, but upon finding certain 'tokens' that suggested she was no virgin, he was unable to stir himself to have sex with her.

Cromwell hastened to see him the next morning, perhaps hoping that, against the odds, the intimacy of the marriage bed would have made his master see Anne in a more favourable light. He soon realised that the opposite was true. Finding the king 'not so pleasant' as he expected, he tentatively asked how he liked his new wife. 'Surely my lord as you know I liked her before not well,' Henry retorted, 'but now I like her much worse.' He went on to confide his suspicions that Anne was 'no maid', judging from the shape of her stomach and breasts, and that he had therefore 'left her as good a maid as I found her'.[31]

It is likely that Henry was being disingenuous. Having latched on to the idea that Anne had been married before, he was clutching at any evidence – no matter how flimsy – to prove it. In fact, judging from Anne's own account of her marital relations with Henry, she was entirely innocent in the ways of men. When her ladies discreetly enquired whether her marriage had been consummated, she replied: 'How can I be a maid . . . and sleep every night with the King? When he comes to bed he kisses me, and takes me by the hand, and bids me, Good night, sweetheart: and in the morning kisses me, and bids me, Farewell, darling. Is this not enough?' It took the outspoken Countess of Rutland to point out: 'Madam, there must be more than this, or it will be long before we have a Duke of York.'[32]

Even now, Cromwell was determined not to give up on the marriage. He therefore instructed Anne's lord chamberlain, the Earl of Rutland, to advise her how to make herself more pleasing to the king.[33] At the same time, he privately instructed Anthony Denny to praise Anne whenever the opportunity presented itself. Of all the men whom Cromwell had placed in the privy chamber, Denny had proved the most acceptable to Henry and was now one of his closest attendants. Greatly though he was esteemed by the king, however, there was little Denny could do to change Henry's opinion of his new wife, and he was soon forced to admit defeat. Henry would hear nothing favourable about Anne, and upbraided the hapless Denny: 'He would utter plainly to him, as to a servant whom he used secretly about him . . . that he could never . . . be provoked and stirred to know her carnally.'[34] Sir Anthony Browne also noted his master's abhorrence for Anne, and feared that his half-brother William Fitzwilliam, who had praised her beauty, would pay the price.

Although the men closest to Henry knew that his new marriage was a sham, it gave heart to the Lutheran princes of the Schmalkaldic League, who dispatched Ludwig von Baumbach to London with instructions to conclude a religious and political alliance. Upon arriving, the envoy at once sought out Cromwell, confident that he was the surest means of bringing this alliance to a happy conclusion. But to his dismay, the chief minister told him that there was nothing he could do to help. Cromwell might have been firmly committed to reform, but he was enough of a political realist to know that pushing his master on the issue at this time would bring nothing but grief. He had enough to do in clawing back favour after the disastrous Cleves match. Refusing to take Cromwell at his word, Baumbach sought an audience with the king himself, but Henry told the envoy frankly that the League was useless to England as a political ally.

By April 1540, Henry had made his displeasure with Cromwell so obvious that everyone at court expected news of his fall to be announced any day. 'Cromwell is tottering,' reported Marillac with satisfaction. He was not alone in predicting that this would lead to a reversal in the religious revolution that the chief minister and his close ally Cranmer had orchestrated, and surmised: 'Within a few days there will be seen in this country a great change in many things.' The French ambassador went on to relate that Henry had been busy planning a change in ministers, 'recalling those he had rejected and degrading those he had raised'.[35]

It is an indication of how embattled Cromwell was feeling at this time that he made friendly overtures to one of his deadliest enemies, Stephen Gardiner. 'Yesterday my lord of Winchester dined at London with my lord Privy Seal,' Wriothesley reported, 'and were more than four hours, and opened their hearts, and so concluded that, and there be truth or honesty in them, not only all displeasures be forgotten, but also in their hearts be now perfect entire friends.'[36] This may have been wishful thinking on the young man's part. Cromwell and Gardiner had been fiercely opposed to each other for too long to settle their differences in the space of an evening.

Wriothesley's loyalty to Cromwell was soon rewarded. Shortly after the dinner with Gardiner, Cromwell secured the young man a place on the council and also resigned the role of principal secretary jointly to him and Ralph Sadler. It seemed that Cromwell, expecting Henry to dismiss him at any moment, had decided to fall on his sword. But this was out of character for a man who always came out fighting when he was under siege from his enemies. Rather, it may have been a deliberate tactic to increase the number of his supporters on the council.

Although in public Henry appeared to be in a state of fury against his chief minister, in private it would soon become apparent that Cromwell had succeeded in talking his way back into favour. Knowing that the Anne of Cleves fiasco had made his royal master lose faith in him, Cromwell had to convince Henry that his loyalty to him superseded all else – even the religious reforms that had become his lifeblood. To demonstrate this, he made an opening speech in the House of Lords in April, reiterating the king's desire for religious accord among his subjects. He then introduced measures to eradicate heresy, some of which led to a reversal of his earlier reforms. The result was a compromise in religion, such as his master had made it clear he desired.

Henry understood the sacrifice that Cromwell had made and he rewarded him richly for it. On 18 April, he made the chief minister Earl of Essex, one of the most ancient and distinguished titles in the land.[37] He also appointed him lord great chamberlain, following the death of John de Vere, fifteenth Earl of Oxford. By making Cromwell an earl, Henry had not only shown to the world that he was forgiven, but had placed him on an equal – if not superior – social standing with his blue-blooded rivals. This was a staggering about-turn, even by Henry's standards. In his next dispatch, a dumbfounded Marillac was forced to admit that Cromwell 'was in as much credit with the King as ever he was, from which he was near being shaken by the Bishop of Winchester and others'.[38]

For Norfolk and Gardiner, it was too much to bear. They had been within a whisker of getting rid of their chief rival for good; now he was back in favour – and in spectacular style. Moreover, the king had strengthened Cromwell's powerbase by showing favour to his allies: Wriothesley and Sadler were knighted on the same day that Cromwell received his honour. But having almost tasted victory, his enemies were not prepared to relinquish it. They therefore resolved on a plan to oust the new Earl of Essex from the king's service on a permanent basis.

Cromwell, too, came out fighting. He knew that his enemies were furious about his restoration to Henry's good graces and were thirsting for vengeance. He therefore resolved to destroy them before they could destroy him. The six or seven weeks that followed his promotion would witness the most vicious battle ever waged between the king's men. The seasoned courtier, Sir Francis Bryan, observed that there was an 'overplus' of 'malice and displeasures'. Marillac concurred that Henry's 'ministers seek only to undo each other to gain credit, and under colour of their master's good each attends to his own. For all the fine words of which they are full they will act only as necessity and interest compel them.' Little wonder that nobody believed Cromwell's assertion that he desired nothing but 'the establishment of one perfect unity in opinion amongst us all'. It was clear from the outset that it would be a fight to the death.

'Here is nothing but every man for himself,' reported Arthur Plantagenet's agent John Hussee.[39]

The day before Henry made his chief minister Earl of Essex, Lord Lisle had returned from Calais. He had been recalled on suspicion of treasonable communications with another member of the Plantagenet clan, Cardinal Reginald Pole. It is likely that Cromwell had been instrumental in persuading the king to take action against his uncle. Lisle was one of Norfolk's greatest allies, and the pair were united by a common loathing for this base-born minister who had overturned the natural order and religion of the kingdom. It was at this moment that William Fitzwilliam and Sir Anthony Browne decided to sever all connections with Cromwell and throw in their lot with Norfolk. The time for vacillating between court factions was over. Henry's men were now ranged into two camps, ready for war.

Robert Radcliffe, Earl of Sussex, was dispatched to Calais on 9 May at the head of a commission to inquire into charges of misgovernment. But he was also to investigate rumours of sacramentarianism, an extreme form of evangelicalism, so it may have been his ally Norfolk, rather than Cromwell, who had persuaded the king to enlist his services.

On 19 May, a little over a month after his arrival in London, Lisle was arrested and taken to the Tower. Any doubt that he was there at Cromwell's behest is erased by the fact that a few days later, Richard Sampson, the conservative Bishop of Chichester, and Dr Nicholas Wilson, a staunch ally of Bishop Gardiner, joined Lisle in the Tower. All three men were the victims of the struggle for power that was raging in Henry's court.

This power struggle also centred upon Henry's marriage. Cromwell grasped at any sign that the king might be warming towards his new wife. When Anne attended the traditional Mayday tournaments with her husband and was accorded every honour, the Earl of Surrey riding out as her chief defender, it stoked rumours that she would soon be crowned. The chief minister duly held discussions about the matter with the ambassador of Cleves, and again urged Anne, through the Earl of Rutland, to do her best to please the king. But while Cromwell was appealing to Henry's political sensibilities,

Norfolk was stoking his passion for his young niece, Katherine. He understood, perhaps better than his rival, how powerful desire and vanity were in influencing the choice of their ageing and obese king.

But there was still a risk that Henry might indulge his passion by keeping Katherine as a mistress, while fulfilling his political duty by maintaining Anne as his wife. Knowing that this would safeguard Cromwell's position and strengthen the cause of reform, Norfolk began a whispering campaign aimed at discrediting his rival. According to the Spanish Chronicle, he started a rumour that Cromwell had received a substantial fee from the Duke of Cleves for brokering the marriage. Together with Edward Seymour, who had now turned decisively against the chief minister, he voiced his suspicions to the king, telling him: 'All the nobles of the realm are surprised that your Majesty should give so much power to the Secretary, who, doubtless, received a large sum from the Duke of Cleves for bringing about your marriage as he did.'[40]

Warming to their theme, the two men hinted that Cromwell was planning some kind of insurrection. As evidence, they cited the fact that he retained more servants than any of the king's other men. 'In all parts of the kingdom people are wearing his livery and calling themselves his servants, under shelter of which they are committing a thousand offences,' they told Henry. They went on to claim that Cromwell had arms in his house to equip more than 7,000 men and that he had been quietly bolstering the king's personal guard with forty men from his own household. Worse still, they said, even in the king's privy chamber, his most secure and intimate domain, there were five 'devoted servants' of the chief minister. 'We do not like the look of it,' they concluded. By the time they had finished speaking, neither did Henry.

It took little to ignite the suspicions of a king who was by now as deeply paranoid about threats to his crown as his father had been. The French ambassador claimed that at this time Henry was a king who would 'fain keep in favour with everybody, but does not trust a single man'.[41] Sir John Russell, who was much closer to Henry, concurred that he was 'a prince of much wisdom and knowledge, yet he was very suspicious and much given to suspicion (suspicion)'.[42] This situation was at least partly of the king's making. He had fostered an atmosphere of suspicion and mistrust through his own fickle behaviour, which had deprived his men of the luxury of feeling secure in his favour. But partly, too, it had been created by the men themselves, who had both encouraged and capitalised upon their royal master's growing paranoia to serve their own ends. It was a situation as volatile as it was toxic.

Though it was only a few short weeks since Henry had appointed Cromwell to the highest offices in the land, the conversation with Norfolk and Seymour had been enough to convince the king that his chief minister must be brought down. 'I promise you I will find a way to take his power away from him,' he assured them.[43] The meeting is not recorded by any other source, and it is possible that the Spanish Chronicle was drawing on rumours that were circulating at court around this time – no doubt sparked by Norfolk and his allies. These rumours rapidly took hold and were embellished along the way. It was even whispered that Cromwell had told Chapuys in a private conversation: 'I hope to be a king myself one day.' The old rumours that he planned to marry Henry's daughter Mary were revived as proof and, although just as groundless as the others, would form one of the most notable charges against him. The Spanish Chronicle claims that when Norfolk and Seymour hastened back to the king with reports of the latest rumours, Henry retorted: 'I may inform you that I greatly suspect him of a design to raise the kingdom and murder me.'[44]

It is easy to imagine the paranoid and irascible king turning against a man whom he had so lately raised to greatness. But if Henry really did harbour private suspicions towards Cromwell, he was careful not to show any hint of them in public. In early June, Marillac reported: 'Things are brought to such a pass that either Cromwell's party or that of the bishop of Winchester must succumb', but added: 'although both are in great authority and favour of the King their master, still the course of things seems to incline to Cromwell's side'.[45] Marillac had good reason for his change of opinion. It was rumoured that Robert Barnes would soon be released. At the same time, a cleric with known 'Popish leanings' had recently been arrested.

But Marillac was about to be proved wrong. On 10 June 1540, an apparently routine meeting of the Privy Council was held. As soon as Cromwell, who arrived late, strode into the chamber, he was arrested by a captain of the guard on charges of treason and heresy. Shocked to the core, the chief minister flew into a rage and 'cast his bonnet on the ground, saying to the Duke of Norfolk and others of the Privy Council assembled there that this was the reward of his services'. In the next breath, though, he 'appealed to their consciences as to whether he was a traitor; but since he was treated thus he renounced all pardon, as he had never thought to have offended, and only asked the King not to make him languish long'.[46]

The speed with which Cromwell seemed to submit to his fate suggests that he, like Henry, had known that it was coming. The battle that he had waged with Norfolk and his faction had grown so fierce in recent weeks that, as Marillac observed, it was obvious to all that the king would never make peace between them. There could only be one victor and, for once, Cromwell had been outwitted.

The intensely personal nature of the rivalry between the king's most powerful men is revealed by the detailed description of what happened next. Norfolk strode up to Cromwell and ripped the order of St George from his neck, as if by doing so he could strip him of all the honours with which this blacksmith's son had tried to cover up the shame of his birth. Eager to show that he was 'as great an enemy in adversity as he had been thought a friend in prosperity', William Fitzwilliam now stepped forward and untied the Garter from Cromwell's knee.[47] The beleaguered minister was then bundled into a waiting boat and taken to the Tower.

The official statement that was released on the day of Cromwell's arrest described the heinousness of his crimes in general, rather than specific terms. Spurred on by his 'sensual appetite', he had 'clean contrary to . . . his grace's most godly intent, secretly and indirectly' drawn the king away from the 'true and virtuous way, which his majesty sought and so entirely desired'. Furthermore, he had 'showed himself so fervently bent to the maintenance of that his outrage, that he hath not spared most privily, most traitorously, to devise how to continue the same and plainly in terms to say, as it hath been justified to his face by good witnesses, that if the king and all his realm would turn and vary from his opinions, he would fight in the field in his own person, with his sword in his hand against him and all other; adding that if he lived a year or two, he trusted to bring things to that frame, that it would not lie in the king's power to resist or let it, if he would'.[48] All of this was mere rumour and conjecture, and hardly enough upon which to build a convincing case of treason. But that mattered little to Henry, or to the men who had brought down his chief minister. Even one of Cromwell's last remaining allies, Thomas Wriothesley, had deserted him: indeed, the statement had been drafted in his hand.

News of Cromwell's arrest spread rapidly across the kingdom and abroad. Marillac, who could barely keep up with the pace of events, hurried off a letter to his master. 'Thomas Cromwell . . . who, since the Cardinal's death, had the principal management of the affairs of this kingdom . . . was, an hour ago, led prisoner to the Tower and all his goods attached,' he reported, adding: 'Cromwell's party seemed the strongest lately . . . The thing is the more marvellous as it was unexpected by everyone.'[49] Edward Hall noted that 'many lamented, but more rejoiced' upon hearing the news, and that Cromwell's enemies 'banqueted, and triumphed together that night'.[50]

In characteristic style, the king now set about removing all trace of his former chief minister. Henry's servants descended upon Cromwell's houses and seized all of his possessions. It was soon clear that the architect of the dissolution had siphoned off some of the spoils for himself. A total of £7,000 sterling (equivalent to more than £2 million today) was taken away, along with silver plates, chalices, crucifixes and 'other spoils of the Church'. They were immediately deposited in the king's treasury, which Marillac rightly interpreted as 'a sign that they will not be restored'.[51] Henry's officials took away evidence, as well as riches. This included correspondence with the Lutheran princes of Germany, which provided ample proof of Cromwell's heretical leanings. When these were shown to the king, he was 'so exasperated against him [Cromwell] that he would no longer hear him spoken of, but rather desired to abolish all memory of him as the greatest wretch ever born in England'.[52] This was typical of the man who loved to extremes, but hated to them too – often in quick succession.

Having so recently raised Cromwell to an earldom, Henry stripped him of all his titles and offices, proclaiming 'that none should call him lord Privy Seal or by any other title of estate, but only Thomas Cromwell, shearman'. In this one sentence, the king had reduced his chief minister to the lowly origins from which he had risen. Referring to Cromwell as a shearman, or shearer of sheep, was a dismissive way of describing his business as a wool merchant. He had been many other things besides, even discounting his court offices, including a property owner, money-lender and – above all – a highly successful lawyer. But Henry wanted to bring Cromwell as low with words as he had done with deeds. Even Cromwell's servants were ordered to set aside their master's livery in case they should act as a reminder of his existence. While most rejoiced that Henry had at last ousted his despised chief minister, the Venetian ambassador shrewdly observed that Cromwell was just another victim of the king's notoriously fickle nature. 'It is thought that he [Cromwell] likewise will make the same end as all the others most in favour with the King', he wrote.[53]

Henry wrote to Marillac shortly afterwards, and it was obvious that the rumours about Cromwell had hit home. He told the ambassador that his minister had been 'working against the intention of the King and of the Acts of Parliament', and had boasted that 'the King with all his power could not prevent it, but rather his own party would be so strong that he would make the King descend to the new doctrines even if he had to take arms against him'. Henry confided that he had heard of Cromwell's plots from 'those who heard them and who esteemed their fealty more than the favour of their master'.[54] Norfolk, Gardiner and Seymour had known exactly what to say to ignite their royal master's paranoia. The fact that Cromwell had only recently proved that he would put the king's wishes ahead of his reforms was quickly forgotten.

But Henry's relationships with the men closest to him were as complex as they were volatile. Echoing his treatment of Wolsey after his arrest eleven years earlier, while in public he denounced Cromwell as a black-hearted villain, in private he showed some sympathy towards him. One eyewitness noticed that the king had been 'very kind' to Cromwell's servants upon his arrest, and had taken many of them into his own service 'to save them from want'.[55] Henry also sent some money to Cromwell in the Tower, which presumably he could use to bribe his gaolers for better food or other comforts, and urged that he keep him informed of how he was being treated. All of this was done with the utmost discretion. Just as Henry had kept his favour towards Wolsey hidden from Anne Boleyn, so he was careful to conceal his sympathy for Cromwell from the men who had brought him down.

The beleaguered minister wrote at once to thank his master for his 'abundant' beneficence, assuring Henry that he was his 'most humble and most obedient and most bounden subject and most lamentable servant and prisoner, prostrate at the feet of your most excellent majesty'. He went on to assure the king of his abiding fidelity and to remind him of the 'labours, pains and travails' he had taken during the decade of his service at court. Cromwell also praised Henry as 'the most bountiful prince to me that ever was king to his subject, yea and more like a dear father, your Majesty not offended, than a master'.[56] His faithfulness to Henry was a recurring theme throughout his imprisonment. When his arch-enemy Norfolk was sent to interrogate him, Cromwell reflected bitterly that he had 'always been pursued by great enemies about the king; so that his fidelity was tried like gold'.[57]

While Cromwell was doing what he could to redeem himself from the Tower, back at court the few allies he had left had quickly abandoned him. Sir John Russell had proved a steadfast friend to the chief minister over the years, but he was enough of a political realist – and pragmatist – to realise the futility of trying to defend him now. The fact that Russell had retained Henry's favour for so long was due largely to his keeping his own political and religious preferences hidden so that he could mould them to those of his royal master. He counted both Catholics and Reformers among his close acquaintances, and his patronage was not bestowed along religious lines. Rather, he seemed to prioritise the king's wishes above religion.

Thomas Cranmer, who together with Cromwell had spearheaded the English reformation, remained loyal to his ally, but paid the price. Marillac reported that the reformist faction 'seems quite overthrown by the taking of the said lord Cromwell, who was chief of his band,

and there remain only on his side the Archbishop of Canterbury, who dare not open his mouth, and the lord Admiral [William Fitzwilliam, Earl of Southampton], who has long learnt to bend to all winds, and they have for open enemies the duke of Norfolk and the others'.[58]

Cranmer did eventually try to defend Cromwell to the king, and wrote an impassioned plea urging Henry to remember everything that his chief minister had done for him. He expressed himself 'sorrowful and amazed that he [Cromwell] should be a traitor against your majesty, he that was so advanced by your majesty . . . he who loved your majesty (as I ever thought) no less than God; he who studied always to set forwards whatsoever was your majesty's will and pleasure; he that cared for no man's displeasure to serve your majesty; he that was such a servant . . . in wisdom, diligence, faithfulness, and experience, as no prince in this realm ever had'. For Cranmer's own part, he averred: 'I loved him as my friend, for so I took him to be; but I chiefly loved him for the love which I thought I saw him bear ever towards your grace, singularly above all other.' But Cranmer ended with a blatant attempt to feather his own nest, praying that God would 'send such a counsellor in his place whom your grace may trust, and who for all his qualities can and will serve your grace like him, and that will have so much solicitude and care to preserve your grace from all dangers as I ever thought he had'.[59]

Cranmer's letter worked no effect. With blind determination, Henry entrusted his assiduous Lord Chancellor Audley with attainting Cromwell, his former friend and ally, through a parliamentary device that offered the accused no chance to defend himself. Audley no doubt appreciated the irony that the man whose legal skills exceeded his own considerable acumen had been denied a trial. But service to the king always exceeded all other concerns for the Lord Chancellor. In recognition of this, the previous year Henry had approved the Act of Precedence, which gave Audley superiority over all but dukes of royal blood in parliament, the Privy Council, and Star Chamber. His status was further enhanced in May 1540, when he was installed as a Knight of the Garter.

The bill of attainder against Cromwell was introduced to the Lords on 17 June. It described the fallen minister as being of 'very base and low degree' and 'the most detestable traitor that has been seen during the King's reign'. There were no fewer than eleven indictments, ranging from heresy and corruption to 'usurping upon your kingly estate power and authority and office, without your grace's commandment or assent'. The many references to Cromwell's lowly birth reveal Norfolk's hand in the drafting. In his eyes, this was Cromwell's real crime. Despite being 'a person of as poor and low degree as few be', so the charges ran, Cromwell had said publicly 'that he was sure of you [the king], and it is detestable that any subject should speak so of his sovereign'.[60] After the bill had been read out, nobody was prepared to speak in Cromwell's defence, and it was passed twelve days later. Even the fallen minister's closest ally, Archbishop Cranmer, voted for it. Cromwell was now a dead man walking.

But Henry had not quite finished with his faithful servant yet. Desperate to untangle himself from the Cleves marriage, he called upon Cromwell to give evidence from the Tower in support of an annulment. Along with the king's physicians and his closest body servants, Sir Anthony Denny and Sir Thomas Heneage, Cromwell was urged to testify that his master 'never for love to the woman consented to marry; nor yet, if she brought maidenhead with her, took any from her by true carnal copulation'.[61] For good measure, Henry dispatched Norfolk, Audley and Fitzwilliam to the Tower so that they might 'move' Cromwell's conscience to provide the evidence that his royal master needed. The former favourite was quick to oblige, rushing off a letter testifying that the marriage had not been consummated, and hinting that the Cleves ambassadors had deliberately concealed Anne's previous betrothal.

Having fulfilled his duty, and realising that this might be his last chance to write to his master, Cromwell pleaded with Henry to show favour to his son, Gregory, fearing that the young man might suffer by association with a condemned traitor. 'Sir, upon my knees I most humbly beseech your gracious majesty to be a good and gracious lord to my poor son, [and] the good and virtuous lady his wife and their poor children.' It was clever of Cromwell to mention his daughter-in-law, thus reminding Henry of Gregory's kinship to the most beloved of all the king's wives. Having done his best to protect his son, Cromwell added a desperate postscript for himself: 'Most gracious prince,' he wrote in a hurried and untidy script, 'I cry for mercy, mercy, mercy.'[62]

According to John Foxe, writing more than twenty years after the event, the king asked for Cromwell's letter to be read to him three times. It evidently worked some effect, for he subsequently conferred some of Cromwell's titles and lands upon his son Gregory.[63] But this was evidently enough to salve Henry's conscience, for he did no more.

On 9 July, Cranmer declared the king's marriage to Anne of Cleves null and void. After speaking out for Cromwell, he was quick to disassociate himself from his former ally. This helped to preserve his favour with the king, but he was probably also saved by the fact that Henry's prospective new bride, Katherine Howard, knew that the archbishop had warned against the Cleves marriage. As if to reward him, the king gave Cranmer formal precedence in the reshaped Privy Council shortly afterwards.

Cromwell's execution was scheduled for the morning of 28 July. Having been stripped of his titles, he was to be beheaded on Tower Green, the site reserved for common traitors. The day before, a delivery of clothes arrived at Hampton Court Palace. They belonged to the man who now only had hours to live. Nicholas Bristowe, the king's assiduous keeper of the wardrobe, recorded every item before distributing them among his master's surviving favourites. They included Sir Thomas Heneage, his groom of the stool, Richard Cecil, a yeoman of the privy chamber, and Robert Radcliffe, Earl of Sussex. Bristowe himself was a recipient. He had no scruple in accepting this macabre gift: Cromwell was one of many deceased or attainted courtiers whose possessions he had redistributed on the king's behalf. Only Cromwell's Garter robes were retained by Henry. They remained at Hampton Court 'by the King's command' for the rest of the reign.[64]

The following morning, Cromwell was escorted to the scaffold by a heavily armed guard, his royal master being fearful of a revolt by the 'common people'. Although the fallen minister had courted widespread hostility by pushing through the seismic religious reforms, he had been one of the most charitable men at court, never ignoring any plea for assistance and giving daily alms to the poor who gathered outside his residences. He had been greatly beloved among the ordinary citizens of London as a result.

The condemned man behaved with dignity and calm acceptance. Having mounted the scaffold, he addressed the crowds. 'Gentlemen, you should all take warning from me, who was, as you know, from a poor man made by the King into a great gentleman, and I, not contented with that, nor with having the kingdom at my orders, presumed to a still higher state, and my pride has brought its punishment. I confess I am justly condemned, and I urge you, gentlemen, study to preserve the good you possess, and never let greed or pride prevail in you. Serve your King, who is one of the best in the world, and one who knows best how to reward his vassals.'[65] With these carefully chosen words, Cromwell seemed to agree with the most vociferous criticism levelled against him: that a man of his lowly birth should not have so far overreached himself. But his speech was intended as a warning, not an apology. Henry's other men who were there that day should have taken heed of their fallen rival and reflected upon the fickle favour of their master.

'He has not been the same man'

AS THE 'RAGGED and butcherly' executioner swung the axe down onto Cromwell's neck for the third time, finally severing his head from his body, the king was joyfully anticipating his fifth wedding, which would take place later that day.[1] With Cromwell's help, he had finally secured an annulment from Anne of Cleves so that he could marry the infinitely more beguiling young Katherine Howard. Cranmer, too, had played his part by chairing a Convocation committee that proved the marriage had been invalid because of a previous contract between Anne and the Duke of Lorraine. That he felt anxious in the wake of his ally's fall is proven by the fact that when some of the clerics involved in drafting the annulment gossiped about the rivalry that had existed between Cromwell and Gardiner, the archbishop had them brought before the council to make an apology.

Henry clearly hoped that Cromwell's death would put an end to the vicious sniping and backbiting between the rival factions at court. While Norfolk and Gardiner may have taken it as a victory for the conservatives, the king made it clear that he wanted to achieve a middle way in religion from now on. He signalled this in typically brutal fashion two days after Cromwell's execution by ordering the burning at the stake of three evangelicals and three conservatives known to be loyal to Rome. There was insufficient evidence against any of them, but Henry was determined to express his desire for unity with their blood.

One man who emerged triumphant from the controversy was Charles Brandon. He had led the team that negotiated the terms of the annulment with Anne of Cleves. Although he had counted Cromwell as an ally for the past three years, he did not suffer by association now. Yet neither had he turned his coat like so many other courtiers by helping to bring down the chief minister. In the new atmosphere of compromise and accord that Henry was trying to promote, his old friend Suffolk fitted in perfectly. Not for the first time in Henry's reign, the duke became a symbol of stability at a time of political turmoil.

In the weeks that followed, Henry betrayed no regret at the execution of his one-time favourite, but instead gave every appearance of a love-struck teenager. If he mentioned Cromwell at all, then it was as a 'knave'. In the meantime, the distribution of the late minister's possessions and offices continued. Thomas Wriothesley, who had been quick to distance himself from his former patron, was granted Cromwell's newly refurbished mansion at Austin Friars. Meanwhile, the king had ordered that some of the choicer pieces of Cromwell's furniture be removed from Austin Friars and given to Anne of Cleves as part of her annulment settlement. The symbolism of the gesture was obvious to all: even in death, Cromwell was paying for the fiasco of his master's fourth marriage.[2]

Meanwhile, among those to profit from the offices that Cromwell had surrendered was his former ally, Sir John Russell, whom Henry appointed Lord High Admiral on the same day that Cromwell was executed. Although he lost out when his royal master, in haste to eradicate all trace of a former favourite, had Cromwell's Council of the West disbanded soon afterwards, the wealth and status that he had given Russell in the region endured and would prove a source of stability there for the crown long into the future.

Marillac gleefully reported on the division of the spoils that followed Cromwell's demise. 'The Privy Seal has been given to the admiral Fitzwilliam, while Master Russell has become Lord High Admiral of England in his room. The bishop of Durham [Cuthbert Tunstall] has been appointed first secretary, or viceregent in ecclesiastical causes . . . For the affairs of justice, the Chancellor [Audley] has been deputed.'[3] Within days, it was as if the king's most powerful servant had never existed. Cromwell's noble rivals crowed in triumph. 'Now is the false churl dead, so ambitious of others' blood,' cried Norfolk's son the Earl of Surrey. 'Now is he stricken with his own staff . . . These new erected men would by their wills leave no nobleman on life.'[4]

By contrast, a number of the king's men found themselves in danger after Cromwell's fall. Even though he had benefited from his former patron's demise, Wriothesley was subjected to an examination by the king's officials soon afterwards. He was even accused by Walter Chandler of slandering the king and of unlawfully retaining some manors near Winchester. To Wriothesley's great relief, the charge was judged malicious, and in December 1540 Chandler was compelled to apologise to Wriothesley before the Privy Council. Shaken by the experience, Wriothesley resolved to ally himself to the conservatives, evidently judging that it was worth sacrificing his principles in order to retain the king's favour. He struck up a close alliance with Gardiner, and it was soon noted that he had 'obtained considerable power' in the wake of Cromwell's fall, and that 'he advised the King in everything'.[5] Wriothesley's alliance with Gardiner also brought him material rewards. For example, in October 1542 the bishop granted him the mastership of the game in Fareham Manor and annuities worth £86, citing his 'great love and singular affection' for Wriothesley.[6] Gardiner's generosity came at a price, though: it was strictly conditional upon the secretary's willingness to further the conservative cause.

Meanwhile, the handful of men who had remained faithful to Cromwell were immediately under the king's suspicion, notably the secretary Sir Ralph Sadler, who had been knighted around the same time that his former patron was made Earl of Essex, and Sir Thomas Wyatt, who had openly wept for the minister at his execution. Both men were arrested in January 1541, along with several others who had been closely connected to Cromwell. This may have been at the behest of Norfolk and his party, rather than Henry. Marillac opined: 'There could be no worse war than the English carry on against each other; for after Cromwell had brought down the greatest of the realm, from the Marquis [of Exeter, Henry Courtenay] to the Grand Esquire Caraud [Sir Nicholas Carew], now others have arisen who will never rest till they have done as much to all Cromwell's adherents, and God knows whether after them others will not recommence the feast. [I] never saw them look more troubled,' he concluded.[7]

Sadler and Wyatt were released two months later. It was partly thanks to Katherine Howard that the latter was pardoned. Like many women before her, she had been charmed by the charismatic poet. The king's own abiding affection for Wyatt had undoubtedly also played a part. Chapuys recorded that Henry imposed a condition on his pardon, namely that he should take back his wife, Elizabeth Brooke, 'from whom he had been separated for upwards of fifteen years'.[8] This was an onerous condition for the poet, who included a veiled reference to her in a later verse as the 'clog' on his wheel. But he was too desirous of the king's renewed favour to gainsay him. Whether he still revered Henry after what he had done to Cromwell is another matter. Soon after his release, Wyatt retired to Allington, his estate in Kent, for a few months, and it may have been during his stay that he composed his penitential psalms on the theme of enemies and tyrannical rulers.

By the time of Wyatt and Sadler's release, Henry was already regretting his haste in having their patron put to death. As early as December 1540, the king had betrayed signs of remorse. That month, he bestowed a barony upon Cromwell's son Gregory. He also showed favour to Cromwell's nephew, Richard, who was later given a sought-after position in the privy chamber.

Even though he had been quick to fill the offices that Cromwell had vacated, Henry had not been able to find another man with the same exceptional ability, shrewdness and capacity for hard work to act as his chief minister. After Wolsey had been ousted from power, Cromwell had soon stepped into his shoes. But there was no man to do so now, and the role would remain vacant for the rest of the reign. Too late, Henry had realised the extent of Cromwell's genius. That he had taken Cromwell for granted during his decade of service had been partly Cromwell's fault for having made it look easy: he had fulfilled every task that Henry had set for him with minimum show and maximum efficiency. Now, as Foxe observed: 'The king did afterwards greatly and earnestly repent his death, but alas too late, who was heard oftentimes to say, that now he lacked his Cromwell.'[9]

In characteristic style, Henry lashed out at others, rather than accepting any measure of the blame. On 3 March 1541, a little over seven months after the former chief minister's execution, Marillac reported that the king regularly reproached his councillors that 'upon light pretexts, by false accusations, they made him put to death the most faithful servant he had ever had'.[10]

But Henry did not brood on his loss for long. Instead, he made a virtue out of necessity and resolved that never again would he allow one of his ministers to enjoy such power as Cromwell – and, before him, Wolsey – had done. Now the forty-nine-year-old king was determined to rule alone for the first time in his reign. His character had undergone a similar, if more gradual, transformation. Gone was the convivial, open-hearted king of his youth; in his place was a suspicious, paranoid and boastful tyrant – 'very stern and opinionated' – who recognised no will but his own and would bring even the greatest of his subjects down on little more than a whim.[11]

'Although formerly everyone condescended to his wishes, still there was some form of justice,' remarked the French ambassador Marillac in August 1540, 'but now will be only the King's pleasure.' He added that Henry had become not merely 'a King to be obeyed, but an idol to be worshipped'.[12] Henry himself declared that he 'would be obeyed whosoever spake to the contrary'.[13] One courtier noted that if the king began a sentence with the word 'Well', everyone knew that his mind was made up and it would be foolhardy to argue.[14] Henry's court, which had long been a dangerous place for those seeking advancement, was now a deadly one.

But for the time being, everything was set fair for Katherine Howard's male relatives and associates following her marriage to Henry. Utterly besotted with his new wife, the king was blind to her faults, as well as to those of the Howards. The principal beneficiary was her uncle, the Duke of Norfolk, who enjoyed both political and material rewards at his sovereign's hands. Two other men rose to prominence after the conclusion of the vows. Katherine's cousin, Henry Howard, Earl of Surrey, became a Knight of the Garter. Meanwhile, Robert Radcliffe, Earl of Sussex, whose son Henry had married Norfolk's daughter Elizabeth, attained the pinnacle of his career in royal service when he was made lord great chamberlain for life.[15] It was particularly satisfying for Norfolk to see Cromwell's former office go to one of his close allies.

But the flighty young queen was a good deal less enamoured of her ageing, obese husband than he was of her. There is reason to suppose that the king was suffering from impotence by the time he married her. Certainly there was little sign that Katherine had fallen pregnant. In fact, she was soon looking elsewhere for sexual gratification.

If Katherine's promiscuous past had come to light, it would have been shocking enough, but she compounded the situation by taking a lover soon after she became Henry's fifth queen. Thomas Culpeper was a 'beautiful youth' who served as gentleman of the king's privy chamber. Distantly related to the new queen through an ancestor in the reign of Edward II, he is first noted at court in 1535, when he began acting on behalf of Arthur, Viscount Lisle, the lord deputy of Calais, and his wife, Honor. By November 1537 he was a gentleman of the king's privy chamber. A further indication of how much the king esteemed him came the following January. One of Culpeper's serving boys had been condemned to death for theft at Westminster Palace, but was reprieved from the gallows when a royal pardon arrived just as the hangman was removing the ladder.

Although Culpeper must have been charming and affable to win such favour with Henry so soon, he had a darker side. In 1539, he was accused of raping a park keeper's wife. One of the villagers who tried to arrest him was killed – whether by Culpeper or a member of his entourage is not clear. In an age when even petty crime could carry the death sentence, this was more than enough to have had Culpeper sent to the gallows. But the king pardoned him, and just a few months later Culpeper attended the reception of Anne of Cleves upon her arrival in England. Trouble never seemed to be far away, though, and in March 1541, some of his servants were imprisoned for their role in a brawl at Southwark, an area of the city notorious for its bawdy houses and taverns.

Quite when the affair between Culpeper and Katherine Howard began is not certain. They had attended many of the same court functions since she became Henry's wife, but the first hint of an attachment came on Maundy Thursday 1541, when the queen presented him with a velvet cap. Culpeper knew the dire consequences that would follow if he bedded the king's wife, but perhaps this piqued his attraction even more. They began to meet in secret, with the assistance of Katherine's lady of the privy chamber, Jane Boleyn, widow of George, and Katherine Tilney, another attendant.

The affair continued throughout the king's progress to the northern counties that summer. Culpeper was later recorded as having visited the queen's bedchamber at several locations en route, including Pontefract and Lincoln. It may have been at the latter place that Katherine penned the now infamous letter to Culpeper. On the surface it appears to be an expression of love and desire – certainly that is how it was later interpreted by the king's officials. Culpeper had been ill, so the couple had not been able to meet for a while, and Katherine expressed a yearning to see him. 'It makes my heart die to think I cannot be always in your company,' she wrote, before signing off: 'Yours as long as life endures.'[16]

This letter may not be all it appears, however. The emotional language could have been driven less by Katherine's desire than by her desperation to escape the plight that she was in. Culpeper had a reputation for lechery as well as violence, and it is easy to imagine him as a dangerous and controlling suitor who refused to let the young queen escape their liaison. Katherine herself was vulnerable to such a domineering and manipulative man. Attractive and vivacious but hopelessly naïve, she had been preyed upon by unscrupulous men since her youth, and seems to have played an essentially passive role, responding to their demands rather than her own inclinations.

The invidious situation in which she now found herself was compounded by the arrival of one of her former lovers, Francis Dereham. Undoubtedly, he was seeking to blackmail the queen into giving him a position at court in return for his silence about their earlier affair. It worked. Four days after his arrival at Pontefract Castle, Katherine appointed Dereham her secretary. But this only bought his silence for a short while, and the hapless Katherine was obliged to offer him further bribes.

By the time that the royal progress reached York in September, the queen had reached breaking point. She sent word to Culpeper that she would not meet him in private again. Predictably, he refused to accept her decision but continued to pester and threaten her. On 6 October, the king and his entourage left Hull, the final stopping place on their tour, and began the slow journey back to London. Unbeknownst to Katherine, events were unfolding there that would seal her fate.

But as far as Henry was concerned, this was one of the happiest periods of his life. He had a beautiful young wife, whom he relished showing off during his progress, and he had also just received news that his 'entirely beloved son' and heir was thriving.[17] Although he is often depicted as a fragile, sickly child, Edward enjoyed robust health for much of his childhood. In the portrait that Holbein painted when the prince was a little over a year old, he has full cheeks and chubby hands. The report that Henry received of his son in October 1541 tactfully described him as 'well fed', but also 'handsome' and 'remarkably tall for his age'.[18] Having just turned three years old, Edward was still under the supervision of Lady Bryan and the other women of his household. It would soon become apparent that Audley's earlier remark about the young prince being too much indulged was justified.

Barely was the ink dry on this dispatch than the king received another, altogether more alarming report of his son. Edward had contracted malaria at Hampton Court. This was one of the most feared diseases of the age, and it carried symptoms akin to influenza, notably high fever. Henry was aghast when he heard the news. Upon Edward's young shoulders rested the entire future of the Tudor dynasty. With rumours of the king's impotence circulating since his short-lived marriage to Anne of Cleves, there was little hope of a 'spare heir'. All of the obsessive care that Henry had lavished upon the upbringing and security of his 'precious jewel' had apparently been in vain. Panic-stricken, Henry at once summoned 'all the doctors in the country', including Dr William Butts, his own personal physician, who had also attended his illegitimate son, Henry FitzRoy. Upon arriving at the prince's bedside, Butts asked him if he 'felt any disposition to vomit'. Edward's reply displayed all the petulance of this indulged four-year-old. 'Go away, fool,' he exclaimed.[19]

As Henry hastened towards Hampton Court, events were conspiring in London that would soon heap more misery upon his shoulders. John Lassells was a sewer in the king's privy chamber and a former servant of Thomas Cromwell. A staunch reformer, he had long desired the downfall of Norfolk and his party, and in early October 1541 he thought that he had found the means. His sister Mary had formerly served in the household of the Dowager Duchess of Norfolk, and she now confided to her brother what she had witnessed involving the young Katherine Howard. Lassells went straight to Archbishop Cranmer, who was no doubt shocked at the revelations. Not wishing to bear the burden of the knowledge alone, he consulted Edward Seymour and Thomas Audley. All three men knew that the only recourse was to relay the news to the king. If they did not, then they could be accused of colluding with the queen's deceit. But they also knew that their royal master was besotted with his young wife and would react to the revelation with shock and fury, lashing out at whichever unfortunate man was to relay it.

Cranmer must have wished that Lassells had not come to him first, because Seymour and Audley insisted that he should be the one to tell Henry as soon as he arrived at Hampton Court. This was not the first time that Cranmer had proved the most resilient when other men had flinched from delivering unpalatable news or advice to the king, as his secretary Richard Morice recalled: 'His estimation was such with his prince, that in matters of great importance wherein no creature durst once move the king, for fear of displeasure or moving the king's patience or otherwise for troubling his mind, then was my lord Cranmer most violently by the holy council obtruded and thrust out, to undertake that danger and peril in hand.'[20]

Now, Cranmer had to undertake the most dangerous move of his career to date. Like Seymour and Audley, he was fully aware that 'the king's affection was so marvellously set upon that gentlewoman as it was never known that he had the like to any woman, so that no man durst take in hand to open to him that wound, being in great perplexity how he would take it'.[21] But the archbishop knew that his master's ire would be greater still if he found out that Cranmer had concealed the news from him. He therefore made his way to Hampton Court to receive his royal master, who arrived on 2 November. By now filled with fear and apprehension, Cranmer stopped short of relaying the news in person, but rather presented the king with a written statement of the allegations.

Having just given thanks for his marriage in the Chapel Royal, Henry's first reaction was one of disbelief. Perhaps thanks to Cranmer's strategy, his royal master did not immediately explode into fury. Rather, he sent his trusted attendant William Fitzwilliam, Earl of Southampton, to interview John Lassells and his sister. He also dispatched Thomas Wriothesley to question Francis Dereham and Henry Manox, Katherine's former music tutor. Both men soon confirmed the truth of the allegations. Devastated and humiliated in equal measure, the king met Wriothesley and the Duke of Norfolk in secret and went with them to an all-night Privy Council meeting at Southwark Palace on 6 November. Only then did he accept the truth about his wayward young wife and he utterly renounced her, vowing never to see her again.

Everything now unravelled with alarming speed. The queen was kept to her chambers at Hampton Court while Cranmer, Audley and Sir William Paulet interrogated her about her relations with Manox and Dereham. The Lord Chancellor detained the Duchess of Norfolk at his house in Aldgate while she was questioned. He and the other men were soon joined by the Duke of Norfolk, no doubt anxious to prove that his loyalty to the king far outweighed any ties of kinship to the beleaguered queen.

Katherine withstood their combined pressure for two days, but then confessed the truth of the allegations to Cranmer alone, perhaps swayed by his gentler persuasions. The archbishop evidently felt some sympathy for the young woman, because in reporting her testimony to Henry, he told him that he had found her in 'lamentation and heaviness, as I never saw no creature; so that it would have pitied any man's heart in the world to have looked upon her'.[22] This echoed his attempt to make his royal master look more kindly upon Anne Boleyn five years earlier. Now it seemed to work to better effect, though, because the king instructed his archbishop to give Katherine hope of clemency – but only after making it clear just how 'grievous' her transgressions were.

Cranmer duly returned to Katherine's chambers and found her almost deranged with fear. He therefore went against his master's instructions by trying to calm her with the hope of Henry's forgiveness first. But rather than being appeased, she lamented that 'this sudden mercy' made her crimes appear even more 'heinous'. The archbishop was a patient and kindly man, and stayed with the queen until he had brought her to 'quietness'. This did not last for long, however, because at about six o'clock, she suffered another 'pang' when she realised that this was the time that the king's groom of the stool, Sir Thomas Heneage, usually brought her a message from her husband.[23]

Henry might have been persuaded by Cranmer to show clemency towards his wife, but he immediately changed his mind when Dereham confessed, under torture, that he had been replaced in the queen's affections by Thomas Culpeper. That his wife had lied about her sexual past was bad enough; this latest revelation shook the king to his core. He was now a cuckold and, worse still, the perpetrator was one of his most intimate servants. The queen was immediately interrogated about Dereham's allegations. At first she denied them, but then she admitted to the affair, blaming Culpeper for pressuring her into it. Even Cranmer could do nothing to help her now. On 12 November, he and the council signed the queen's statement, and the following day Wriothesley went to see her at Hampton Court and 'declared certain offences that she had done in misusing her body with certain persons afore the king's time, wherefore he there discharged all her household'.[24] The day after, Katherine was moved to the former monastery of Syon, west of London.

The king's only solace in the midst of the crisis was that Prince Edward had recovered. Dr William Butts was now even higher in his royal master's favour than he had been before. But the episode had been a salutary reminder of the vulnerability of Henry's regime. Thanks to his rejection of papal authority, he had alienated the most powerful potentates of Europe. His own health was beginning to fail, and if his only son and heir were to succumb to another disease – fatally this time – then his kingdom might be seized by his continental rivals.

For now, though, Henry had more immediate concerns. His wife's lover was being subjected to intense interrogation. Culpeper insisted that Katherine had initiated their meetings, but did not admit to having sex with her, only that he had desired her. But his admission of motive was enough to condemn him, since the Treason Act of

1534 recognised intent to harm the king as high treason. He was convicted with Dereham by a special commission held on 1 December and attended by all of the king's most influential men, including Lord Chancellor Audley, the dukes of Norfolk and Suffolk, and Sir William Fitzwilliam. Nine days later, both of the accused were put to death. Culpeper was beheaded at Tyburn, an unusual location since beheadings were usually carried out at Tower Hill. But the king's council wished to make an example of him in this more public place, and also decreed that he should be taken there strapped to a hurdle pulled by a horse. Dereham, meanwhile, suffered the full horrors of a traitor's death, being hanged, disembowelled, beheaded, and quartered.

What had begun as a clandestine scandal now became a witch hunt, as numerous other relatives of the queen were rounded up – so many, in fact, that they exceeded the capacity of the Tower. Ralph Sadler applied his energies to gathering evidence of the queen's adultery, which he knew would help to discredit his former patron's adversary, Norfolk. Displaying the same ruthlessness that had characterised many of his late master's dealings, he did everything he could to transform a case of treason into a purge of those who had orchestrated Cromwell's downfall.

Spying an opportunity for further advancement, Sadler's former colleague Wriothesley was also prominent in the interrogations of the Duchess of Norfolk and her household. The Duke of Norfolk himself must have feared that he would soon be summoned, but in the event he escaped implication, and those who had been imprisoned were all eventually pardoned and released. Katherine herself was condemned under a bill of attainder and beheaded at the Tower on 13 February 1542. Her cousin Henry Howard, Earl of Surrey, was among the small crowd that assembled to witness the macabre spectacle. Soon afterwards, he penned a lament to the tragedies that had befallen the Howards. Casting them as the 'white lion' and the Seymours as the 'white wolf', he vowed:

I shall be glad to feed on that
that would have fed on me.[25]

Even after the release of the various family members who had been sent to the Tower in the wake of Katherine's fall, the Howards remained under suspicion. Surrey himself found this to his cost when in July 1542 he was imprisoned in the Fleet, ostensibly for challenging John à Leigh to a duel. But there was clearly more to it than that, for he later attested that he had been charged with matters concerning his fidelity to the king. John à Leigh was accused of maintaining a treasonable association with Cardinal Pole. Surrey himself was suspected of retaining a servant who had been in Italy with Pole, and of employing as a jester an Italian man who was reputedly a spy. He was released the following month and accompanied his father on an expedition to Scotland in October. But the king remained suspicious of him ever after.

In contrast to the demise of his former marriages, which, with the exception of Jane Seymour, Henry had met with a combination of self-righteousness and cold indifference, Katherine Howard's betrayal plunged him into a deep depression. His councillors were dismayed to see the king so distressed. They wrote to Sir William Paget, who, as well as serving as secretary to three of Henry's wives, had performed a number of diplomatic missions for the king and was his now ambassador to France. Upon receiving the council's letter, he learned how their royal master was so choked with sorrow that for a while he could not give vent to it, but that at last he had wept 'plenty of tears'.[26] Henry's melancholy had not lifted two months after his fifth wife's execution, when Chapuys reported to the emperor: 'Since he heard of his late wife's conduct he has not been the same man, and Chapuys has always found him sad, pensive and sighing.'[27]

It would be the beginning of a steady decline for the king, which none of his men could halt. Culpeper's betrayal made Henry watchful and suspicious of the other men who served him. Never again would he trust any of them to the same extent. From now on, he increasingly ruled by fear, abandoning the desire for unity that he had expressed in the wake of Cromwell's execution.

16

'My dearest son in Christ'

BY THE END of his fifth marriage, Henry was painfully aware that he was far from the man he had once been. He had gained a colossal amount of weight since the jousting accident of 1536, his waist expanding to a staggering fifty-two inches and his chest to fifty-eight. 'The King was so stout that such a man has never been seen,' remarked one contemporary chronicler. 'Three of the biggest men that could be found could get inside his doublet.'[1] Henry's weight gain had exacerbated the wound on his leg, which had become ulcerated, tormenting the king with constant, often excruciating, pain. It also caused several bouts of fever – one of which, in 1538, had almost proved fatal. His physicians privately expressed the fear that their master was 'not of constitution to live long'.[2]

After Katherine Howard's demise, the king retreated to his privy apartments, away from the prying eyes of the court. But thanks to having dramatically expanded the number of male attendants in his privy chamber earlier in his reign, he found that it was no longer private enough for his needs. Whereas before, he had loved to be surrounded by like-minded, boisterous young men, now he had neither the energy nor the patience for their company. He therefore commissioned new 'secret lodgings' at Hampton Court and his other favourite palaces. These were like palaces in miniature and included everything the king might need – from a bedroom and bathroom to a chapel, library, wardrobe and jewel house – so that he could live in them for several weeks at a time and only rarely venture out into the public rooms beyond. Foxe reflected that the king 'used very seldom, being not well at ease, to stir out of his Chamber or Privy Gallery. And few of his Council, but by especial commandment, resorted unto him.'[3]

Henry selected just a handful of favoured companions to attend him in his new privy lodgings. They included his most intimate body servants, who were lodged in apartments nearby. Principal among them was the groom of the stool, whose accommodation was directly adjacent to the king's bedchamber. Thanks to an embarrassing health complaint that he had developed in recent years, Henry was increasingly reliant upon the man who filled this position. His meat-rich diet, combined with a lack of physical exercise, had left the king suffering from severe constipation.

Although the groom of the stool was one of the most sought-after positions in the royal household because of the unique access to the king that it provided, the men who were appointed to it in later years had to earn their keep more than their predecessors had. Thomas Heneage, who had been groom of the stool since 1536, attended his master during his most debilitating moments. For example, in June 1539 the king was in so much discomfort with his bowels that Heneage was obliged to administer a painful enema, which he admitted, though effective, left his master with 'a little soreness in his body'.[4]

By now, Heneage was adept at taking advantage of his privileged (if unpleasant) position, and had gained in riches and status during the preceding years. Among the honours he had received was a knighthood in October 1537, following the birth of Prince Edward. He had always headed the privy chamber at important official occasions, such as the reception of Anne of Cleves. By the beginning of the 1540s, it was widely known that he was one of the surest means of access to the king. Almost everyone who corresponded with other members of the court asked to be commended to Heneage.

The king still retained a number of gentlemen of the privy chamber, although they were rather different in character to the notorious 'minions' who had led him astray in his youth. Sir Thomas Cawarden was typical of the new breed, who were assiduous, hard-working and of lower birth than their predecessors. The son of a London fuller, he became a mercer before attracting the attention of Thomas Cromwell, who recognised his ability and also approved of his reformist ideals. Cromwell had secured him a position in the king's privy chamber, but his rapid rise in favour thereafter was due to his own efforts and personality. By 1540 he was listed as one of the gentlemen, and the following year he received a generous New Year gift from his sovereign.

Another favourite companion of the king in private was his fool, Will Somer. An illustration contained in a psalter that was presented to Henry in 1540 reveals the closeness of their relationship. Somer is shown attending the king in his privy chamber, and is listening while his master – who appears more aged than in the authorised portraits of the time – strums on a harp. A few years later, Somer appeared in another intimate portrait. This one shows the king with his three children. His cherished son Edward is to his left, but in between them, standing a pace behind, is Will Somer. It is a striking illustration of just how greatly Somer was esteemed by his royal master. Few other men had managed to hold on to the king's favour so consistently. The shrewd politicians and lauded intellects who crowded into the public rooms beyond would have done well to heed the example of this so-called fool.

As well as lifting the king's mood, Somer might also have been employed by Henry to relieve his increasingly frequent bouts of ill health. The Tudors took a holistic approach to their health and well-being. They believed that the body consisted of four humours: choler (yellow bile), phlegm, black bile and blood – each of which needed to be kept in balance. One of the ways to achieve this was to ensure the presence of mirth in a person's life. The physician Andrew Boorde, in his *First Book of Knowledge*, published in 1542, asserted: 'Mirth is one of the chiefest things of Physic.'

Mirth meant laughter, but also good company, lively conversation and being merry with one another. This is where the fools such as Will Somer could be so important. A contemporary chronicle notes that he had 'admission to the King [at all times], especially when sick and melancholy', which suggests that Henry relied on Somer in his lowest moments. This is confirmed in a later book by Robert Armin, who wrote:

Few men were more beloved than was this Fool
Whose merry prate kept with the King much rule.
When he was sad, the King and he could rhyme,
Thus Will exiled sadness many a time.[5]

Will Somer's ability to lighten the king's mood, as well as his natural honesty, unfettered by political ambition or guile, made him one of the most highly valued members of the king's household. Little wonder that Henry sought his company more and more during his later years.

Among the other companions who remained by Henry's side during the difficult months following Katherine Howard's execution was Sir John Russell. His loyalty to the king had always remained beyond question, but he too was growing frail. Hans Holbein the younger made a sketch of Russell in the late 1530s. Then in his mid-fifties, the courtier appears quite aged, with a skullcap and full white beard. His face is drawn in partial profile to conceal his right eye, which had been injured years earlier, and his expression is both serious and determined. While others clamoured for power and profit, what mattered to him most was his unswerving loyalty to the king. Despite his increasing paranoia, Henry clearly recognised this and rewarded Russell richly for it. On 3 December 1542, he was promoted to Lord Privy Seal, a position that he retained for the remainder of his life and one that boosted his already considerable yearly salary by £365 (equivalent to around £112,000).

The king's frailty was mirrored by a number of his other longer-serving associates. His illegitimate uncle Arthur Plantagenet had remained a prisoner in the Tower until 1542, despite being innocent of the charges brought against him as part of the power struggle between Cromwell and the conservatives. Henry then restored him to favour, and in January the Garter was returned to him as a symbol that he had been exonerated. But when Wriothesley went to the Tower to relay the happy tidings to him on 3 March, the elderly man was so overcome that he collapsed and died of a heart attack. His stepson, John Dudley, who was still endeavouring to further his court career, inherited his title of Viscount Lisle.

Later that year, Henry lost another of his men. Sir Thomas Wyatt had been swiftly rehabilitated after narrowly escaping a charge of treason in the wake of Cromwell's demise. The king had showered him with grants of land and offices, and in August 1542 he was rumoured to have been appointed Vice Admiral of the fleet against France. But he had suffered increasing bouts of ill health in recent years, and had often complained of violent headaches. He was concerned enough to make a will in June 1541. Nevertheless, the king continued to keep him gainfully employed. On 3 October 1542 he was appointed to conduct the Earl of Tyrone to his royal master. But on the same day, Wyatt was sent to meet the Spanish envoy Montmorency de Courrière at Falmouth. Exhaustion weakened his already fragile constitution, and he contracted a fever on his return. He was obliged to seek refuge at the house of Sir John Horsey in Sherborne, Dorset, and died there on about 6 October.

Henry was devastated when he received the news. The French ambassador Marillac claimed that 'there was no one with whom the King was more private, nor to whom he gave greater demonstrations of love'.[6] There was some justification for this statement. Among his personal possessions at Hampton Court, Henry kept Wyatt's seal and a set of hawking rings. The king had always been drawn to irreverent men, and Wyatt's combination of frankness, wit and learning had ensured that even when he had overstepped the mark, he had always been forgiven. According to the seventeenth-century historian David Lloyd, it had been Wyatt's humour and verbal dexterity that had prompted the English reformation. He had apparently once jested to Henry 'that a man cannot repent him of his sin but by the Pope's leave'.[7] Although Wyatt had certainly been an adherent of the reformist faith, it is unlikely that he can claim such credit. But the anecdote captures some of the appeal that he held for Henry.

Henry felt keenly the loss of those men who had been among his closest and longest-standing companions. Although he had proved many times how swiftly he could turn against even cherished favourites, sending them to their deaths with apparently no hesitation, it was a different matter when his men died while still in favour. As well as missing their company, their deaths served as a salutary reminder to Henry of his own mortality. Now in his early fifties and plagued by ill health, he faced the grim prospect that he would soon follow them to the grave. This was made worse by the knowledge that he would be plunging the kingdom into the uncertainty of a minority rule by his young son Edward.

Although the number of Henry's old companions had dwindled

by the closing years of his reign, one of the few who survived was Sir Francis Bryan. He was still in robust health and, according to Roger Ascham, perennially youthful, despite the many years he had spent travelling. His scandalous conduct in France, together with his dalliances with known papists, had cost him his position as chief gentleman, but he continued to serve the king in his privy chamber. His influence was a poor reflection of what it had been in the glory days of his friendship with Henry, but he still enjoyed the fruits of their earlier intimacy in the form of numerous grants of land, pensions, and offices. Despite his religious sympathies, Bryan was also among the beneficiaries of the dissolved monastic lands, all of which made him a wealthy man.

Neither had Henry completely lost faith in Bryan's diplomatic abilities. In January 1543, he appointed his old companion Vice Admiral with orders to sail to the Firth of Forth and intercept the ship carrying Claude de Lorraine, first Duc de Guise, to Scotland. This was Bryan's chance to redeem himself, but in characteristically reckless fashion, he threw it away. While at sea, his ship was beset by storms and he flouted the orders of the Lord Admiral, John Dudley. His command was revoked at the end of February. Surprisingly, though, Henry did not give up on him. Indeed, he entrusted Bryan with a diplomatic mission of considerable importance in October, when he appointed him ambassador to Charles V with instructions to cement the Anglo–Imperial alliance and make plans for their common war against France. This time, Bryan seems to have conducted himself well, and his embassy continued – with some interruptions for other service – until the end of December 1544, during which time there is no hint of any controversy.

The early 1540s also witnessed the ongoing rehabilitation of those men among Henry's entourage who had been closely associated with his former chief minister, Thomas Cromwell. Foremost among them was Sir Ralph Sadler, who was appointed to the prestigious post of keeper of the wardrobe in 1543. Henry had soon come to appreciate Sadler's talents as much as Cromwell had done. In Sadler he had a highly capable and industrious young man, who would regularly begin work at 4 a.m. and not retire until midnight. In order to be close to Henry, Sadler acquired a house in Hackney (now Sutton

House), and was also given accommodation at the palaces of Westminster, Whitehall and Hampton Court. Before long, he was in great demand from his royal master, to the extent that he was obliged to deputise some of his new duties as keeper of the wardrobe to his long-time associate, Thomas Wriothesley.

In March 1543, the king appointed Sadler as his resident ambassador in Scotland and charged him with negotiating a marriage between the infant Mary, Queen of Scots, only child of James V, and Henry's son Edward. Henry's old rival James had died the previous December, shortly after the English army triumphed over the Scottish at the Battle of Solway Moss. The encounter had been sparked by James's refusal to break with the Roman Catholic Church, as his English counterpart had done, which had incited the latter to launch a major raid into south-west Scotland. The victorious Henry now sought to push home his advantage with a favourable alliance.

So highly did the English king esteem his new ambassador that he even proposed that Sadler's wife should be appointed governess to his own daughter. This was wholly inappropriate, given that Ellen Sadler was of humble birth, as her husband was obliged to tactfully point out to his master. Despite Sadler's attempts to broker an alliance, Henry continued to adopt an aggressive stance towards his northern neighbour, which put his ambassador in a difficult situation. Scottish hostility towards the English soon became apparent, and several attempts were made on Sadler's life. Frustrated and angry, he railed against the Scots, declaring: 'Under the sun live not more beastly and unreasonable people than here be of all degrees.'[8] By the end of the year, Henry had declared war on Scotland, prompting Sadler to abandon his embassy and return to England. The proposed marriage between Henry's son and Mary, Queen of Scots, came to nothing.

It was also in 1543 that a man who had striven for years to gain recognition from the king, finally enjoyed his moment in the sun. John Dudley, Viscount Lisle, was the son of Edmund, whom Henry had executed early in his reign, and had served both Wolsey and Cromwell before finally coming within the king's orbit as a naval and military commander. He had undertaken a number of military and diplomatic commissions during the 1520s and 30s. Knighted in

1523, at the age of nineteen, he had appeared in a description of the Christmas revels at court the following year. Of a sharp and pragmatic mind, he was also strongly committed to religious reform and had been working steadily towards that cause since the early days of Cromwell's ascendancy. In November 1542, Henry had appointed Dudley warden-general of the Scottish marches and he had acquitted himself well during the complex diplomatic situation that followed the Battle of Solway Moss. It may have been this that had finally persuaded the king to bring Dudley more fully into his orbit, and on 26 January 1543 he was appointed Lord High Admiral. This carried with it *ex officio* membership of the Privy Council, and Dudley was sworn into this inner sanctum on 23 April.

Dudley was quick to justify the king's faith in him. If he was less talented than the likes of Wolsey and Cromwell, he was hardworking, competent and did as he was bidden – all qualities that appealed to Henry. As Lord High Admiral, he proved a resounding success, transforming the ramshackle administration of the royal navy into the most sophisticated structure of any navy in Europe. This gave the king an important advantage over his rivals in mobilisation, supply, victualling and logistics.

So far, the year 1543 had also proved kind to Archbishop Cranmer. He had emerged from the crisis of the king's fifth marriage with his favour not just intact, but enhanced, thanks at least partly to his role in persuading Katherine to confess. Since Cromwell's demise, he had been the most prominent member of the evangelical faction at court, but it was not a role with which he felt comfortable. A mild and peaceable man, 'he so behaved himself to the whole world, that in no manner of condition he would seem to have any enemy', recounted a contemporary. But in the turbulent world of Henry's court, no man could enjoy unfettered authority, and the archbishop was observed to have 'many great and secret enemies'. While his late ally Cromwell had faced down opposition with ruthlessness, Cranmer behaved towards his adversaries 'with such countenance and benevolence that they could never take good opportunity to practise their malice against him but to their great displeasure and hindrance in the end'.[9]

That did not stop them from trying. In spring 1543, Cranmer faced a greater threat from his conservative enemies than ever before. The so-called 'Prebendaries' Plot' was orchestrated by a combination of disaffected Canterbury Cathedral clergy and their allies at Oxford University, together with conservative Kentish gentry. But the man who was discreetly pulling the strings of the whole controversy was Bishop Gardiner who, having destroyed Cromwell, was confident that his ally would soon follow.

In April 1543, Cranmer's enemies presented a raft of accusations against him to the king. They ought to have found a willing ear, for Henry's conservative revision of the Bishops' Book had recently been finalised in Convocation, despite the archbishop's protests. Shortly afterwards, parliament passed an act 'for the advancement of true religion', which restricted the reading of the Bible to those of a certain status. This represented a significant reversal of the reforms for which Cranmer and Cromwell had fought for so many years. True to form, the archbishop offered little resistance to the changes. What might be taken as weakness by others was, as ever, valued by the king, whose confidence in Cranmer was fully restored, and he 'was so grown in estimation with the king's highness, that none of these complaints could prevail'.[10]

The same month, Henry concluded a treaty with Emperor Charles V. This was due in no small part to the efforts of Eustace Chapuys, who had arrived back in England in July 1540, just missing the execution of his old sparring partner Cromwell. Not long afterwards, the king had been furious upon discovering that Francis I had been sending aid to England's enemies in Scotland. Seizing the opportunity to conclude an Anglo–Imperial treaty, in July 1542, Chapuys had journeyed to Brussels to consult with Charles. Increasingly house-bound by gout, he had been provided with a sedan chair for the journey by Henry.

It was also in April 1543 that William Paget was appointed as joint principal secretary with Ralph Sadler and admitted to the Privy Council. A shrewd politician and diplomat, Paget had served Henry with impressive dedication and efficiency for more than a decade, and he was quick to take advantage of his new promotion. Before long, he was the most senior member of the council and one of the most powerful members of Henry's government. As principal secretary, he controlled his royal master's correspondence and became the essential conduit for information. He also acted as the king's spokesperson and was the lynchpin for his intelligence network. Like other men before him, he appreciated the potential that his position offered to secure close and regular attendance upon the king, and once observed: 'Men may better speak or do, being present than absent.'[11]

Although no man had been able to fill Cromwell's shoes, Paget perhaps came closest. Both men had risen to prominence in Henry's service through hard work rather than birth: Paget, like Cromwell, was the son of a shearman. Little wonder that Henry, who was increasingly hampered by his physical infirmities, came to rely upon him more and more.

Meanwhile, the Duke of Norfolk, who was still struggling to rehabilitate himself in the wake of his niece's disgrace, persuaded Henry that he fully supported the new policy of aggression towards France. In June 1543 he declared war on Francis I on the king's behalf and was appointed lieutenant-general of the army. The Anglo–Imperial treaty set out plans for a two-pronged invasion, with Charles and his army advancing from the east and Henry's forces from Calais. The English king wasted no time in amassing a huge army with which to invade France.

The following month, Henry married for the sixth and final time. As soon as Katherine Howard had been executed, speculation had begun as to who the king would marry next. The fact that he enjoyed amicable relations with his fourth wife, Anne of Cleves, who had remained in England after the annulment of her marriage and been afforded every courtesy as the king's 'sister', had led some to believe that the pair would marry again. But another lady had caught Henry's eye: the twice-widowed Katherine Parr. Aged thirty and of a calm and steady nature, she presented a welcome contrast to her flighty young predecessor. She was also exceptionally well educated and strongly committed to the reformed religion. This spelt danger for the likes of Norfolk and Gardiner, and they knew it. Even before Henry married Lady Parr in July 1543, they began plotting against her.

Although Katherine had had little choice but to accept the king's

advances, she was deeply in love with another man at court: Thomas
Seymour, the attractive and reckless younger brother of Edward,
Lord Hertford. When the king heard of this, he was plagued with
jealousy and found an excuse to have Seymour sent away from court.
The king's sixth wedding duly went ahead on 12 July 1543. It was a
low-key affair, taking place in the queen's private apartments at
Hampton Court Palace and attended by just eighteen guests.

Distracted by his new marriage, as well as by the warlike plans
he was making with his council, Henry made no move to follow up
the allegations that had been made against Archbishop Cranmer.
But one evening in early September, he took a boat trip from
Whitehall to Lambeth Palace. 'Ah, my chaplain, I have news for you,'
Henry said to Cranmer upon arriving at the archbishop's residence.
'I know now who is the greatest heretic in Kent,' he teased, and
pulled out a paper summarising the charges. In characteristic fashion,
Cranmer meekly submitted himself to the royal justice. 'Oh Lord
God!' Henry exclaimed, 'What fond simplicity you have, to let yourself be imprisoned, so that every enemy of yours may take advantage
against you . . . I have better regard unto you, than to permit your
enemies so to overthrow you.'[12] Ignoring Cranmer's protests, the
king told him to appoint himself as chief investigator of the affair
and to choose his colleagues in commission. He then presented the
archbishop with a ring as a symbol of his support. There could be
no clearer indication of how little credence he had given to Cranmer's
enemies.

Everything turned out as Henry had arranged. Cranmer made
his way to the council chamber, but was deliberately kept waiting
outside the door 'amongst serving men and lackeys' for more than
three-quarters of an hour.[13] When he was at last admitted, Gardiner
and his cronies began to bully him, refusing to let him argue his
case and telling him to prepare to go at once to the Tower, as
Cromwell had done three years earlier. But Cranmer calmly produced
the ring and told them that the king 'by this token hath resumed
this matter into his own hand, and dischargeth you thereof'. He
then accompanied them to a humiliating audience with their royal
master, who threw out their accusations. 'Ah, my lords, I thought I
had a discreet and wise Council,' he chided, 'but now I perceive that

I am deceived. How have ye handled here my Lord of Canterbury? What make ye of him? A slave? Shutting him out of the council chamber among serving men?'[14] He then ordered them all to shake hands with the archbishop and never to so malign him in future.

'Nevermore after no man durst spurn [Cranmer] during the king Henry's life,' declared the archbishop's faithful secretary, Richard Morice.[15] This was no idle boast. Although there would be other conservative plots and threats during the years to come, none of them came close to shaking Henry's faith in Cranmer. He knew that the archbishop's devotion to his service and utter veneration for his master's will would always supersede all else. This won Cranmer if not immunity, then certainly a degree of protection from the increasingly deadly world of court rivalries and factions. If it meant compromising some of his personal principles and ideals, then it was worth the sacrifice.

Although he had many adversaries at court, Cranmer did enjoy the friendship of an influential member of Henry's personal staff. Dr William Butts was well known for his reformist sympathies, and his defence of the archbishop was later represented by Shakespeare in *Henry VIII*. There is a scene in which Cranmer is under threat from a plot by his enemies on the council. Butts hears of it and assures him: 'This is a piece of malice. I am glad I came this way so happily: the king shall understand it presently.'[16] That Butts used his position of trust and intimacy with the king to influence his decisions is also attested by the fact that he secured advancement for his fellow reformers Hugh Latimer and Sir John Cheke. This demonstrates the extent to which Henry's personal and political life were intermingled. Even those men who, like Butts, were assigned very specific medical or domestic roles that had nothing to do with politics were able to exploit their proximity to the king to shape his opinions and policies.

Instead it was Gardiner who soon found himself in hot water. His nephew Germayne had been involved in the plot and now became its scapegoat. He was accused of conspiring with Reginald Pole and was executed at Tyburn in March 1544. Henry ordered that Gardiner himself be investigated for treason. He was persuaded to do so by his old friend the Duke of Suffolk, who had visited Henry in his chambers one evening to discuss the matter. Had Suffolk taken care to speak in a lower voice, his plan might have succeeded, but as he recalled: 'our talk was not so secret, but that some of his [Gardiner's] friends in the Privy Chamber . . . suspecting the matter, sent him word thereof'.[17] Having been forewarned, Gardiner hastened to the king early the following morning and threw himself on his mercy. In an uncharacteristically benevolent mood, the king offered him a pardon.

To set the seal on Gardiner's misery, and that of his conservative allies, the king soon promoted a number of men who were closely associated with his new wife. They included Sir William Parr, uncle to the new queen. Born in 1480, Sir William was one of the oldest men at court, and had begun his royal service under the king's father. An excellent soldier who preferred the field of combat to court politics, he had been knighted by Henry VIII for his efforts at Tournai in 1513 and had gone on to serve him in a number of other campaigns. Sir William was a forceful character, whose bluff and quarrelsome nature set him at odds with other, more seasoned courtiers. But he appreciated the greater potential for advancement that was on offer at court, compared to his more natural habitat of the battlefield. An avid reformer, he had therefore applied his energies in Cromwell's service during the late 1530s, and had been his chief agent for the dissolution in Northamptonshire.

Parr might have remained a royal servant of middling rank had it not been for the marriage of his niece to the king. In the same month, he was appointed a chamberlain of her household, and later that year he became a privy councillor, Knight of the Garter and Earl of Essex. Honours now followed in quick succession, and the following February, 1544, Parr received a substantial grant of lands in Bedfordshire and Northamptonshire. Quite what Henry thought of his wife's uncle is not clear, but he was content to show him favour for her sake, and when he went on campaign to France in the summer of 1544, he appointed Parr to Katherine's regency council.

Another Parr relative rose to prominence after Katherine's marriage to Henry. Her brother-in-law, William Herbert, had been in the king's service intermittently since 1526, when he was named as one of his spears or gentlemen pensioners. Variously described

as 'Black Will Herbert' and a 'mad fighting fellow', he had a somewhat dubious reputation. In 1527, he murdered a man in Bristol, then
fled to France, where he served in the army and won favour with
Francis I. He had returned to England by 1531, when he was referred
to as a member of the royal household. Four years later, he was an
esquire of the body, and by 1540 he had been promoted to gentleman
of the privy chamber. But it was largely thanks to his sister-in-law's
marriage that his prospects were suddenly enhanced. Within six
months of Katherine's becoming queen, Herbert had been knighted.
Other grants and honours soon followed.

The year 1543 witnessed another milestone, beside the king's sixth
and final marriage. On 12 October, Prince Edward turned six. The
Tudors considered this the age at which a child became an adult. As
a result, Henry ordered that his son's apartments be remodelled so
that they exactly mirrored those of the king. New furnishings were
ordered, which were even more lavish than those they had replaced
and included Flemish tapestries showing the classical and biblical
scenes that the king favoured. Edward's books were embellished
with covers of enamelled gold set with rubies, sapphires and
diamonds, and his cutlery and napery glittered with precious stones
and gold and silver thread. The prince was also given a new wardrobe
of clothes so that he could dress like his father. Soon, he was decked
out in sable furs, doublets of crimson velvet and black satin, decorated with buttons of Venice gold.[18]

The other significant change in Edward's upbringing was that his
female attendants were dismissed and he was assigned to the care
and tutelage of a predominantly male household. Richard Cox and
John Cheke, both highly respected scholars, were appointed as his
tutors. The latter was greatly impressed with the young prince, and
later declared that he 'has accomplished at this early period of his
life more numerous and important objects, than others have been
able to do when their age was more settled and matured'. Another
renowned scholar, Roger Ascham, concurred: 'He is wonderfully in
advance of his years.'[19] This studious boy was even more precocious
than his father had been, and applied himself with greater discipline
than Henry had shown at a similar age.

The king selected the sons of some of his favourites as companions for the prince. They included Henry and Charles Brandon, and Robert, son of John Dudley. The prince's cousins, Edward and Henry Seymour, sons of Lord Hertford, were also among the new household. The king was clearly eager for his heir to be surrounded by young men from the same mould as those who had kept him entertained during his own youth. Edward's companions not only joined his lessons, but accompanied him in hunting, hawking and dancing.

Henry took a close interest in his son's education, and although he accepted that it should follow humanist lines, with an emphasis on Latin, Greek, grammar and rhetoric, he insisted that Edward should also be taught fencing, horseback riding, music, and other courtly pursuits that Erasmus had once dismissed as 'foolish'.[20] He no doubt approved of the fact that the prince also showed a keen interest in gambling, and Edward's account books testify that he was allowed to indulge this a great deal. It may have been the king who encouraged his son's interest in astronomy, astrology and the mystical arts. The inventory of Edward's apartments lists five astronomical instruments, as well as some 'small tools of sorcery'.[21] He shared this pursuit with his half-sister, Elizabeth, who also joined his studies for much of the time.

The king also ensured that his son received a religious education that was at least broadly evangelical. After all, it was crucial that his heir should respect and promote the royal supremacy over the Church. Religious conservatives were therefore excluded from the prince's schoolroom. The young prince's religious views were shaped by the Archbishop of Canterbury, as well as by his tutors. Cranmer had been careful to cultivate the king's son and heir, increasingly mindful of the need to safeguard the 'true religion' in the next reign. In October 1544, the prince wrote to thank the archbishop for his 'very kind letter', and assured him: 'I am not unmindful either of your attention to me or your kindness which you study every day to show me.'

The same letter suggests that Cranmer supplied the fatherly role that Henry had failed to fulfil. In a stark contrast to the formality of Edward's dealings with the king, his words are filled with genuine warmth. 'I affectionately receive and honour that truly paternal affection which you have expressed,' Edward told Cranmer, 'and I hope that you may live many years, and continue to be my honoured father by your godly and wholesome advice.' For his part, the archbishop called the prince 'my dearest son in Christ', and assured him: 'My life is not to be called living unless you are in health and strength.'[22]

While Cranmer supplied Edward's spiritual needs, his father continued to supply his material ones. In ensuring that his son had everything that his heart could desire, Henry was conforming to what he understood was required for a king in waiting. Edward's childhood also continued to reflect Henry's own in terms of the distance that his father maintained between them, although he was afforded far greater luxury than Henry VII had given his second son. Having been indulged by his female attendants during his infancy, Edward was used to having his own way by the time he transferred to his sumptuous new all-male household. The result was inevitable: the prince grew into a spoilt young man, and when provoked, his temper was every bit as vicious as his father's. Reginald Pole recalled how Edward once flew into a rage and tore a living falcon into four pieces in front of his tutors. If he heard of such behaviour, Henry did nothing to check it.

In fact, it was Edward's latest stepmother, not his father, who exerted the greatest positive influence upon his upbringing. In contrast to Henry, she was very affectionate towards the prince and his sisters, showering them with attention. Thanks to her, their visits to court became more frequent and prolonged, and they enjoyed a greater sense of familial closeness than they had ever known. The alacrity with which Edward responded suggests that he had longed for the affection that had been so notably lacking from his father.

Edward's fondness for his new stepmother is revealed in the letters that they exchanged. He referred to her as 'Mater Charissima' (my dearest mother) and assured her that she held 'the chief place in my heart'.[23] Katherine took a particular interest in Edward's schooling, and it was thanks to her that he had been appointed tutors such as John Cheke, whose religious views chimed with those of the new queen. The prince was effusive in his gratitude and wrote to thank Katherine for encouraging him 'to go forward in such things wherein your grace beareth me on hand that I am already entered'.[24] It is clear that Henry's last wife had helped to fill the gaping void in Edward's life left by the king's aloof – but entirely traditional – style of royal parenting.

In the same month that Prince Edward celebrated his transition to adulthood, his father enlisted Henry Howard, Earl of Surrey, to help strengthen his relations with the emperor. Although Surrey had taken part in various military campaigns in the past, he had never really lived up to the warlike credentials of his ancestors. Now, though, he was given another opportunity to do so by joining Charles V's campaign in northern France. He seems to have acquitted himself well, because the following month Charles wrote in praise of Surrey's noble heart and talents. But there were subsequently rumours that the earl had exceeded his commission by entering into secret conference with 'divers great captains' and had become 'the Emperor's man'.[25] If Henry heard these rumours, he appeared not to heed them. When Charles V's emissary, the Duke of Najera, visited the English court in February 1544, Surrey was appointed to act as his guide. At the end of May, he was sent with a large retinue to meet the Spanish Duke of Albuquerque, and at about this time he was created cupbearer to the king.

By contrast, Surrey's father, the Duke of Norfolk, was losing ground to his rivals. Principal among them was Edward Seymour, Earl of Hertford, who now dominated Henry's council. His alignment with the new religion, as espoused by Queen Katherine Parr, was a key factor in his rise. Norfolk, on the other hand, remained staunchly conservative and hostile to 'stirrers-up of heresy', as the Spanish envoy observed.[26] This set him at odds not only with Seymour's faction, but with the king himself.

Delighted with his new wife, Henry now seemed once more reconciled to the cause of reform. This made his ongoing patronage of his favourite artist all the more natural. Hans Holbein had undertaken numerous commissions for the king and his courtiers during the eleven or so years since taking up residence in England. The Anne of Cleves affair had been quickly forgotten, and there is no suggestion that Henry had laid any blame on Holbein's shoulders for the flattering portrait he had supplied. The fact that Holbein was so highly valued by the king meant that he was in constant demand from the other members of court, all of whom clamoured for the honour of having their portrait painted by the most celebrated artist of the age. Holbein's commissions cut across the rivalries and factions among the king's men, and he accepted work from both religious conservatives, such as the Duke of Norfolk, and reformers such as Edward Seymour. He may have naturally favoured the latter, but he never allowed his principles to get in the way of business.

As a result, by 1543 Holbein was a wealthy man. The records show that he was paid more than any other court painter during his lifetime. An indication of his prosperity had been revealed by his visit to Basel in 1538, when his fine clothes had attracted attention and he had been described as a wealthy man. Although he received a smaller number of commissions from the king during Henry's later years, this was due to the fact that there were fewer prospective wives whose image the king wished him to capture. Tellingly, in a painting completed in 1542, the subject matter was physicians rather than wives. Holbein had been commissioned to paint the king with the newly formed Barber Surgeons' Company. Although Henry was now far from a strident image of majesty, Holbein depicted him in a similarly powerful frontal pose as his Whitehall mural of 1537.

Among the eighteen other men in the painting were the king's personal physicians, William Butts and John Chambre, and his apothecary Thomas Alsop. Butts was pre-eminent among them, having served the king for almost twenty years, as well as his queens, Anne Boleyn and Jane Seymour, his daughter Mary, and his sons Edward and Henry FitzRoy. Butts had also attended some of the most prominent men among the king's entourage, including Cardinal Wolsey, the Duke of Norfolk and George Boleyn. Henry rewarded him handsomely for his service, and he received an annual salary of £100, one of the highest in the royal household.

John Chambre's service stretched back even further. Aged seventy-two by the time the painting was completed, he appears grim-faced and rather severe. He studied at Oxford, where he was elected fellow of Merton College, and went on to study medicine in Italy, graduating at Padua in 1506. Upon his return to England, he served as physician to Henry VII and retained his position under his son. In

1518, he was among the six founders of the College of Physicians. Like Butts, Chambre attended Jane Seymour, and a letter that he wrote describing her health still survives. He combined his medical career with one in the Church and was awarded a number of prestigious ecclesiastical appointments by Henry VIII, including the archdeaconries of Bedford and Meath, and the canonry of Windsor. He built the beautiful cloisters of St Stephen's Chapel, Westminster, at his own cost, but saw them demolished during the Reformation. If he bore any grudge against the king for it, he was always careful to swear allegiance to him as head of the new church.

Thomas Alsop was a more recent appointee. He had entered Henry's service as a gentleman apothecary in September 1540. Nothing is known of his early life, but he was a citizen and grocer of London, and was established in business by 1538, when he supplied medicine to the king's son Edward. A number of his accounts still survive in The National Archives and reveal that he attended various members of the king's circle, including his niece Margaret Douglas, for whom he supplied 'water of virgin's milk', a medicinal wash for a skin complaint; lotion for her husband's eyes; and a 'treacle' or compound for her pet monkey.

For Henry himself, Alsop supplied an array of different remedies during the closing years of his reign, which reveal the myriad complaints from which the king was suffering. They included an eyewash made from 'eyebright' (*Euphrasia officinalis*); almond oil for the lips; rhubarb pills; 'fennel-flower (*Nigella sativa*) bruised in a tied cloth'; bags with sponges, herbs, musk and civet for Henry to bathe in; and a remedy described as 'fomentation' for piles. The king was evidently so delighted with Alsop's potions that he also ordered some 'succade' (candied fruit), liquorice and sugar for his beloved hounds, as well as 'horehound water' for his hawks.

It is a sign of how much this increasingly reclusive king trusted Holbein that as well as the Barber Surgeons painting, he commissioned him to undertake one last portrait of himself during his declining years. It was a risky commission for Holbein, who knew that Henry was highly sensitive about his physical frailties. But he executed it brilliantly, showing Henry in magnificent attire that included a rich red coat trimmed with ermine and cloth of gold that detracted attention from his white-flecked hair and the staff upon which he was leaning.

Up to now Holbein, who was in his mid-forties, had enjoyed much better health than his royal master. But in October 1543, he was struck down by a sudden illness and died the following month. He had drawn up a hasty will on 7 October, which reveals that he had a second family in England. Despite accruing considerable wealth thanks to the king's patronage, Holbein's will mentions no property or other assets, and he died with debts amounting to more than half a year's salary. But he left a legacy that far exceeded his worldly goods.

Holbein's influence upon Henry's personal life had been profound. The portraits that he painted of the king's prospective wives had influenced Henry's choice far more than the political or religious motives that were championed by his ministers. Moreover, through his genius in art and propaganda, he had established Henry as the epitome of magisterial power, magnificence and invincibility – both in the king's own lifetime and forever after. Of all the king's men, it was arguably to Holbein that Henry owed the greatest debt.

Five months later, Henry lost another of his male attendants. On 21 April 1544, Thomas Audley gave up the Great Seal, declaring himself no longer able to perform his duties 'through infirmity of body'. He had been the mainstay of the king's legal affairs for eleven years, and since Cromwell's execution he had been the most active member of the Privy Council, undertaking a wide range of business in central and local government and acting as a point of contact for foreign ambassadors. Of particular use to the king had been his expertise on issues of treason. But from 1543, his health had started to seriously falter, and he had been largely absent from parliamentary meetings. He died peacefully, aged fifty-six, at his home in Aldgate, London, on 30 April 1544, and was buried at Saffron Walden in Essex.

'The stone is not harder, nor the marble blacker, than the heart of him who lies beneath,' remarked the seventeenth-century historian Thomas Fuller, of the black marble tomb containing the former Lord Chancellor's remains.[27] By the time of his death, Audley had earned a reputation for rapaciousness. But that may have been more due to the fact that he applied the same thoroughness to his own legal and financial affairs as he did to the king's. Rather more balanced is the assessment provided by another seventeenth-century commentator, David Lloyd, who described Audley as 'quick, solid, apprehensive and judicious'. He added the shrewd observation: 'Patience can weather out the most turbulent age, and a solid judgment the most intricate times; the reserved and quiet man is the most secure.'[28] Although his character does not shine forth from the original sources with the same vibrancy as some of his peers, the Lord Chancellor always appeared calm, temperate and judicious. These qualities, together with his ability to bend to political storms rather than rage against them, had helped Audley to retain Henry's favour throughout his life. Few of the king's other men could boast such an accomplishment.

Audley did not live to see his royal master's last-gasp attempts at military glory. In May 1544, Henry declared war against Scotland and dispatched two of his most trusted men to help administer the expedition: Edward Seymour and Ralph Sadler. They conducted a well-organised and brutally effective raid on Edinburgh – the first major action in Henry's so-called 'Rough Wooing' of his northern rival. The groundwork had already been laid by the king's longest-standing favourite, the Duke of Suffolk. He had been active in Henry's military service since the Pilgrimage of Grace, and between times had attended the Privy Council more regularly than ever before. In recognition of his competence as a military commander, Henry had appointed him as his lieutenant of the north in January 1543, and he served in this post until March 1544. It was a highly responsible position, demanding both military and diplomatic skill. Suffolk executed it with impressive efficiency, and Seymour and Sadler had benefited from his efforts.

In the summer of 1544, Henry embarked upon his third invasion of France. His intention was to seize Boulogne in retaliation for the French having sent aid to his enemies in Scotland. But the English king had clearly learned nothing from the crippling expense of his previous two forays across the Channel, which had brought little reward. Despite being severely incapacitated by his ulcerated leg and rapidly expanding girth, Henry was set upon recapturing the glories of his youth. He therefore gathered about him those old sporting companions who still drew breath – the dukes of Suffolk and Norfolk principal among them – and began the preparations for war.

Having proven himself on the northern border, Suffolk was now assigned the command of the French expedition. He and Henry's forces marched upon the key coastal town of Boulogne and, with characteristic bravery and skill, laid siege to it on 19 July 1544. Sir John Russell, who was also approaching sixty, was appointed commander of the vanguard, which consisted of 13,000 men. Sir Francis Bryan was also enlisted in the royal forces, and took leave of his embassy to Charles in order to take up a command at Montreuil. Henry Howard joined the forces there as marshal and was wounded during a failed attempt to storm the town.

The king himself was determined to share in the glory, and soon set out to join his men. Before doing so, he established a regency council headed by his wife. Among its more prominent members was Thomas Wriothesley, who had been elevated to the peerage as Baron Wriothesley in January 1544 and appointed Lord Chancellor in May, following the death of Audley. Wriothesley revelled in his newfound status, and whenever he appeared in public he was preceded by his gentlemen and followed by his yeomen clad in velvet and gold chains.

Content that his realm was in safe hands, Henry set sail for France in late summer 1544. Chapuys was obliged to accompany him, with much grumbling. Henry, who was in no better state himself, ignored his complaints and insisted that camp life had improved Chapuys' health. Upon arriving at Boulogne, he immediately took command of his forces, and was triumphant when the French at last surrendered on 13 September. He invited his old friend Suffolk to occupy Boulogne the following day. Suffolk was soon joined by the Duke of Norfolk and Sir Anthony Browne. The king returned to England in triumph at the end of the month.

But no sooner had the king returned than news reached him that his ally Charles V had concluded a peace with Francis, leaving Henry to face the French alone. This sparked a series of furious rows between the English king and Charles's ambassador, Chapuys, who defended his master by insisting that Henry had agreed to the peace. The king called him a liar and argued that by the terms of his own treaty with the emperor, Charles was obliged to help him defend Boulogne. The wranglings went on for months, thwarting Chapuys' hopes for retirement. Although a successor, François Van der Delft, was sent to England in December 1544, Chapuys was obliged to stay with him until he was fully conversant with the complex diplomatic relations with England. In April 1545, Chapuys at last gave up his commission and went to the Netherlands, although he was given the task of managing commercial negotiations with England until July.

Chapuys' relationship with Henry had been fraught with difficulty. It is to his credit that he had never allowed himself to be cowed by this indomitable man, but had upheld his own and his master's principles throughout. Upon Chapuys' retirement, William Paget described him as being 'as wilful a man and as glorious, as ever I had to do with all', but one who said 'whatever came into his mouth without respect of honesty or truth, so it might serve his turn'.[29] This remark was borne more of Paget's frustration at being outwitted by the seasoned diplomat than by an accurate assessment of his character. True, Chapuys had often employed the art of dissimulation during his long sojourn at Henry's court, but that was an essential part of any diplomat's arsenal. Although he had sometimes been just as frustrated by Chapuys as Paget was, Henry appreciated that fact. As a result, Chapuys retained the king's respect to the end of his embassy. His real legacy, though, was the collection of long and brilliantly detailed descriptions of Henry and his court that have survived down the centuries. Although they inevitably betray Chapuys' natural bias, particularly against those associated with religious reform, they provide an unrivalled source for the inner workings of the Henrician court.[30]

Meanwhile, things were going from bad to worse for Henry's French campaign. The dukes of Norfolk and Suffolk proceeded to disobey his order to remain in Boulogne, and on 3 October 1544 they left John Dudley, Viscount Lisle, with 4,000 men to defend the city. Russell subsequently joined forces with Norfolk in a siege against Montreuil, but made no secret of his disapproval of the duke's strategy. He was right: the siege ended in ignominious failure, and by the autumn Russell and his forces were forced to retreat first to

Boulogne, then Calais. Outnumbered, the English army was now trapped in the city, which enabled the French to launch an attack on Boulogne. They almost succeeded in recapturing it, but were beaten back when the troops prematurely turned to looting. It was obvious, though, that Henry's beleaguered forces would not long be able to withstand a fresh assault. Norfolk realised this and withdrew with his troops, which earned him a stinging rebuke from the king. But Henry could not afford to lose the duke as a commander, and the following year he appointed him captain-general of the army raised in East Anglia in 1545 to resist an anticipated French invasion.

Having witnessed first-hand the futility – and cost – of his master's enterprise, Sir John Russell was determined to bring Henry to his senses. Although a number of other councillors were beginning to mutter against the French campaign, only this long-standing servant was brave enough to complain directly to the king, telling him in no uncertain terms that it was an expensive and 'wild war . . . without any gain'.[31] The subject was a sensitive one for Henry, who must have known that the campaign would be his last, but for once he chose not to shoot the messenger. Rather, he rewarded Russell for his honesty by appointing him lord lieutenant in June 1545. As such, he was responsible for supervising coastal defences and recruiting mariners and ships in the south-west. Russell eyed an opportunity to secure gainful employment for his old friend Sir Francis Bryan, who joined him the following month in a review of the region's coastal defence. Russell assured the king that Bryan, despite his chequered career, was the best man to deputise for him.

The king was right to focus upon his coastal defences, because in the summer of 1545, Francis launched an invasion fleet against England. Comprising 200 ships and 30,000 soldiers, this was larger than the more famous Armada fleet of 1588 and constituted the most serious threat to Henry's sovereignty that he had faced in four decades of rule. On 16 July, the majority of the French fleet entered the Solent, a strait between mainland England and the Isle of Wight. The English had eighty ships in place to oppose them, but retreated into Portsmouth harbour because their fighting vessels were most effective in sheltered water. The king went there to inspect his fleet and was accompanied by several of his leading commanders, including Henry Howard, who joined him on board his flagship, the *Henry Grace à Dieu*. While dining with the ship's commander, John Dudley, the king presented George Carew, a relative of the late Sir Nicholas Carew and Henry Courtenay, with the command of his magnificent ship, the *Mary Rose*, and made him Vice Admiral of the fleet. Three days later, however, Henry was among the spectators who watched in horror as the ship sank in the Solent. Carew and 400 of his crew drowned.

Despite this major setback, Henry's fleet was triumphant and the French retreated on 22 July. But his troops in France were struggling to retain their hold on Boulogne, so in August he dispatched reinforcements. Henry Howard was appointed to command the vanguard of the royal army. He marshalled a considerable body of men to bolster the king's cause, and his efforts were rewarded in early September when he was appointed lieutenant-general on sea and land for all England's continental possessions. John Welsbourne, who had served in Henry's privy chamber for more than twenty years, also won recognition for his part in the campaign.

Meanwhile, the king charged the Duke of Suffolk, who had recently helped to fortify the key coastal town of Portsmouth, to prepare to lead an army to the relief of Boulogne. He had soon forgiven his old friend for the unauthorised retreat from the city, and in February 1545 had rewarded him for his loyal service by selling him the lands of Tattershall College in Lincolnshire at less than half the standard price. Thanks in no small part to the generosity of his royal master in the preceding years, Suffolk's landed income was now higher than it had ever been. But he would not live to enjoy it, or to fulfil his commission in Boulogne, for on 22 August he died at Guildford in Surrey. The cause of his death is not known, but at the age of sixty-one he was one of the longest lived of all Henry's men. He was also one of the greatest survivors of his master's increasingly brutal regime.

Charles Wriothesley echoed the thoughts of many when he declared that 'all true Englishmen may greatly lament' Suffolk's death.[32] As well as his enduring favour with Henry, Brandon had been one of the most popular members of the king's court. The reason for his success had lain partly in his ability to adapt to the ever-shifting world of court policy and allegiance. Although at heart a traditionalist in religion, he had worked happily with fellow councillors of a more reformist bent, notably William Paulet, Edward Seymour and John Dudley. He had also patronised known reformers, such as Hans Holbein, and the clergy who had benefited from his largesse included both committed Protestants and former monks. His softening towards reform could have in part been due to the influence of his young wife, who had joined Katherine Parr's circle at court.

Suffolk's ambiguous religious and political stance mirrored that of his royal master. Both men were obliged to seek compromise in their later years, in order to reconcile the conflicting demands of those who called upon their favour or alliance. Their characters and temperaments had been closely aligned since the very beginning of their friendship, and it was probably this fact that had saved Suffolk from the fate of so many of his peers. Although he had occasionally lost his master's favour, it had only ever been temporary. Henry loved the duke too much to suffer his absence for long. For his part, Suffolk had justified the king's faith in him by serving him faithfully to his last breath. His motto – *Loyaulte me oblige* – was a fitting one.

Henry's reaction to the news of Suffolk's death is not recorded, but he decreed that the duke should be buried 'at the King's costs' at St George's Chapel, Windsor, the final resting place of his beloved third queen, Jane Seymour.[33] There could have been no more powerful expression of the affection and esteem that he cherished towards his old friend.

Many at court predicted that the void left by Suffolk's death would soon be filled by John Dudley, Viscount Lisle. He had distinguished himself during the French campaign of 1544–5, and the ever-observant Eustace Chapuys had claimed that he had emerged as one of the king's most influential advisers. But this was overstating the case. While Henry certainly appreciated Dudley's abilities, he lacked the qualities that the king sought in a close adviser and confidant. He was competent and hard-working, but had none of the charisma, charm and courtly accomplishments that transformed a member of Henry's entourage from a mere official to an esteemed companion. Nevertheless, his service did not go unrewarded, and the king granted him several former ecclesiastical properties, as well as a privileged position in the privy chamber. By the end of the reign, Dudley was one of the richest men in the kingdom.

Other men besides Dudley had been keen to fill Suffolk's place, particularly in the military arena. Having at last channelled his warlike ancestors, there was no stopping the Earl of Surrey. Throughout the autumn and winter of 1545, he encouraged the king in his desire to conquer more of France. This ran counter to the advice of Henry's privy councillors who, mindful of the crippling expense, urged their master to give up Boulogne. Even Norfolk, who could usually be relied upon to advocate an aggressive foreign policy, warned his son not to encourage the king to defend the city. Surrey seems to have ignored his advice because in early November, his father was calling for his removal from command. Although Henry had been beguiled by the image of military glory that Surrey had so vividly brought to mind, when he heard of his reckless activities, his faith in the earl was shattered.

Meanwhile, the king was also maintaining his aggression towards Scotland. Seymour led another bloody campaign during 1545 and was again accompanied by the able Sadler. The latter was arguably of greater value to Henry at the centre of government, but during his protracted absences from court, he was replaced as principal secretary by William Paget, who had proved himself a 'master of practices' since taking up the position two years earlier.[34] The two men were allies, though, and it was thanks to Paget's efforts that Sadler was able to regain some political influence at court. In October 1545, he attended a meeting of the council after an absence of more than two years.

Sadler's favour with the king was soon threatened by a personal scandal, however. His wife Ellen had formerly been married to a London tradesman called Matthew Barre, who had abandoned her and their two children. Before marrying Sadler, she had enquired after Barre, but eventually presumed him dead. However, in November 1545 one of Wriothesley's servants overheard a drunken Barre boasting that he was Lady Sadler's husband. Barre was seized and interrogated, and the truth of his claims established. Sadler appealed to parliament, employing all of his skills of reasoning, and managed to secure passage of a private bill, passed on 24 December, that legitimised his children. Ellen, however, remained legally Barre's wife, and it may have been years before Sadler's marital status was regularised. Humiliated by the scandal, he was also deeply attached to Ellen and 'took this matter very heavily'.[35]

Sadler subsequently retreated with his wife to his mansion at Standon, Hertfordshire. This not only provided refuge from the gossips in London, but also gave him an excuse not to attend the many revels and masques at court, which he seemed to find distasteful. But distancing himself from court life – and thereby his royal master – came at a price: for all his considerable talents, he would never enjoy the greatest promotions that were on offer in Henry's service. Nevertheless, he remained a trusted and efficient royal servant, working alongside Sir Richard Rich in the collection of debts due to the crown, and playing a leading role in the reorganisation of the courts of augmentations and of general surveyors. As well as the salaries from his court offices, he amassed property in twenty-five counties in England and Wales, which brought him an annual income of around £372 (£115,000 in today's money).

Sadler's former associate Wriothesley also continued to wield significant influence during the mid-1540s, and the king showed him many signs of favour. Chapuys claimed that he was one of the men 'who enjoy nowadays most authority and have the most influence and credit with the king'.[36] On 23 April 1545, he was elected a Knight of the Garter, and the following day Henry stood as godfather at the baptism of Wriothesley's son, who was named in the king's honour. Buoyed by such signs of favour, during the rest of the year he worked hard to enhance his already considerable influence as Lord Chancellor. In characteristic fashion, he continued to ally himself to conservatives and reformists alike, according to which could best serve his purpose at any given moment. It was a tactic that served him well during the intrigues and uncertainties that always attended the close of a reign.

17

'I have been young, and now am old'

O N CHRISTMAS EVE 1545, the king appeared before his parliament
to deliver the closing speech. Hauling his huge body up to
standing, he leaned heavily on his stick and winced occasionally at
the pain in his leg. He was a piteous sight compared to the thrusting,
athletic 'Adonis' of his younger days, and many of those present
shed a tear as they feared it might be the last time they ever saw
him.

'My loving subjects,' he began, 'study and take pains to amend
one thing which is surely amiss and far out of order, to the which
I most heartily require you, which is that charity and concord is not
amongst you, but discord and dissensions beareth rule in every place
. . . what love and charity is amongst you when the one calleth the
other heretic and Anabaptist, and he calleth him again papist, hypo-
crite and Pharisee? Be these tokens of charity amongst you? Are
these the signs of fraternal love between you?'

They were the words of a man worn down by years of bitter
in-fighting between his courtiers, by frailty of body and by dejection
of spirit. Once he might have encouraged divisions among his most
powerful men so that he could more easily subdue and rule them;
now he was tired of the endless controversies, backbiting and jeal-
ousies. The religious reforms that he had set in train had sparked
fierce conflict not just between courtiers, but between subjects across
the kingdom. Henry had realised, too late, that this conflict, once
unleashed, could not be reined in. And though he ended with a final
plea to live 'in charity one with another, like brother and brother',
he knew that his words had come too late. He would live out his
days as an almost futile witness to the struggles that were tearing
his kingdom apart.

The sombre mood at court was hardly alleviated by news that soon arrived from France. The Earl of Surrey suffered an ignominious defeat at St Étienne in January 1546. Convinced that he had lost the king's favour, he became depressed and disaffected, and looked on in despair as his debts mounted. The following month, he received word that Edward Seymour would replace him as lieutenant-general, and on 21 March the Privy Council ordered him home. This served to deepen his growing antipathy towards the Seymour brothers. To Surrey's dismay, he learned that as well as receiving reports of irregularities and mismanagement in his command, the king had heard whispers that he had been engaged in treacherous activities. The earl arrived at court on 27 March, but was met with a cold reception and was denied access to the king – an ominous sign. Increasingly isolated and vulnerable, Surrey's only ally was his father. But Norfolk had proved quick to abandon members of his family in the past, so his support was far from reliable.

Surrey soon relinquished any hope of winning back favour with the king. But he was consoled by the fact that Henry's health was now fading rapidly, so the earl focused his efforts upon the future. In the spring of 1546 he became embroiled in a vicious debate about the regency council that would rule after the king's death. Prince Edward was only eight years old, and even if the king's health improved, it was obvious to all that he would not live to see his son reach maturity. Surrey insisted that the Howards had the strongest claim to control the protectorate, but his opponents argued that their adherence to the old religion disqualified them.

Chief among them was George Blagge, Henry's esquire of the body, whom he affectionately called 'pig', for reasons unknown. Blagge was an ambitious social climber who had attached himself to various patrons, including Thomas Wyatt and the Earl of Surrey, before entering royal service. He argued that 'such as the king should specially appoint thereto should be meetest to rule the Prince'. But his former patron Surrey insisted that 'his father was meetest both for good services done and for estate'. A furious row erupted, with Blagge swearing that 'rather than it should come to pass that the Prince should be under the government of your father or you, I would bide the venture to thrust this dagger in you'.[1] The issue was about more than the regency: it was a battle between the officials of court, represented by Blagge, who wanted to see things arranged through the proper channels, and the 'old order', who believed in the natural right of the aristocracy to bear rule. This same battle had raged since the very beginning of Henry's reign.

Another candidate for the regency was the queen. Increasingly outspoken in her support for the new religion, Katherine Parr had alienated the conservatives in her husband's court, and in February 1546, they hatched a plot to destroy her. Gardiner started rumours of her imminent demise, and even prompted gossip about the women who might replace her. His confidence was not entirely misplaced. Tormented by the pain from his ulcerated leg, and suffering a range of other health complaints, Henry had become increasingly short-tempered with those around him, his sixth wife included. He had once complained to Gardiner about her forthrightness in the religious discussions she had had with her husband. The bishop needed no further encouragement to put his plan into action.

Gardiner's fellow conspirators included Sir Richard Rich, who had helped bring down Sir Thomas More a decade earlier and had subsequently been appointed chancellor of augmentations. More surprising choices were two men who had been associated with religious reform: Sir Thomas Wriothesley, Lord Chancellor, and William Paget, who had been closely allied to the Seymour faction. These three men now dominated Henry's council and, together, represented a dangerous threat to anyone who crossed their path. When John Dudley struck Gardiner in the face at the council table, he was banished from court for a month.

Together, these men now sought proofs of heresy that would seal Katherine's fate. Gardiner's first move was to try to implicate the queen in the case of a woman named Anne Askew, who had recently been imprisoned on suspicion of heresy. Desperate to incite Anne to name the queen, Gardiner ordered that she be subjected to horrific torture. According to Foxe, using what he claimed was Anne's own account, this was carried out by Gardiner's associates Wriothesley and Rich, who did not hesitate 'to rack me with their own hands, till I was nigh dead'.[2] In so doing, the two men were taking a huge risk. Anne should have been protected by law, both because she was a gentlewoman and because she had already been condemned, so to torture her without the king's sanction was overstepping the bounds of their authority. But the prize they sought was worth it: if they secured evidence of the queen's heresy, they would wield even greater political power. Though she fainted away from the pain on several occasions, Anne refused to give Wriothesley and Rich what they wanted. In the course of her ordeal, she demanded of Wriothesley 'how long he would halt on both sides?'[3] It was a shrewd observation of the man who had always placed political expediency ahead of personal principles.

Changing tack, Gardiner and his supporters focused instead on the queen's library. They knew that she and some of her ladies kept a number of forbidden books in their chambers. Katherine herself had gone to the trouble of concealing hers in her garderobe, and they eventually managed to procure evidence of this, despite the fact that Sir William Parr had smuggled most of them out. At around the same time as Anne Askew was burned at the stake on 16 July, the Bishop of Winchester issued a warrant for the arrest of the queen. Having seen two of his royal master's wives sent to the block, he was confident of success. Wriothesley, who had witnessed Anne Askew's grisly execution, was assigned the task of arresting Katherine, and was accompanied by a body of armed men.

In the event, Henry's sixth wife was only saved by a twist of fate. One of the court doctors happened to see the warrant when it was accidentally dropped, and he went at once to warn the queen. For all her terror, Katherine was quick to act. She took to her bed and had it given out that she was mortally ill. The king duly came rushing to her side and, in an impressive performance, Katherine pleaded that her illness stemmed from fear that she had displeased him. She also assured Henry that she had only engaged him in spiritual debates in order to take his mind off his many ailments, as well as to learn from his responses. Katherine had played to Henry's vanity perfectly.

The king forgave his wife at once, and proceeded to rail against Gardiner, Wriothesley and their fellow conspirators for daring to question the queen's loyalty. He angrily rebuffed the Lord Chancellor, calling him knave, beast and fool, and drove him from his presence. But while Wriothesley was soon restored to favour and received a visit from his master at his magnificent residence at Titchfield, Gardiner would never recover Henry's trust. Relations between them took another downturn towards the end of November 1546, when Henry flew into a rage with Gardiner for declining a proposed exchange of lands with the king. The bishop begged for forgiveness, and in a letter to Paget lamented: 'I hear no specialty of the king's majesty's miscontentment in this matter of lands, but confusedly, that my doings should not be well taken.'⁴ In vain, Gardiner claimed that he had never denied any request for the lands, but Henry continued to upbraid him, declaring that he had 'utterly refused any conformity'.⁵

Among the king's men who almost fell foul of Gardiner's machinations was Sir Anthony Denny. His wife Joan had been caught up in the controversy against Katherine, and the fact that Anne Askew was a distant relative of her uncle, Sir Gawain Carew, had not helped matters. Anne had admitted that Lady Denny's servant had supplied her with money, but this was insufficient to have her convicted, and both she and her husband survived the storm.

Archbishop Cranmer had also been a target for Gardiner's plot, but had escaped any reprisals. However, a number of his associates were arrested on heresy charges in May 1546, and some were put to the flames that summer. The archbishop wisely kept a low profile, and even after the queen had been restored to her husband's affections, Cranmer took no chances. It seems that, during this period and under the influence of his chaplain Nicholas Ridley, Cranmer moved towards an understanding of Christ being spiritually, as opposed to physically, present in the Eucharist. This would become an important and openly expressed part of his theology in later years, but for now he kept extremely quiet about it. He had served the king long enough to know that even though he seemed to now favour the reformists once more, it would take little to make him swing the other way.

In fact, the attempted coup would be the last battle in the long war that had raged between the two religious factions among Henry's men. It quickly became obvious that it had dealt a decisive blow to the conservatives and all those associated with them. Thomas Wriothesley soon learned the truth of this. The same year, he ordered the arrest of George Blagge on suspicion of heresy. He went on to superintend Blagge's trial at the Guildhall, and sentenced him to death by burning. But when the king learned of this he was 'sore offended' and ordered Wriothesley 'to draw out his pardon himself'. A grateful Blagge told his royal master: 'If your Majesty had not been better to me than your bishops were, your pig had been roasted ere this time!'[6]

The secret of the reformist party's success lay more in practical than in political or ideological considerations. Access to the ageing – and ailing – king remained the principal means by which favour and influence could be won. With Henry leading an increasingly reclusive life, the number of those granted an audience diminished sharply. They included his wife, his archbishop, his physicians and his privy chamber attendants, almost all of whom were evangelicals. Henry had always liked to be surrounded by bright young men who could provide intellectual stimulation and lively debate, even if his own opinions were formed more slowly and, often, unpredictably. It is therefore no coincidence that towards the end of Henry's reign, his policy shifted ever more towards the new religion. Norfolk, Gardiner and their allies might still dominate the debates in council, but the real power lay with those men who attended the king during his increasing number of private hours.

Although he had long numbered himself among the conservatives, Sir Francis Bryan had now changed allegiance, abandoning his Howard cousins in favour of the Seymours. It was a shrewd move. In October 1546, the king conferred upon him the freedom of the City of London, as if to signal his place in the new political order. The same month, the queen's brother-in-law William Herbert was promoted to the position of chief gentleman of the privy chamber. Herbert had evidently impressed the king during the previous few years because in 1545 he had been returned to parliament as one of the knights of the shire for Wiltshire, and on 21 February 1546 he was made steward for life of the Duchy of Lancaster estates in that county. Now, as chief gentleman of the privy chamber, he stood to gain substantially in terms of both influence and wealth, and would soon take advantage.

Meanwhile, the Duke of Norfolk was, for once, attempting a more conciliatory strategy. In June 1546, he again proposed a marriage between his daughter Mary and Thomas Seymour. This was anathema to Surrey, who instead tried to encourage his sister to seduce the ageing king and become his mistress, assuring her that she would thereby 'wield as much influence on him as Madame d'Etampes doth about the French King'.[7] Outraged, Mary furiously rejected her brother's scheme, and when she told his friends of it they distanced themselves from him.

On 21 August, Surrey was in attendance upon the king in the foremost rank at the reception of Claude d'Annebault, Admiral of France, who had commanded the French fleet during the invasion attempt the previous summer. The Admiral was a commissioner for the Anglo–French treaty that had been signed on 7 June, putting an end to the hostility that had simmered between the two kings for several years. His visit to England was marked by the last, brilliant flowering of courtly magnificence that had defined Henry's reign in its heyday. The man who masterminded the opulent spectacle was Sir Thomas Cawarden, who had been appointed Master of the Office of the Revels and Tents that year. Edward Hall, who had witnessed numerous such entertainments, could hardly find the words to describe them, and simply concluded: 'You would much marvel, and scant believe' their scale and magnificence.[8] Henry was deeply grateful to Cawarden for breathing new life into a fading reign and reminding him of past glories, and he bequeathed him a generous legacy 'in token of special love'.[9]

Shortly after d'Annebault's departure, Henry's favoured privy chamber servant, Sir Richard Long, died at the age of fifty-two. He had served Henry faithfully to the end, and was greatly mourned. But the king himself had also fallen dangerously ill, and was again reported to be sick in October. He was attended by a member of his privy chamber staff, whom he now decided to raise to the position of chief gentleman.

As the 1540s progressed, Anthony Denny had become increasingly indispensable to his royal master. In 1544, he had accompanied the king to Boulogne and had been knighted there on 30 September. A year after receiving his knighthood, he and his brother-in-law, John Gates, and their assistant William Clerk had been licensed by the king to affix the royal stamp on all of the documents that were sent out in his name. This was an indication of Henry's growing infirmity and his increasing reliance upon the men who served him, and enabled Denny and his companions to wield considerable influence from that day forward.

Denny's pre-eminence was confirmed in October 1546, when, along with William Herbert, he replaced Sir Thomas Heneage as chief gentleman of the privy chamber. It is possible that Heneage retired on the grounds of age, since he was then sixty years old. He retained his links to Henry's inner sanctum because he was cited in the contemporary records as a gentleman extraordinary of the privy chamber. But now it was Denny who reigned supreme in that arena. As groom of the stool, he automatically assumed responsibility for the privy purse. However, Henry had also appointed him keeper of Westminster Palace in 1537. Denny thus became *de facto* treasurer of the cash reserves that Henry had built up at Westminster during the early 1540s, as well as of his most precious plate and jewels. This was a weighty responsibility and one that was open to abuse. Whether Denny fell prey to temptation is difficult to tell, but he certainly profited from these years of service to the ailing king.[10]

Denny's 'gentle' and godly manner appealed to a king who was increasingly subject to brooding and melancholy. An illumination of around 1545 shows Henry reading in his bedchamber, and his texts were often religious. Against verse 25 of Psalm 37, which reads: 'I have been young, and now am old; yet I have not seen the righteous forsaken, nor his seed begging bread', he wrote: 'A painful saying.'[11] Denny's closeness to the king was expressed in the gifts that they regularly exchanged. For example, Denny commissioned Hans Holbein to design a beautiful clock salt, which he gave as a gift to the king at the beginning of 1545. The chief gentleman would later be described in a royal patent as 'the most intimate of Henry VIII's council and chamber'.[12]

Although Denny had proved a firm supporter of the Reformation, he had been careful not to push his religious views forward too forcefully (perhaps learning from the example of his former patron Cromwell), and had always made it clear that his loyalty to, and friendship with the king was paramount. As if to demonstrate this, he had exposed a number of heretical books to Henry's officials. As a result, he had won favour from both sides of the religious divide: the Catholic Henry Howard, Earl of Surrey, and the evangelical humanist Sir John Cheke both wrote in his praise.

But those closest to Denny knew that he cherished a 'sincere affection to God and his holy word' and could be relied upon to support the cause of reform.[13] Both Cranmer and Seymour used Denny's proximity to the king to influence policy, knowing that it was Henry's habit to discuss state business with him in private, after he had done so with his council. This provided an opportunity that Seymour and the archbishop were quick to exploit. One such occasion was when Denny supported Cranmer's recommendations against the 'vain ceremonies' of traditional religion. Little wonder that he would later be hailed as 'an enemy to the Pope and his superstition'.[14] The fact that his wife Joan, who was also a committed evangelical, served in the new queen's household further strengthened his hand with the king.

A similar tactic was employed with another of Henry's private servants: his favourite physician William Butts, who worked hand in glove with Denny to influence their royal master. For example, in 1544 – the year in which Butts received a knighthood from Henry – he and Denny had intervened on Cranmer's behalf to protect his radical curate, Richard Turner, who had been accused of 'free and bold preaching against popish errors'. The archbishop had been too concerned about his own position to petition the king himself, so had asked Denny and Butts to help. He knew that Butts could be relied upon because he had interceded on Cranmer's behalf during the Prebendaries' Plot. Both he and Denny were also long practised in judging the most apposite time to approach their master, and Denny, 'spying a time when the King was in trimming and washing . . . pleasantly and merrily beginneth to insinuate unto the King the effect of the matter'. So successful were the two men that 'whereas before he [Henry] had commanded the said Turner to be whipped out of the country, he now commanded him to be retained as a faithful subject'.[15]

Butts' influence was well known throughout the court and it won him significant powers of patronage. He was referred to as 'a considerable man of affairs', and had grown very wealthy during his years in the king's service. This was only brought to an end by his death, at the age of sixty, in November 1545. Henry was alarmed as well as saddened by his loss, given that his own health was now seriously faltering and he had more need than ever of his old physician's skills. Butts was replaced by a physician named Thomas Wendy. Although competent enough in medicine, he lacked his predecessor's intellectual abilities, which he was made him a poor substitute in Henry's eyes.

On 10 December 1546, while he was staying at Oatlands in Surrey, the king's condition worsened once more. Those closest to him knew that he could not live for much longer. This intensified the atmosphere of suspicion at court. A week before the king's latest illness was reported, the Earl of Surrey was arrested after Richard Southwell, a member of the Privy Council, claimed 'that he knew certain things of the Earl that touched his fidelity to the King'.[16] Surrey's attempts to influence the regency were cited, as were his slanders against the council, his scheme to make his sister Henry's mistress, and his plans to flee the kingdom.

When Surrey heard of this, in characteristically reckless style he offered to fight Southwell in his shirt. Other men subsequently attested to his conspiracy to murder the council and take control of Prince Edward. Eager to claw back favour, Wriothesley switched sides with practised ease and assisted his royal master in drawing up the accusations against Surrey. He detained the earl in his house for several days while he examined him, and subsequently drafted the charges and a list of interrogatories.

On 12 December, Surrey, who had been denied his retinue, was led through the streets of London to the Tower, along with his father Norfolk, who was clearly implicated by association. This humiliating ordeal was arranged by Wriothesley, who never flinched from inflicting suffering upon those whom he had chosen to oppose. Meanwhile, the Howard family seat at Kenninghall and other residences were searched by a delegation led by Anthony Denny's brother-in-law John Gates, by now an influential privy chamber servant, and the earl's associates were interrogated.

Norfolk was quicker to rally himself than his son. The very next day, he wrote to the king pleading his innocence and offering his lands to Henry as proof of his loyalty. In an echo of his arch-rival Cromwell's arrest six years earlier, he begged 'that he may know what is laid to his charge and have some word of comfort from his Majesty'. Just as Cromwell had been kept in ignorance of the charges against him, however, so was Norfolk. He therefore also wrote to the Privy Council, asking 'that he meet his accusers face to face before the King or else before the Council'.[17] But the duke received no 'word of comfort' from Henry, who the day after arriving at Whitehall on 23 December had amended a draft of articles against Surrey and his father. Neither could Surrey hope for assistance from his fellow councillors. His former ally, Sir Anthony Browne, was among the men who were now involved in proceedings against him and his father.

Back at court, Norfolk's long-standing ally Gardiner was also under siege. Edward Seymour may have been behind the rumours that began to circulate that the Bishop of Winchester had secretly plotted to restore England to the papal fold. He had been quick to capitalise upon the king's failing health and prolonged absences to get the better of his rivals. At Christmas, the Imperial ambassador Van der Delft reported in some alarm that most of the council now supported Seymour, and that 'the majority of the people are of these perverse sects and in favour of getting rid of the bishops and they do not conceal their wish to see Winchester and other adherents of the ancient faith in the Tower with the Duke [of Norfolk]'. He added: 'This misfortune to the house of Norfolk may have come from that party [i.e. Seymour's].'[18] How much Henry himself knew of all this is not certain. Seymour probably kept him largely in ignorance, relaying only those details that were most advantageous to his own position.

On 26 December, the king, whose life was now quickly ebbing away, sent for a small group of confidants. They included Edward Seymour, John Dudley, Sir William Paget and Sir Anthony Denny. The king ordered Denny to bring his will. After hearing it read, he told Paget to make certain amendments, including the removal of Gardiner's name from the list of executors and councillors who were to rule during his son's minority. According to Paget's own account, he and the bishop's other allies tried to persuade their royal master to restore Gardiner to the list. But the king was adamant and declared that he 'had the same bishop of suspicion of misliking his highness's proceedings in some things of religion'. He added, for good measure, that Gardiner was 'much bent to the popish party', 'a wilful man and not meet to be about his son'.[19] Henry Neville, who had continued to rise in favour since being appointed a groom of the privy chamber, later confirmed that the king harboured a great hatred towards the bishop.

Edward Seymour took evident satisfaction in attesting that Henry had referred to Gardiner as 'a troublesome man; and that he would trouble all the rest [of the executors] if he were named among them'.[20] Seymour's ally Denny, who made little secret of his antipathy towards Gardiner, corroborated his testimony and claimed that Henry had told him that if the bishop 'were in my testament, and one of you, he would cumber you all, and you should never rule him, he is of so troublesome a nature. Marry, I myself could use him, and rule him to all manner of purposes as seemed good to me; but so shall you never do, and therefore talk no more of him to me in this behalf.'[21]

Although Henry had already appointed the sixteen men who were to form the regency council during his son's minority, another one tried to muscle in during the closing days of the old king's reign. Edward Seymour's younger brother Thomas had been appointed to the Privy Council on 23 January, but the king had just enough grasp of his mental faculties to prevent this feckless younger brother from seizing more power after his death. According to Foxe, Henry 'being on his deathbed, and hearing [Seymour's] name among those elected to the [regency] Council, cried out "no, no!", though his breath was failing him'.[22] The fact that Seymour benefited from Henry's will suggests that it was amended after the king's death.

The revised will was signed with the dry stamp on 30 December 1546.[23] It was sealed with the signet and witnessed before Henry handed it to Edward Seymour. William Paget, who was working in cahoots with Seymour, made an agreement with him in the gallery outside Henry's chamber that the provisions their master had made should be amended to give Seymour seniority over his fellow councillors. In return, Seymour promised to make Paget his principal adviser.

Meanwhile, 'troublesome' to the end, Gardiner doggedly insisted on continuing to attend Privy Council meetings until as late as 16 January 1547, but his exclusion from power in the next reign had been assured. Nevertheless, the fact that Henry's will had been signed with the dry stamp, rather than his own hand, left the way open for his final wishes to be reinterpreted to suit those who clamoured for power in the new reign. Among them was William Paget, who told the Privy Council that the king 'being remembered in his deathbed that he had promised great things to divers men . . . willed in his testament that whatever should in any wise appear to his Council to have been promised by him, the same should be performed'.[24]

By the dawning of the new year, Henry was fading fast. On 8 January, the French ambassador reported that the 'King has been so ill for the past fifteen days that he was reported dead'. Given that he now lived almost entirely in seclusion, and that his own father's death had been kept secret until the succession had been secured, many people 'believe him so, seeing that, whatever amendment is announced, few persons have access to his lodgings and his chamber'.[25]

It was treason for any of the king's subjects to speak of his death, so although it was obvious to all of the men who attended him that he would not live much longer, only one dared to say it. Sir Anthony Browne, who, though fickle towards his allies at court, had served Henry faithfully for almost thirty years, told his royal master that he was close to death, perhaps so that the king might prepare himself. He suffered no repercussions from this: indeed, Henry rewarded his honesty with a bequest of £300 and made him an executor of his will.

Meanwhile, on 7 January 1547, a grand jury was summoned to try the Earl of Surrey. None of the charges cited by Southwell were included. Instead, the sole charge was, rather obscurely, that on 7 October 1546 at Kenninghall, Surrey had displayed the royal arms and insignia in his own heraldry. His servant testified that Surrey had claimed that the Saxon king Edward the Confessor had bestowed the arms of England upon the earl's predecessors. Laying claim to the inheritance of the Saxon kings was a threat to the Tudor heirs of William the Conqueror so, tenuous though it all was, it served to strengthen the case against Surrey.

In the end, it would be his own father's testimony that would seal Surrey's fate. On 12 January, Norfolk submitted a confession, pleading: 'I have offended the King in opening his secret counsels at divers times to sundry persons to the peril of his Highness and disappointing of his affairs. Likewise I have concealed high treason, in keeping secret the false acts of my son, Henry Earl of Surrey, in using the arms of St. Edward the Confessor, which pertain only to kings.'[26] Norfolk again offered up his estates, asking that they might go to Prince Edward. If this was intended as a gesture, the king took it seriously and seized all of them, with the exception of certain properties in Sussex and Kent.

The duke's former ally Wriothesley had witnessed his confession, and the following day he joined the other commissioners who had been appointed to try Norfolk's son at the Guildhall. They included William Paget, whom Henry had instructed to ensure the earl's condemnation. Surrey pleaded not guilty and vehemently defended himself. But it was to no avail. He was convicted of treason and executed on Tower Hill six days later. In what had by now become a well-practised move, Henry gifted the executed earl's gown of gold to one of his other men: Sir Francis Bryan. His old companion perhaps reflected how close he had come in the past to having his own clothes taken from his back and given to another.

The Earl of Surrey was the last victim of Henry VIII's increasingly brutal regime. As he was led to the block, the king was at Whitehall Palace, having retreated there from the Christmas celebrations at Greenwich. It was obvious to the handful of men who attended him that he would soon breathe his last. On 17 January, two days before Surrey's execution, Henry had received both the French and Imperial ambassadors. Apologising for the fact that his illness had hindered their business, he was graceful and charming, and betrayed no hint – verbally, at least – of how much pain he must have been in. It would be the last time that Henry was seen by anyone other than his private attendants.

Meanwhile, the Duke of Norfolk was still languishing in the Tower. Despite testifying against his son and forfeiting the bulk of his lands, he had received no sign of mercy from the king. Instead, his reputation had been blackened further by the testimony provided by his family, including his estranged wife, his daughter Mary, and his mistress. The latter claimed that her lover had boasted that the king 'loved him [Norfolk] not because he was too much loved in his country', and that the duke had predicted Henry would soon die.[27]

On the morning of 27 January, Henry saw his confessor and received Holy Communion. Later that day, he discussed certain matters of state with his councillors. One of his last acts as king was to give his assent, via Wriothesley and the other commissioners, to the Duke of Norfolk's execution. It was given by letters patent signed by the dry stamp on 27 January, and it was rumoured that Norfolk would die the next day. Quite how conscious Henry was of the decision is not clear, but there is an undeniable poignancy in the fact that, at the end of his own life, he had condemned one of his longest-serving men to his death. It reflects the king's increasingly ruthless and changeable behaviour during his later years, which had rendered even his closest male companions hapless players in a dangerous and volatile game of survival.

By the evening, the king had lapsed into a perilous state. Judging that his royal master could only have a few hours left, Denny gently urged his royal master 'to prepare himself to death . . . and to call upon God . . . for grace and mercy'.[28] He asked his royal master if he wished to speak to any 'learned man'. Henry replied 'that if he had any, it should be Dr Cranmer'. When Denny enquired whether the archbishop should be sent for, the king told him: 'I will first take a little sleep, and then as I feel myself, I will advise upon the matter.'

They were the last words that Henry ever spoke. By the time that Cranmer arrived, his royal master was beyond speech. Cranmer now ministered to him not as a servant to a king, but as a priest to a dying man. John Foxe described the scene that followed Cranmer's arrival at Whitehall. 'Then the archbishop, exhorting him to put his trust in Christ, and to call upon his mercy, desired him, though he could not speak, yet to give some token with his eyes or with his hand, that he trusted in the Lord. Then the King, holding him with his hand, did wring his hand in his as hard as he could.'[29]

Henry died shortly afterwards, at two o'clock in the morning of 28 January. Whether he was conscious enough, in his final moments, to realise that it would have been his father's ninetieth birthday must rest with conjecture. But given how often at times of crisis he had been plagued by memories of the man whose shadow he had never quite managed to cast off, it is likely that the significance of the date had not been lost upon him.

Although Henry had vacillated between conservatism and reform for many years, his death was taken as a sign that he had at last accepted the latter. There had been no Latin chants, no anointing, as was traditional for the Catholic last rites; instead, the king had simply acknowledged his trust in Christ. Henry therefore died in the faith that his loyal archbishop had long espoused, but had never forced upon his royal master. The fact that he was incapable of doing more was overlooked by those who claimed this as a victory for reform.

Cranmer was genuinely grief-stricken upon his royal master's death and was seen to shed tears at the bedside. From that moment onwards, he allowed his beard to grow. For some, this represented a sign of Cranmer's move to a more obvious rejection of Catholicism, since many of the continental reformers had also allowed their facial hair to grow. Others took a rather different view and claimed that it was done in memory of his beloved king.

It is telling that in his final hours, Henry had chosen to be attended only by men. Even his wife Katherine and daughter Mary had been denied admittance to his chamber at Whitehall. Racked by pain and humiliated by his bloated, stinking body, Henry had only been able to bear the company of his most trusted male servants.

To his last breath, Henry's relationships with the men who surrounded him had both reflected and influenced his character and behaviour. It was they who had stoked and suffered his ruthlessness and paranoia, they who had been made and unmade by him, inspired his affection and trust, and, in the end, exploited his vulnerability. The final glimpse we have of Henry is as a king – and a man – defined not by his six wives, but by the men who had at turns entertained, advised, angered, delighted and shaped him for fifty-six years.

Epilogue

'Some special man'

In the closing days of January, Prince Edward received two visitors from his father's court. One was his uncle, Edward Seymour, and the other was Sir Anthony Browne. They had ridden to the prince's residence at Hertford as soon as his father had breathed his last. Henry VIII's death was concealed from his subjects for a further two days, just as his own father's had been, in order to allow time for his councillors to arrange a smooth succession. Meals continued to be taken into his privy chamber so that the servants beyond would have no inkling that anything was amiss.

Meanwhile, Henry's son and successor was moved to Enfield, where Princess Elizabeth was staying. The young prince was filled with excited anticipation because he knew that his formal creation as Prince of Wales was being actively considered, so he hoped that Seymour might be bringing news of its confirmation. But as soon as Edward was with his sister, the two men told them of their father's death. Distraught, Edward rushed into his sister's arms and they wept together for several hours while the councillors looked on, aghast. Yet in his diary, Edward recorded only that there was 'great lamentation and weeping' when his father's death was announced to the people of London, and mentions nothing of his own feelings.[1]

Edward soon set out for London. He arrived in the capital on 31 January and was given a rousing reception, to his 'great felicity'.[2] Following tradition, he resided at the Tower until his coronation. On the same day as Edward's arrival, a tearful Wriothesley announced his royal master's death to parliament. The sincerity of this arch-politician is questionable. After all, his position in the new reign seemed assured. Henry had named him one of the sixteen executors to sit on his son's regency council. He had also bequeathed the Lord Chancellor £500 in his will and the earldom of Southampton, which he duly inherited on 16 February.

Edward Seymour showed no such regret, feigned or otherwise, in the days following the old king's death. Instead, one of his first acts after conveying the news to his nephew was to seize the jewels that Henry had bestowed upon his sixth wife. This rather aggressive action triggered a long-running and bitter dispute with Katherine, who was already aggrieved at being deprived of any powers of regency. It did not help matters that Seymour's wife was seen wearing the jewels at the coronation the following month.

Seymour and his fellow executors met on 31 January and agreed 'that being a great number appointed to be executors with equal and like charge, it should be more than necessary as well for the honour, surety and government of the most royal person of the king our sovereign lord that now is as for the more certain and assured order and direction of his affairs, that some special man of the number and company aforesaid should be preferred in name and place before others'.[3] They decided to create two posts: Governor of the King's Person and Protector of the Realm.

Of all the men in whom Henry had entrusted power during his son's reign, Edward Seymour stood head and shoulders above the rest. He had spent years planning for this moment and made sure that the transfer of authority to him would be as smooth as it had been from Henry to his son. As the new king's uncle, he was a natural choice as Lord Protector, and he was more politically shrewd than most of his rivals. But he was so greedy for power that he also persuaded the executors to make him Governor of the King's Person too. This sparked the resentment of his brother Thomas, who had expected that this title would go to him.

Thomas Seymour was not the only man who had cause to feel aggrieved. The new Lord Protector's ally, William Paget, had been instrumental in laying the path to Seymour's promotion during the closing days of Henry's reign, but he was denied the rewards that had been held out as an enticement. 'Remember what you promised me in the gallery at Westminster, before the breath was out of the body of the King that dead is,' Paget urged him. 'Remember what you promised me immediately after, devising with me concerning the place which you now occupy.'[4]

On the same day as Seymour's position was decided, the French ambassador, Odet de Selve, reported to his master that the Duke of Norfolk had been secretly beheaded on the previous day. In fact, the duke had been spared the same fate as his son by the king's death. The new Lord Protector, Edward Seymour, resisted the temptation to deal the killer blow because he and his council judged that it would be more politic to begin the new reign peaceably. Instead, they contented themselves with keeping Norfolk in the Tower and plundering his estates. As he was the wealthiest peer in England, these were considerable.

Initially, there was little change in the court personnel after Henry's death. The only senior officer to lose his place was Lord St John, who was obliged to cede his post as lord great chamberlain to John Dudley. Anthony Denny continued to wield influence in the new king's privy chamber. An executor of his master's will, he also received a substantial bequest, although there are hints that Denny abused his position as keeper of the privy purse to extract even more of his late master's bounty. He was also made a privy councillor and would be vested with an increasing level of power by his ally, the Lord Protector, even deputising for him on occasion. He died in service, on 10 September 1549, but his heirs would enjoy similar prominence in the reigns of the later Tudors and their successors, the Stuarts.

Some of the other privy chamber posts were filled by men who had attended Edward as prince. They included John Fowler, John Philpot and Robert Maddox, to each of whom the new king had grown attached. But otherwise this department, like the others, remained largely untouched.

Ralph Sadler was one of the privy councillors deputed to arrange the king's funeral in his capacity as master of the great wardrobe. The late king's apothecary, Thomas Alsop, supplied perfumed substances to place in the coffin. Henry had left Alsop a generous bequest in his will, so the apothecary was no doubt glad to perform this final service for his former master. His royal patronage had won him a host of wealthy clients, and he had also maintained his business interests as a member of the Grocers' Company. By the time of his own death in 1558, Alsop was a man of considerable means, with assets that included sixteen properties in London.

Henry's enormous body began its last journey from Westminster to Windsor on 14 February, and he was laid to rest two days later in St George's Chapel. His son Edward did not attend, as was customary. Nor did most of his council: they were too busy fighting over the terms of the late king's will. Henry Grey, Marquess of Dorset, was assigned the role of chief mourner – not because he was the most highly favoured of Henry's men by the time of his death, but because he was the closest in blood to him, after Prince Edward.

The two most senior members of the late king's privy chamber took pride of place in the funeral procession, as a contemporary account described: 'Then set at the head and feet of the said corpse Sir Anthony Denny and Sir William Herbert, two of the chief of his privy chamber.'[5] The king's former groom of the stool, Sir Thomas Heneage, also attended the funeral as a gentleman of the privy chamber extraordinary. Meanwhile, Bishop Gardiner directed the funeral mass. Given Henry's often-expressed antipathy towards 'wily Winchester', it is doubtful whether his late master would have approved.

Henry's choice of Windsor for his final resting place has long been taken as proof of his esteem for Jane Seymour, who was buried there. But it was also a sign of his enduring affection towards one of his men. The mortal remains of Charles Brandon, Duke of Suffolk, had lain there since his death almost eighteen months before. Now his royal master was interred close by. And so these two brothers in arms, who had so closely resembled each other in life and whose friendship had endured for more than four decades, were reunited in death.

Although Edward Seymour's position seemed assured until his nephew reached maturity, it would soon become obvious that vesting so much power in one man was a recipe for disaster. The fatal flaw in the arrangement was the fact that, although the council had decreed that the Lord Protector 'shall not do any act but with the advice and consent of the rest of the coexecutors', Seymour had no intention of adhering to what they envisaged as an honorary presidency. He meant to be regent, and soon began to exercise the executive powers of the crown. In short, as one contemporary observed: 'He was all but king.'[6]

This was not what Henry had intended, but even he could not rule beyond the grave. Before his death, he had, though, had plans to restore what he regarded as a 'greatly decayed' nobility, thanks to so many of their lands having reverted to the crown during his reign. William Paget claimed that the late king had 'willed me to make unto him a book of such as he did choose to advance'.[7] This document still exists in The National Archives, and the many amendments reflect the king's constant changes of mind about which of his men should benefit from his largesse. It was therefore open to interpretation, and the fact that most of the men who were put forward for ennoblement were favourable to Seymour and his regime suggests that the latter had helped to decide what the old king intended. Seymour was to receive the highest honour as Duke of Hertford, Exeter or Somerset; John Dudley was to be Earl of Coventry; Sir John Russell was to be Earl of Northampton; Thomas Wriothesley and Sir William Paulet were both earmarked for the earldom of Winchester; and William Parr was to become a marquess.

The council declared themselves satisfied that these were Henry's intended beneficiaries, but they postponed the final decision until a more appropriate time. They did not have long to debate the issue, however, because it was important that the new titles be conferred in time for Edward's coronation. On 16 February, the young king duly distributed the new honours. His uncles, Edward and Thomas Seymour, became Duke of Somerset and Baron Seymour of Sudeley respectively, while John Dudley was made Earl of Warwick and Katherine Parr's brother William became the Marquess of Northampton. Neither Sir John Russell nor Sir William Paulet were granted their intended titles at this time, although they were promoted to the earldoms of Bedford and Wiltshire respectively in January 1550.

Four days later, Henry's nine-year-old son was crowned Edward VI amid magnificent pomp and pageantry that called to mind the heyday of his father's reign. According to John Foxe, although the new king was 'but tender in years', he had matured into a young man of whom his father would have been proud: 'For his sage and mature ripeness in wit and all princely ornaments . . . I see but few to whom he may not be equal.'[8]

Henry's long-serving attendant, Sir Anthony Browne, rode next to the young king in his coronation procession. Although he had tried to persuade the dying king to admit Gardiner into his regency council, Browne had swiftly changed sides upon Edward's accession and was one of the first to accept Seymour as Lord Protector. But he did not live long enough to make an impact in the new reign, for he died on 6 May 1548 at his estate in Surrey.

On 22 February, as part of the celebrations that followed the coronation, Edward took part in a court masque, along with his companion Henry Brandon, the twelve-year-old Duke of Suffolk. Those members of the audience who could remember the heyday of his father's reign must have been struck by how little had changed. Like his father, Edward showed an enthusiasm for martial displays of all kinds, but because of his youth and his status as the sole male Tudor heir, his own participation was limited to archery and 'running at the ring'.

Edward also shared enough of his father's sense of humour to keep Henry's favourite jester in employment. Although Will Somer disappears from the records for a while after his old master's death, he is listed in the court entertainments at Christmas 1550, and appears regularly thereafter. For one festivity, he was kitted out with several elaborate new costumes and ordered to take part in a mock combat that the young king had devised.

In early April 1547, news arrived at court that the late king's fiercest rival, Francis I, had died. He had bested Henry even in death, for he had left his throne not to a minor, but to an accomplished, twenty-eight-year-old son. But it seems that this charismatic and pleasure-loving king had lost heart towards the end, for he was said to have 'died complaining about the weight of a crown that he had first perceived as a gift from God'.[9] Wriothesley thought he knew the reason for the French king's melancholy: 'It was said that he never rejoiced since he had heard of the King's Majesty's [Henry VIII's] death.'[10]

As Edward's reign began to settle, a number of his father's long-standing servants found favour with the new king. Among them was

Sir John Russell. In recognition of his unstinting loyalty, the late king had bequeathed him the princely sum of £500 (c. £120,000) and named him an executor on Edward's council. Although there seemed to be little love lost between Russell and Seymour, the former was prepared to support his protectorship without allying too closely with him. It would prove a wise strategy, enabling Russell to survive the turbulence of the young king's reign. So successful was he, in fact, that he also found favour in the next. He would serve Mary Tudor until his death, aged about seventy, on 14 March 1555. Admired for his honesty as well as for his pragmatism to the end of his days, Russell had been one of only a handful of Henry's men whose steadfast and loyal service had contributed significantly to the stability of the Tudor dynasty.

Russell's old friend Sir Francis Bryan also fared well in his service to Edward VI. His change of loyalty to the Seymours in the dying months of Henry's reign was rewarded. In September 1547, he was given the command of the horse in an expedition against Scotland led by the new Lord Protector and was made knight-banneret. The last service of this most peripatetic of courtiers lay in Ireland, where, at the age of fifty-eight, he at last took a wife: the powerful widow Joan Butler, Dowager Countess of Ormond. Bryan was subsequently appointed lord marshal, commanding Edward VI's forces against the Irish rebels. He died there in February 1550, and his last words were reported at the English court: 'I pray you, let me be buried amongst the good fellows of Waterford (which were good drinkers).'[11]

Everything had seemed set fair for the new Earl of Southampton as he held the sword of state at Edward's coronation. But a little over two weeks later, on 6 March, Wriothesley was deprived of the Great Seal and confined to his home at Ely Place. His alleged crime was the abuse of his authority, and he was accused of having 'menaced divers of the said learned men [of Edward's regency council] and others'.[12] But his real offence was in abandoning his long-practised strategy of changing alliance to suit the political climate. Instead, he had miscalculated by making an enemy of Edward Seymour. He made little attempt to counter the charges. His compliance was rewarded at the end of June, when he was released and subsequently regained his place on the Privy Council.

By this time, Thomas Seymour had already married Henry VIII's widow, Katherine Parr. The speed with which the Dowager Queen took another husband sent shockwaves throughout the court. Henry's eldest daughter Mary was so appalled that she refused to have anything more to do with her former stepmother. Princess Elizabeth was more pragmatic. She adored Katherine and accepted her invitation to live with her and Seymour at Chelsea. But it would have disastrous consequences. Seymour soon began a dangerous game of flirtation with the late king's youngest daughter, which resulted in Elizabeth being thrown out of Chelsea. Undeterred, when Katherine died after giving birth to a short-lived daughter in September 1548, Seymour renewed his advances towards the princess.

Meanwhile, thanks to his close alliance with Edward Seymour, as well as his ideological alignment with the new king, Thomas Cranmer retained his position as Archbishop of Canterbury. For all that he regretted the late king's passing, he experienced a sense of relief, too, for he could live openly with his wife and children now that Edward's first parliament had repealed the Act of Six Articles. Early in the new reign, he wrote to the young king, urging him 'to finish and bring to pass that your father did most godly begin'.[13] Edward needed little persuasion. His passion for reform belied his tender years, thanks in no small part to Cranmer's assiduity in cultivating his favour during the preceding years.

During the course of Edward's short reign, Cranmer would oversee the establishment of a strongly reformed doctrine in England, encapsulated in the Book of Common Prayer, issued in March 1549, which was followed by an even more radical version three years later. This would be Cranmer's greatest and most lasting achievement. He had, at last, been given free rein to express the views that he had so often been obliged to temper and suppress during Henry's reign. Though it was not at all what his late master would have wanted, it was a dazzling achievement.

But it was all too brief. The accession of Edward's sister Mary, who was determined to return England to the Roman Catholic fold, spelt disaster for those who had promoted the cause of reform. Cranmer would be the most high-profile victim of the Marian burnings.

Although Cranmer had signed a recantation of his Protestant beliefs towards the end, when he went to his death in March 1556, he stretched out his right hand into the flames, declaring that it had 'offended'.[14] There is a profound tragedy in the fact that, having survived the many and dangerous vicissitudes of Henry's reign, Cranmer met his end at the orders of his daughter.

By contrast, having weathered the storm of Edward's reign, Cranmer's long-standing rival the Duke of Norfolk enjoyed great favour during the ascendancy of Mary Tudor. Recognising his unstinting dedication to the old religion, the queen showered him with honours. By the time of his death in August 1554, the eighty-one-year-old duke was Lord High Steward, Earl Marshal and a privy councillor.

Meanwhile, Edward Seymour had soon paid the price for his 'excessive arrogance' and overweening authority. As one contemporary observed, he had sought to make himself 'the king of the king', and 'had no one here superior to him in any degree of honour'.[15] He was ruthless in his quest for absolute authority, not flinching even to have his own brother Thomas put to death in March 1549 on charges of plotting to kidnap the king, marry his sister Elizabeth and make himself Lord Protector. His arrogance soon made an enemy of his erstwhile ally John Dudley. When Seymour realised that Dudley was conspiring to deprive him of power, he pursued him 'with the most unrelenting hatred'.[16] But it was Dudley who would triumph. In October 1549, with the assistance of Wriothesley and a number of other prominent religious conservatives, he led a coup to oust the Protector from office. The young king himself was persuaded to order his uncle's arrest.

Although Seymour was subsequently released and readmitted to the Privy Council, he was deprived of any real power from that day forward. Dudley was now the dominant force, and those who had helped him to power were quick to benefit. Prominent among them was Thomas Wriothesley, who was appointed to attend upon the young king. 'Wriothesley . . . is lodged . . . next to the king. Every man repaireth to Wriothesley, honoureth Wriothesley, sueth unto Wriothesley . . . and all things be done by his advise,' observed one contemporary.[17] But within a few short weeks, he had been thrown out of office and placed under house arrest on suspicion of abusing his authority. By now, Wriothesley was seriously ill, and he died on 30 July 1550 at the age of forty-five.

John Dudley soon became as blinded by ambition as his predecessor, and held sway with increasing tyranny. Having secured himself the dukedom of Northumberland in October 1551, he had Seymour arrested a few days later on trumped-up charges of treason. The former Lord Protector was executed in January 1552. This merely served to increase the ranks of Dudley's enemies, but, undeterred, he ruled with ever greater tyranny.

If he had known of the chaos and disorder into which his son's reign would descend, Henry VIII would have been appalled. He had not been alone in predicting great things for his successor, who was described by Vergil as 'a youth who most assuredly was destined for rule, for virtue and for wisdom. He is endowed with the highest talents and has aroused the greatest expectations among all men.'[18] At least the young king's subjects could look forward to the day when, aged eighteen, he would claim the full inheritance that his father had bequeathed him.

But Edward's reign – and his life – would end far sooner than anyone could have predicted. In April 1552, he contracted measles. Although he recovered, his immune system was fatally weakened, and he soon fell prey to tuberculosis. On 6 July 1553, Henry's precious son and heir died, aged just fifteen.

After a short-lived coup by John Dudley that placed his daughter-in-law (and Henry VIII's great-niece), Lady Jane Grey, on the throne, the late king's daughter Mary claimed her inheritance. But her reign, too, would be as brief as it was turbulent, and it was left to her half-sister Elizabeth to rescue the fortunes of the Tudor dynasty.

It is one of history's greatest ironies that, having focused all of his efforts on producing a male heir, it was Henry's forgotten younger daughter who would realise the hopes that had been articulated in the inscription on Prince Edward's portrait of 1539: 'Little one, imitate your father and be the heir of his virtue, the world contains nothing greater . . . Surpass him . . . and none will ever surpass you.' In the male-dominated world of sixteenth-century monarchy, Elizabeth, not Edward, would imitate her father – and surpass him.

ACKNOWLEDGEMENTS

Historical subjects do not get much bigger – in all respects – than Henry VIII. This most famous of monarchs strides across the pages of history as he did the times in which he lived and ruled. Writing his biography is not for the faint-hearted, and I am greatly indebted to a number of historians who have forged the path ahead of me, notably Alison Weir, Derek Wilson and David Starkey.

The idea for the book came at the very end of a conversation with my agent, Julian Alexander, in which we had discussed future writing projects. I mentioned in passing that it was a long-cherished ambition to write a biography of Henry VIII, but feared the ground was too well-trodden. There was a pause, then Julian asked: 'What about the men?' It was one of those light bulb moments and I will be forever in his debt.

This is the third book for which I have been lucky enough to work with Maddy Price, my brilliant editor at Hodder. It is thanks to her enthusiasm, clarity of vision and thoughtful guidance that the book has taken shape in the way it has, always with Henry at its focus. I am also indebted to Becca Mundy and Caitriona Horne for their endlessly creative marketing and publicity, and to the exhaustive efforts of the picture researcher, Juliet Brightmore. Warmest thanks are also due to Geraldine Beare for her assiduous work on the index.

I am grateful to a number of colleagues at Historic Royal Palaces, in particular Alden Gregory for sharing some fascinating nuggets of his research on the Field of Cloth of Gold and my line manager Adrian Philips for all his support. I would also like to thank my friend, the Reverend Stephen Kuhrt, for providing much-needed guidance on the complexities of Henrician theology and for reading the book through in its entirety as soon as I had submitted it.

I would not have been able to tackle the gargantuan task of writing about Henry VIII without the ongoing support of my family and friends. Particular thanks are due to my parents, John and Joan Borman, and my parents-in-law, Joy and John Ashworth. I am also deeply grateful to my husband Tom for managing not to roll his eyes whenever I panicked about not meeting the deadline, and for supplying me with a glass or two of wine at apposite moments. And finally to my daughter Eleanor for sharing her own perspective on Henry, gleaned from many happy hours watching Horrible Histories.

Abbreviations

BL MS	British Library Manuscript
CSPF	Calendar of State Papers, Foreign Series
CSPS	Calendar of State Papers, Spanish
CSPV	Calendar of State Papers, Venetian
Hall, *Chronicle*	Hall, Edward, *Chronicle; containing the History of England, during the reign of Henry the fourth and the succeeding monarchs, to the end of the reign of Henry VIII*
HMC	Historical Manuscripts Commission
LP Henry VIII	*Letters and Papers, Foreign and Domestic, of the Reign of Henry VIII, 1509–47*
TNA	The National Archives

Author's Note

All spelling and punctuation has been modernised for ease of reference.

BIBLIOGRAPHY

Selected Archival Sources

BL Additional MS 500001, fo.22 – Elizabeth of York's Book of Hours.

BL Royal MS 2 A xviii, fo.30v – Lady Margaret Beaufort's Book of Hours.

TNA E404/81/1 – Prince Henry's christening, 1491.

BM MS Cotton Julius B XII fo.91 – Prince Henry is created Duke of York and a Knight of the Bath, 1494.

BL Egerton MS 1651 fo.1 – Erasmus's poem to Prince Henry, 1499.

BL Additional MS 21404 fo.9 – Prince Henry's letter to Philip the Handsome, 1506.

BL Additional MS 31922 – A volume of songs compiled by Sir Henry Guildford, including lyrics written by Henry VIII.

TNA SP1/5, fos.76–7 – Wolsey's 'purge' of Henry VIII's privy chamber, 1519.

BL Cotton MS Titus B I fo.188 – Henry VIII agrees to Cardinal Wolsey's reform of his household, 1519.

BL MS Cotton Titus B.i, fo.192 – A 'privy remembrance' from Wolsey to Henry VIII, urging him to take measures for his security, 1520.

TNA PRO, SP 1/20, fos.42–3 – Sir Nicholas Wingfield's letter to Wolsey regarding arrangements for the Field of Cloth of Gold, 1520.

TNA SP 1/49 fos.7–7v – The will of Sir William Compton, 1528.

BL MS Cotton Vitellius B.XII fo.173 – Thomas Alward's description of Henry VIII's last meeting with Wolsey, October 1529.

BL Cotton MS Titus B i fos.261r, 264 – Thomas Cromwell's letters to Henry VIII.

TNA PROB 11/25, fo.243v – William Blount, Lord Mountjoy's will, 1534.

BM Harleian MS 283 fo.134 – Letter from Sir William Kingston, Constable of the Tower of London, regarding the preparations for the executions of Anne Boleyn and her alleged lovers, 1536.

BL MS Cotton Otho CX – Henry Percy's letter to Cromwell, insisting he had not been pre-contracted to Anne Boleyn, 1536.

TNA SP 3/7, fo.28r – Sir John Russell's letter to Arthur Plantagenet, announcing Henry VIII's marriage to Jane Seymour, 1536.

BL Harley MS 282 fos.211–12 – Letter from Cromwell to Sir Thomas Wyatt, announcing the birth of Henry VIII's son Edward, 1537.

TNA KB 8/11 fo.2 – The evidence against Henry Courtenay, Marquess of Exeter, 1538.

BL Cotton MS Titus B I – Letter from Cromwell to the Earl of Rutland, urging him to make Anne of Cleves more pleasing to the king, 1540.

BL Cotton MS Titus B i fos.267–9, Otho CX fo.242 – Cromwell's letters to Henry VIII from the Tower, 1540.

BL Additional MS 48028 fos.160–5 – The indictment against Cromwell, 1540.

TNA SP 1/189 fo.151r – Sir John Russell's letter to Henry VIII, complaining about the expense and futility of the war with France, 1545.

TNA SP 4/1 – The dry stamp register, 1546.

TNA E23/4 fo.16 – Henry VIII's will, 1546.

BL Harley MS 1419 A – The inventory of Henry VIII's possessions, 1547.

BM Cotton MS Nero C x, fo.12 – Edward VI's diary, recording the death of his father, Henry VIII, 1547.

Society of Antiquaries, London, MS 123, fo.1r – Edward VI's reception into London, upon being proclaimed king, 1547.

Printed Primary Sources

A Collection of Ordinances and Regulations for the Government of the Royal Household, Made in Divers Reigns. From King Edward III to King William and Queen Mary (London, 1790).

Allen, P.S. and H.M. (eds), Letters of Richard Fox: 1486–1527 (Oxford, 1929).

Bacon, F., The Historie of the raigne of King Henry the seventh, and other works of the 1620s, ed. Kiernan, M. (Oxford, 2012).

Barlowe, J. and Roy, W., Rede me and be not wrothe, ed. Parker, D.H. (Toronto, 1992).

Bray, G. (ed.), Documents of the English Reformation (Cambridge, 1994).

Brewer, J.S. and Bullen, W. (eds), Calendar of the Carew Manuscripts, preserved in the Archiepiscopal Library at Lambeth, 1515–1574 (London, 1867).

Brewer, J.S., et al. (eds), Letters and Papers, Foreign and Domestic, of the Reign of Henry VIII, 1509–47, 21 vols and 2 vols addenda (London, 1862–1932).

Brown, R. (ed.), Calendar of State Papers and Manuscripts, Relating to English Affairs, Existing in the Archives and Collections of Venice, Vols I–V (London, 1864–73).

Brown, R. (ed. and trans.), *Four years at the court of Henry VIII: Selection of despatches written by the Venetian Ambassador, Sebastian Giustinian, and addressed to the Signory of Venice, January 12th 1515, to July 12th 1519,* 2 vols (London, 1854).

Byrne, M. St C. (ed.), *The Letters of King Henry VIII* (London, 1936).

Byrne, M. St C. (ed.), *The Lisle Letters,* 6 vols (Chicago and London, 1981).

Calendar of the Close Rolls preserved in the Public Record Office: Henry VII 1485–1509 (London, 1955).

Calendar of Letters, Despatches, and State Papers, relating to the negotiations between England and Spain, preserved in the archives at Simancas and elsewhere, Vols II–VI, Part I (London, 1866–90).

Calendar of Patent Rolls, preserved in the Public Record Office, Henry VII, Vol. I 1485–1494 (London, 1914).

Campbell, W., *Materials for a History of the Reign of Henry the Seventh: from Original Documents preserved in the Public Record Office,* 2 vols (London, 1873, 1877).

Cattley, S.R. and Townsend, G. (eds), *John Fox, Acts and Monuments* (London, 1838).

Cherbury, Lord Herbert of, *The Life and Raigne of King Henry the eighth* (1649).

Coates, T. (ed.), *Letters of Henry VIII, 1526–29* (London, 2001).

Collected Works of Erasmus (Toronto, 1974).

Correspondencia de Gutierre Gomez de Fuensalida, Embajador en Alemania, Flandes é Inglaterra (1496–1509) (Madrid, 1907).

Cox, J.E. (ed.), *The Works of Thomas Cranmer, Archbishop of Canterbury, Martyr, 1556,* 2 vols (Cambridge, 1844, 1846).

Crapelet, G.A., *Lettres de Henri VIIIième à Anne Boleyn* (Paris, 1835).

Dasent, J.R., *Acts of the Privy Council of England,* Vols I and II (London, 1890).

Dillon, J., *Performance and Spectacle in Hall's Chronicle* (London, 2002).

Doran, S., *The Tudor Chronicles, 1485–1603* (London, 2008).

Dyce, A. (ed.), *John Skelton, Works* (London, 1843).

Ellis, H., *Original Letters illustrative of English History,* First Series, Vols I and II (London, 1969).

Fisher, J., *The English Works of John Fisher, Bishop of Rochester, 1469–1535,* ed. Hatt, C.A. (Oxford, 2002).

Froude, J.A. (ed.), *The Pilgrim: A Dialogue of the Life and Actions of King Henry VIII, by William Thomas, Clerk of the Council to Edward VI* (London, 1861).

Fuller, T., *The Church History of Britain*, ed. Brewer, J.S., new edn, 6 vols (London, 1845).

Gairdner, J. (ed.), *Letters and Papers Illustrative of the Reigns of Richard III and Henry VII*, 2 vols (London, 1861–3).

Gairdner, J., *The Paston Letters, 1422–1509*, Vols III–VI (London, 1875–1904).

Grafton, R., *A Chronicle at large* (London, 1809).

Hall, E., *The union of the two noble and illustre femelies of Lancastre and York* (London, 1548).

Hall, E., *A Chronicle; Containing The History of England, During The Reign of Henry the fourth and the succeeding monarchs, to the end of the reign of Henry VIII* (London, 1809).

Halliwell, *Letters of the Kings of England*, 2 vols (London, 1846–8).

Hay, D. (ed. and trans.), *The Anglica Historia of Polydore Vergil, A.D. 1485–1537*, Camden Series, Vol. LXXIV (London, 1950).

Haynes, A., *Collection of State Papers Relating to Affairs in the Reigns of King Henry VIII, King Edward VI, Queen Mary and Queen Elizabeth, From the Year 1542 to 1570 . . . Left by William Cecil, Lord Burghley . . . at Hatfield House* (London, 1740).

Hillerbrand, H.J. (ed.), *Erasmus and His Age: Selected Letters of Desiderius Erasmus* (New York, 1970).

Historical Manuscripts Commission, *Calendar of the Manuscripts of the Most Honourable Marquis of Salisbury, Preserved at Hatfield House, Hertfordshire*, Vol. I (London, 1883).

Historical Manuscripts Commission, *Calendar of the Manuscripts of the Most Honourable the Marquess of Bath, preserved at Longleat, Wiltshire, 1533–1659*, Vol. V (London, 1968).

Historical Manuscripts Commission, *Report on the Manuscripts of Lord De L'Isle & Dudley, preserved at Penshurst Place*, Vol. I (London, 1925).

Historical Manuscripts Commission, *The Manuscripts of His Grace the Duke of Rutland, preserved at Belvoir Castle*, Vol. I (London, 1888).

Hitchcock, E.V. (ed.), Roper, W., *The Lyfe of Sir Thomas Moore, knighte*, Early English Text Society, Vol. XCVII (London, 1935).

Hume, M.A. (ed. and trans.), *Chronicle of King Henry VIII of England . . . written in Spanish by an unknown hand* (London, 1889).

Jenkyns, H., *The remains of Thomas Cranmer, D.D., archbishop of Canterbury*, 4 vols (Oxford, 1833).

Jordan, W.K. (ed.), *The Chronicle and Political Papers of King Edward VI* (1966).

Kaulek, J. (ed.), *Correspondance politique de MM. de Castillon et de Marillac, ambassadeurs de France en Angleterre (1537–1542)* (Paris, 1885).

Kingsford, C.L. (ed.), *Chronicles of London* (Oxford, 1905).

Lloyd, D., *The states-men, and favourites of England since the Reformation* (London, 1665).

Luders, A., et al. (eds), *Statutes of the realm*, 11 vols, Record Commission (London, 1810–28).

Mattingly, G., *Catherine of Aragon* (London, 1963).

Mayer, T. (ed.), *Correspondence of Reginald Pole, Volume I: A Calendar, 1518–1546* (Aldershot, 2002).

Merriman, R.B. (ed.), *Life and Letters of Thomas Cromwell*, 2 vols (Oxford, 1902).

More, T., *A Dyaloge of Syr Thomas More* (London, 1529).

Muller, J.A., *Letters of Stephen Gardiner* (Cambridge, 1933).

Mynors, R.A.B. and Thomson, D.F.S. (eds), *The Correspondence of Erasmus* (Toronto, 1975).

Nicholl, A. and J. (eds), *Holinshed's Chronicle, As Used in Shakespeare's Plays* (London, 1955).

Nichols, F.M., *The Epistles of Erasmus*, 3 vols (1901–18).

Nichols, J.G. (ed.), *Literary Remains of King Edward the Sixth*, 2 vols (London, 1857).

Nichols, J.G. (ed.), *Narratives of the Days of the Reformation, chiefly from the manuscripts of John Foxe the Martyrologist*, Camden Society, old series, Vol. LXXVII (London, 1859).

Pithy pleasaunt and profitable workes of maister Skelton, Poete Laureate. Nowe collected and newly published (London, 1568).

Pocock, N. (ed.), *Records of the Reformation: The Divorce, 1527–1533* (Oxford, 1870).

Pratt, J. (ed.), *Actes and Monuments of John Foxe*, 8 vols (London, 1877).

Puttenham, G., *The Arte of English Poesie* (London, 1589).

Rebholz, R.A. (ed.), *Sir Thomas Wyatt: The Complete Poems* (London, 1978).

Robinson, H. (ed.), *Original Letters Relative to the English Reformation*, 2 vols (Cambridge, 1846–7).

Rogers, E.F. (ed.), *The Correspondence of Sir Thomas More* (Princeton, 1947).

Scattergood, J. (ed.), *John Skelton: The Complete English Poems* (New Haven and London, 1983).

Singer, W.S. (ed.), *The Life of Cardinal Wolsey by George Cavendish his Gentleman Usher* (London, 1827).

Stapleton, T., *Plumpton Correspondence: A series of letters, chiefly domestic, written in the Reigns of Edward IV, Richard III, Henry VII and Henry VIII* (London, 1839).

State Papers published under the authority of His Majesty's Commission, King Henry the Eighth, 11 vols (London, 1830–52).

Statutes of the Realm, 11 vols (London, 1963).

Stow, J., *Annales: or, A General Chronicle of England* (London, 1631).

Strype, J., *Ecclesiastical Memorials, Relating Chiefly to Religion, and the Reformation of it . . . under King Henry VIII, King Edward VI and Queen Mary I*, 3 vols (Oxford, 1822).

Strype, J., *Memorials of Thomas Cranmer*, 3 vols (London, 1840).

Surtz, E. and Hexter, J.H. (eds), *The Complete Works of Thomas More*, Vol. III (New Haven, 1965).

Toulmin Smith, L. (ed.), *The Itinerary of John Leland . . . With an appendix of extracts from Leland's Collectanea* (London, 1906–10).

Turnbull, W.B., *Calendar of State Papers, Foreign Series, of the Reign of Edward VI* (London, 1861).

Tyndale, W., *The Practice of Prelates* (London, 1530).

Williams, C.H. (ed.), *English Historical Documents 1485–1558* (London, 1967).

Wood, M.A.E., *Letters of Royal and Illustrious Ladies of Great Britain*, 3 vols (1846).

Wriothesley, C., *A Chronicle of England During the Reigns of the Tudors, from AD 1485 to 1559*, ed. Hamilton, W.D., 2 vols, Camden Society, new series, 11, 20 (London, 1875–7).

Wyatt, G., *Extracts from the Life of the Virtuous Christian and Renowned Queen Anne Boleigne*, in Singer, W.S. (ed.), *The Life of Cardinal Wolsey by George Cavendish his Gentleman Usher* (London, 1827).

Wyatt, T., *Collected Poems*, ed. Daalder, J. (Oxford, 1975).

Yorke, P. (ed.), *Miscellaneous State Papers. From 1501 to 1726*, Vol. I (London, 1778).

Secondary Sources

Ackroyd, P., *The Life of Thomas More* (London, 1998).

Anglo, S., *Spectacle and Pageantry and Early Tudor Policy* (Oxford, 1997).

Bagley, J.J., *Henry VIII and His Times* (London, 1962).

Baldwin-Smith, L., *Henry VIII: The Mask of Royalty* (London, 1971).

Bernard, G.W., 'The Rise of Sir William Compton, Early Tudor Courtier', *English Historical Review*, Vol. XCVI, no. 381 (October 1981), pp. 754–77.

Bernard, G.W., *The Tudor Nobility* (Manchester and New York, 1992).

Bernard, G.W., *Power and Politics in Tudor England* (Aldershot, 2000).

Borman, T., *Thomas Cromwell: The Untold Story of Henry VIII's Most Faithful Servant* (London, 2014).

Borman, T., *The Private Lives of the Tudors* (London, 2016).

Casady, E., *Henry Howard, Earl of Surrey* (New York, 1938).

Chapman, H., *The Last Tudor King: A Study of Edward VI* (Bath, 1961).

Chapman, H.W., *Two Tudor Portraits: Henry Howard, Earl of Surrey and Lady Katherine Grey* (London, 1960).

Childs, J., *Henry VIII's Last Victim* (London, 2008).

Chrimes, S.B., *Henry VII* (New Haven and London, 1999).

Coby, J.P., *Thomas Cromwell: Henry VIII's Henchman* (Stroud, 2012).

Cokayne, G.E., *The Complete Peerage of England, Scotland, Ireland, Great Britain and the United Kingdom* (London, 1913).

Cunningham, S., *Henry VII* (London, 2007).

Dodds, H.M. and Dodds, R., *The Pilgrimage of Grace, 1536–7, and the Exeter Conspiracy*, 2 vols (Cambridge, 1915).

Doran, S. (ed.), *Henry VIII: Man and Monarch* (London, 2009).

Dunham, W.H., 'The Members of Henry VIII's Whole Council, 1509–1527', *English Historical Review*, Vol. LIX (London, 1944).

Dutton, R., *English Court Life: From Henry VII to George II* (London, 1963).

Edwards, A.S.G., *Skelton: The Critical Heritage* (London, 1981).

Edwards, H.L.R., *Skelton: The Life and Times of an Early Tudor Poet* (London, 1949).

Elton, G.R., *Thomas Cromwell: Secretary, Minister and Lord Privy Seal* (Oxford, 1991).

Foister, S., *Holbein in England* (London, 2006).

Foss, E., *The Judges of England: with sketches of their lives and miscellaneous notices connected with the courts at Westminster, from the time of the Conquest*, Vol. V (London, 1857).

Fraser, A., *The Six Wives of Henry VIII* (London, 1993).

Gunn, S., *Henry VII's New Men and the Making of Tudor England* (Oxford, 2016).

Gunn, S.J., *Charles Brandon, Duke of Suffolk c.1484–1545* (Oxford, 1988).

Gunn, S.J., 'The Courtiers of Henry VII', *English Historical Review*, Vol. CVIII (London, 1993).

Gunn, S.J. (ed.), *Early Tudor Government* (Basingstoke, 1995).

Guy, J.A., *The Cardinal's Court: The Impact of Thomas Wolsey in Star Chamber* (Hassocks, 1977).

Guy, J.A., *Tudor England* (Oxford, 1988).

Guy, J.A., *Thomas More* (London, 2000).

Gwyn, P., *The King's Cardinal: The Rise and Fall of Thomas Wolsey* (London, 1990).

Harris, B.J., *Edward Stafford, Third Duke of Buckingham, 1478–1521* (Stanford, 1986).

Hayward, M., *Dress at the Court of Henry VIII* (Leeds, 2007).

Hayward, M. (ed.), *The Great Wardrobe Accounts of Henry VII and Henry VIII* (Woodbridge, 2012).

Head, D., *The Ebbs and Flows of Fortune: Life of Thomas Howard, Third Duke of Norfolk* (Athens, 1995).

Hoak, D., 'The Secret History of the Tudor Court: The King's Coffers and the King's Purse, 1542–1553', *Journal of British Studies*, Vol. XXVI, no. ii (Chicago, April 1987), pp. 208–31.

Hoyle, R.W., *The Pilgrimage of Grace and the Politics of the 1530s* (Oxford, 2001).

Hughes, P.L. and Larkin, J.F., *Tudor Royal Proclamations* (London, 1964).

Hunt, W. and Poole, L. (eds), *The Political History of England*, Vol. V (London, 1906).

Hutchinson, R., *Young Henry: The Rise to Power of Henry VIII* (London, 2011).

Ives, E.W., 'Faction at the Court of Henry VIII: The Fall of Anne Boleyn', *History*, Vol. LVII (1972).

Ives, E.W., *Faction in Tudor England* (London, 1979).

Ives, E.W., *Anne Boleyn* (Oxford, 1986).

Johnson, L., 'All the King's Fools: Mirth & Medicine' (unpublished research for Historic Royal Palaces, September 2011).

Lehmberg, S.E., *The Later Parliaments of Henry VIII, 1536–1547* (Cambridge, 1977).

Loades, D., *Tudor Government: Structures of Authority in the Sixteenth Century* (Oxford, 1997).

Loades, D., *Intrigue and Treason: The Tudor Court 1547–1558* (Harlow, 2004).

Loades, D., *Henry VIII: Court, Church and Conflict* (Kew, 2007).

Loades, D., *Henry VIII* (Stroud, 2011).

Loades, D., *Thomas Cromwell: Servant to Henry VIII* (Stroud, 2013).

Lynn, E., *Tudor Fashion: Dress at Court 1485–1603* (Yale, 2017).

MacCulloch, D., 'Two Dons in Politics: Thomas Cranmer and Stephen Gardiner, 1503–1533', *Historical Journal*, Vol. XXXVII, no. i (Cambridge, March 1994), pp. 1–22.

MacCulloch, D., *The Reign of Henry VIII: Politics, Policy and Piety* (London, 1995).

MacCulloch, D., *Thomas Cranmer: A Life* (New Haven and London, 1996).

Mackay, L., *Inside the Tudor Court: Henry VIII and His Six Wives through the Eyes of the Spanish Ambassador* (Stroud, 2015).

Mackie, J.D., *The Earlier Tudors, 1485–1558* (Oxford, 1994).

Marius, R., *Thomas More* (New York, 1984).

Mathew, D., *The Courtiers of Henry VIII* (London, 1970).

Miller, H., *Henry VIII and the English Nobility* (Oxford, 1986).

Murphy, B., *The Bastard Prince: Henry VIII's Lost Son* (Stroud, 2004).

Murphy, B.A., 'The Life and Political Significance of Henry FitzRoy, Duke of Richmond, 1525–1536', PhD diss., University of Wales (1997).

Norwich, J.J., *Four Princes: Henry VIII, Francis I, Charles V, Suleiman the Magnificent and the Obsessions that Forged Modern Europe* (London, 2016).

Penn, T., *Winter King: The Dawn of Tudor England* (London, 2011).

Redworth, G., *In Defence of the Church Catholic: The Life of Stephen Gardiner* (Oxford, 1990).

Richardson, W.C., *Stephen Vaughan, Financial Agent of Henry VIII: A Study of Financial Relations with the Low Countries* (Louisiana, 1953).

Ridley, J., *Thomas Cranmer* (Oxford, 1962).

Ridley, J.G., *The Statesman and the Fanatic: Thomas Wolsey and Thomas More* (London, 1982).

Ridley, J.G., *Henry VIII* (London, 1984).

Roberts, J., *Holbein and the Court of Henry VIII* (Edinburgh, 1993).

Robinson, J.M., *The Dukes of Norfolk* (Chichester, 1995).

Russell, J.G., *The Field of the Cloth of Gold: Men and Manners in 1520* (London, 1969).

Samman, N., 'The Henrician Court during Cardinal Wolsey's Ascendancy, c.1514–1529', PhD diss., University of Wales (1988).

Scarisbrick, J.J., *Henry VIII* (New Haven and London, 1997).

Schofield, J., *The Rise and Fall of Thomas Cromwell: Henry VIII's Most Faithful Servant* (Stroud, 2011).

Schwarz, A.L., *Vivat Rex! An Exhibition Commemorating the 500th Anniversary of the Accession of Henry VIII* (New York, 2009).

Sessions, W.A., *Henry Howard the Poet Earl of Surrey: A Life* (Oxford, 1990).

Sil, N.P., 'King's Men, Queen's Men, and Statesmen: A Study of the Careers of Sir Anthony Denny, Sir William Herbert, and Sir John Gate, Gentlemen of the Tudor Privy Chamber', PhD diss., University of Oregon (1978).

Skidmore, C., *Edward VI: The Lost King of England* (London, 2007).

Southworth, J., *Fools and Jesters at the English Court* (Stroud, 1998).

Starkey, D. (ed.), *The English Court: From the Wars of the Roses to the Civil War* (London and New York, 1987).

Starkey, D., 'Court, Council and the Nobility in Tudor England', in Asch, R.G. and Birkie, A.M. (eds), *Princes Patronage and the Nobility: The Court at the Beginning of the Modern Age, c.1450–1650* (Oxford, 1991).

Starkey, D., *The Reign of Henry VIII: Personalities and Politics* (London, 2002).

Starkey, D., *Six Wives: The Queens of Henry VIII* (London, 2003).

Starkey, D., *Henry: Virtuous Prince* (London, 2008).

Starkey, D. (ed.), *Henry VIII: A European Court in England* (London, 1991).

Streitberger, W.R., *Court Revels, 1485–1559* (Toronto, 2012).

Strong, R., *Holbein and Henry VIII* (London, 1967).

Temperley, G., *Henry VII . . . Illustrated* (Connecticut, 1914).

Thomson, P., *Sir Thomas Wyatt and His Background* (Stanford, 1964).

Thurley, S., *The Royal Palaces of Tudor England: Architecture and Court Life 1460–1547* (New Haven and London, 1993).

Walker, G., *John Skelton and the Politics of the 1520s* (Cambridge, 1988).

Walker, G., 'The Expulsion of the Minions Reconsidered', *The Historical Journal*, Vol. XXXII, no. i (Cambridge, March 1989), pp. 1–16.

Wegg, J., *Richard Pace, Tudor Diplomat* (London, 1937).

Weir, A., *Children of England: The Heirs of King Henry VIII, 1547–1558* (London, 1996).

Weir, A., *Henry VIII: King and Court* (London, 2001).

Weir, A., *The Six Wives of Henry VIII* (London, 2007).

Weir, A., *Mary Boleyn: 'The Great and Infamous Whore'* (London, 2011).

Willen, D., *John Russell, First Earl of Bedford, One of the King's Men* (London, 1981).

Williams, N., *Henry VIII and His Court* (London, 1971).

Williams, N., *The Cardinal and the Secretary* (London, 1975).

Wilson, D., *In the Lion's Court: Power, Ambition and Sudden Death in the Reign of Henry VIII* (London, 2002).

Wilson, D., *Uncrowned Kings of England: The Black Legend of the Dudleys* (London, 2013).

Wilson, D., *A Brief History of Henry VIII: Reformer and Tyrant* (London, 2016).

NOTES

PREFACE

1. Hymans, H., *Le Livre des Peintres de Carel van Mander* (Amsterdam, 1979), p. 218.
2. Translation provided by Derek Wilson in *A Brief History of Henry VIII: Reformer and Tyrant* (London, 2016), pp. 23–4.

INTRODUCTION: 'THE CHANGABLENESS OF THIS KING'

1. *LP Henry VIII*, Vol. VII, no. 1554; Vol. XVI, no. 590; Hume, M.A. (ed. and trans.), *Chronicle of King Henry VIII of England . . . written in Spanish by an unknown hand* (London, 1889), p. 105.

CHAPTER 1: 'THE KING'S SECOND BORN SON'

1. Hay, D. (ed. and trans.), *The Anglica Historia of Polydore Vergil, A.D. 1485–1537*, Camden Series, Vol. LXXIV (London, 1950), p. 3.
2. *Polydore Vergil*, p. 145; Bacon, F., *The Historie of the raigne of King Henry the seventh, and other works of the 1620s*, ed. Kiernan, M. (Oxford, 2012), p. 168.
3. *Polydore Vergil*, p. 145.
4. *CSPV*, Vol. I, p. 298.
5. *CSPV*, Vol. I, p. 158.
6. The contemporary accounts record that Arthur's household cost 1,000 marks per year, equivalent to around £300,000 today.
7. There is some hint in the contemporary sources that during this time Elizabeth gave birth to a short-lived prince named Edward. Some historians place his date of birth as early as 1487 or 1488, while others argue that it was between 1499 and 1502.
8. The patent rolls record some small matters of business that the king attended to there at this time. *Calendar of Patent Rolls, preserved in the Public Record Office, Henry VII, Vol. I: 1485–1494* (London, 1914), pp. 332, 333.

9. *Polydore Vergil*, p. 67.

10. BL Royal MS 2 A xviii, fo.30v. For a commentary on the manuscript, see Doran, S. (ed.), *Henry VIII: Man and Monarch* (London, 2009), pp. 13, 18.

11. Williams, C.H. (ed.), *English Historical Documents 1485–1558* (London, 1967), p. 387.

12. TNA E404/81 fo.1. See also Doran (ed.), *Henry VIII*, pp. 13, 19.

13. A rare example of Elizabeth of York's handwriting can be seen in her Book of Hours. BL Additional MS 50000I, fo.22.

14. Penn, T., *Winter King: The Dawn of Tudor England* (London, 2011), p. 101.

15. Penn, *Winter King*, p. 101.

16. Bacon, *Historie*, p. 179.

17. Bacon, *Historie*, p. 166.

18. *Calendar of Patent Rolls*, Vol. I, p. 423.

19. BM MS Cotton Julius B XII fo.91; *Calendar of the Close Rolls preserved in the Public Record Office: Henry VII 1485–1509* (London, 1955), no. 797, p. 237. See also Kingsford, C.L. (ed.), *Chronicles of London* (Oxford, 1905), p. 201. Allhallowtide was celebrated from 31 October to 2 November.

20. BL MS Cotton Julius B XII fo.91.

21. Gairdner (ed.), *Letters and Papers*, Vol. I, pp. 388–402.

22. Gairdner (ed.), *Letters and Papers*, Vol. I, pp. 388–402; Kingsford (ed.), *Chronicles of London*, pp. 201–3.

23. *Calendar of the Close Rolls*, no. 845, p. 248.

24. *Calendar of the Close Rolls*, no. 894, pp. 263–4. See also no. 1193, p. 355.

25. *Calendar of the Close Rolls*, no. 969, p. 287.

26. *CSPV*, Vol. I, p. 250.

27. His family name may derive from one of the six places called Skelton in Yorkshire, and a number of his early poems are connected with that county.

28. Edwards, A.S.G., *Skelton: The Critical Heritage* (London, 1981), p. 43.

29. Dyce, A. (ed.), *Poetical Works of John Skelton* (1843), Vol. I, p. 129.

30. *Pithy pleasaunt and profitable workes of maister Skelton, Poete Laureate. Nowe collected and newly published* (London, 1568). For examples of Skelton's works at Eltham, see Scattergood, J. (ed.), *John Skelton: The Complete English Poems* (New Haven and London, 1983), pp. 345–6.

31. *Polydore Vergil*, p. 93.

32. *CSPV*, Vol. I, pp. 263–4; Bacon, *Historie*, p. 167.

33. *Calendar of the Close Rolls*, no. 894, pp. 263–4, nos. 1080, 1081, p. 319.

34. Bacon, *Historie*, p. 179.

35. *Collected Works of Erasmus* (Toronto, 1974), Vol. I, p. 12.

36. Wilson, D., *In the Lion's Court* (London, 2002), p. 76.

37. Mynors, R.A.B. and Thomson, D.F.S. (eds), *The Correspondence of Erasmus*, Letters 142–297, 1501–1514 (Toronto, 1975), p. 100.

38. Edwards, *Skelton: The Critical Heritage*, p. 44.

39. *CSPV*, Vol. III, p. 447.

40. John More was later appointed serjeant-at-law (1503), judge of the common pleas (1518) and judge of the king's bench (1520). His wife, Agnes Graunger, was also from a prosperous family, being the daughter of an alderman and later sheriff of London.

41. Roper, W., *The lyfe of Sir Thomas Moore, knighte*, ed. Hitchcock, E.V. (London, 1935), p. 5.

42. Doran, *Henry VIII*, p. 157.

43. Roper, *Thomas Moore*, p. 5.

44. Wilson, *In the Lion's Court*, p. 25.

45. Mynors and Thomson (eds), *The Correspondence of Erasmus*, p. 299.

46. This still survives and is now in the collections of the Folger Shakespeare Library.

47. BL Egerton MS 1651 fo.1; Penn, *Winter King*, p. 110.

48. Skelton, J., *Speculum Principis*, reproduced in Salter, F.M. (ed.), *Speculum*, Vol. IX, no. 1 (January 1934), pp. 25–37.

49. Scattergood (ed.), *John Skelton*, p. 43.

50. Edwards, H.L.R., *Skelton: The Life and Times of an Early Tudor Poet* (London, 1949), pp. 288–9.

51. Kingsford (ed.), *Chronicles of London*, pp. 231–2.

52. Mattingly, G., *Catherine of Aragon* (London, 1963), pp. 32–7.

53. Tremlett, G., *Catherine of Aragon: Henry's Spanish Queen* (London, 2010), p. 76.

54. Tremlett, *Catherine of Aragon*, pp. 80, 83.

55. Licence, A., *In Bed with the Tudors: The Sex Lives of a Dynasty from Elizabeth of York to Elizabeth I* (Stroud, 2013), p. 52.

56. Weir, A., *Elizabeth of York: The First Tudor Queen* (London, 2013), p. 374.

57. Hall, E., *A Chronicle; Containing The History of England, During The Reign of Henry the fourth and the succeeding monarchs, to the end of the reign of Henry VIII* (London, 1809), p. 494.

58. *LP Henry VIII*, Vol. IV, Part iii, no. 5773.

59. Mackie, J.D., *The Earlier Tudors, 1485–1558* (Oxford, 1994), p. 192; Penn, *Winter King*, pp. 66–7.

60. Licence, *In Bed with the Tudors*, p. 54.

CHAPTER 2: 'HAVING NO AFFECTION OR FANCY UNTO HIM'

1. Falkus, C. (ed.), *The Private Lives of the Tudor Monarchs* (London, 1974), pp. 12–13.
2. Penn, *Winter King*, p. 177.
3. The sewer would wash the king's hands in specially heated and scented water, and dry them on a linen towel. Although this sounds quite menial work, touching the royal person was considered an enormous honour and was only accorded to the most favoured members of Henry's entourage.
4. More, T., *A Rueful Lamentation* (London, 1503).
5. Gairdner (ed.), *Letters and papers*, Vol. I, pp. 233, 239.
6. Penn, *Winter King*, p. 141.
7. *CSPV*, Vol. I, p. 298.
8. *Polydore Vergil*, p. 335.
9. *Rotuli Parliamentorum*, Vol. VI, p. 522.
10. Hazlitt, W.C., *Remains of the Early Popular Poetry of England* (1864–6), Vol. II, pp. 109–30; *CSPV*, Vol. IV, p. 184.
11. Weir, A., *Henry VIII: King and Court* (London, 2001), p. 7.
12. Penn, *Winter King*, p. 179.
13. *Polydore Vergil*, p. 79.
14. Gairdner (ed.), *Letters and Papers Illustrative of the Reigns of Richard III and Henry VII*, Vol. I, p. 180.
15. *CSPS*, Vol. I, no. 588: Vol. II, no. 12.
16. Weir, *Henry VIII*, p. 7.
17. See, for example, Gairdner (ed.), *Letters and Papers Illustrative of the Reigns of Richard III and Henry VII*, Vol. I, p. 372; Vol. II (London, 1863), p. 135.
18. Brown, R. (ed. and trans.), *Four years at the court of Henry VIII: Selection of despatches written by the Venetian Ambassador, Sebastian Giustinian, and addressed to the Signory of Venice, January 12th 1515, to July 26th 1519*, Vol. I (London, 1854), p. 76.
19. Thurley, S., *The Royal Palaces of Tudor England* (New Haven and London, 1993), p. 179.
20. *CSPS*, Vol. I, 1485–1509, no. 398.
21. *Polydore Vergil*, p. 151. See also Stow, J., *Annales: or, A General Chronicle of England* (London, 1631), p. 486.
22. Penn, *Winter King*, p. 321; *CSPS*, Vol. I, no. 552.
23. Weir, *Henry VIII*, p. 98.
24. Hume (ed. and trans.), *Chronicle*, p. 134.
25. Bacon, *Historie*, p. 148.
26. Penn, *Winter King*, p. 309.

27. Bacon, *Historie*, p. 167.

28. Gairdner (ed.), *Letters and Papers Illustrative of the Reigns of Richard III and Henry VII*, Vol. II, pp. 241–2.

29. *CSPS*, Vol. I, 1485–1509, no. 459.

30. Loades, D., *Henry VIII* (Stroud, 2011), p. 40.

31. *CSPV*, Vol. I, p. 313.

32. *Polydore Vergil*, p. 139.

33. Gairdner (ed.), *Letters and Papers Illustrative of the Reigns of Richard III and Henry VII*, Vol. II, p. 147.

34. BL Additional MS 21404 fo.9; Gairdner (ed.), *Letters and Papers Illustrative of the Reigns of Richard III and Henry VII*, Vol. I, p. 285.

35. BL Additional MS 21404 fo.9; Gairdner (ed.), *Letters and Papers Illustrative of the Reigns of Richard III and Henry VII*, Vol. I, p. 285.

36. Falkus (ed.), *The Private Lives of the Tudor Monarchs*, p. 19.

37. Weir, *Henry VIII*, p. 7.

38. Bacon, *Historie*, p. 164.

39. Puttenham, G., *The Arte of English Poesie* (London, 1589), p. 246.

40. Williams (ed.), *English Historical Documents*, p. 387; *Polydore Vergil*, p. 151. See also Stow, *Annales*, p. 486.

41. *Polydore Vergil*, p. 151. See also Stow, *Annales*, p. 486.

42. Williams (ed.), *English Historical Documents*, p. 387.

43. Bacon, *Historie*, pp. 165, 167.

44. *CSPS*, Vol. I, pp. 177–8.

45. *Polydore Vergil*, Ap.129.

46. *CSPS*, Vol. I, nos. 551, 553; *CSPS* Supplement to vols I and II, no. 23.

47. Penn, *Winter King*, pp. 311, 317.

48. Williams (ed.), *English Historical Documents*, p. 387.

49. Penn, *Winter King*, p. 317.

50. *Correspondencia de Gutierre Gomez de Fuensalida, Embajador en Alemania, Flandes é Inglaterra (1496–1509)*, p. 449.

51. *Polydore Vergil*, p. 145.

52. Bacon, *Historie*, p. 164.

53. *Polydore Vergil*, pp. 127, 129.

54. *CSPS* Supplement to vols I and II, no. 2.

55. Not to be confused with Thomas Wriothesley, first Earl of Southampton (1505–50), who became a key member of Henry VIII's government.

56. Penn, *Winter King*, p. 344.

57. Penn, *Winter King*, p. 345.

CHAPTER 3: 'LUSTY BACHELORS'

1. *CSPV*, Vol. I, p. 345.
2. Hall, E., *The union of the two noble and illustre famelies of Lancastre and York* (1548), f.ii; Dillon, J., *Performance and Spectacle in Hall's Chronicle* (London, 2002), p. 17.
3. Anglo, S., *The Great Tournament Roll of Westminster* (Oxford, 1968), p. 1.
4. Singer, W.S. (ed.), *The Life of Cardinal Wolsey by George Cavendish his Gentleman Usher* (London, 1827), pp. 78–9.
5. *Polydore Vergil*, p. 151.
6. Dillon, *Performance and Spectacle*, p. 17.
7. Bacon, *Historie*, p. 169.
8. Chrimes, S.B., *Henry VII* (New Haven and London, 1999), p. 314.
9. Starkey, D., *The Reign of Henry VIII: Personalities and Politics* (London, 2002), p. 28.
10. *CSPV*, Vol. I, p. 347.
11. *CSPV*, Vol. IV, p. 293.
12. *CSPV*, Vol. II, p. 400.
13. *CSPV*, Vol. II, pp. 78, 400.
14. Carlson, D.R. (ed.), 'The Latin Writings of John Skelton', *Texts and Studies*, Vol. 88, no. 4 (North Carolina, 1991), no. X.
15. Weir, *Henry VIII*, p. 2; Williams (ed.), *English Historical Documents*, pp. 388–91; Surtz, E. and Hexter, J.H. (eds), *The Complete Works of Thomas More*, Vol. III (New Haven, 1965).
16. Elizabeth was born in 1506, Cicely in 1507 and John in 1509.
17. *Collected Works of Erasmus* (Toronto, 1974), Vol. II, pp. 147–8.
18. Bacon, *Historie*, p. 179.
19. Grafton, R., *A Chronicle and Mere History* (1809), pp. 235–6.
20. Dillon, *Performance and Spectacle*, p. 17.
21. Grafton, *A Chronicle and Mere History*, pp. 235–6.
22. Wilson, *In the Lion's Court*, p. 80.
23. Bacon, *Historie*, p. 166.
24. There were forty-two noblemen at Henry's accession, and fifty-one by the time of his death. But this distorts the considerable number of new creations that he made during the course of his reign. By its end, over half of the surviving noblemen owed their titles to Henry. See Miller, H., *Henry VIII and the English Nobility* (Oxford, 1986), pp. 35, 256–7.
25. Hall, *Chronicle*, p. 502.
26. Dillon, *Performance and Spectacle*, pp. 20–9.
27. Bacon, *Historie*, p. 180.

28. *CSPV*, Vol. I, p. 346.

29. Bacon, *Historie*, p. 180; *CSPV*, Vol. II, p. 559.

30. Bacon, *Historie*, p. 180.

31. Loades, *Henry VIII*, p. 9.

32. *LP Henry VIII*, Vol. XI, no. 957.

33. Allen, P.S. and H.M. (eds), *Letters of Richard Fox: 1486–1527* (Oxford, 1929), p. xi.

34. Allen, P.S. and H.M. (eds), *Letters of Richard Fox*, p. 44.

35. BL Additional MS 19398 fo.44; *CSPS*, Vol. II, p. 71.

36. Loades, *Henry VIII*, p. 68.

37. Dillon, *Performance and Spectacle*, p. 31.

38. Dillon, *Performance and Spectacle*, p. 42.

39. Weir, *Henry VIII*, p. 97.

40. Dillon, *Performance and Spectacle*, p. 42.

41. Merriman, R.B. (ed.), *Life and Letters of Thomas Cromwell*, 2 vols (Oxford, 1902), Vol. I, p. 414.

42. Dillon, *Performance and Spectacle*, p. 55.

43. Wilson, *In the Lion's Court*, pp. 78–9. It must have been satisfying for Compton when he received orders to arrest the Duke of Buckingham in 1521. Although there is no evidence, beyond gossip, that Compton and Anne were guilty of adultery, in 1523 Henry's groom took the unusual step of bequeathing land to her in his will. He also directed his executors to include Anne in the prayers for his kin.

44. *LP Henry VIII*, Vol. I, Part i, nos. 474, 734; Vol. I, Part ii, no. 3502; Vol. III, Part I, no. 1321.

45. Dillon, *Performance and Spectacle*, p. 31.

46. BL Additional MS 31922.

47. Weir, *Henry VIII*, pp. 99–100.

48. His brother George was also a prominent courtier and regularly took part in great occasions, such as ambassadorial receptions and tournaments.

49. Nicoll, A. and J. (eds), *Holinshed's Chronicle, as used in Shakespeare's Plays* (London, 1955), p. 186; Cavendish, George, *The Life of Cardinal Wolsey by George Cavendish his Gentleman Usher* (London, 1827), pp. 27–8.

50. *LP Henry VIII*, Vol. III, Part ii, no. 765.

51. *CSPV*, Vol. IV, p. 295.

52. *CSPV*, Vol. IV, p. 295.

53. Allen, P.S. and H.M. (eds), *Letters of Richard Fox*, p. 54.

54. *LP Henry VIII*, Vol. I, no. 880.

55. *A Collection of Ordinances and Regulations for the Government of the Royal*

Household (London, 1790), pp. 154–7; Miller, *Henry VIII and the English Nobility*, p. 85.

56. *LP Henry VIII*, Vol. I, p. 152.

57. Richard's son was William Cecil, who later became chief adviser, Secretary of State, and Lord High Treasurer to Elizabeth I.

58. Lynn, E., *Tudor Fashion: Dress at Court 1485–1603* (Yale, 2017). He was followed by John Malte, who served until his death in 1545, and then by John Bridges who dressed the king for the last two years of his reign and was tailor to all three of his successors.

CHAPTER 4: 'HIS MAJESTY'S SECOND SELF'

1. *CSPV*, Vol. II, p. 559; Streitberger, W.R., *Court Revels, 1485–1559* (Toronto, 2012), p. 92.

2. *Polydore Vergil*, p. 131.

3. *CSPV*, Vol. IV, p. 293.

4. Cavendish, *Cardinal Wolsey*, p. 7.

5. Tyndale, W., *The Practice of Prelates* (London, 1530), p. 307.

6. Cavendish, *Cardinal Wolsey*, p. 80.

7. *Four years at the court of Henry VIII*, Vol. I, p. 128.

8. *Polydore Vergil*, 196n.

9. Cavendish, *Cardinal Wolsey*, pp. 11–12, 79.

10. Cavendish, *Cardinal Wolsey*, p. 12.

11. Cavendish, *Cardinal Wolsey*, p. 82.

12. Cavendish, *Cardinal Wolsey*, p. 12.

13. Hume (ed. and trans.), *Chronicle*, p. 1.

14. Williams (ed.), *English Historical Documents*, p. 402.

15. Wilson, *In the Lion's Court*, p. 127; *Four years at the court of Henry VIII*, Vol. I, p. 128.

16. Cavendish, *Cardinal Wolsey*, pp. 13, 83.

17. *Polydore Vergil*, p. 247.

18. Cavendish, *Cardinal Wolsey* p. 25.

19. Cavendish, *Cardinal Wolsey*, pp. 80–1.

20. Strype, J., *Ecclesiastical Memorials, Relating Chiefly to Religion, and the Reformation of it . . . under King Henry VIII, King Edward VI and Queen Mary I* (Oxford, 1822), Vol. I, Part i, p. 6.

21. Cavendish, G., *Cardinal Wolsey*, pp. 11–12.

22. Tyndale, W., *The Practice of Prelates* (London, 1530), p. 307.

23. Cavendish, *Cardinal Wolsey*, pp. 11–12.

24. Cavendish, *Cardinal Wolsey*, pp. 11–12.

25. Dillon, *Performance and Spectacle*, pp. 36–7.

26. Hall, *Chronicle*, p. 518; Streitberger, *Court Revels*, p. 75.

27. No blame was placed on the nursery staff. Elizabeth Poyntz was rewarded for her service with an annuity of £20 (£6,000).

28. Wilson, *In the Lion's Court*, p. 102.

29. The same title was used by Jean Maillard, Henry VIII's French secretary.

30. Carlson, D.R. (ed.), 'The Latin Writings of John Skelton', *Texts and Studies*, Vol. 88, no. 4 (North Carolina, 1991), no. XVI, ll. 12–14. Skelton later wrote a Latin elegy for the tomb of Henry's grandmother, Lady Margaret Beaufort, which was completed by Pietro Torregiano in 1516 and lay close to that of her son, Henry VII.

31. *Polydore Vergil*, p. 187.

32. Allen, P.S. and H.M. (eds), *Letters of Richard Fox*, p. 58.

33. *Polydore Vergil*, p. 175.

CHAPTER 5: 'THE SERVANT IS NOT GREATER THAN HIS LORD'

1. *LP Henry VIII*, Vol. I, Part ii, no. 2171.

2. Streitberger, *Court Revels*, p. 77.

3. *Polydore Vergil*, p. 223.

4. *Four years at the court of Henry VIII*, Vol. I, p. 87.

5. *LP Henry VIII*, Vol. II, Part i, xxvii–viii.

6. *Polydore Vergil*, p. 223.

7. BL, Cotton MS Caligula D. vi, fo.186r. *LP Henry VIII*, Vol. II, Part I, no. 80.

8. *LP Henry VIII*, Vol. II, Part i, no. 106.

9. *LP Henry VIII*, Vol. II, Part i, nos. 103, 203.

10. *LP Henry VIII*, Vol. II, Part i, no. 138.

11. *LP Henry VIII*, Vol. II, Part i, no. 222.

12. *LP Henry VIII*, Vol. II, Part i, no. 224.

13. Norwich, J.J., *Four Princes: Henry VIII, Francis I, Charles V, Suleiman the Magnificent and the Obsessions that Forged Modern Europe* (London, 2016), p. 4.

14. Bacon, *Historie*, p. 179.

15. *Four years at the court of Henry VIII*, Vol. I, pp. 90–1.

16. *Four years at the court of Henry VIII*, Vol. I, p. 86.

17. The debt was later reduced by Henry.

18. *CSPV*, Vol. II, p. 244.

19. *Four years at the court of Henry VIII*, Vol. I, p. 119.

20. Dillon, *Performance and Spectacle*, p. 106.

21. Dillon, *Performance and Spectacle*, p. 117.

22. *Four years at the court of Henry VIII*, Vol. I, p. 128.

23. *Polydore Vergil*, p. 225.

24. *CSPV*, Vol. II, pp. 380, 521; Vol. III, p. 79.

25. *Four years at the court of Henry VIII*, Vol. I, pp. 110, 139, 155; *LP Henry VIII*, Vol. II, Part ii, Appendix, no. 12.

26. *Polydore Vergil*, pp. 225, 231.

27. Williams (ed.), *English Historical Documents*, p. 402.

28. Cattley, S.R. and Townsend, G. (eds), John Foxe, *Acts and Monuments* (London, 1838), Vol. V, pp. 416–17.

29. *Polydore Vergil*, pp. 231, 233.

30. Williams (ed.), *English Historical Documents*, p. 402.

31. Foss, E., *The Judges of England: with sketches of their lives and miscellaneous notices connected with the courts at Westminster, from the time of the Conquest* (London, 1857), Vol. V, p. 212.

32. Ellis, H. (ed.), *Original Letters Illustrative of English History*, Vol. I (London, 1969), p. 269; Doran, *Henry VIII*, p. 8; British Library, Cotton MS Vespasian F xiii fo.138.

33. Ellis (ed.), *Original Letters*, Vol. I, p. 126.

34. *Four years at the court of Henry VIII*, Vol. I, p. 181.

35. *Four years at the court of Henry VIII*, Vol. I, pp. 191–5.

36. *LP Henry VIII*, Vol. II, Part i, ccxiv.

37. Grafton, R., *A Chronicle and Mere History* (1809), pp. 382–3.

38. Grafton, *A Chronicle and Mere History*, pp. 382–3.

CHAPTER 6: 'YOUTHS OF EVIL COUNSEL'

1. Dillon, *Performance and Spectacle*, p. 56.

2. Starkey, *Henry VIII*, p. 55.

3. Hall, *Chronicle*, pp. 67, 68v.

4. Rebholz, R.A. (ed.), *Sir Thomas Wyatt: The Complete Poems* (1978), p. 151.

5. Starkey, *Henry VIII*, pp. 51–2.

6. Starkey, *Henry VIII*, pp. 53–4.

7. Starkey, *Henry VIII*, pp. 56–7. Coffin went on to become a gentleman usher, sewer of the chamber, and Master of the Horse to both Anne Boleyn and Jane Seymour. He was knighted in October 1537, following the birth of Prince Edward. He died the following year, probably of the plague, and bequeathed all of his hawks and his best horses to the king.

8. *Four years at the court of Henry VIII*, Vol. II, p. 271. Greg Walker casts doubt upon the theory that Wolsey deliberately 'purged' the privy chamber in

this way, in 'The Expulsion of the Minions Reconsidered', *The Historical Journal*, Vol. 32, no. 1 (Cambridge, March 1989), pp. 1–16.

9. BL Cotton MS Titus B I fo.188.

10. Starkey, *Henry VIII*, p. 62.

11. Hall, *Chronicle*, pp. 597–8.

12. *Four years at the court of Henry VIII*, Vol. II, pp. 270–1.

13. Hall, *Chronicle*, pp. 597–8.

14. Hall, *Chronicle*, pp. 597–8.

15. Hall, *Chronicle*, pp. 597–8.

16. *LP Henry VIII*, Vol. II, no. 4034.

17. Starkey, *Henry VIII*, p. 61.

18. *LP Henry VIII*, Vol. I, Part ii, no. 2366; TNA SP1/5, ff.76–7; *Four years at the court of Henry VIII*, Vol. II, p. 271.

19. *LP Henry VIII*, Vol. III, no. 17.

20. *CSPV*, Vol. II, nos. 1220, 1230.

21. Lehmberg, S.E., *The Later Parliaments of Henry VIII, 1536–1547* (Cambridge, 1977), p. 202.

22. Roper, *Thomas Moore, knighte*, ed. Hitchcock, E.V. (London, 1935), p. 11.

23. Rogers, E. (ed.), *St Thomas More: Selected Letters* (Princeton, 1961), p. 94.

24. Hughes, P.L. and Larkin, J.F., *Tudor Royal Proclamations*, Vol. I (1964), pp. 84–5.

25. *LP Henry VIII*, Vol. II, Part i, no. 1959.

26. Nicholl, A. and J. (eds), *Holinshed's Chronicle, As used in Shakespeare's Plays* (London, 1955), p. 178.

27. *LP Henry VIII*, Vol. II, Part ii, no. 4057.

28. *LP Henry VIII*, Vol. III, Part i, no. 1.

29. BL MS Cotton Titus B.i, fo.192.

30. Nicholl, A. and J. (eds), *Holinshed's Chronicle*, p. 178.

31. TNA PRO, SP 1/20, ff.42–3.

32. Dillon, *Performance and Spectacle*, p. 77.

33. Dillon, *Performance and Spectacle*, p. 77.

34. Dillon, *Performance and Spectacle*, pp. 79–80.

35. Dillon, *Performance and Spectacle*, pp. 92–5.

36. These had belonged to the Duke of Buckingham before his indictment for treason in 1521.

37. *LP Henry VIII*, Vol. I, Part i, no. 157.

38. Nicholl, A. and J. (eds), *Holinshed's Chronicle*, pp. 178, 182.

39. Hall, *Chronicle*, p. 599.

40. *LP Henry VIII*, Vol. III, Part i, no. 1284 (3).

41. Dillon, *Performance and Spectacle*, p. 101.
42. Dillon, *Performance and Spectacle*, p. 98.
43. Dillon, *Performance and Spectacle*, p. 100.
44. Luders, A., et al. (eds), *Statutes of the Realm* (1820–40), Vol. III, p. 246.
45. Vergil claims that Pace eventually had to resign the secretaryship because his mind was 'so impaired that he shortly after began to have periods of madness'. *Polydore Vergil*, p. 329.
46. *CSPV*, Vol. III, p. 319.
47. Hall, *Chronicle*, p. 696.
48. *LP Henry VIII*, Vol. IV, Part i, no. 1318.
49. Hall, *Chronicle*, p. 700.
50. Scattergood (ed.), *John Skelton*, p. 239.
51. Scattergood (ed.), *John Skelton*, p. 293.

CHAPTER 7: 'THE MOST RASCALLY BEGGAR IN THE WORLD'

1. Dillon, *Performance and Spectacle*, p. 120.
2. *CSPV*, Vol. I, no. 517.
3. Cavendish, *Cardinal Wolsey*, p. 118.
4. *CSPV*, Vol. IV, p. 365.
5. Weir, *Henry VIII*, p. 256.
6. Henry never forgot the service that Moody had performed. Upon the latter's retirement from court in 1540, he was granted a coat of arms 'for miraculously saving his [Henry VIII's] life at Hitchin, County of Herts, when leaping over a ditch with a pole which brake; that if the said Edmund, a footman in the King's retinue, had not leapt into ye water and lifted up the King's head, he had drowned'.
7. *CSPV*, Vol. III, no. 1053.
8. *CSPV*, Vol. III, no. 1053; Weir, *Henry VIII*, p. 253.
9. Nicoll, A. and J. (eds), *Holinshed's Chronicle*, p. 197.
10. *LP Henry VIII*, Vol. II, Part i, no. 1935. See also Bernard, G.W., 'The Rise of Sir William Compton, Early Tudor Courtier', *English Historical Review*, Vol. 96, no. 381 (October 1981), p. 775.
11. *Polydore Vergil*, pp. 308–9.
12. Crapelet, G.A., *Lettres de Henri VIIIième à Anne Boleyn* (1835), p. 184.
13. Cherbury, Edward, Lord Herbert of, *The life and raigne of King Henry the Eighth* (1649), p. 8.
14. TNA SP 1/49 fos.7–7v; *LP Henry VIII*, Vol. IV, Part ii, no. 4442(1).
15. Daalder, J. (ed.), *Thomas Wyatt: Collected Poems* (1975), p. 192.
16. 'Ordinances for the Household made at Eltham in the XVII year of King

Henry VIII in 1526', in *A Collection of Ordinances and Regulations for the Government of the Royal Household* (London, 1790), pp. 154, 157.

17. Dillon, *Performance and Spectacle*, p. 122.

18. *LP Henry VIII*, Vol. IV, no. cci.

19. Cavendish, *Cardinal Wolsey*, p. 119.

20. *LP Henry VIII*, Vol. IV, no. 2665.

21. *State Papers published under the authority of His Majesty's Commission. King Henry the Eighth*, 11 vols (London, 1830–52), Vol. I, p. 195.

22. Allen, P.S., et al. (eds), *Opus epistolarum Des. Erasmi Roterodami*, 12 vols (1906–58), Vol. VI, p. 392, no. 1740.

23. Leviticus 20:21.

24. *State Papers . . . King Henry the Eighth*, Vol. I, p. 278.

25. *LP Henry VIII*, Vol. IV, Part ii, no. 3318.

26. *LP Henry VIII*, Vol. IV, Part ii, no. 3644.

27. Dillon, *Performance and Spectacle*, p. 121.

28. Hall, *Chronicle*, p. 733.

29. *LP Henry VIII*, Vol. IV, Part ii, no. 4507.

30. *LP Henry VIII*, Vol. IV, Part ii, no. 4468.

31. *LP Henry VIII*, Vol. IV, Part ii, no. 4649.

32. *LP Henry VIII*, Vol. IV, Part ii, no. 5458.

33. *LP Henry VIII*, Vol. IV, Part ii, no. 5275.

34. Rebholz (ed.), *Sir Thomas Wyatt*, p. 151.

35. Allen, P.S. and H.M. (eds), *Letters of Richard Fox*, p. 93.

36. *State Papers . . . King Henry the Eighth*, Vol. VII, no. 169.

37. Weir, *Henry VIII*, p. 256.

38. *LP Henry VIII*, Vol. IV, no. 5806.

39. *LP Henry VIII*, Vol. IV, no. 5806.

40. *LP Henry VIII*, Vol. IV, no. 5806.

41. Foxe, *Acts and Monuments*, Vol. III, p. 585.

42. Williams (ed.), *English Historical Documents*, p. 422.

43. Williams (ed.), *English Historical Documents*, pp. 423, 425.

44. *Polydore Vergil*, p. 331. Hall corroborated this account and added that Catherine also accused Wolsey of tyranny, pride, vainglory, a voluptuous life, lechery and malice to the emperor.

45. Cavendish, *Cardinal Wolsey*, pp. 93–4. See also Hall, *Chronicle*, p. 759.

46. Cavendish, *Cardinal Wolsey*, pp. 93–4.

47. Wilson, *In the Lion's Court*, p. 341.

48. Hall, *Chronicle*, p. 759.

49. BL MS Cotton Vitellius B.XII f.173.

50. BL MS Cotton Vitellius B XII f.173.
51. Mackay, L., *Inside the Tudor Court* (Stroud, 2015), p. 30.
52. Mackay, *Inside the Tudor Court*, p. 47.
53. Mackay, *Inside the Tudor Court*, p. 48.
54. *CSPS*, Vol. IV, Part I, p. 189.

CHAPTER 8: 'THE INCONSTANTNESS OF PRINCES' FAVOUR'

1. Stow, *Annales*, pp. 547–9.
2. *LP Henry VIII*, Vol. IV, Part iii, no. 6019.
3. Cavendish, *Cardinal Wolsey*, p. 105.
4. Cavendish, *Cardinal Wolsey*, p. 111.
5. Cavendish, *Cardinal Wolsey*, p. 112.
6. *LP Henry VIII*, 4/3, no. 6030.
7. Foxe, *Acts and Monuments*, Vol. V, p. 363.
8. Ellis (ed.), *Original Letters*, first series, Vol. II, pp. 1–2.
9. *LP Henry VIII*, Vol. IX, no. 862.
10. Cavendish, *Cardinal Wolsey*, pp. 169, 170.
11. Cavendish, *Cardinal Wolsey*, p. 105.
12. Hall, *Chronicle*, p. 764.
13. Erasmus, D., *Epistolae*, Vol. VIII, p. 294.
14. *CSPV*, Vol. III, p. 447; Roper, *Thomas Moore*, p. 21.
15. Wilson, *In the Lion's Court*, p. 220.
16. Roper, *Thomas Moore*, pp. 56–7.
17. Cavendish, *Cardinal Wolsey*, pp. 183–4.
18. *Parliamentary or Constitutional History of England, 1751–1762*, Vol. III, pp. 42–55.
19. Cavendish, *Cardinal Wolsey*, p. 275.
20. *LP Henry VIII*, Vol. IV, no. 6447; Cavendish, *Cardinal Wolsey*, pp. 471–82.
21. *CSPS*, Vol. V, Part i, p. 228.
22. *LP Henry VIII*, Vol. XV, no. 486.
23. *CSPS*, Vol. V, Part II, p. 56.
24. *LP Henry VIII*, Vol. XV, no. 486.
25. *LP Henry VIII*, Vol. IV, nos. 6076, 6199.
26. Cavendish, *Cardinal Wolsey*, p. 119.
27. *LP Henry VIII*, 4/3, no. 6114.
28. Cavendish, *Cardinal Wolsey*, p. 287.
29. Cavendish, *Cardinal Wolsey*, pp. 507–8.
30. *CSPS*, Vol. IV, Part i, p. 692.
31. *LP Henry VIII*, Vol. IV, no. 6196.

32. Cavendish, *Cardinal Wolsey*, pp. 128ff.; *LP Henry VIII*, Vol. IV, Part iii, no. 6295.

33. *LP Henry VIII*, Vol. IV, no. 2827.

34. *LP Henry VIII*, Vol. IV, Part iii, no. 6205.

35. Hume (ed. and trans.), *Chronicle*, p. 105.

36. *CSPF, 1547–53*, no. 491.

37. Hume (ed. and trans.), *Chronicle*, p. 105.

38. *LP Henry VIII*, Vol. IV, Part iii, nos. 6335, 6344.

39. *CSPS*, Vol. IV, Part iii, p. 6738.

40. *CSPS*, Vol. IV, Part i, p. 354.

41. *State Papers . . . King Henry the Eighth*, Vol. VII, p. 212.

42. *LP Henry VIII*, Vol. IV, Part iii, no. 6720.

43. *State Papers . . . King Henry the Eighth*, Vol. VII, p. 213.

44. Cavendish, *Cardinal Wolsey*, p. 170.

45. Cavendish, *Cardinal Wolsey*, p. 375.

46. Cavendish, *Cardinal Wolsey*, p. 376.

47. Cavendish, *Cardinal Wolsey*, pp. 174, 377.

48. Cavendish, *Cardinal Wolsey*, pp. 387–8. It is possible that the cause of Wolsey's death was adult-onset diabetes. This often resulted in looseness of the bowels, which tended to be termed 'dysentery'. Wolsey's refusal to eat after his arrest, and his subsequent dysentery and vomiting, could have resulted in a diabetic coma.

49. Wriothesley, C., *A chronicle of England during the reigns of the Tudors from AD 1485 to 1559*, ed. Hamilton, 2 vols, Camden Society, new series, 11, 20 (1875–7), Vol. I, p. 16.

50. Tyndale, W., *The Practice of Prelates*, p. 307.

51. Foxe, *Acts and Monuments*, Vol. IV, p. 616.

52. Hall, *Chronicle*, p. 774. See also Nicoll, A. and J. (eds), *Holinshed's Chronicle*, pp. 204–5.

53. *State Papers . . . King Henry the Eighth*, Vol. VII, p. 213; Norton, E., *The Anne Boleyn Papers* (Stroud, 2013), p. 149.

54. Cavendish, *Cardinal Wolsey*, pp. 396–9.

55. Dillon, *Performance and Spectacle*, p. 134.

56. *CSPV*, Vol. IV, pp. 266, 268. All that now remains of Wolsey's tomb is the sarcophagus and base. In 1808, these were moved to St Paul's Cathedral to house the body of Lord Nelson.

57. Cavendish, *Cardinal Wolsey*, p. 404.

CHAPTER 9: 'THE MAN WHO ENJOYS MOST CREDIT
WITH THE KING'

1. Foxe, *Acts and Monuments*, Vol. III, p. 648.
2. *CSPS*, Vol. IV, Part ii, p. 759.
3. *Four years at the court of Henry VIII*, Vol. I, p. 237.
4. *CSPS*, Vol. IV, Part i, pp. 451–2.
5. *CSPS*, Vol V, Part ii, p. 257.
6. *LP Henry VIII*, Vol. XV, no. 486.
7. Wood, M.A.E., *Letters of Royal and Illustrious Ladies of Great Britain*, 3 vols (London, 1846), Vol. II, p. 66.
8. *LP Henry VIII*, Vol. IV, no. 6554.
9. *CSPS*, Vol. V, pp. 356–9.
10. Merriman (ed.), *Life and letters*, Vol. I, pp. 17–18; Hume (ed. and trans.), *Chronicle*, pp. 31, 87.
11. Foxe, *Acts and Monuments*, Vol. V, pp. 366–8.
12. Williams (ed.), *English Historical Documents*, p. 393.
13. Pratt (ed.), *Actes and Monuments of John Foxe*, Vol. V, p. 364.
14. Foxe, *Actes and Monuments*, Vol. III, p. 645.
15. Hume (ed. and trans.), *Chronicle*; *CSPS*, Vol. V, Part ii, pp. 207, 239.
16. Cavendish, G., *Metrical Visions*, in Singer (ed.), *The Life of Cardinal Wolsey*, Vol. II, p. 52.
17. *CSPV*, Vol. IV, pp. 294–5.
18. Merriman (ed.), *Life and letters*, Vol. II, pp. 20, 23.
19. *LP Henry VIII*, Vol. V, no. 628.
20. Merriman (ed.), *Life and letters*, Vol. I, pp. 90–1.
21. *LP Henry VIII*, Vol. V, no. 1452.
22. *LP Henry VIII*, Vol. V, no. 1239.
23. *CSPS*, Vol. IV, Part ii, p. 669.
24. *CSPS*, Vol. IV, Part ii, pp. 76–7.
25. *CSPS*, Vol. V, Part i, p. 484.
26. Strype, *Ecclesiastical Memorials*, Vol. I, Part i, p. 221.
27. Merriman (ed.), *Life and letters*, Vol. I, p. 348.
28. Allen et al. (eds), *Opus epistolarum Des*, Vol. X, p. 193, no. 2788.
29. *LP Henry VIII*, Vol. VI, no. 1306.
30. Nichols, J.G. (ed.), *Narratives of the days of the Reformation*, Camden Society old series, Vol. LXXVII (London, 1859), p. 219.
31. Nichols (ed.), *Narratives*, pp. 241–2.
32. Cox, J.E. (ed.), *The Works of Thomas Cranmer, Archbishop of Canterbury, Martyr, 1556*, Vol. II (Cambridge, 1846), p. 237.

33. Nichols (ed.), *Narratives*, pp. 241–2.

34. Nichols (ed.), *Narratives*, pp. 244–5.

35. Cox (ed.), *Works of Thomas Cranmer*, Vol. II, p. 237.

36. Cox (ed.), *Works of Thomas Cranmer*, Vol. II, p. 241.

37. Nichols (ed.), *Narratives*, p. 258.

38. Nichols (ed.), *Narratives*, pp. 249–50.

39. Cox (ed.), *Works of Thomas Cranmer*, Vol. II, p. 271.

40. Williams (ed.), *English Historical Documents*, p. 418.

41. Hume (ed. and trans.), *Chronicle*, p. 102.

42. Merriman (ed.), *Life and letters*, Vol. I, p. 135; *LP Henry VIII*, Vol. VII, no. 1554.

43. Bray, G. (ed.), *Documents of the English Reformation* (Cambridge, 1994), p. 59.

44. Lehmberg, S.E., *The Reformation Parliament, 1529–1536* (Cambridge, 1970), p. 146.

45. Cox (ed.), *Works of Thomas Cranmer*, Vol. II, p. 304.

46. Hall, *Chronicle*, p. 788.

47. Rogers (ed.), *St Thomas More*, p. 172.

48. Allen et al. (eds), *Opus epistolarum Des*, Vol. X, p. 2831.

49. Foxe, *Acts and Monuments*, Vol. IV, pp. 657–8.

50. Roper, *Thomas Moore*, p. 50.

51. *LP Henry VIII*, Vol. V, no. 171.

52. Hillerbrand, H.J. (ed.), *Erasmus and His Age, Selected Letters of Desiderius Erasmus* (New York, 1970), pp. 270–1.

53. *LP Henry VIII*, Vol. XII, Part ii.

54. In Greek mythology, Priam was King of Troy during the Trojan War. Jones, E. (ed.), *Henry Howard, Earl of Surrey: Poems* (Oxford, 1964), 27, II.3–4.

55. Weir, *Henry VIII*, p. 330.

56. *LP Henry VIII*, Vol. IX, no. 528.

57. *LP Henry VIII*, Vol. XV, no. 804.

58. *LP Henry VIII*, Vol. IX, no. 172.

59. Dillon, *Performance and Spectacle*, p. 140.

60. Dillon, *Performance and Spectacle*, p. 151.

61. Wilson, *In the Lion's Court*, p. 380.

62. Roper, *Thomas Moore*, p. 57.

63. Roper, *Thomas Moore*, p. 57.

64. *State Papers . . . King Henry the Eighth*, Vol. I, p. 408.

65. TNA PROB 11/25, fo.243v.

CHAPTER 10: 'I SHALL DIE TODAY AND YOU TOMORROW'

1. *CSPS*, Vol. V, Part i, p. 294.
2. Merriman, p. 374.
3. Merriman (ed.), *Life and letters*, Vol. I, pp. 373–9.
4. Roper, *Thomas Moore*, p. 71.
5. Roper, *Thomas Moore*, p. 71.
6. Rogers, E.F. (ed.), *The Correspondence of Sir Thomas More* (Princeton, 1947), pp. 488–91.
7. Roper, *Thomas Moore*, p. 69.
8. Roper, *Thomas Moore*, p. 72.
9. Rogers, *Correspondence*, pp. 491–501.
10. Wriothesley, *Chronicle*, Vol. I, p. 29.
11. Rogers, *Correspondence*, pp. 491–501.
12. Rogers, *Correspondence*, p. 250.
13. Rogers, *Correspondence*, p. 553.
14. Rogers, *Correspondence*, pp. 555–9.
15. Rogers, *Correspondence*, p. 553.
16. Weir, *Henry VIII*, p. 363.
17. *CSPV*, Vol. V, p. 26.
18. *CSPS*, Vol. V, Part i, p. 466.
19. Roper, *Thomas Moore*, p. 263.
20. Roper, *Thomas Moore*, p. 185.
21. Roper, *Thomas Moore*, pp. 193, 196.
22. Roper, *Thomas Moore*, p. 103.
23. When Margaret's husband William died and was buried in January 1578, her body and More's head were transferred to the Roper vault in St Dunstan's, Canterbury.
24. Roper, *Thomas Moore*, p. 104.

CHAPTER 11: 'RESISTING EVIL COUNSELLORS'

1. Granger, J., *A biographical history of England from Egbert the Great to the revolution*, 5th edn, I (1824), p. 149.
2. Weir, *Henry VIII*, p. 251.
3. 1 Corinthians 1:25.
4. Southworth, J., *Fools and Jesters at the English Court* (Stroud, 1998), p. 9.
5. *LP Henry VIII*, Vol. VII, Part ii, no. 1257.
6. *LP Henry VIII*, Vol. X, no. 901.
7. Merriman (ed.), *Life and letters*, Vol. I, p. 414.

8. *CSPS*, Vol. V, Part i, p. 542.

9. Janelle, P. (ed), *Obedience in Church and State: Three Political Tracts* (Cambridge, 1930), p. 72.

10. Perry, M., *The Word of a Prince* (London, 1990), p. 23.

11. Luders, A., et al. (eds), *Statutes of the realm*, Vol. III, p. 680.

12. *LP Henry VIII*, Vol XII, Part ii, no. 1013.

13. Weir, A., *The Six Wives of Henry VIII* (London, 1991), p. 293.

14. Merriman (ed.), *Life and letters*, Vol. I, p. 439.

15. Merriman (ed.), *Life and letters*, Vol. II, p. 1.

16. Merriman (ed.), *Life and letters*, Vol. II, p. 3.

17. *LP Henry VIII*, Vol. X, no. 141.

18. Wriothesley, *Chronicle*, Vol. I, p. 33; *LP Henry VIII*, Vol. X, p. 102.

19. *LP Henry VIII*, Vol. X, no. 351.

20. *LP Henry VIII*, Vol. X, no. 351.

21. *Statutes of the Realm*, 11 vols (London, 1963), Vol. III, pp. 575–8.

22. Hume (ed. and trans.), *Chronicle*, p. 26.

23. *LP Henry VIII*, Vol. XIII, Part ii, no. 401.

24. Byrne, M, St C. (ed.), *The Lisle Letters*, 6 vols (Chicago and London, 1981), Vol. IV, p. 1001.

25. *CSPF Edward VI*, no. 471.

26. Wilson, *In the Lion's Court*, p. 497.

27. *CSPS*, Vol. IV, Part II.ii, p. 841.

28. Norton, *Anne Boleyn Papers*, p. 288. Cromwell was later obliged to surrender one of these rooms to Jane Seymour in order to facilitate her courtship with his master.

29. *CSPS*, Vol. V, Part i, p. 484; Part ii, p. 81; *LP Henry VIII*, Vol. X, no. 601.

30. *LP Henry VIII*, Vol. X, no. 699.

31. Cox (ed.), *Works of Thomas* Cranmer, Vol. II , p. 314.

32. Starkey, *Henry VIII*, p. 101.

33. *CSPV*, Vol. V, p. 47.

34. See, for example: BL Cotton MS Titus B i fos.261r, 264; Merriman (ed.), *Life and letters*, Vol. II, p. 298.

35. *LP Henry VIII*, Vol. X, no. 752.

36. *LP Henry VIII*, Vol. X, no. 351.

37. *LP Henry VIII*, Vol. X, no. 699.

38. *LP Henry VIII*, Vol. X, no. 699.

39. *LP Henry VIII*, Vol. X, no. 699.

40. *LP Henry VIII*, Vol. X, no. 700.

41. *LP Henry VIII*, Vol. X, no. 699.

42. *LP Henry VIII*, Vol. X, no. 700.

43. Merriman (ed.), *Life and letters*, Vol. II, p. 196.

44. *CSPS*, Vol. II, pp. 453–4.

45. *LP Henry VIII*, Vol. X, no. 351.

46. *CSPS*, Vol. V, Part ii, p. 137.

47. *CSPS*, Vol. V, Part ii, p. 137.

48. Cavendish, *Cardinal Wolsey*, p. 30.

49. Cavendish, *Cardinal Wolsey*, p. 452.

50. Starkey, *Reign of Henry VIII*, p. 119.

51. Merriman (ed.), *Life and letters*, Vol. II, p. 12.

52. Another George Boleyn, who became Dean of Lichfield in the reign of Elizabeth I, is often rumoured to have been Lord Rochford's son, but the evidence for this is questionable, and he may have been illegitimate. Lord Rochford's inquisition post mortem made no mention of the young man and instead named his sister, Mary Boleyn, as his heir.

53. *LP Henry VIII*, Vol. XVI, no. 467.

54. Hume (ed. and trans.), *Chronicle*, p. 66.

55. *LP Henry VIII*, Vol. X, no. 699; *CSPS*, Vol. V, Part ii, p. 198.

56. *CSPF Elizabeth*, Vol. I 1558–9 (London, 1863); Weir, A., *The Lady in the Tower* (London, 2009), p. 99.

57. Weir, *Lady in the Tower*, p. 5.

58. Dillon, *Performance and Spectacle*, p. 154.

59. *Lisle Letters*, Vol. III, p. 165; *LP Henry VIII*, Vol. X, no. 909.

60. Wriothesley, *Chronicle*, Vol. I, p. 53.

61. Weir, *Henry VIII*, p. 379.

62. Muir, K., *Life and Letters of Sir Thomas Wyatt* (Liverpool, 1963), p. 201.

63. Hume (ed. and trans.), *Chronicle*, pp. 63–4.

64. Wriothesley, *Chronicle*, Vol. I, p. 36.

65. Merriman (ed.), *Life and letters*, Vol. II, p. 12.

66. Wriothesley, *Chronicle*, Vol. I, p. 37.

67. Wriothesley, *Chronicle*, Vol. I, pp. 38–9.

68. *LP Henry VIII*, Vol. X, no. 792; Cox (ed.), *Works of Thomas Cranmer*, Vol. II, pp. 323–4.

69. BL Harleian MS 283 f.134.

70. Ives, E.W., *Anne Boleyn* (Oxford, 1986), p. 392. Wriothesley, *Chronicle*, Vol. I, pp. 39–40. Despite winning numerous sums from the king at tennis and other sports, Weston died with debts totalling £925 – equivalent to around £285,000 today.

71. *CSPV*, Vol. V, p. 43.

72. Wriothesley, *Chronicle*, Vol. I, p. 40.
73. BL MS Cotton Otho CX.
74. Merriman (ed.), *Life and letters*, Vol. II, pp. 12, 21.

CHAPTER 12: 'EVERY MAN HERE IS FOR HIMSELF'

1. TNA SP 3/7, fo.28r.
2. *CSPS*, Vol. V, Part i, p. 420.
3. *LP Henry VIII*, Vol. X, no. 973.
4. *LP Henry VIII*, Vol. X, no. 1110; Merriman (ed.), *Life and letters*, pp. 17–18.
5. *LP Henry VIII*, Vol. X, no. 24.
6. A cap of maintenance is a ceremonial hat of crimson velvet lined with ermine. It is reserved only for persons of nobility or special honour.
7. Wriothesley, *Chronicle*, Vol. I, p. 53.
8. Weir, *Henry VIII*, p. 395.
9. After the dissolution of Thetford Priory, FitzRoy's remains were interred in St Michael's Church, Framlingham, Suffolk.
10. TNA SP 1/105 f.245v.
11. *CSPS*, Vol. V, Part ii, p. 198.
12. *LP Henry VIII*, Vol. XI, no. 148.
13. Denny also subsequently secured a place in the household of the king's younger daughter for his sister-in-law, Katherine Astley, who would go on to become one of Elizabeth's greatest favourites.
14. Starkey, *Henry VIII*, pp. 110–11. Maecenas was a Roman diplomat and counsellor, and patron of such poets as Virgil and Horace.
15. Mayer, T. (ed.), *Correspondence of Reginald Pole, Volume 1: A Calendar, 1518–1546* (Aldershot, 2002), p. 98.
16. *LP Henry VIII*, Vol. XI, no. 147.
17. Hume (ed. and trans.), *Chronicle*, p. 36.
18. [Anon.] 'The Life and death of Thomas Lord Cromwell', in *The Ancient British Drama*, Vol. I (London, 1810), p. 368.
19. Cox (ed.), *Works of Thomas Cranmer*, Vol. II, p. 322.
20. The three sacraments promoted by the articles were baptism, the Eucharist and penance.
21. Merriman (ed.), *Life and letters*, Vol. I, p. 142.
22. *CSPS*, Vol. V, Part i, p. 500.
23. *CSPS*, Vol. V, Part i, p. 427.
24. Williams (ed.), *English Historical Documents*, p. 394.
25. Merriman (ed.), *Life and letters*, Vol. II, p. 35.
26. *LP Henry VIII*, Vol. VIII, Part i, no. 995.

27. Merriman (ed.), *Life and letters*, Vol. II, p. 30.
28. *LP Henry VIII*, Vol. XI, no. 786 (3).
29. *LP Henry VIII*, Vol. XII, Part i, no. 163.
30. *LP Henry VIII*, Vol. XI, no. 576.
31. *LP Henry VIII*, Vol. VII, no. 1581, Vol. VIII, no. 178, Addenda I, nos. 1090, 1116, 1144.
32. *LP Henry VIII*, Vol. XI, no. 714.
33. *LP Henry VIII*, Vol. XI, no. 576.
34. *LP Henry VIII*, Vol. XI, nos. 601, 602, 603.
35. *CSPS*, Vol. V, Part ii, no. 268.
36. *LP Henry VIII*, Vol. XI, no. 576; *CSPS*, Vol. V, Part ii, p. 268.
37. Willen, D., *John Russell, First Earl of Bedford, One of the King's Men* (London, 1981), pp. 26–7.
38. *LP Henry VIII*, Vol. XI, no. 1143.
39. *LP Henry VIII*, Vol. XI, no. 816.
40. *LP Henry VIII*, Vol. XI, no. 1103.
41. *LP Henry VIII*, Vol. XII, Part i, no. 976.
42. Jones (ed.), *Henry Howard, Earl of Surrey*, 27, II.51–2.
43. Jones (ed.), *Henry Howard, Earl of Surrey*, 18, I.3
44. Hume (ed. and trans.), *Chronicle*, p. 36; *CSPS*, Vol. V, Part ii, p. 313.
45. *LP Henry VIII*, Vol. XIV, Part ii, pp. 328–44, no. 782.
46. Cox (ed.), *Works of Thomas Cranmer*, Vol. II, p. 322.
47. *LP Henry VIII*, Vol. XII, Part i, nos. 594, 636.
48. *LP Henry VIII*, Vol. XII, Part i, no. 118.
49. Merriman (ed.), *Life and letters*, Vol. II, p. 53.

CHAPTER 13: 'A GOODLY PRINCE'

1. Wriothesley, *Chronicle*, Vol. I, p. 64; Merriman (ed.), *Life and letters*, p. 60.
2. *LP Henry VIII*, Vol. XII, Part ii, no. 629. Seymour's prayers were soon answered, for Elizabeth proved a fertile wife to Gregory, giving him a son the year after their wedding and five more children (three sons and two daughters) in the years that followed.
3. Hume (ed. and trans.), *Chronicle*, p. 73.
4. Dillon, *Performance and Spectacle*, p. 154.
5. Wriothesley, *Chronicle*, Vol. I, pp. 66–7.
6. BL Harley MS 282 fos.211–12; Merriman (ed.), *Life and letters*, Vol. II, p. 94.
7. Although as the king's firstborn son, Edward was also Prince of Wales, he was never formally proclaimed in this title.

8. Wriothesley, *Chronicle*, Vol. I, p. 68. In fact, Edward was not invested with these titles until later in his father's reign.

9. Although it has long been assumed that Jane died of puerperal fever, recent research by Alison Weir has made a convincing case for the cause being food poisoning and a resulting infection.

10. *LP Henry VIII*, Vol. XII, Part ii, no. 972.

11. Wriothesley, *Chronicle*, Vol. I, p. 71.

12. *LP Henry VIII*, Vol. XIII, Part ii, no. 732.

13. *LP Henry VIII*, Vol. XIII, Part i, no. 1375.

14. *LP Henry VIII*, Vol. IX, no. 1086.

15. Merriman (ed.), *Life and letters*, Vol. II, pp. 151–4.

16. Cox (ed.), *Works of Thomas* Cranmer, Vol. II, p. 344.

17. *State Papers . . . King Henry the Eighth*, Vol. II, p. 551n.

18. *State Papers . . . King Henry the Eighth*, Vol. II, pp. 551–3n.

19. *State Papers . . . King Henry the Eighth*, Vol. II, pp. 551–3n.

20. Strype, *Ecclesiastical Memorials*, Vol. I, Part i, p. 530.

21. Foxe, *Acts and Monuments*, Vol. III, p. 646.

22. Muller, J.A. (ed.), *The Letters of Stephen Gardiner* (Cambridge, 1933), p. 399.

23. Norton, *Anne Boleyn Papers*, p. 278.

24. Thurley, *The Royal Palaces of Tudor England*, p. 141.

25. Jordan, W.K. (ed.), *The Chronicle and Political Papers of King Edward VI* (1966), p. 3

26. Nichols, J.G. (ed.), *Literary Remains of King Edward the Sixth* (1857), Vol. I, pp. xxxvii–xxxviii.

27. Chapman, *The Last Tudor King: A Study of Edward VI* (Bath, 1961), p. 40.

28. Skidmore, C., *Edward VI: The Lost King of England* (London, 2007), p. 22.

29. Elton, G.R., *Thomas Cromwell: Secretary, Minister and Lord Privy Seal* (Oxford, 1991), p. 19.

30. *CSPS*, Vol. VI, Part i, pp. 40, 53.

31. Foxe, *Acts and Monuments*, Vol. III, p. 589.

32. *LP Henry VIII*, Vol. XIII, Part ii, no. 732.

33. Hume (ed. and trans.), *Chronicle*, p. 131.

34. Merriman (ed.), *Life and letters*, Vol. II, p. 214.

35. *LP Henry VIII*, Vol XI, no. 451.

36. *LP Henry VIII*, Vol. XIII, Part ii, no. 979.7.

37. *LP Henry VIII*, Vol. XIII, Part ii, no. 979.7. Gertrude was attainted for treason on 1 July 1539, but later released.

38. *LP Henry VIII*, 13/2, no. 804.

39. TNA KB 8/11 fo.2.

40. *LP Henry VIII*, Vol. 13, Part ii, no. 804.

41. Dodds, H.M. and Dodds, R., *The Pilgrimage of Grace, 1536–7, and the Exeter conspiracy*, 2 vols (Cambridge, 1915), Vol. II, p. 320.

42. Merriman (ed.), *Life and letters*, Vol. II, p. 162.

43. Fuller, T., *The Worthies of England* (London, 1608–61), Vol. III, p. 234.

44. *LP Henry VIII*, Vol. XIV, Part i, no. 290.

45. Hall, *Chronicle*, p. 827.

46. Carew's remains must have been later removed because the antiquarian John Stow records them as being interred in the London church of St Botolph, Aldgate.

47. Wood, *Letters of Royal and Illustrious Ladies of Great Britain*, Vol. III, p. 112.

48. *Lisle Letters*, Vol. V, p. 639. Russell was subsequently appointed JP for Cornwall, Devon, Dorset and Somerset.

CHAPTER 14: 'THE GREATEST WRETCH EVER BORN IN ENGLAND'

1. Ralegh, W., *The History of the World*, ed. Patrides, C.A. (1971), p. 56.

2. Merriman (ed.), *Life and letters*, Vol. II, p. 97.

3. Merriman (ed.), *Life and letters*, Vol. II, p. 175.

4. Merriman (ed.), *Life and letters*, Vol. II, p. 200.

5. Chapman, *The Last Tudor King*, pp. 44–5.

6. Merriman (ed.), *Life and letters*, Vol. I, p. 262; Hume (ed. and trans.), *Chronicle*, p. 88.

7. *LP Henry VIII*, Vol. XIV, Part i, no. 655. By 'device', Cromwell meant an Act or statute.

8. *CSPS*, Vol. V, Part i, p. 442.

9. *Calendar of State Papers, Venice*, Vol. V, p. 26.

10. *LP Henry VIII*, Vol. XI, no. 42.

11. *LP Henry VIII*, 13/2, no. 280.

12. Merriman (ed.), *Life and letters*, Vol. II, pp. 216–19.

13. Bray (ed.), *Documents of the English Reformation*, pp. 222–3; Luders, A., et al. (eds), *Statutes of the Realm* (1820–40), Vol. III, pp. 739–43.

14. Nichols (ed.), *Narratives*, p. 254.

15. MacCulloch, D., *Thomas Cranmer* (New Haven and London, 1996), p. 251.

16. Nichols (ed.), *Narratives*, p. 258.

17. *LP Henry VIII*, Vol. XIV, Part i, no. 1260.

18. MacCulloch, *Thomas Cranmer*, p. 258.

19. Merriman (ed.), *Life and letters*, Vol. II, p. 238; Hume (ed. and trans.), *Chronicle*, p. 90.

20. *LP Henry VIII*, Vol. XVI, no. 466.

21. Wriothesley, *Chronicle*, Vol. I, pp. 109–10.

22. Merriman (ed.), *Life and letters*, Vol. II, p. 271; Strype, *Ecclesiastical Memorials*, Vol. I, Part ii, pp. 555–6.

23. Merriman (ed.), *Life and letters*, Vol. II, pp. 268–76; *LP Henry VIII*, Vol. XV nos. 823, 824.

24. Merriman (ed.), *Life and letters*, Vol. II, p. 270.

25. Wilson, *In the Lion's Court*, p. 386.

26. Hume (ed. and trans.), *Chronicle*, pp. 94–5.

27. Strype, *Ecclesiastical Memorials*, Vol. I, Part ii, Appendix 462; Merriman (ed.), *Life and letters*, Vol. II, p. 270.

28. Hume (ed. and trans.), *Chronicle*, pp. 92–3.

29. Hume (ed. and trans.), *Chronicle*, p. 94.

30. Merriman (ed.), *Life and letters*, Vol. II, pp. 269–70.

31. Merriman (ed.), *Life and letters*, Vol. II, p. 271; Strype, *Ecclesiastical Memorials*, Vol. I, Part ii, pp. 555–6.

32. Strype, *Ecclesiastical Memorials*, Vol. I, Part ii, p. 462.

33. BL Cotton MS Titus B i.

34. Starkey, *Henry VIII*, pp. 98–9.

35. *LP Henry VIII*, Vol. XV, no. 486.

36. *LP Henry VIII*, Vol. XV, no. 429.

37. The title had become vacant upon the death of Henry Bourchier in a riding accident on 12 March.

38. Merriman (ed.), *Life and letters*, Vol. I, p. 290.

39. Starkey, *Henry VIII*, p. 17; Williams (ed.), *English Historical Documents*, p. 394; *Lisle Letters*, Vol. IV, p. 359; Vol. V, p. 1403.

40. Hume (ed. and trans.), *Chronicle*, pp. 96–7, 99.

41. Williams (ed.), *English Historical Documents*, p. 394.

42. Miller, *Henry VIII and the English Nobility*, p. 254.

43. Hume (ed. and trans.), *Chronicle*, pp. 96–7, 99.

44. Hume (ed. and trans.), *Chronicle*, p. 97.

45. *LP Henry VIII*, Vol. XV, no. 737.

46. *LP Henry VIII*, Vol. XV, no. 804. See also Hume (ed. and trans.), *Chronicle*, p. 98.

47. *LP Henry VIII*, Vol. XV, no. 804.

48. *State Papers . . . King Henry the Eighth*, Vol. VIII, p. 349.

49. *LP Henry VIII*, Vol. XV, nos. 767, 804.

50. Doran, S., *The Tudor Chronicles, 1485–1603* (London, 2008), p. 181.

51. *LP Henry VIII*, Vol. XV, no. 804.

52. *LP Henry VIII*, Vol. XV, no. 804.

53. *CSPV*, Vol. V, p. 84.

54. *LP Henry VIII*, Vol. XV, no. 766; *CSPS*, Vol. VI, Part i, pp. 537–9.

55. Spanish Chronicle, p. 99. The varying fortunes of Cromwell's servants after his fall are described by Mary Robertson: 'Thomas Cromwell's Servants: The Ministerial Household in Early Tudor Government and Society', PhD diss., University of California, Los Angeles (1975), pp. 400–8.

56. BL Cotton MS Titus B i fos.267–9.

57. Burnet, G., *History of the Reformation of the Church of England* (London, 1865), Vol. III, p. 296. Upon his own arrest six years later, Norfolk demanded the same privilege. He 'prayed the lords to intercede with the King, that his accusers might be brought face to face, to say what they had against him; and he did not doubt but it should appear he was falsely accused'. Ibid.

58. *LP Henry VIII*, Vol. XV, no. 767.

59. Cox (ed.), *Works of Thomas Cranmer*, Vol. II, p. 401; *LP Henry VIII*, Vol. XV, no. 770.

60. BL Additional MS 48028 fos.160–5; *LP Henry VIII*, Vol. XV, no. 498. A transcript of the indictment is printed in Burnet, *History of the Reformation of the Church of England*, Vol. IV, pp. 416–21.

61. *LP Henry VIII*, Vol. XV, no. 825.

62. BL Cotton MS Otho CX fo.242; Merriman (ed.), *Life and letters*, Vol. II, pp. 268–76; *LP Henry VIII*, Vol. XV, no. 824. Another (edited) version is provided at no. 823.

63. *LP Henry VIII*, Vol. XVI, no. 578.

64. Lynn, *Tudor Fashion*, p. 166; *LP Henry VIII*, Vol. XV, p. 454 and XVI, p. 187.

65. Hume (ed. and trans.), *Chronicle*, pp. 103–4.

CHAPTER 15: 'HE HAS NOT BEEN THE SAME MAN'

1. Foxe, *Acts and Monuments*, Vol. III, p. 654; Hall, *Chronicle*, p. 839.

2. Hume (ed. and trans.), *Chronicle*, p. 105; Holder, N., 'The Medieval Friaries of London', PhD thesis, University of London (2011), p. 169.

3. *CSPS*, Vol. VI, Part i, p. 541.

4. Starkey, *Henry VIII*, p. 127.

5. Hume (ed. and trans.), *Chronicle*, p. 105.

6. Redworth, G., *In Defence of the Church Catholic: The Life of Stephen Gardiner* (1990), p. 180.

7. *LP Henry VIII*, Vol. XVI, no. 467.

8. *CSPS*, 1538–42, 314.

9. Foxe, *Acts and Monuments*, Vol. III, p. 654.

10. *LP Henry VIII*, Vol. XVI, no. 590; Kaulek, J. (ed.), *Correspondance politique de MM. de Castillon et de Marillac, ambassadeurs de France en Angleterre (1537–1542)* (Paris, 1885), p. 274.

11. John Foxe, quoted in Weir, *Henry VIII*, p. 465.

12. Williams (ed.), *English Historical Documents*, p. 393.

13. *State Papers . . . King Henry the Eighth*, Vol. I, p. 79.

14. *Lisle Letters*, Vol. III, p. 412.

15. Sussex did not enjoy it for long, however. He died two years later, in November 1542.

16. *LP Henry VIII*, Vol. XVI, no. 1134.

17. Luders, et al. (eds), *Statutes of the Realm*, Vol. III, p. 955.

18. Skidmore, *Edward VI*, p. 27.

19. Chapman, *The Last Tudor King*, p. 52.

20. Nichols (ed.), *Narratives*, p. 259.

21. Nichols (ed.), *Narratives*, pp. 259–60.

22. Cox (ed.), *Works of Thomas Cranmer*, Vol. II, p. 408.

23. Cox (ed.), *Works of Thomas Cranmer*, Vol. II, p. 409.

24. Wriothesley, *Chronicle*, Vol. I, pp. 130–1.

25. Howard, Henry, 'Eache beast can chuse his feere', cited in Hughey, R. (ed.), *The Arundel Harington manuscript of Tudor poetry*, 2 vols (Ohio, 1960), Vol. I, p. 78, l.68.

26. *LP Henry VIII*, Vol. XVI, no. 1334.

27. *LP Henry VIII*, Vol. XVII, Appendix B, no. 13.

CHAPTER 16: 'MY DEAREST SON IN CHRIST'

1. Hume (ed. and trans.), *Chronicle*, p. 108.

2. Weir, *Henry VIII*, p. 457.

3. Starkey, *Henry VIII*, p. 120.

4. *LP Henry VIII*, Vol. XIV, Part ii, no. 153.

5. Armin, R., *Nest of Ninnies* (London, 1608)

6. Kaulek, J. (ed.), *Correspondance politique de MM. de Castillon et de Marillac, ambassadeurs de France en Angleterre (1537–1542)* (Paris, 1885), p. 263.

7. Lloyd, D., *The states-men, and favourites of England since the Reformation* (1665); Beal, P., *English Literary Manuscripts*, Vol. I (London, 1980), p. 46.

8. *LP Henry VIII*, Vol. XVIII, Part ii, no. 175.

9. Nichols (ed.), *Narratives*, p. 245.

10. Nichols (ed.), *Narratives*, p. 252.

11. Haynes, A., *Collection of State Papers Relating to Affairs in the Reigns of King Henry VIII, King Edward VI, Queen Mary and Queen Elizabeth, From the Year 1542 to 1570 . . . Left by William Cecil, Lord Burghley . . . at Hatfield House* (London, 1740), p. 7.

12. Nichols (ed.), *Narratives*, pp. 252–3.

13. Nichols (ed.), *Narratives*, p. 256.

14. Foxe, *Acts and Monuments*, Vol. VIII, p. 26.

15. Nichols (ed.), *Narratives*, p. 258.

16. Shakespeare, W., *Henry VIII*, Act V, scene ii.

17. Starkey, *Henry VIII*, p. 116.

18. Lynn, *Tudor Fashion*.

19. Williams (ed.), *English Historical Documents*, p. 395.

20. Pollnitz, A., 'Humanism and Court Culture in the Education of Tudor Royal Children', in Betteridge, T. and Riehl, A., *Tudor Court Culture* (New Jersey, 2010), p. 47.

21. Skidmore, *Edward VI*, pp. 33–4.

22. Cox (ed.), *Works of Thomas Cranmer*, Vol. II, p. 413.

23. Fraser, A., *The Wives of Henry VIII* (London, 1993), p. 385.

24. James, S.E., *Kateryn Parr: The Making of a Queen* (Stroud, 1999), p. 141.

25. Thomas, W., *The Pilgrim*, ed. Froude, J.A. (London, 1861), pp. 73–4.

26. *CSPS*, Vol. VIII, 1545–6, pp. 555–6.

27. Purnell, E.K., *Magdalen College* (Cambridge, 1904), p. 37.

28. Lloyd, D., *State-worthies, or, The statesmen and favourites of England since the Reformation* (London, 1670), pp. 72, 75.

29. *State Papers . . . King Henry the Eighth*, Vol. X, pp. 466–8.

30. Chapuys died in January 1556 in the Belgian town of Louvain, where he had lived since leaving England. It must have been a source of great satisfaction to him that Henry's ardently Roman Catholic daughter Mary, whom Chapuys had long supported, was now on the throne, and was married to Charles V's son Philip. He could not have predicted how disastrous and brief her reign would be.

31. TNA SP 1/189, fo.151r.

32. Wriothesley, *Chronicle*, Vol. I, p. 160.

33. Wriothesley, *Chronicle*, Vol. I, p. 160.

34. Starkey, *Henry VIII*, p. 131.

35. Bindoff, S.T., *The History of Parliament: The House of Commons 1509–58*, Vol. I (London, 1982), p. 251.

36. *CSPS*, Vol. IV, Part ii, 1531–3, no. 244; Vol. VI, Part ii, 1542–3, nos. 14, 74, 85.

CHAPTER 17: 'I HAVE BEEN YOUNG, AND NOW AN OLD'

1. Starkey, *Henry VIII*, p. 126.
2. Pratt (ed.), *Actes and Monuments of John Foxe*, Vol. V, p. 547.
3. Pratt (ed.), *Actes and Monuments of John Foxe*, Vol. V, p. 544.
4. Muller, *Letters of Stephen Gardiner*, p. 247.
5. Foxe, *Acts and Monuments*, Vol. VI, p. 138.
6. Pratt (ed.), *Actes and Monuments of John Foxe*, Vol. V, p. 564.
7. Hart, K., *The Mistresses of Henry VIII* (Stroud, 2009), pp. 194–7. Anna Jeanne de Pisseleu d'Heilly, Duchess of Étampes (1508–80), was one of the favourite mistresses of Francis I.
8. Hall, *Chronicle*, p. 867.
9. Streitberger, *Court Revels*, p. 161.
10. See Hoak, D., 'The Secret History of the Tudor Court: The King's Coffers and the King's Purse, 1542–1553', *Journal of British Studies*, Vol. 26, no. 2 (Chicago, April 1987), pp. 208–31.
11. Starkey, *Henry VIII*, p. 110.
12. Sil, N.P., 'King's Men, Queen's Men, and Statesmen: A Study of the Careers of Sir Anthony Denny, Sir William Herbert, and Sir John Gate, Gentlemen of the Tudor Privy Chamber', PhD diss., University of Oregon (1978), pp. 197–8.
13. Starkey, *Henry VIII*, p. 110.
14. Dowling, M., *Humanism in the Age of Henry VIII* (1986), p. 63.
15. Sil, 'King's Men, Queen's Men, and Statesmen', p. 22; Starkey, *Henry VIII*, p. 115.
16. Starkey, *Henry VIII*, p. 133.
17. *LP Henry VIII*, Vol. XI, Part ii, nos. 540, 554.
18. *LP Henry VIII*, Vol. XXI, Part ii, no. 605.
19. Foxe, *Acts and Monuments*, Vol. VI, p. 163.
20. Foxe, *Acts and Monuments*, Vol. VI, p. 170.
21. Foxe, *Acts and Monuments*, Vol. VI, pp. 691–2.
22. Starkey, *Henry VIII*, p. 138.
23. The original is held by The National Archives. E23/4 fo.16v.
24. Starkey, *Henry VIII*, p. 138.
25. Starkey, *Henry VIII*, p. 142.
26. *LP Henry VIII*, Vol. XI, Part ii, no. 696.
27. Cherbury, Edward, Lord Herbert of, *The life and raigne of King Henry the Eighth* (1649), p. 627.
28. Sil, 'King's Men, Queen's Men, and Statesmen', p. 196.
29. Foxe, *Acts and Monuments*, Vol. V, p. 689.

EPILOGUE: 'SOME SPECIAL MAN'

1. BM Cotton MS Nero CX, f.12.
2. Society of Antiquaries, London, MS 123, fo.1r.
3. Dasent, J.R. (ed.), *Acts of the Privy Council of England* (London, 1890), Vol. II, p. 17.
4. Starkey, *Henry VIII*, p. 140.
5. Sil, N.P., 'King's Men, Queen's Men, and Statesmen', pp. 197–8.
6. Williams (ed.), *English Historical Documents*, p. 415.
7. *Acts of the Privy Council*, Vol. II, p. 16.
8. Williams (ed.), *English Historical Documents*, p. 394.
9. Cavendish, R., 'The Marriage of Mary, Queen of Scots', in *History Today*, Vol. 58, Issue 4 (April 2008).
10. Wriothesley, *Chronicle*, Vol. I, p. 183.
11. 'The letters of Richard Scudamore to Sir Philip Hoby', *Camden Miscellany*, 30, CS, 4th series, Vol. XXXIX (1990), pp. 121–2.
12. *Acts of the Privy Council*, Vol. II, p. 56.
13. Cox (ed.), *Works of Thomas Cranmer*, Vol. II, pp. 418–19.
14. MacCulloch, *Thomas Cranmer*, pp. 601–4.
15. Williams (ed.), *English Historical Documents*, p. 415.
16. Williams (ed.), *English Historical Documents*, pp. 415–16.
17. Ponet, J., *A short treatise of politike power* (1556), in *Theatrum orbis terrarum* (1972), sig.Iiii–iiiv.
18. *Polydore Vergil*, p. 337.

INDEX

PICTURE ACKNOWLEDGEMENTS

Alamy: text page iii/Great Seal of Henry VIII, 4 below right/artist unknown/ photo Keith Corrigan, 7 above right/miniature attributed to Gerard Hornebolt, 12 above right/English school/Longleat House Wiltshire UK, 13 above left/State Collection of Prints and Drawings Munich Germany, 15 below left/English school/Knole Kent UK, 15 centre right/engraving by Wenceslas Hollar after Hans Holbein the Younger. Bridgeman Images: 1 left/English school/Hever Castle Kent UK, 1 below right/English school/The Berger Collection at the Denver Art Museum USA, 2 above left/English school/Society of Antiquaries of London UK, 2 above right/English school/Belvoir Castle Leicestershire UK, 2 below and 5 below and 15 above left/© British Library Board All Rights Reserved, 3 above/artist unknown/National Portrait Gallery London UK photo © Stefano Baldini, 4 below left/Hardwick Hall Derbyshire UK portrait by Hans Holbein the Younger, 5 above right/Italian school/private collection photo © Philip Mould Ltd London, 7 below left/Uffizi Gallery Florence Italy, 7 below right and 9 centre left (engraving by Robert White) and 13 below/private collections, 8/Walker Art Gallery National Museums Liverpool UK, 9 above left/English school/Hardwick Hall Derbyshire UK, 9 centre right/school of Hans Holbein/The Trustees of the Weston Park Foundation UK, 11 above right/ portrait by Hans Holbein the Younger/National Gallery of Art Washington DC, 11 below/Castle Howard Yorkshire UK, 12 below left/portrait by Hans Holbein the Younger/Metropolitan Museum of Art New York USA, 13 below right/engraving by Francis Delaram/private collection, 14 above/Hans Holbein the Younger/private collection/De Agostini Picture Library, 14 below left/Hans Holbein the Younger/Isabella Stewart Gardner Museum Boston USA, 14 below right/Hans Holbein the Younger/The Vyne Hampshire UK, 16 above left/ portrait by Hans Holbein the Younger and 16 below English school/both National Portrait Gallery London UK. © College of Arms London UK 2018: 3 below/detail from the 1511 Westminster Tournament Roll. © National Archives London UK: 6 centre/E30-114 (detail from manuscript of 1527). Royal Collection Trust © Her Majesty Queen Elizabeth II 2018/Bridgeman Images: 1 above right, 4 above left and above right/portraits by Hans Holbein the Younger, 6 above/ early 19th century engraving by J Brown, 6 below/detail from The Field of the Cloth of Gold c. 1545 English school, 7 above left/portrait by Hans Holbein the Younger, 9 below/anonymous engraving mid 16th century, 10 above left/ portrait by Lucas Horenbout, 10 above right/portrait by Hans Holbein the Younger, 10 below/copy after Holbein's original mural by Remigius van Leemput, 12 above left/portrait by Hans Holbein the Younger.